Math 65

An Incremental Development

Second Edition

Math 65

An Incremental Development

Second Edition

Stephen Hake

John Saxon

Saxon Publishers, Inc.

Math 65: An Incremental Development
Second Edition

Copyright 2001 by Stephen Hake and John Saxon

Printed in the United States of America.

ISBN: 1-56577-036-6

Production Supervisor: David Pond

Production Coordinator: Joan Coleman

Graphic Artists: Matthew Arrington,
            John Chitwood, and
            Tim Maltz

Manufacturing Code: 11S0501

Printed on recycled paper.

┌─ ***Reaching us via the Internet*** ─┐
│   │
│ **WWW:** www.saxonpub.com   │
│ **E-mail:** info@saxonpub.com   │
└───────────────────────────────────────┘

Saxon Publishers, Inc.
2450 John Saxon Blvd.
Norman, OK 73071

Contents

vi   Contents

viii   **Contents**

Preface

To The Student

This book will take you from basic arithmetic through the foundation of many areas of mathematics, including geometry, measurement, algebra, and scale and graph reading. We study mathematics because it is an important part of our daily lives. Our school schedule, our trip to the store, the preparation of our meals, and many of the games we play all involve mathematics. Most of the word problems you will see in this book are drawn from our daily experiences.

Mathematics is even more important in the adult world. In fact, your personal future in the adult world may depend in part upon the mathematics you have learned. This book was written with the hope that more students will learn mathematics and learn it well. For this to happen, you must use this book properly. As you work through the pages of this book, you will find similar problems presented over and over again. **Solving these problems day after day is the secret to success.**

Each lesson begins with practice of basic number facts and mental math. These exercises will improve your speed, your accuracy, and your ability to do math "in your head." The accompanying pattern and problem-solving activities will give you practice using strategies that can help you solve more complicated problems. Near the end of the lesson is a set of practice problems that focus on the topic of the lesson. Following each lesson is a problem set that reviews the skills you are learning day by day. **Work every problem in every practice set and in every problem set. Do not skip problems. With honest effort you will experience success and true learning which will stay with you and serve you well in the future.**

Acknowledgments

We thank Shirley McQuade Davis for her ideas on teaching word problem thinking patterns.

Stephen Hake
Temple City, California

John Saxon
Norman, Oklahoma

LESSON
1

Counting Sequences • Identifying Digits

Facts Practice: 100 Addition Facts (Test A in Test Masters)[†]

Mental Math: Count by tens from 10 to 100. Count by hundreds from 100 to 1000.

a. 3 + 3	**b.** 30 + 30	**c.** 300 + 300
d. 40 + 50	**e.** 200 + 600	**f.** 50 + 50
g. 20 + 20 + 20	**h.** 500 + 500 + 500	

Problem Solving: The counting numbers are 1, 2, 3, 4, and so on. How many one-digit counting numbers are there?

Counting sequences

Counting is a math skill that we learn early. Counting by ones, we say the numbers

$$1, 2, 3, 4, 5, 6, \ldots$$

These numbers are called **counting numbers.** We may also count by a number other than one. Here we show the first five numbers for counting by twos. Then we show the first five numbers for counting by fives.

$$2, 4, 6, 8, 10, \ldots$$

$$5, 10, 15, 20, 25, \ldots$$

A counting pattern is a **sequence.** The three dots mean that the sequence continues even though the numbers are not written. We can study a sequence to discover the counting pattern or rule used. Then we can figure out more numbers in the sequence. We will practice discovering the counting patterns in some sequences.

Example 1

What are the next three numbers in this sequence?

3, 6, 9, 12, __15__ , __18__ , __21__ , ...

[†]For instructions on how to use the boxed activities, please consult the preface.

Solution   The pattern is "Count by threes." We may count by threes or we may count by ones and emphasize every third number, as "One, two, **three,** four, five, **six,** ...." We find the next three numbers are **15, 18,** and **21.**

Example 2   What is the next number in this sequence?

56, 49, 42, 35 , ...

Solution   This sequence counts down. How much is counted down each time? Reading a sequence backward may help us determine the rule. We find the rule of this sequence is "Count down seven." Counting down seven from 42 gives us **35.**

Identifying digits   There are ten digits in our decimal system. They are 0, 1, 2, 3, 4, 5, 6, 7, 8, and 9. The number 385 has three digits, and the last digit is 5. The number 148,567,896,094 has 12 digits, and the last digit is 4.

Example 3   The number 186,000 has how many digits?

Solution   The number 186,000 has **six digits.**

Example 4   What is the last digit of 26,348?

Solution   The number 26,348 has five digits. The last digit is **8.**

Practice   Write the next three numbers in each sequence:

a. 6, 8, 10, 12 , 14 , 16 , ...

b. 7, 14, 21, 28 , 35 , 42 , ...

c. 4, 8, 12, 16 , 20 , 24 , ...

d. 21, 18, 15, 12 , 9 , 6 , ...

e. 45, 40, 35, 30 , 25 , 20 , ...

f. 12, 18, 24, 30 , 36 , 42 , ...

How many digits are in each of these numbers?

g. 36,756   h. 8002   i. 1,287,495

What is the last digit of each of these numbers?

j. 17   k. 3586   l. 654,321

Problem set 1

Write the next number in each sequence:

1. 10, 15, 20, _25_, ...   2. 56, 49, 42, _35_, ...

3. 8, 16, 24, _32_, ...   4. 18, 27, 36, 45, _54_, ...

5. 24, 21, 18, _15_, ...   6. 32, 28, 24, 20, _16_, ...

Write the missing number in each sequence:

7. 7, 14, _21_, 28, 35, ...   8. 40, _35_, 30, 25, 20, ...

9. 20, _24_, 28, 32, 36, ...   10. 24, 32, _36_, 48, ...

11. _42_, 36, 30, 24, ...   12. 21, 28, _35_, 42, ...

Write the next three numbers in each sequence:

13. 3, 6, 9, 12, _15_, _18_, _21_, ...

14. 8, 16, 24, _32_, _40_, _48_, ...

15. 6, 12, 18, _24_, _29_, _36_, ...

16. 40, 35, 30, _25_, _20_, _15_, ...

17. 18, 21, 24, _27_, _30_, _33_, ...

18. 9, 18, 27, _36_, _45_, _54_, ...

19. What word names an ordered list of numbers?

How many digits are in each number?

20. 186,000   21. 73,842   22. 30,004,091

What is the last digit of each number?

23. 26,348   24. 347   25. 9,675,420

LESSON
2

Identifying Even and Odd Numbers

Facts Practice: 100 Addition Facts (Test A in Test Masters)

Mental Math: Count up and down by tens between 10 and 100. Count up and down by hundreds between 100 and 1000.

a. 6 + 6   **b.** 60 + 60
c. 600 + 600   **d.** 60 + 70
e. 70 + 80   **f.** 300 + 300 + 300
g. 90 + 90   **h.** 50 + 50 + 50 + 50

Problem Solving: How many two-digit counting numbers are there?

Whole numbers are the counting numbers and 0.

0, 1, 2, 3, 4, 5, 6, ...

Counting by twos, we say these numbers.

2, 4, 6, 8, 10, 12, 14, 16, 18, 20, ...

This is a special sequence. These numbers are **even numbers.** The number 0 is also an even number. The sequence of even numbers continues without end. The numbers 36 and 756 and 148,567,896,094 are also even. We can tell that a whole number is even by the last digit. If the last digit is 0, 2, 4, 6, or 8, then the number is even.

An even number of objects can be paired. Twelve is an even number. Here we have drawn 12 dots and have paired them. Notice that every dot has a "partner."

Next we draw 13 dots and pair them. We find that there is an "odd fellow" without a "partner."

So 13 is not even.

The whole numbers that are not even are **odd.** We make a list of the odd numbers by beginning with one, and then adding two to get the following numbers. The sequence of the odd numbers is

1, 3, 5, 7, 9, 11, 13, 15, 17, ...

Thus, if the last digit is 1, 3, 5, 7, or 9, then the number is odd. All whole numbers are either odd or even.

Example 1 Which of these numbers is even?

3586   2345   2223

Solution Even numbers are the numbers we say when counting by twos. We may look at the last digit to see if the number is odd or even. If the last digit is even, then the number is even. The last digits of these three numbers are 6, 5, and 3, respectively. Since the digit 6 is even, the even number is **3586.**

Example 2 Which of these numbers is not odd?

123,456   654,321   353,535

Solution All whole numbers are either odd or even. A number that is not odd is even. The last digits of these numbers are 6, 1, and 5, respectively. Since 6 is even (not odd), the number that is not odd is **123,456.**

Practice Tell whether each of these numbers is odd or even:

a. 0   **b.** 1234   **c.** 20,001

d. 999   **e.** 3000   **f.** 391,048

Problem set 2

†**1.** If a whole number is not even, then what is it?
(2) odd

What is the last digit in each number?

2. 47,286,560
(1) 0

3. 296,317
(1) 7

For each number, write either "odd" or "even":

4. 15 even
(2) even

5. 196
(2) even

6. 3567
(2) odd

7. Which of these numbers is even?
(2)

      3716   2345   2223

8. Which of these numbers is odd?
(2)

    45,678   56,789   67,890

9. Which of these numbers is not odd?
(2)

    333,456   654,321   353,535

10. Which of these numbers is not even?
(2)

    300   232   323

Write the next three numbers in each sequence:

11. 9, 12, 15, ____, ____, ____, ...
(1)

12. 16, 24, 32, 40, 48, 56, ...
(1)

13. 120, 110, 100, 90, 80, 70, ...
(1)

---

†The italicized numbers within parentheses underneath each problem number are called *lesson reference numbers*. These numbers refer to the lesson(s) in which the major concept of that particular problem is introduced. If additional assistance is needed, reference should be made to the discussion, examples, practice, or problem set of that lesson.

Gabi

14. 28, 24, 20, _____, _____, _____, ...
(1)

15. 55, 50, 45, _____, _____, _____, ...
(1)

16. 18, 27, 36, _____, _____, _____, ...
(1)

17. 36, 33, 30, _____, _____, _____, ...
(1)

18. 18, 24, 30, _____, _____, _____, ...
(1)

19. 14, 21, 28, _____, _____, _____, ...
(1)

20. 66, 60, 54, _____, _____, _____, ...
(1)

21. 48, 44, 40, _____, _____, _____, ...
(1)

22. 99, 90, 81, _____, _____, _____, ...
(1)

23. 88, 80, 72, _____, _____, _____, ...
(1)

24. 84, 77, 70, _____, _____, _____, ...
(1)

25. If all of the students in a class can form two equal lines
(2) of students, then the number of students in the class
could not be how many?

A. 30   B. 31   C. 32

LESSON
3

Using Money to Illustrate Place Value

Facts Practice: 100 Addition Facts (Test A in Test Masters)

Mental Math: Count up and down by tens between 10 and 200. Count up and down by hundreds between 100 and 2000.

a. 30 + 70	**b.** 20 + 300	**c.** 320 + 20
d. 340 + 200	**e.** 250 + 40	**f.** 250 + 400
g. 120 + 60	**h.** 600 + 120	

Problem Solving: How many three-digit counting numbers are there?

Materials needed:

- Each student will need copies of $1, $10, and $100 bills, a place value template, and storage materials.

- Masters for $1, $10, and $100 bills are available in the *Math 65 Test Masters*. Each student will need 20 bills of each denomination.

- A master for the *Place Value Template* is also in the *Math 65 Test Masters*. One place value template is needed for each student.

- A locking plastic bag and paper clips are convenient for storage. This "money pouch" may be useful for many weeks.

Preparation for activity:

- Distribute bills, storage materials, and place value templates to students.

Activity Place twelve $1 bills on the template in the ones' position.

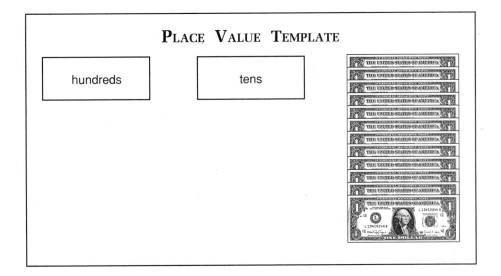

There are twelve $1 bills on the template. We can use fewer bills to make $12 by exchanging ten $1 bills for one $10 bill. Take ten of the $1 bills from the template and replace them with one $10 bill in the tens' position.

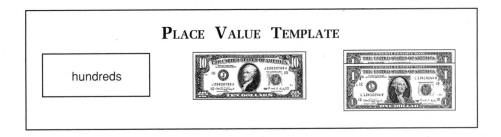

The bills on the template illustrate the **expanded form** of 12.

Expanded form: 1 ten + 2 ones

Example Place $312 on the place value template using the fewest bills necessary. Then write "312" in expanded form.

Solution

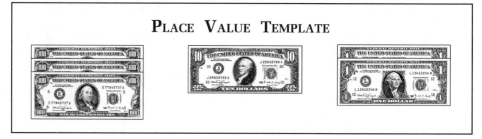

PLACE VALUE TEMPLATE

In expanded form, 312 is

3 hundreds + 1 ten + 2 ones

Practice

a. Place twelve $10 bills on the place value template. Then exchange ten of the bills for one $100 bill and write the result in expanded form.

b. Place twelve $1 bills and twelve $10 bills on the template. Then exchange bills so that the same amount of money is on the template using the fewest number of bills. Write the result in expanded form.

c. Which digit in 365 shows the number of tens?

d. Write the number for 3 hundreds plus 5 tens.

e. How much money is one $100 bill plus ten $10 bills plus fifteen $1 bills? You may use your bills to help you find the answer.

Problem set 3

1. Write the number for 5 hundreds plus 7 tens plus
   (3) 8 ones.

2. Write the number for 2 hundreds plus 5 tens plus
   (3) 0 ones.

3. In 560, which digit shows the number of tens?
   (3)

4. In 365, which digit shows the number of ones?
   (3)

5. Ten tens is the same as one what?
   (3)

6. Which number is not odd?
(2)
A. 365   B. 653   C. 536

7. Which number is not even?
(2)
A. 1234   B. 2345   C. 3456

8. The greatest two-digit odd number is 99. What is the
(2) greatest two-digit even number?

9. Two teams have an equal number of players. The total
(2) number of players on both teams could not be:

A. 22   B. 25   C. 50

10. We can count to 12 by 2's or by 3's. We do not count to
(1) 12 when counting by:

A. 1's   B. 4's   C. 5's   D. 6's

Write the next three numbers in each sequence:

11. 9, 12, 15, _____, _____, _____, ...
(1)

12. 54, 48, 42, _____, _____, _____, ...
(1)

13. 8, 16, 24, _____, _____, _____, ...
(1)

14. 80, 72, 64, _____, _____, _____, ...
(1)

15. 16, 20, 24, _____, _____, _____, ...
(1)

16. 40, 36, 32, _____, _____, _____, ...
(1)

17. 27, 36, 45, _____, _____, _____, ...
(1)

18. 81, 72, 63, _____, _____, _____, ...
(1)

19. 10, 20, 30, _____, _____, _____, ...
(1)

20. 33, 30, 27, _____, _____, _____, ...
(1)

21. What number equals four tens?
(3)

22. What number equals five hundreds?
(3)

23. How much money is two $100 bills plus twelve $10
(3) bills plus fourteen $1 bills? You may use your bills to
help you find the answer.

24. The number 80 means eight tens. The number 800
(3) means eight what?

25. The fifth number in the sequence 4, 8, 12, 16, ..., is 20.
(1) What is the ninth number in this sequence?

LESSON 4

Comparing Whole Numbers

Facts Practice: 100 Addition Facts (Test A in Test Masters)

Mental Math: Count up and down by tens between 0 and 200.
Count up and down by hundreds between 0
and 2000.

a. 300 + 300 + 20 + 20   **b.** 250 + 50
c. 300 + 350   **d.** 320 + 320
e. 300 + 300 + 50 + 50   **f.** 250 + 60
g. 340 + 600   **h.** 240 + 320

Problem Solving: The two-digit counting numbers that have
a 1 and 2 are 12 and 21. There are six
three-digit counting numbers that have a 1,
2, and 3. One of these numbers is 213.
What are the other five numbers?

When we count from one to ten, we count in order of size
from least to greatest.

$$1, 2, 3, 4, 5, 6, 7, 8, 9, 10$$

least   greatest

Of these numbers, the least is one and the greatest is ten.
With these numbers in order, we can see that five is
greater than four and that five is less than six.

Sometimes we use mathematical symbols to compare numbers.

$$5 = 5 \quad \text{is read} \quad \text{"Five is equal to five."}$$

$$5 > 4 \quad \text{is read} \quad \text{"Five is greater than four."}$$

$$5 < 6 \quad \text{is read} \quad \text{"Five is less than six."}$$

When the "greater than/less than" symbol is used to show the comparison, it may point either to the left or to the right. When the symbol is properly placed between two numbers, the smaller end points to the smaller number.

Example 1 Write the numbers 64, 46, and 54 in order from least to greatest.

Solution From least to greatest means from smallest to largest. We write the numbers in this order:

46, 54, 64

Example 2 Show each comparison by replacing the circle with the proper comparison symbol:

(a) 7 ◯ 7   (b) 6 ◯ 4   (c) 6 ◯ 8

Solution If two numbers are equal, we show the comparison with an equal sign.

(a) **7 = 7**

If two numbers are not equal, we place the "greater than/less than" symbol so that the smaller end points toward the smaller number.

(b) **6 > 4**   (c) **6 < 8**

Example 3 Write this comparison using digits and a comparison symbol:

Six is less than ten.

Solution   We translate the words into digits and a comparison symbol.

$$6 < 10$$

Practice   Write each comparison using mathematical symbols:

a. Twenty is less than thirty.

b. Twelve is greater than eight.

c. Write the numbers 324, 243, and 423 in order from least to greatest.

Compare each pair of numbers by replacing the circle with the proper comparison symbol:

d. 36 ◯ 63

e. 110 ◯ 101

f. 90 ◯ 90

g. 112 ◯ 121

Problem set 4   Write each comparison using digits and a comparison symbol:

1. Four is less than ten.
(4)

2. Fifteen is greater than twelve.
(4)

Compare each pair of numbers by replacing the circle with the proper comparison symbol:

3. 7 ◯ 10
(4)

4. 34 ◯ 43
(4)

5. Write the number for 3 hundreds plus 6 tens plus 5 ones.
(3)

6. Which digit shows the number of hundreds in 675?
(3)

7. Which digit shows the number of ones in 983?
(3)

8. One hundred equals ten what?
(3)

For each number, write either "odd" or "even":

9. 36,275   **10.** 36,300   **11.** 5,396,428
(2)   (2)   (2)

12. The greatest two-digit odd number is 99. What is the
(2) greatest three-digit odd number?

13. We can count to 18 by 2's or by 3's. We do not count to
(1) 18 when counting by:

     A. 1's   B. 4's   C. 6's   D. 9's

14. Write 435, 354, and 543 in order from least to greatest.
(4)

15. The fourth number in the sequence 6, 12, 18, …, is 24.
(1) What is the **ninth** number in this sequence?

16. How much money is five $100 bills, thirteen $10 bills,
(3) and ten $1 bills? You may use your bills to help you
find the answer.

Write the next three numbers in each sequence:

17. 20, 24, 28, _____, _____, _____, …
(1)

18. 106, 104, 102, _____, _____, _____, …
(1)

19. 0, 6, 12, _____, _____, _____, …
(1)

20. 0, 7, 14, _____, _____, _____, …
(1)

21. 40, 32, 24, _____, _____, _____, …
(1)

22. 45, 36, 27, _____, _____, _____, …
(1)

23. What number equals nine tens?
(3)

24. What number equals eleven tens?
(3)

25. What is the **seventh** number in this sequence?
(1)
                    8, 16, 24, …

LESSON 5

Naming Whole Numbers Through Hundreds • Dollars and Cents

Facts Practice: 100 Addition Facts (Test A in Test Masters)

Mental Math: Count up and down by tens between 0 and 200. Count up and down by hundreds between 0 and 2000.

a. 200 + 60 + 300   **b.** 20 + 600 + 30
c. 350 + 420   **d.** 250 + 250
e. 400 + 320 + 40   **f.** 30 + 330 + 100
g. 640 + 250   **h.** 260 + 260

Problem Solving: Write all the three-digit numbers that each have the digits 2, 3, and 4.

Naming whole numbers through hundreds

If numbers are to be our "friends," we should get to know their names. Naming numbers is not difficult if we pay attention to place values. In order to name larger numbers, we should first be able to name numbers which have three digits.

Look at the number 365.

365 means: three hundreds + six tens + five ones

365 is named: three hundred   sixty   five

We will use words to name a number that we see and use digits to write a number that is named. Look at these examples.

18	eighteen
80	eighty
81	eighty-one
108	one hundred eight
821	eight hundred twenty-one

Notice that we do not use the word *and* when naming whole numbers. For example, we name the number 108, "one hundred eight," **not** "one hundred and eight." Also, notice that we use a hyphen when using words to write the numbers from 21 to 99 which do not end with zero. For example, we write 21, "twenty-one," **not** "twenty one."

Dollars and cents   Dollars and cents are written with a dollar sign and a decimal point. We first name the number of dollars and then name the number of cents. We use "and" between the number of dollars and the number of cents. For example, $324.56 is written as three hundred twenty-four dollars and fifty-six cents.

Practice†   **a.** Use words to name $563.45.

b. Name 101 using words.

c. Use words to name 111.

d. Use digits to write two hundred forty-five.

e. Write four hundred twenty using digits.

f. Use digits to write five hundred three dollars and fifty cents.

Problem set 5   **1.** Use digits to write three hundred seventy-four dollars and twenty cents.
   (5)

2. Use words to name $623.15.
(5)

3. Use digits to write two hundred five.
(5)

4. Use words to name 109.
(5)

---

†All lessons with practice sets starred with an asterisk (*) have supplemental practice sets in the appendix. These sets may be used as needed for additional practice.

5. Write this comparison using digits and a comparison
(4)   symbol:

> *One hundred fifty is greater than one hundred fifteen.*

6. Compare: 346 ◯ 436
(4)

7. Use digits to write the number for 5 hundreds plus 7
(3)   tens plus 9 ones.

8. Arrange these four numbers in order from least to
(4)   greatest:

462	624	246	426

9. Which digit shows the number of tens in 567?
(3)

10. Counting by tens, what number comes after 90?
(1)

For each number, write either "even" or "odd":

11. 363,636   **12.** 36,363   **13.** 2000
(2)   (2)   (2)

14. The greatest three-digit odd number is 999. What is
(2)   the greatest three-digit even number?

15. We can count to 20 by 2's or by 10's. We do not count
(1)   to 20 when counting by:

   A. 1's   B. 3's   C. 4's   D. 5's

16. There is an equal number of boys and girls in the
(2)   room. Which could **not** be the number of students in
   the room?

   A. 12   B. 29   C. 30   D. 44

17. How much money is six $100 bills, nine $10 bills, and
(3)   twelve $1 bills? You may use your bills to help you
   find the answer.

Write the next four numbers in each sequence:

18. 0, 9, 18, _____, _____, _____, _____, ...
(1)

19. 25, 30, 35, _____, _____, _____, _____, …
(1)

20. 6, 12, 18, _____, _____, _____, _____, …
(1)

21. 100, 90, 80, _____, _____, _____, _____, …
(1)

22. 90, 81, 72, _____, _____, _____, _____, …
(1)

23. 88, 80, 72, _____, _____, _____, _____, …
(1)

24. 7, 14, 21, _____, _____, _____, _____, …
(1)

25. What is the ninth number in this sequence?
(1)
3, 6, 9, …

LESSON
6

Adding One-Digit Numbers • Practicing the Addition Algorithm

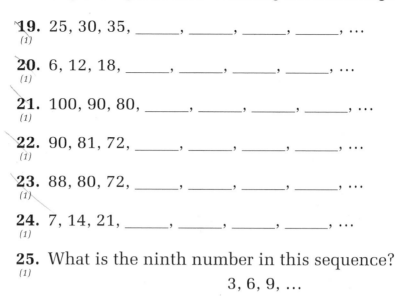

Facts Practice: 100 Addition Facts (Test A in Test Masters)

Mental Math: Count up and down by 20's between 0 and 200. Count up and down by 200's between 0 and 2000.

a. 400 + 50 + 300 + 40   b. 320 + 300
c. 320 + 30   d. 320 + 330
e. 60 + 200 + 20 + 400   f. 400 + 540
g. 40 + 250   h. 450 + 450

Problem Solving: Write all six three-digit numbers that each have the digits 3, 4, and 5. Then arrange the six numbers in order from least to greatest.

Adding one-digit numbers

Numbers that are added are called **addends.** The answer to an addition problem is the **sum.** We may add numbers in any order to find the sum. For example, the sum of 5 + 6 equals the sum of 6 + 5. When adding more than two numbers, we may still add in any order. Here are three ways to add 6, 3, and 4. We show the two numbers we added first. Sometimes we can find pairs of numbers that add up to 10. This makes the addition easier.

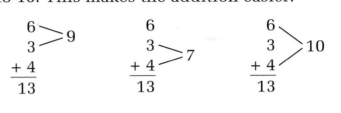

Example 1 What is the sum of 7, 4, 3, and 6?

Solution The "sum" is the answer when we add. We may add the numbers as they are written or align them in a column. Here we write the numbers in a column and add in an order that makes the work a little easier.

$$10 \Big\langle \begin{matrix} 7 \\ 4 \\ 3 \\ +\ 6 \end{matrix} \Big\rangle 10 \\ \overline{20}$$

Practicing the addition algorithm An **algorithm** is a procedure for getting an answer. Algorithms were invented to get answers quickly and easily. In this lesson we will practice a common addition algorithm.

When we add, we are careful to add like things. As the saying goes, "You cannot add apples and oranges and get oranges." When we add numbers, we are careful to add digits that have the same place value. Digits that are in the same column have the same place value.

Adding money may help us understand the addition algorithm. Two students may want to act out the story in this example.

Example 2 Tom had $462. Maria paid Tom $58 rent when she landed on his property. Then how much money did Tom have?

Solution First we will use bills to illustrate the story: Tom had $462.

Maria paid Tom $58 rent.

When Tom added the money Maria paid him to the money he already had, he ended up with four $100 bills, eleven $10 bills, and ten $1 bills.

Tom may exchange the ten $1 bills for one $10 bill. That will give Tom twelve $10 bills. Then he may exchange ten $10 bills for one $100 bill. That will give Tom five $100 bills and two $10 bills.

After Maria paid Tom, he had **$520.**

Now we will show a paper-and-pencil solution.

Tom had $462. $462
Maria paid Tom $58.   + $ 58
Then Tom had …

First we add the ones, then the tens, and then the hundreds.

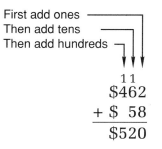

First add ones
Then add tens
Then add hundreds

    1 1
$462
+ $ 58
$520

Notice we exchange ten ones for one ten. Then we exchange ten tens for one hundred.

Practice* Find the sum for each of these addition problems. While adding, look for combinations which add up to 10.

a. 8 + 6 + 2   **b.** 4 + 7 + 3 + 6

c. 9 + 6 + 4   **d.** 4 + 5 + 6 + 7

e. 7 + 3 + 4   **f.** 2 + 6 + 3 + 5

g. 6 + 7 + 5   **h.** 8 + 7 + 5 + 3

Use the addition algorithm to find the sum of each of these addition problems. When putting the numbers into columns, remember to line up the last digits one above the other.

i. $463 + $158   **j.** 674 + 555   **k.** $323
$142
l. 543 + 98   **m.** $47 + $485   + $365

Problem set 6

1. You may use bills to help you answer the question in
(6) this story:

> *Tom had $520. Mike paid him $86 rent. Then how much money did Tom have?*

2. Use words to name $212.50.
(5)

3. In 274, which digit shows the number of hundreds?
(3)

For each number, write either "even" or "odd":

4. 1234   **5.** 12,345   **6.** 1,234,567
(2)   (2)   (2)

7. Use digits to write five hundred eight dollars.
(5)

8. Use words to name 580.
(5)

Find each sum. Look for combinations of 10.

9. 1 + 6 + 9
(6)

10. 7 + 6 + 4
(6)

11. 8 + 3 + 1 + 7
(6)

12. 4 + 5 + 6 + 7
(6)

13. $436
(6)   + $527

14.   592
(6)   + 408

15.   963
(6)   + 79

16. $180
(6)   + $747

17. All the books were put into two piles. There was one
(2)   more book in one pile than in the other pile. The total
      number of books in both piles could not be:

A. 28   B. 29   C. 33   D. 55

Find the **eighth** number in each sequence:

18. 10, 20, 30, …
(1)

19. 6, 12, 18, …
(1)

20. 7, 14, 21, …
(1)

21. 8, 16, 24, …
(1)

22. Compare:
(4)
        Nine hundred sixteen ◯ nine hundred sixty

23. Write this comparison using digits and a comparison
(4)   symbol:

        Six hundred ninety is greater than six
        hundred nine.

24. Compare: 5 + 5 + 5 ◯ 4 + 5 + 6
(4)

25. The smallest even two-digit whole number is 10. What
(2)   is the smallest odd two-digit whole number?

LESSON 7

Place Value • Writing Numbers Through Hundred-Thousands'

Facts Practice: 100 Addition Facts (Test A in Test Masters)

Mental Math: Count up and down by 20's between 0 and 200. Count up and down by 200's between 0 and 2000.

a. $25 + $25	**b.** $300 + $450	**c.** $250 + $250
d. 30 + 450	**e.** $75 + $25	**f.** $750 + $250
g. $50 + $350	**h.** 360 + 360	

Problem Solving: The sum of 12 and 21 is 33. What is the sum of the six three-digit numbers that have the digits 1, 2, and 3? What is the sum of the digits in each column? Why is the sum of the digits in each column the same?

Place value   The value of a digit depends upon its place in a number. The table below lists the values of the first six whole number places.

$$\underline{\hspace{1.2cm}}\ \underline{\hspace{1.2cm}}\ \underline{\hspace{1.2cm}}\ ,\ \underline{\hspace{1.2cm}}\ \underline{\hspace{1.2cm}}\ \underline{\hspace{1.2cm}}$$

hundred-thousands' | ten-thousands' | thousands' | hundreds' | tens' | ones'

Writing numbers through hundred-thousands'   We have practiced naming whole numbers with up to three digits. In this lesson we begin naming whole numbers with four, five, and six digits.

Sometimes commas are used to write whole numbers with more than three digits to make the numbers easier to read. To write commas in a whole number, we count digits from the right-hand end of the whole number and place a comma after every three digits.

54,321

Count from the right. Insert a comma
after three places.

The comma in this number marks the end of the
thousands. To read this number, we read the number
formed by the digits in front of the comma, and then say
"thousand" when we get to the comma. Next, we read the
number formed by the last three digits.

54,321

Fifty-four thousand, three hundred twenty-one

Notice that we write a comma after the word *thousand*
when we use words to name the number. The list below
shows samples of named numbers.

5,281	Five thousand, two hundred eighty-one
$27,050	Twenty-seven thousand, fifty dollars
125,000	One hundred twenty-five thousand
203,400	Two hundred three thousand, four hundred

Example 1 Use words to name 52370.

Solution We begin by writing the number with a comma: 52,370.
Then we name the number formed by the digits in front of
the comma, write "thousand" and a comma, and then we
name the number formed by the digits after the comma.
We name 52,370 as **fifty-two thousand, three hundred
seventy.**

Example 2 Using digits, write one hundred fifty thousand, two
hundred thirty-four.

Solution We use digits to write "one hundred fifty" and write a
comma for the word *thousand.* Then we use digits to write
"two hundred thirty-four": **150,234.**

Numbers used to name position or order are called **ordinal numbers.** This table of examples shows two ways to write ordinal numbers.

Examples of Ordinal Numbers

first	1st	seventh	7th
second	2nd	eighth	8th
third	3rd	ninth	9th
fourth	4th	tenth	10th
fifth	5th	eleventh	11th
sixth	6th	twelfth	12th

Example 3 Tom was the fourth person in a line of ten people waiting in line for a movie. How many people were in front of Tom? How many people were behind Tom?

Solution We will draw a sketch to illustrate the problem.

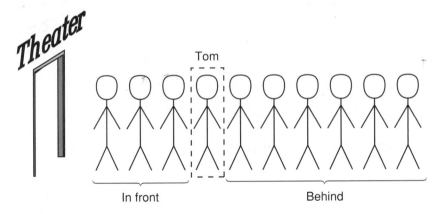

There were **three people in front** of Tom and **six people behind** him.

Practice* Use words to name each number. (*Hint:* Begin by putting the comma in place.)

    a. 36420

    b. $12300

    c. 4567

Use digits to write each number:

   d. Sixty-three thousand, one hundred seventeen

   e. Two hundred fifty-six thousand, seven hundred

   f. Fifty thousand, nine hundred twenty-four

   g. Seven hundred fifty thousand dollars

Problem set 7

1. You may use bills to help you find the answer to the
(6) question in the story:

> *Mike had $462. He was paid $88 rent. Then
> how much money did Mike have?*

2. Which digit is in the tens' place in 567?
(7)

3. Use digits to write seven hundred seven.
(5)

4. Use words to name 717,452.
(7)

5. Find the sum of 54 and 246.
(6)

Find each sum:

  6. $463   **7.** $286   **8.**   709
  (6)   + $364   (6)   + $414   (6)   + 314

Find the **seventh** number in each sequence:

  9. 10, 20, 30, …   **10.** 5, 10, 15, …
  (1)   (1)

  11. 6, 12, 18, …   **12.** 7, 14, 21, …
  (1)   (1)

  13. 8, 16, 24, …   **14.** 9, 18, 27, …
  (1)   (1)

15. Compare: two hundred fifty $\bigcirc$ two hundred fifteen
(4)

16. Compare: $3 + 8 + 7 \bigcirc 5 + 7 + 5$
(4)

Find each sum:

17.
(6)
$436
$72
+ $54

18.
(6)
361
493
+ 147

19.
(6)
506
79
+ 434

20. Write this comparison using digits and a comparison
(4) symbol:

> *Four hundred eight is less than four hundred
> eighty.*

21. We can count to 24 by 2's or by 3's. We do not count to
(1) 24 when counting by:

A. 4's   B. 5's   C. 6's   D. 8's

For each number, write "even" or "odd":

22. 1969
(2)

23. 1492
(2)

24. 1776
(2)

25. The smallest even three-digit number is 100. What is
(2) the smallest odd three-digit number?

LESSON
8

Subtraction Facts •
Fact Families

Facts Practice: 100 Addition Facts (Test A in Test Masters)

Mental Math: Count up and down by 50's between 0 and 500.
Count up and down by 500's between 0 and 5000.

    a. 3000 + 3000   **b.** 5000 + 5000   **c.** 350 + 450
    d. 370 + 580   **e.** $275 + $25   **f.** $350 + $500
    g. 750 + 750   **h.** 250 + 750

Problem Solving: The sum of the six numbers that have the digits 1, 2, and 3 is 1,332. What is the sum of the six three-digit numbers that have the digits 2, 4, and 6? What do you notice about the two sums?

Subtraction facts

Subtraction is taking one number from another number. If five birds were perched on a branch and three flew away, then two birds would be left on the branch.

A number sentence for this story is

$$5 - 3 = 2$$

We read this number sentence, "Five minus three equals two." The dash (–) between the 5 and the 3 is called a **minus sign. The minus sign tells us to subtract the number to the right of the sign from the number to the left of the sign**. Order matters when we subtract. The subtraction 5 − 3 means to start with 5 and subtract 3.

When a subtraction problem is written in a column with one number above another number, we start with the top number and subtract the bottom number. These two forms mean the same thing. Both tell us to start with 5 and subtract 3.

$$5 - 3 \qquad\qquad \begin{array}{r} 5 \\ -\ 3 \\ \hline \end{array}$$

The answer when we subtract is called the **difference.**

Example 1 When 7 is subtracted from 12, what is the difference?

Solution We start with 12 and subtract 7. If we write the numbers in a line, we write the 12 first. If we write the numbers in a column, we write the 12 on top and write the 7 below the 2 so that the digits with the same place values are in the same column. We subtract and find that the difference is **5.**

$$12 - 7 = 5 \qquad\qquad \begin{array}{r} 12 \\ -\ \ 7 \\ \hline 5 \end{array}$$

Example 2 What is 8 minus 3?

Solution The word *minus* means to take away. Here we are to find what is left when we take 3 away from 8. When we see the word *minus*, we may put a **minus sign** (−) in its place.

$$8 - 3 = \mathbf{5} \qquad\qquad \begin{array}{r} 8 \\ -\ 3 \\ \hline \mathbf{5} \end{array}$$

Fact families Addition and subtraction are closely related. The three numbers that form an addition fact also form a subtraction fact. For example, the numbers 2, 3, and 5 form two addition facts and two subtraction facts.

$$\begin{array}{r} 2 \\ +\ 3 \\ \hline 5 \end{array} \qquad \begin{array}{r} 3 \\ +\ 2 \\ \hline 5 \end{array} \qquad \begin{array}{r} 5 \\ -\ 2 \\ \hline 3 \end{array} \qquad \begin{array}{r} 5 \\ -\ 3 \\ \hline 2 \end{array}$$

We call the numbers 2, 3, and 5 a *fact family*.

Example 3   Write two addition facts and two subtraction facts for the fact family 3, 4, and 7.

Solution

$$3 + 4 = 7 \qquad 4 + 3 = 7$$
$$7 - 3 = 4 \qquad 7 - 4 = 3$$

Practice   **a.** 17 − 9   **b.** 12 − 8   **c.** 15 − 9

d. 11 − 5   **e.** 17 − 8   **f.** 16 − 8

Write two addition facts and two subtraction facts for each fact family:

g. 7, 8, 15

h. 5, 7, 12

Problem set 8

1. Which digit is in the thousands' place in 3654?
(7)

2. List the five odd one-digit numbers.
(2)

3. When seven is subtracted from 15, what is the difference?
(8)

4. When 56 is added to 560, what is the sum?
(6)

5. What is seven minus four?
(8)

6. What is sixty-four plus two hundred six?
(6)

7. Use words to name $812,000.
(7)

8. Use digits to write eight hundred two.
(5)

9. Write a two-digit odd number using 5 and 6.
(2)

10. Use words to name the number for 4 hundreds plus 4 tens plus 4 ones.
(3)

Write the **ninth** number in each sequence:

11. 6, 12, 18, …   **12.** 3, 6, 9, …
(1)   *(1)*

13. Write two addition facts and two subtraction facts for
(8) the fact family 4, 8, 12.

14. Think of two odd numbers and add them. Is the sum
(2) odd or even?

Subtract to find each difference:

15. 18 − 9   **16.** 15 − 7   **17.** 12 − 5
(8)   (8)   (8)

18. 11 − 8   **19.** 14 − 6   **20.** 13 − 9
(8)   (8)   (8)

Add to find each sum:

21. $36 + $403 + $97   **22.** 572 + 386 + 38
(6)   (6)

23. 47 + 135 + 70   **24.** $590 + $306 + $75
(6)   (6)

25. Look at this list of numbers. If the greatest odd number
(4,2) in this list is added to the smallest even number in
this list, what is the sum?

364   287   428   273

LESSON 9

Practicing the Subtraction Algorithm

Facts Practice: 100 Subtraction Facts (Test B in Test Masters)

Mental Math: Count up and down by 50's between 0 and 500.
Count up and down by 500's between 0 and 5000.

a. $250 + $250   **b.** 6000 + 6000   **c.** $75 + $125
d. 750 + 750   **e.** 60 − 20   **f.** 600 − 200
g. 6000 − 2000   **h.** 860 + 70

Problem Solving: The letters P, T, and A can be arranged in
six different orders. Write the six possible
orders and circle the ones that spell words.

We may find a subtraction answer by counting, by using
objects, or by remembering combinations. When
subtracting larger numbers, it is helpful to have a method.

We remember that a method is called an *algorithm*. In this lesson we will practice an algorithm for subtraction. We will use a money example to help us understand the algorithm. You may want to use some bills from your money pouch to act out this story.

Maria has $524. She needs to pay Tom $58 for rent. After she pays Tom, how much money will she have?

We will use five $100 bills, two $10 bills, and four $1 bills to show how much money Maria has.

5　　　　　　2　　　　　　4

From $524 Maria needs to pay Tom $58, which is five $10 bills and eight $1 bills. Maria has enough money to pay Tom, but she doesn't have enough $10 bills and $1 bills to pay him with tens and ones. Before Maria pays Tom, she may exchange one $10 bill for ten $1 bills. Then she will have enough ones but not enough tens.

5　　　　　　1　　　　　　14

She may also exchange one $100 bill for ten $10 bills. Then she will have enough tens.

4　　　　　　11　　　　　　14

From these bills, Maria can pay Tom with five $10 bills and eight $1 bills. Taking away five tens and eight ones leaves this much.

| 4 | 6 | 6 |

After she pays Tom, Maria will have $466.

We exchanged bills to show the subtraction. We also use exchange with the pencil-and-paper algorithm. We write the subtraction problem and begin subtracting the ones.

Subtract ones

↓

$524

− $ 58

We cannot subtract $8 from $4. We need more ones. We look at the tens' column and see 2 tens. We exchange 1 ten for 10 ones, which gives us 1 ten and 14 ones. Now we can subtract the ones.

$5 2̸¹4

− $ 5 8

6

Next we subtract the tens. We cannot subtract 5 tens from 1 ten, so again we will exchange. This time we exchange 1 hundred for 10 tens, which gives us 4 hundreds and 11 tens. Now we finish subtracting.

$ ⁴5̸ ¹2̸¹4

− $ 5 8

$ 4 6 6

Since the value of every column is 10 times the value of the column to its right, we may follow this method whenever we come to a column where we cannot subtract. Study the example and solution below to see how this is done.

Example Use the subtraction algorithm to find the differences.

(a) $346
     − $264

(b) 219 − 73

(c)   600
     − 123

Solution (a) $ $\overset{2}{\cancel{3}}\overset{1}{4}6$
     − $ 2 6 4
       $ 8 2

(b) $\overset{1}{\cancel{2}}\overset{1}{1}9$
    −   7 3
      1 4 6

(c) $\overset{5}{\cancel{6}}\,\overset{9}{\cancel{0}}\overset{1}{0}$ or $\overset{5\ 9}{\cancel{6}\cancel{0}}\overset{1}{0}$
   − 1 2 3   − 1 2 3
    4 7 7   4 7 7

Notice part (c). Since there are no tens in the tens' column, we must go to the hundreds' column to create some tens. We show a second way of dealing with this situation. We may think of 600 as 60 tens. Taking 1 of the tens leaves 59 tens. Some people think this is a neater and easier way to subtract across zeros.

Practice*   **a.** $496
        − $157

b.   400
     − 136

c. $315
      − $264

d. $500
     − $63

e.   435
     −   76

f.   800
    − 406

g. 86 − 48   **h.** $132 − $40   **i.** 203 − 47

Problem set 9

1. You may use bills to help you find the answer to the
_(9)_   question in this story:

> *Mike had $550. He paid a tax of $75. Then how much money did he have?*

2. List the five even one-digit numbers.
_(2)_

3. Which digit shows the number of tens in 596?
_(3)_

4. One hundred is equal to how many tens?
_(3)_

5. When seven is subtracted from 15, what is the
(8) difference?

6. Write two addition facts and two subtraction facts for
(8) the fact family 7, 8, 15.

7. What is the sum of one hundred ninety and one
(6) hundred nineteen?

8. Write this comparison using digits and a comparison
(4) symbol:

>   *Five hundred forty is greater than five
>   hundred fourteen.*

9. Using digits and symbols, the sentence "Three plus
(4) two equals five" can be written 3 + 2 = 5. Use digits
and symbols to write the following sentence:

>   *Sixty plus sixteen equals seventy-six.*

10. Write a three-digit even number less than 200 using
(2) the digits 1, 2, and 3.

11. $346   **12.**   56   **13.** $219   **14.**   600
(9) − $178   (9)   − 38   (9)   − $73   (9)   − 321

15.   300   **16.** $500   **17.**   608   **18.**   415
(9) − 124   (9)   − $246   (9) − 314   (9) − 378

19. $787   **20.**   573   **21.** $645   **22.**   429
(6) $156   (6)   90   (6) $489   (6)   85
+ $324   + 438   + $65   + 671

Write the **ninth** number in each sequence:

23. 7, 14, 21, ...   **24.** 9, 18, 27, ...   **25.** 8, 16, 24, ...
(1)   (1)   (1)

**LESSON
10**

Missing Numbers in Addition

Facts Practice: 100 Subtraction Facts (Test B in Test Masters)

Mental Math: Count up and down by 25's between 0 and 200. (Think quarters.) Count up and down by 20's between 0 and 200.

a. 5000 + 4500	**b.** 6000 − 4000	**c.** $750 + $250
d. 380 + 90	**e.** 500 − 400	**f.** 125 + 125
g. 640 + 260	**h.** 6 + 6 − 2 + 5	

Problem Solving: Arrange the letters E, T, and A in six different orders. Circle the arrangements that spell words.

In this number sentence there is a missing addend. A letter is used to stand for the missing addend. We used *W*, but any letter may be used. The letter may be upper case or lowercase.

$$8 + W = 15$$

A number sentence with an equal sign is often called an *equation*. Since eight plus seven equals 15, we know that the missing addend in this equation is seven. Notice that we can find a missing addend by subtracting. In this number sentence we subtract eight from 15 to find the missing number.

$$15 - 8 = 7$$

Example 1   Find the missing addend:

$$\begin{array}{r} 24 \\ +\ M \\ \hline 37 \end{array}$$

Solution   There are two addends and the sum.

$$\begin{array}{rl} 24 & \text{addend} \\ +\ M & \text{addend} \\ \hline 37 & \text{sum} \end{array}$$

One of the addends is 24. The sum is 37. We subtract 24 from 37 and find that the missing addend is **13.** Then we use the number in the original problem to be sure the answer is correct.

$$
\begin{array}{r} 37 \\ -\ 24 \\ \hline 13 \end{array}
\qquad
\begin{array}{r} 24 \\ +\ 13 \\ \hline 37 \end{array}
$$

Example 2   Find the missing addend: $15 + 20 + 6 + W = 55$

Solution   In this equation, there are four addends and the sum. The known addends are 15, 20, and 6. Their total is 41.

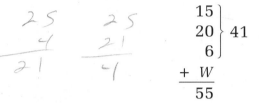

$$
\begin{array}{r}
\left.\begin{array}{r} 15 \\ 20 \\ 6 \end{array}\right\} 41 \\
+\ W \\ \hline 55
\end{array}
$$

So 41 plus W equals 55. We can find the missing addend by subtracting 41 from 55, which is **14.** Then we check the answer.

$$
\begin{array}{r} 55 \\ -\ 41 \\ \hline 14 \end{array}
\qquad
\begin{array}{r} 15 \\ 20 \\ 6 \\ +\ 14 \\ \hline 55 \end{array}
$$

We see that the answer checks.

Practice   Find the missing addend in each equation:

a. $35 + m = 67$ **b.** $n + 27 = 40$

c. $5 + 7 + 9 + f = 30$ **d.** $15 + k + 10 + 25 = 70$

Problem set 10   **1.** You may use bills to help you find the answer to the
(6) question in this story:

> *Maria passed GO and collected $200. If she had $466 before she passed GO, how much money did she have after she passed GO?*

2. For the fact family 4, 5, 9, make two addition facts and
_(8)_ two subtraction facts.

3. Use the digits 4, 5, and 6 to make a three-digit odd
_(2)_ number that is greater than 500.

4. Write this comparison using digits and a comparison
_(4)_ symbol:

> _Six hundred thirteen is less than six hundred
> thirty._

5. $34 + m = 61$
_(10)_

6. What is five hundred ten minus fifty-one?
_(9)_

7. Which digit shows the number of hundreds in
_(3)_ 325,985?

8. We can count to 30 by 3's or by 10's. We do not count
_(1)_ to 30 when counting by:

    A. 2's   B. 4's   C. 5's   D. 6's

9. Think of one odd number and one even number and
_(2)_ add them. Is the sum odd or even?

10. Compare: $100 - 10 \bigcirc 100 - 20$
_(4)_

11. _(9)_ $\begin{array}{r} \$363 \\ - \$179 \\ \hline \end{array}$	**12.** _(9)_ $\begin{array}{r} 400 \\ - 176 \\ \hline \end{array}$	**13.** _(9)_ $\begin{array}{r} \$570 \\ - \$91 \\ \hline \end{array}$	**14.** _(9)_ $\begin{array}{r} 504 \\ - 175 \\ \hline \end{array}$

15. _(6)_ $\begin{array}{r} \$367 \\ \$48 \\ + \$135 \\ \hline \end{array}$	**16.** _(6)_ $\begin{array}{r} 179 \\ 484 \\ + 201 \\ \hline \end{array}$	**17.** _(6)_ $\begin{array}{r} \$305 \\ \$897 \\ + \$725 \\ \hline \end{array}$	**18.** _(6)_ $\begin{array}{r} 32 \\ 248 \\ + 165 \\ \hline \end{array}$

19. $\$463 - \$85$ **20.** $432 + 84 + 578$
_(9)_   _(6)_

21. $18 + w = 42$ **22.** $12 + r = 80$
_(10)_   _(10)_

Write the next four numbers in each sequence:

23. 3, 6, 9, 12, …   **24.** 4, 8, 12, 16, …   **25.** 6, 12, 18, 24, …
_(1)_   _(1)_   _(1)_

LESSON 11

"Some and Some More" Stories

Facts Practice: 100 Subtraction Facts (Test B in Test Masters)

Mental Math: Count up and down by 25's between 0 and 200. Count up and down by 250's between 0 and 2000.

a. 6000 + 3200   **b.** 5000 − 3000   **c.** 375 + 125
d. 570 + 250   **e.** 350 − 300   **f.** 540 − 140
g. 7 + 6 − 3 + 4   **h.** 10 − 3 + 7 + 10

Problem Solving: Find three different letters that can be arranged to spell at least two different words. Can you think of three different letters that can be arranged to spell three different words?

In an action story, a heroic character often risks danger to rescue someone who is in trouble. The details and characters of the story may differ, but the underlying idea, the plot, is the same.

Although we consider many stories in mathematics, there are only a few kinds of stories or plots. One kind of math story is a "some and some more" story. Here are three "some and some more" stories:

Tom paid Mike $120 rent. Then Mike had $645. How much money did Mike have before Tom paid him rent?

Cheryl counted 18 children on the playground. When the bell rang, more children ran onto the playground. Then Cheryl counted 98 children. How many children ran onto the playground when the bell rang?

The school football team scored 6 points in the first quarter, 13 points in the second quarter, 7 points in the third quarter, and 6 points in the fourth quarter. How many points did the team score in all four quarters?

In each of these stories there was "some." Then "some more" was added to make a total. "Some and some more" stories have an addition pattern.

$$\begin{array}{r}\text{Some} \\ +\ \text{Some More} \\ \hline \text{Total}\end{array} \qquad \text{Some} + \text{Some More} = \text{Total}$$

To answer a question in a "some and some more" story, we will:

1. Draw the pattern.
2. Find the missing number.
3. Check the answer to see if the answer is sensible and the arithmetic correct.

Example 1   Tom paid Mike $120 rent. Then Mike had $645. How much money did Mike have before Tom paid him rent?

Solution   Mike had some money. Tom paid him some more money. We draw the pattern.

$$\begin{array}{ll}\text{Mike had some money.} & M \\ \text{Tom paid Mike \$120.} & +\ \$120 \\ \text{Then Mike had \$645.} & \overline{\quad \$645}\end{array}$$

The missing number is how much money Mike had before Tom paid him. We can find a missing addend by subtracting.

$$\begin{array}{r}\$645 \\ -\ \$120 \\ \hline \$525\end{array}$$

Now we check the answer to see if it is sensible and correct. Is it sensible that Mike had $525 before Tom paid him? We return to the original problem and add to check the answer.

$$\begin{array}{ll}\text{Mike had some money.} & \$525 \\ \text{Tom paid Mike \$120.} & +\ \$120 \\ \text{Then Mike had \$645.} & \overline{\quad \$645}\end{array}$$

Before Tom paid him, Mike had **$525.**

Example 2   Cheryl counted 18 children on the playground. When the bell rang, more children ran onto the playground. Then Cheryl counted 98 children. How many children ran onto the playground when the bell rang?

Solution   We draw the pattern.

Some	18 children
+ Some More	+ M children
Total	98 children

The missing number is one of the addends. We can find a missing addend by subtracting.

$$\begin{array}{r} 98 \text{ children} \\ - 18 \text{ children} \\ \hline 80 \text{ children} \end{array}$$

We check the answer to see if it is sensible and correct. Is it sensible that 80 children ran onto the playground when the bell rang?

$$\begin{array}{r} 18 \text{ children} \\ + 80 \text{ children} \\ \hline 98 \text{ children} \end{array}$$

When the bell rang, **80 children** ran onto the playground.

Example 3   The school football team scored 6 points in the first quarter, 13 points in the second quarter, 7 points in the third quarter, and 6 points in the fourth quarter. How many points did the team score in all four quarters?

Solution   The team scored some points, then some more and some more and some more. We draw the pattern.

Some	6 points
Some More	13 points
Some More	7 points
+ Some More	+ 6 points
Total	

The missing number is the total. We add to find the total.

$$
\begin{array}{r}
6 \text{ points} \\
13 \text{ points} \\
7 \text{ points} \\
+ \ \ 6 \text{ points} \\
\hline
\textbf{32 points}
\end{array}
$$

Is the answer sensible? Is the arithmetic correct? One way to check column addition is to add the numbers in a different order.

Practice   For each story, draw a "some and some more" pattern. Then find the missing number and check the answer.

a. Tammy wants to buy a camera. She has $24. The camera costs $41. How much more money does Tammy need?

b. Simon was swimming laps when his mother came to watch. She watched Simon swim 16 laps. If Simon swam 30 laps in all, how many laps did Simon swim before his mother came?

Problem set 11

1. Kerry scored 21 points in the game. If she scored 13 points in the first half of the game, how many points did she score in the second half?
(11)

2. Michael and his brother want to put their money together to buy skates. Michael has $18. His brother has $15. The skates cost $56. How much more money do they need?
(11)

3. The Lees traveled 397 miles one day and 406 miles the next day. Altogether, how many miles did the Lees travel in two days?
(11)

4. For the fact family 8, 9, 17, write two addition facts and two subtraction facts.
(8)

5. What is the greatest three-digit even number that can be made using the digits 1, 2, and 3?
(2)

6. Compare: $8 + 7 + 6 \bigcirc 6 + 7 + 8$
(4)

7. Write this comparison using digits and a comparison
(4) symbol:

*Eight hundred twenty is greater than eight
hundred twelve.*

8. Write the following sentence using digits and
(4) symbols:

Forty minus fourteen equals twenty-six.

9. Think of two odd numbers and one even number. Add
(2) them all together. Is the sum odd or even?

10. Use digits to write four hundred eight dollars and
(5) seventy cents.

11. $\begin{array}{r} \$872 \\ -\ \$56 \end{array}$ **12.** $\begin{array}{r} 706 \\ -\ 134 \end{array}$ **13.** $\begin{array}{r} \$800 \\ -\ \$139 \end{array}$ **14.** $\begin{array}{r} 365 \\ -\ 285 \end{array}$
(9)   (9)   (9)   (9)

15. $\begin{array}{r} 578 \\ +\ \ A \\ \hline 600 \end{array}$ **16.** $\begin{array}{r} \$640 \\ \$152 \\ +\ \$749 \end{array}$ **17.** $\begin{array}{r} 365 \\ 294 \\ +\ 716 \end{array}$ **18.** $\begin{array}{r} \$475 \\ \$233 \\ +\ \ \$76 \end{array}$
(10)   (6)   (6)   (6)

19. $\$317 - \$58$ **20.** $433 + 56 + Q = 497$
(9)   (10)

21. $7 + w = 15$ **22.** $15 + y = 70$
(10)   (10)

Write the next four numbers in each sequence:

23. 9, 18, 27, 36, ...   **24.** 8, 16, 24, 32, ...
(1)   (1)

25. 7, 14, 21, 28, ...
(1)

LESSON
12

Reading and Drawing Number Lines, Part 1 • Tally Marks

Facts Practice: 100 Subtraction Facts (Test B in Test Masters)

Mental Math: Count up and down by 25's between 0 and 300.
Count up and down by 50's between 0 and 500.

a. 6500 + 500	**b.** 1000 − 500	**c.** 75 + 75
d. 750 + 750	**e.** 460 − 400	**f.** 380 − 180
g. 20 + 30 − 5	**h.** 16 − 8 + 4 − 2 + 1	

Problem Solving: Larry, Moe, and Joe lined up side by side for a picture. Then they changed their order. Then they changed their order again. List all the possible arrangements. Three students may demonstrate the possible arrangements.

Reading and drawing number lines, part 1

In mathematics we study numbers. We also study shapes such as circles, squares, and triangles. The study of shapes is called **geometry.** The simplest shapes of geometry are the **point** and the **line.** A line does not end. Part of a line is called a **line segment** or just a segment. Here we illustrate a point, a line, and a segment. The arrowheads show that the line does not end.

•   ←————→   ————

Point   Line   Line segment

By carefully marking and numbering a line we can make a **number line. A number line shows numbers at a certain distance from zero.** On the following number line, the distance from 0 to 1 is a segment of a certain length, which we call a unit segment. The distance from 0 to 5 is five of those segments. The arrowheads show that the number line continues in both directions. Numbers to the left of zero are called **negative numbers.** The small marks by each number are **tick marks.**

Example 1   Draw a number line with whole numbers marked from 0 to 5.

Solution   Begin by drawing a line segment. Arrowheads should be drawn on the ends to show that the number line continues without end. Make a tick mark for zero and label it "0." Make **equally spaced** tick marks to the right of zero for the numbers 1, 2, 3, 4, and 5, and label them respectively. When you have finished, your number line should look like the number line above.

To count on a number line, it is important to focus our attention more on the **segments** than on the tick marks. To help us concentrate on the segments, we will answer questions like the following.

Example 2   How many unit segments are there from 2 to 5 on the number line?

Solution   **A unit segment is the distance from 0 to 1 on the number line.** Looking at the number line above, we see one unit segment from 2 to 3, another from 3 to 4, and a third from 4 to 5. The number of unit segments from 2 to 5 is **3.**

Tally marks   Tally marks are used to keep track of a count. Each tally mark counts as one. Here we show the tallies for one through six.

One	Two	Three	Four	Five	Six

Notice that the tally mark for five is a diagonal mark crossing four vertical marks.

Example 3   What number is represented by this tally?   ⊮ ⊮ ⊮ ‖

Solution   We see three groups of five, which is 15, and we see two more tally marks, which makes **17.**

Practice   **a.** Which of these represents a line segment?

A. ——————   B. ⟷   C. •

b. Draw a number line with whole numbers marked and numbered from 0 to 10.

c. How many unit segments are there from 3 to 7 on the number line?

d. What whole number is 6 unit segments to the right of 2 on the number line?

e. What number is represented by this tally?   ⊮ ⊮ ‖‖‖‖

Problem set 12   **1.** How many unit segments are there from 2 to 7 on the
(12)   number line?

2. Use tally marks to show the number 7.
(12)

3. Gilbert weighs 94 pounds. Andy weighs 86 pounds. If
(11)   they both step on a scale, what will they weigh together?

4. Andy weighs 86 pounds. With his book bag on, Andy
(11)   weighs 110 pounds. How much does Andy's book bag weigh?

5. 862
(9) $- \ \ 79$

6. $\$420$
(9) $- \$137$

7. 508
(9) $- \ \ 96$

8. $\$500$
(9) $- \$136$

9. $\$248$
(6) $\$514$
   $+ \ \ \$18$

10. 907
(6) 45
   $+ \ 653$

11. $\$367$
(6) $\$425$
   $+ \$740$

12. W
(10) $+ \ 427$
   568

13. 38 + 427 + P = 475   **14.** $580 − $94
(10)   (9)

15. The number 57 is between which pair of numbers?
(4)
    A. 40 and 50   B. 50 and 60   C. 60 and 70

16. Write this comparison using digits and a comparison
(4) symbol:

Eighteen is less than eighty.

17. Write two addition facts and two subtraction facts for
(8) the fact family 4, 6, 10.

18. Think of an odd number and an even number.
(2) Subtract the smaller number from the larger number.
Is the answer odd or even?

In problems 19 and 20, find the missing number that
makes each equation true:

19. 18 + m = 150   **20.** 12 + y = 51
(10)   (10)

21. Compare: 952 ◯ 947
(4)

Write the next six numbers in each sequence:

22. 2, 4, 6, ...   **23.** 3, 6, 9, ...
(1)   (1)

24. 4, 8, 12, ...   **25.** 5, 10, 15, ...
(1)   (1)

LESSON
13

Multiplying to Perform Repeated Addition • Adding and Subtracting Dollars and Cents

Facts Practice: 100 Subtraction Facts (Test B in Test Masters)

Mental Math: Count by 25¢ from 25¢ to $3.00 and from $3.00 to 25¢.

a. 6500 − 500	**b.** 2000 − 100	**c.** 225 + 225
d. 750 + 750	**e.** 360 − 200	**f.** 425 − 125
g. 50 + 50 − 25	**h.** 8 + 8 − 1 + 5 − 2	

Problem Solving: Copy this addition problem and fill in the missing digits.

$$\begin{array}{r} 3\_4 \\ + 23\_ \\ \hline \_03 \end{array}$$

Multiplying to perform repeated addition

In a room there are 5 rows of desks with 6 desks in each row. How many desks are in the room?

There are many ways to find an answer to this question. One way is to count each desk by counting by ones. Another way is to count the desks in one row and then count the number of rows. Since there are 5 rows of 6 desks, we can add 5 sixes together, as we show here.

$$6 + 6 + 6 + 6 + 6$$

We can also **multiply** to find the number of desks. Whenever we need to add the same number over and over, we may multiply. To find the sum of 5 sixes, we may multiply 5 and 6. We show two ways to write this.

$$5 \times 6 \qquad \begin{array}{r} 6 \\ \times 5 \\ \hline \end{array}$$

The × is called a **times sign.** We read 5 × 6 by saying "Five times six." Five times six means the total of 5 sixes. Multiplication is another way of adding the same number (the second number) the number of times shown by the first number.

In the picture on the previous page, we see 5 rows of desks with 6 desks in each row. However, if we turn the book sideways, we see 6 rows of desks with 5 desks in each row. So we see that **6 fives is the same as 5 sixes.**

Five sixes (5 × 6) means 6 + 6 + 6 + 6 + 6, which equals 30.

Six fives (6 × 5) means 5 + 5 + 5 + 5 + 5 + 5, which also equals 30.

We see that the answer to 6 × 5 is the same as the answer to 5 × 6. This shows us that we may multiply in any order.

Example 1 Change this addition problem to a multiplication problem:

$$7 + 7 + 7 + 7$$

Solution We are asked to change the addition problem into a multiplication problem. We are not asked to find the sum. We see 4 sevens added together. We can write 4 sevens as a multiplication problem by writing **4 × 7.** This is also equal to 7 × 4.

Adding and subtracting dollars and cents

To add and subtract dollars and cents, we align the decimal points so that we add digits with the same place value.

Example 2 (a) $3.45 + $6.23 + $0.50   (b) $4.50 − $3.80

Solution (a)
$$
\begin{array}{r}
\overset{1}{}\$\ 3.45 \\
\$\ 6.23 \\
+\ \$\ 0.50 \\
\hline
\$10.18
\end{array}
$$

(b) $\overset{3}{\cancel{4}}\overset{1}{.}50$
     $- \$ 3.80$
     $\overline{\quad \$ 0.70}$

Solution (b) is 70 cents. The zero to the left of the decimal point shows that there are no dollars.

Practice* Write a multiplication problem for each of these addition problems:

a. $8 + 8 + 8 + 8$ **b.** $25 + 25 + 25$

c. $9 + 9 + 9 + 9 + 9 + 9$

Add or subtract as shown:

d. $\$5.26$ **e.** $\$3.27$
      $+ \$8.92$ $- \$2.65$

Problem set 13

1. Draw a number line with whole numbers marked from
$^{(12)}$ 0 to 8. How many unit segments are there from 3 to 7 on the number line?

2. Use tally marks to show the number 9.
$^{(12)}$

3. Corina hiked 33 miles in one day. If she hiked 14
$^{(11)}$ miles in the afternoon, how many miles did she hike in the morning?

4. Change this addition problem to a multiplication
$^{(13)}$ problem:

$$7 + 7 + 7 + 7 + 7 + 7$$

5. Write two addition facts and two subtraction facts for
$^{(8)}$ the fact family 3, 7, 10.

6. Jim paddled the canoe down the river 25 miles each
$^{(11)}$ day for 5 days. How far did he travel in 5 days?

7. 300
(9) − 114

8. $5.60
(13) − $2.84

9. 203
(9) − 87

10. $512
(9) − $123

11. 432
(10) + B
        683

12. $2.54
(13) $5.36
      + $0.75

13. 387
(6)   496
     + 874

14. $97
(6) $436
     + $468

15. Use digits and symbols to write "Fifteen minus five
(4) equals ten."

16. Think of two even numbers and one odd number. Add
(2) them together. Is the sum odd or even?

17. $4.56 + $13.76
(13)

18. $5127 − $49
(9)

19. N + 27 + 123 = 153
(10)

20. 2510 − 432
(9)

21. Compare: 3 + 3 + 3 + 3 ◯ 4 + 4 + 4
(4)

Write the next six numbers in each sequence:

22. 6, 12, 18, ...
(1)

23. 7, 14, 21, ...
(1)

24. 8, 16, 24, ...
(1)

25. 9, 18, 27, ...
(1)

**LESSON
14**

Missing Numbers in Subtraction

Facts Practice: 100 Subtraction Facts (Test B in Test Masters)

Mental Math: Count by 25¢ from 25¢ to $3.00 and from $3.00 to 25¢. Count by 50¢ from 50¢ to $5.00 and from $5.00 to 50¢.

   a. 2500 + 500   **b.** 2500 − 500   **c.** 390 + 450
   d. $7.50 + $2.50   **e.** 10 + 10 − 5 + 10 − 5
   f. How much money is 2 quarters? 3 quarters? 4 quarters?

Problem Solving: Copy this addition problem and fill in the missing digits.

$$\begin{array}{r} 52\_ \\ + \ \_94 \\ \hline \_0\_2 \end{array}$$

An addition fact read in the reverse direction forms a subtraction fact.

READING DOWN:			**READING UP:**
Three plus four is seven.	↓	$\begin{array}{r} 3 \\ + 4 \\ \hline 7 \end{array}$	↑ Seven minus four is three.

Likewise, a subtraction fact read in the reverse direction forms an addition fact.

READING DOWN:			**READING UP:**
Nine minus five is four.	↓	$\begin{array}{r} 9 \\ - 5 \\ \hline 4 \end{array}$	↑ Four plus five is nine.

Example 1   Reverse the order of these numbers to make an addition equation:

$$68 - 45 = 23$$

Solution   We write the numbers in reverse order.

$$23 \quad 45 \quad 68$$

Then we write in the plus and equal signs to make an equation.

$$\mathbf{23 + 45 = 68}$$

Example 2   Reverse the order of these numbers to make an addition equation:

$$\begin{array}{r} 77 \\ -\ 23 \\ \hline 54 \end{array}$$

Solution   We write the numbers in reverse order with an addition sign.

$$\begin{array}{r} \mathbf{54} \\ +\ \mathbf{23} \\ \hline \mathbf{77} \end{array}$$

In this lesson we will practice finding missing numbers in subtraction problems. There are three numbers in a subtraction problem. Any one of the three numbers may be missing. Sometimes changing a subtraction problem to an addition problem can help us find the missing number.

Example 3   Find the missing number:

$$\begin{array}{r} F \\ -\ 15 \\ \hline 24 \end{array}$$

Solution   We need to find the first number in this subtraction problem. When 15 is subtracted from F, 24 are left. So F must be more than 24. We will read this subtraction problem in the reverse direction as an addition problem.

READING DOWN:		READING UP:
F minus fifteen is twenty-four.	$\begin{array}{r} F \\ -\ 15 \\ \hline 24 \end{array}$	Twenty-four plus fifteen is F.

Reading up, we see that 24 plus 15 is F. This means we can find F by adding 24 and 15.

$$\begin{array}{r} 24 \\ +\ 15 \\ \hline 39 \end{array}$$

We find that F is **39.** Now we use 39 in place of F in the original problem to check our work.

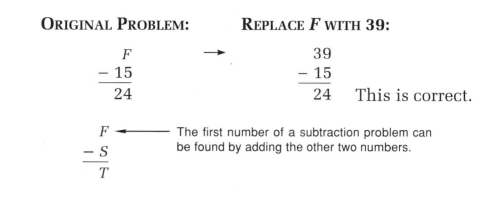

ORIGINAL PROBLEM:

$$\begin{array}{r} F \\ -\ 15 \\ \hline 24 \end{array}$$

REPLACE _F_ WITH 39:

$$\begin{array}{r} 39 \\ -\ 15 \\ \hline 24 \end{array}$$ This is correct.

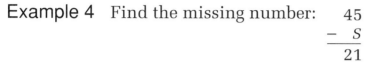

$$\begin{array}{r} F \\ -\ S \\ \hline T \end{array}$$ ⟵ The first number of a subtraction problem can be found by adding the other two numbers.

Example 4   Find the missing number: $$\begin{array}{r} 45 \\ -\ S \\ \hline 21 \end{array}$$

Solution   We need to find the second number in this subtraction problem. When _S_ is subtracted from 45, 21 are left. So _S_ must be less than 45. We will read this problem in both directions.

READING DOWN:		**READING UP:**
Forty-five minus _S_ is twenty-one.	$$\begin{array}{r} 45 \\ -\ S \\ \hline 21 \end{array}$$	Twenty-one plus _S_ is forty-five.

Reading up, we see that 21 plus _S_ is 45. Reading the problem this way, _S_ is a missing addend. We find a missing addend by subtracting.

$$\begin{array}{r} 45 \\ -\ 21 \\ \hline 24 \end{array}$$

We find that _S_ is **24.** Now we replace _S_ with 24 in the original problem to check the answer.

ORIGINAL PROBLEM:

$$\begin{array}{r} 45 \\ -\ S \\ \hline 21 \end{array}$$

REPLACE _S_ WITH 24:

$$\begin{array}{r} 45 \\ -\ 24 \\ \hline 21 \end{array}$$ This is correct.

$$\begin{array}{r} F \\ -\ S \\ \hline T \end{array}$$ ⟵ The second or third number of a subtraction problem can be found by subtracting.

Practice   Reverse the order of the numbers to change each subtraction equation to an addition equation:

a. $34 - 12 = 22$

b.
$$\begin{array}{r} 56 \\ -\ 29 \\ \hline 27 \end{array}$$

Find the missing number in each subtraction problem:

c. $w - 8 = 6$

d. $23 - y = 17$

e.
$$\begin{array}{r} N \\ -\ 24 \\ \hline 48 \end{array}$$

f.
$$\begin{array}{r} 63 \\ -\ P \\ \hline 20 \end{array}$$

g.
$$\begin{array}{r} Q \\ -\ 36 \\ \hline 14 \end{array}$$

h.
$$\begin{array}{r} 42 \\ -\ R \\ \hline 24 \end{array}$$

**Problem set
14**

1. Draw a number line with whole numbers marked and
(12) numbered from 0 to 10. How many unit segments are there from 1 to 5?

2. Use words to name $4.48.
(5)

3. Use digits to write eight hundred eighteen thousand,
(7) eighty.

4. John used tally marks to keep track of the number of
(12) votes each candidate received. Use tally marks to show the number 11.

5. Janet is reading a 260-page book. She has read 85
(11) pages. How many more pages does she have left to read?

6. Change this addition problem to a multiplication
(13) problem:

$$10 + 10 + 10 + 10$$

7. Write this comparison using digits and a comparison
(4) symbol:

Fifty-six is less than sixty-five.

8. Write the largest three-digit even number that has the
(2) digits 1, 2, and 3.

9.
(13)
$43.10
− $1.54

10.
(13)
$3.01
− $1.03

11.
(14)
600
− M
─────
364

12.
(9)
4625
− 1387

13.
(13)
$3.67
$4.12
+ $5.01

14.
(6)
$573
$96
+ $427

15.
(6)
68
532
+ 176

16.
(10)
436
+ Y
─────
634

17.
(14)
$100 − N = 48$

18.
(13)
$31.40 − $13.40

19.
(10)
$6 + 48 + 9 + W = 100$

20.
(6)
$3714 + 56 + 459$

21.
(14)
Reverse the order of the numbers to change this subtraction equation to an addition equation:

$$50 − 18 = 32$$

22.
(1)
What number is missing in this sequence?

$$..., 35, 42, 49, \underline{\hspace{1cm}}, 63, ...$$

23.
(8)
Write two addition facts and two subtraction facts for the fact family 2, 8, 10.

24.
(14)
N
− 17
─────
12

25.
(14)
P
− 175
─────
125

LESSON 15

Making a Multiplication Table

Facts Practice: 100 Multiplication Facts (Test C in Test Masters)

Mental Math: Count up and down by 50's between 0 and 500.

    a. 50 + 50 + 50   **b.** 500 + 500 + 500   **c.** 24 + 26
    d. 240 + 260   **e.** 480 − 200   **f.** 30 + 15
    g. 270 + 280   **h.** $4.50 − $1.25
    i. How much money is 3 quarters? 5 quarters? 6 quarters?
    j. 10 + 6 − 1 + 5 + 10

Problem Solving: Billy, Ron, and Sherry finished first, second, and third in the race, though not necessarily in that order. List the different orders in which they could have finished. Three children may demonstrate the possible orders.

Here we list together several sequences of numbers. Together these sequences form an important pattern.

Zeros	0	0	0	0	0	0
Ones	1	2	3	4	5	6
Twos	2	4	6	8	10	12
Threes	3	6	9	12	15	18
Fours	4	8	12	16	20	24
Fives	5	10	15	20	25	30
Sixes	6	12	18	24	30	36

This pattern is sometimes called a **multiplication table.** From a multiplication table we can find the answer to questions like, "How much is 3 fours?" To determine the answer, we will use rows and columns on a multiplication table, as shown on the next page. Rows run left to right and columns run top to bottom.

Column

↓

	0	1	2	3	4	5	6
0	0	0	0	0	0	0	0
1	0	1	2	3	4	5	6
2	0	2	4	6	8	10	12
3	0	3	6	9	(12)	15	18
4	0	4	8	12	16	20	24
5	0	5	10	15	20	25	30
6	0	6	12	18	24	30	36

Row →

To find 3 × 4, we locate the row which begins with 3 and the column which begins with 4. Look for the number where the row and column meet.

$$4$$
$$\downarrow$$
$$3 \longrightarrow 12$$

The numbers that are multiplied together are called **factors.** The factors in this problem are 3 and 4. The answer to a multiplication problem is called a **product.** From the table we see that the product of 3 and 4 is 12.

Activity The multiplication table above has 7 columns and 7 rows. Make a multiplication table with 10 columns and 10 rows. Be sure to line up the numbers carefully. Use your multiplication table to answer the practice questions.

Practice In a multiplication table, find where the row and column meet and write that number for each problem.

a.   4   **b.**   2   **c.**   6   **d.**   10
            ↓   ↓   ↓   ↓
    5 → ?   6 → ?   3 → ?   8 → ?

Find each product:

e. 6 × 7   **f.** 8 × 9

g. 8 × 4   **h.** 3 × 10

i. The answer to a multiplication problem is called the *product*. What do we call the numbers that are multiplied together?

Problem set 15

1. Draw a number line with whole numbers marked and
(12) numbered from 1 to 13. How many unit segments are there from 6 to 11?

2. Gilbert was the ninth person in line. How many
(7) people were in front of him?

3. Mary used tally marks to count the number of trucks,
(12) cars, and motorcycles that drove by her house. Use tally marks to show the number 13.

4. Write two addition facts and two subtraction facts for
(8) the fact family 1, 9, 10.

5. Use digits to write eight hundred eighty dollars and
(5) eight cents.

6. Khanh weighs 105 pounds. Sammy weighs 87 pounds.
(9) Sammy weighs how many pounds less than Khanh?

7. 3 × 6   **8.** 4 × 8
(15)   (15)

9. 7 × 9   **10.** 9 × 10
(15)   (15)

11.
(14)
$$\begin{array}{r} A \\ -\ 819 \\ \hline 100 \end{array}$$

12.
(13)
$$\begin{array}{r} \$6.00 \\ -\ \$5.43 \\ \hline \end{array}$$

13.
(9)
$$\begin{array}{r} \$501 \\ -\ \$256 \\ \hline \end{array}$$

14.
(14)
$$\begin{array}{r} 510 \\ -\ \ Q \\ \hline 256 \end{array}$$

15.
(6)
$$\begin{array}{r} \$564 \\ \$796 \\ +\ \$287 \\ \hline \end{array}$$

16.
(10)
$$\begin{array}{r} N \\ +\ 96 \\ \hline 432 \end{array}$$

17.
(6)
$$\begin{array}{r} 608 \\ 930 \\ +\ 762 \\ \hline \end{array}$$

18.
(13)
$$\begin{array}{r} \$4.36 \\ \$2.18 \\ +\ \$3.94 \\ \hline \end{array}$$

19. $360 + 47 + B = 518$ **20.** $\$41.32 - \$9.18$
(10)   (13)

21. Write the smallest three-digit even number that has
(2)   the digits 1, 2, and 3.

22. Compare: $5 + 5 + 5 \bigcirc 3 \times 5$
(4)

23. Use digits and symbols to write "Twelve equals ten
(4)   plus two."

24. What number is missing in this sequence?
(1)
$$\ldots, 32, 40, 48, \underline{\hspace{1cm}}, 64, \ldots$$

LESSON **16**	# Horizontal, Vertical, and Oblique • "Some Went Away" Stories

---

Facts Practice: 100 Multiplication Facts (Test C in Test Masters)

Mental Math: Follow this pattern to answer questions **a-f.**

$3 \times 4 = 12$ $3 \times 40 = 120$ $3 \times 400 = 1200$

a. 3×5 **b.** 3×50 **c.** 3×500
d. 5×6 **e.** 5×60 **f.** 5×600
g. $\$3.75 - \$2.50$ **h.** $140 + 16$ **i.** $30 + 12$
j. $20 + 15 - 5 + 10 + 4$

Problem Solving: Copy this addition problem and fill
in the missing digits.

$$\begin{array}{r} \_6\_ \\ + 37\_ \\ \hline \_248 \end{array}$$

Horizontal, vertical, and oblique

Lines and segments may be **horizontal,** **vertical,** or **oblique.** The term *horizontal* comes from the word *horizon.* The horizon is that line in the distance where the earth and sky seem to meet. A horizontal line is level with the horizon, extending left and right.

Horizontal line

A vertical line extends up and down.

Vertical line

A line or segment that is neither horizontal nor vertical is oblique. An oblique line appears to be "slanted."

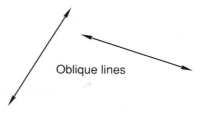

Oblique lines

"Some went away" stories "Some and some more" stories carry the thought of addition. "Some went away" stories carry the thought of subtraction. "Some went away" stories fit this pattern.

$$\begin{array}{r} \text{Some} \\ - \text{ Some Went Away} \\ \hline \text{What is Left} \end{array}$$

Example 1 Jack had $28. He spent $12. Then how much money did Jack have?

Solution Jack had some money, $28. Then he spent some of his money, so some went away. He still had some money left. We draw the pattern.

$$\begin{array}{r} \text{Some} \\ - \text{ Some Went Away} \\ \hline \text{What is Left} \end{array} \qquad \begin{array}{r} \$28 \\ - \$12 \\ \hline W \end{array}$$

To find what is left, we subtract.

$$\begin{array}{r} \$28 \\ - \$12 \\ \hline \$16 \end{array}$$

Then we check to see if the answer is sensible and the arithmetic is correct. We can check subtraction by "adding up."

$$\begin{array}{r} \$28 \\ - \$12 \\ \hline \$16 \end{array}$$

ADD UP:

$16 plus $12 is $28.

The answer is correct.

After spending $12, Jack had **$16** left.

Example 2   After losing 234 pounds, Jumbo still weighed 4368 pounds. How much did Jumbo weigh before he lost the weight?

Solution   We draw a "some went away" pattern.

Before, Jumbo weighed... W pounds
Then Jumbo lost... $- \ 234$ pounds
                                   _____
Jumbo still weighed...   4368 pounds

To find the first number of a subtraction, we add.

$$\begin{array}{r} \overset{1\ 1}{4368} \text{ pounds} \\ + \quad 234 \text{ pounds} \\ \hline 4602 \text{ pounds} \end{array}$$

Then we check the answer. Is it sensible? Is the arithmetic correct? We can check the arithmetic by using the answer in the original pattern.

$$\begin{array}{r} W \longrightarrow \quad 4\,6\,0\,2 \\ - \ 234 \qquad\qquad - \ \ 2\,3\,4 \\ \hline 4368 \qquad\qquad \ \ 4\,3\,6\,8 \end{array}$$ This is correct.

Before losing weight, Jumbo weighed **4602 pounds.**

Example 3   Four hundred runners started the race but many dropped out along the way. If 287 runners finished the race, then how many dropped out of the race?

Solution We draw a "some went away" pattern.

Four hundred started...	400 runners
Some dropped out...	− D runners
287 finished...	287 runners

We find the missing number by subtracting.

$$\overset{3\;9}{\cancel{4\,\cancel{0}}}{}^{1}0 \text{ runners}$$
$$-2\,8\,7 \text{ runners}$$
$$\overline{1\,1\,3 \text{ runners}}$$

Check: Is the answer reasonable? Is the arithmetic correct?

$$\begin{array}{r} 400 \\ -\quad D \\ \hline 287 \end{array} \longrightarrow \begin{array}{r} \overset{3\;9}{\cancel{4\,\cancel{0}}}{}^{1}0 \\ -1\,1\,3 \\ \hline 2\,8\,7 \end{array} \quad \text{This is correct.}$$

There were **113 runners** who dropped out of the race.

Practice Use the word *horizontal*, *vertical*, or *oblique* to describe each line or segment:

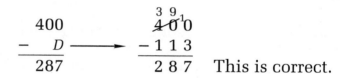

a.   **b.**   **c.**   **d.**

Draw each of the following:

e. A vertical line   **f.** An oblique line

g. A horizontal line segment

Use a "some went away" pattern to answer these questions:

h. After paying $85 rent, Tom still had $326. How much money did Tom have before he paid the rent?

i. Five hundred runners started the race. Only 293 finished the race. How many runners dropped out of the race?

Problem set 16

1. The price went up from $26 to $32. By how much did
    (11) the price increase? Draw a "some and some more"
    pattern.

2. Use tally marks to show the number 15.
    (12)

3. Use words to name $205.50.
    (5)

4. For the fact family 6, 8, 14, write two addition facts
    (8) and two subtraction facts.

5. What word is used to describe a line that goes straight
    (16) up and down?

6. The custodian put away 24 chairs. Then there were 52
    (16) chairs in the room. How many chairs were in the room
    before the custodian put some away? Draw a "some
    went away" pattern.

7. Jill had $24. She spent $8. Then how much money did
    (16) Jill have left? Draw a "some went away" pattern.

8. 3 × 7   **9.** 6 × 7
(15)   (15)

10. 3 × 8   **11.** 7 × 10
(15)   (15)

12. (14)	**13.** (14)	**14.** (13)	**15.** (9)
B − 256 ——— 56	900 − C ——— 90	$4.18 − $2.88 ———	$406 − $278 ———

16. (6)	**17.** (10)	**18.** (6)	**19.** (13)
$357 $946 + $130 ———	G + 843 ——— 1000	365 52 + 548 ———	$3.15 $2.87 + $1.98 ———

20. Think of two one-digit odd numbers. Multiply them.
    (2) Is the product odd or even?

21. Which of these is a horizontal line?
    (16)
    A. ╱   B. ↕   C. ←→

22. Use digits and a comparison symbol to write the
$^{(4)}$ following:

> *Eight hundred forty is greater than eight
> hundred fourteen.*

23. What number is missing in this sequence?
$^{(1)}$

> ..., 24, 30, 36, _____, 48, 54, ...

24. Compare: 4 × 3 ◯ 2 × 6
$^{(4)}$

25. The letter y stands for what number in this equation?
$^{(10)}$

> $$36 + y = 63$$

LESSON 17

Multiplying by One-Digit Numbers

Facts Practice: 100 Multiplication Facts (Test C in Test Masters)

Mental Math: Count up and down by 5's between 1 and 51.
(1, 6, 11, 16, ...) Count by 50¢ to $5.00 and from
$5.00 to 50¢.

a. 4 × 6	**b.** 4 × 60	**c.** 4 × 600
d. 5 × 8	**e.** 5 × 80	**f.** 5 × 800
g. 80 + 12	**h.** 160 + 24	**i.** 580 − 60
j. 5 × 6 + 12 − 2 + 10 − 1		

Problem Solving: Quarters are put into rolls of 40 quarters.
Dimes are put into rolls of 50 dimes. One
roll of quarters has the same value as how
many rolls of dimes?

We may solve the following problem either by adding or
by multiplying.

> *A ticket to the basketball game cost $24. How
> much would three tickets cost?*

To find the answer by adding, we add the price of three tickets.

$$
\begin{array}{r}
\overset{1}{\$24} \\
\$24 \\
+\ \$24 \\
\hline
\$72
\end{array}
$$

To find the answer by multiplying, we multiply $24 by 3. First we multiply the 4 ones by 3. This makes 12 ones, which is the same as 1 ten and 2 ones.

$$
\begin{array}{r}
\overset{1}{\$24} \\
\times\ \ \ 3 \\
\hline
2
\end{array}
$$

We write the 2 ones below the line and the 1 ten above the tens' column. Next we multiply the 2 tens by 3, making 6 tens. Then we add the 1 ten to make 7 tens.

$$
\begin{array}{r}
\overset{1}{\$24} \\
\times\ \ \ 3 \\
\hline
\$72
\end{array}
$$

Example 1 Find the product: $0.25 × 6

Solution Mentally we can figure out that 6 quarters is $1.50. We will use this problem to practice the pencil-and-paper algorithm for multiplication. Think of $0.25 as 2 dimes and 5 pennies. First we multiply 5 pennies by 6, which makes 30 pennies.

$$
\begin{array}{r}
\overset{3}{\$0.25} \\
\times\ \ \ \ \ 6 \\
\hline
0
\end{array}
$$

Since 30 pennies is 3 dimes and 0 pennies, we write "0" below the line and "3" above the dimes' column. Next we multiply 2 dimes by 6, making 12 dimes. Then we add the 3 dimes to make 15 dimes.

$$\begin{array}{r} \overset{1\ 3}{} \\ \$0.25 \\ \times \qquad 6 \\ \hline \mathbf{\$1.50} \end{array}$$

Fifteen dimes equals 1 dollar and 5 dimes. We write "5" below the line and "1" above the dollars' column. There are no dollars to multiply, so we write the 1 in the dollars' place below the line and place the decimal point two places from the right-hand end and the dollar sign.

Example 2   6 × 325

Solution   We follow the same method when we multiply three-digit numbers. We multiply 5 ones by 6 to get 30. Next we multiply 2 tens by 6, making 12 tens, and add 3 tens to get 15 tens. We

$$\begin{array}{r} \overset{1\ 3}{325} \\ \times \quad 6 \\ \hline 1950 \end{array}$$

write the 5 below the line and the 1 above the next digit. Then we multiply 3 hundreds by 6 and add the 1 hundred. The product of 6 × 325 is **1950.**

Practice*
a. $36 × 5

b. 50 × 8

c. 7 × $0.43

d. $\begin{array}{r} 340 \\ \times \quad 8 \\ \hline \end{array}$

e. $\begin{array}{r} \$7.68 \\ \times \quad 4 \\ \hline \end{array}$

f. $\begin{array}{r} 506 \\ \times \quad 6 \\ \hline \end{array}$

g. $\begin{array}{r} \$394 \\ \times \quad 7 \\ \hline \end{array}$

h. $\begin{array}{r} 607 \\ \times \quad 9 \\ \hline \end{array}$

i. $\begin{array}{r} \$9.68 \\ \times \quad 3 \\ \hline \end{array}$

Problem set 17

1. Draw a vertical line segment.
(16)

2. These tally marks represent what number?   ЖЖ ЖЖ ІІІ
(12)

3. Rick read 3 books. Each book had 120 pages. How many pages did Rick read? Find the answer once by adding and again by multiplying.
(17)

4. After buying a notebook for $1.45, Jeremy had $2.65.
(16) How much money did Jeremy have before he bought
the notebook?

5.   24   **6.** $36   **7.**   45   **8.** $56
(17) $\times$ 3   (17) $\times$ 4   (17) $\times$ 5   (17) $\times$ 6

9. $3.25   **10.**   432   **11.** $2.46
(17) $\times$ 6   (17) $\times$ 9   (17) $\times$ 7

12.   364   **13.** C **14.** $4.20
(17) $\times$ 8   (10) $+\ 147$ (13) $-\ $3.75
                   316

15.   604   **16.** M
(14) $-$ W (14) $-$ 73
     406   800

17. $3 + N + 15 + 9 = 60$
(10)

18. $96.75 + $7.98
(13)

19. Find the answer to this problem by multiplying
(17) instead of adding:

$$23 + 23 + 23 + 23 + 23 + 23 + 23 + 23$$

20. Find the product: 26×7
(17)

21. Think of two one-digit even numbers. Multiply them.
(2) Is the product odd or even?

22. Compare: $5 \times 12 \bigcirc 6 \times 10$
(4)

23. Use digits and a comparison symbol to write the
(4) following:

*Five hundred four is less than five hundred
fourteen.*

24. What number is missing in this sequence?
(1)

$$..., 21, 28, 35, \underline{\hspace{1cm}}, 49, 56, ...$$

25. Which digit shows the number of hundreds in 375?
(3)

LESSON 18

Multiplying Three Factors • Missing Numbers in Multiplication

---

Facts Practice: 100 Multiplication Facts (Test C in Test Masters)

Mental Math: Count up and down by 5's between 1 and 51. Count up and down by 200's between 0 and 2000.

a. 3 × 30 plus 3 × 2   **b.** 4 × 20 plus 4 × 3
c. 5 × 30 plus 5 × 4   **d.** 6 × 700
e. 1000 − 100   **f.** 320 + 32
g. $3.75 − $1.25   **h.** 6 × 4 + 1 + 10 − 5 + 3

Problem Solving: All of the digits 1 through 9 are used in this addition problem. Copy the problem and fill in the missing digits.

$$\begin{array}{r} 3\_\_ \\ + 452 \\ \hline \_\_\_ \end{array}$$

Multiplying three factors

In this lesson we will learn how to find the product when three or more numbers are multiplied.

$$9 \times 8 \times 7$$

Numbers that are multiplied together are called *factors*. In the problem above there are three factors. To do multiplication problems with three factors, we multiply two of the factors together. Then we multiply the product we get by the third factor.

First we multiply 9 × 8 to get 72.

Then we multiply 72 × 7 to get 504.

$$\underbrace{9 \times 8}_{72} \times 7 = \\ \times 7 = 504$$

We may multiply numbers in any order. Sometimes changing the order of the factors can make a problem easier to do.

Example 1 Find the product: $6 \times 3 \times 5$

Solution To find the product of three factors, we first multiply two factors. Then we multiply that product by the third factor. We may choose an order of factors that makes the problem easier to do. In this problem we choose to multiply 6×5 first; then we multiply by 3.

$$6 \times 3 \times 5$$
$$30 \quad \times 3 = \mathbf{90}$$

Example 2 $5 \times 7 \times 12$

Solution The order in which we choose to multiply can change the difficulty of the problem. If we multiply 5×7 first, then we must multiply 35×12. If we multiply 5×12 first, then we can multiply 7×60. The second way is easier and can be done mentally. We will rearrange the factors to show the order we choose to multiply.

$$5 \times 12 \times 7$$
$$60 \quad \times 7 = \mathbf{420}$$

Missing numbers in multiplication We should learn the multiplication facts well enough to find a missing factor if we know one factor and the product.

Example 3 Find each missing factor:

(a) $3 \times N = 18$

(b)
$$\begin{array}{r} W \\ \times\ 3 \\ \hline 24 \end{array}$$

Solution There are many ways to find a missing factor. In these examples we could count how many 3's add to equal 18 and 24. We could also use a multiplication table by looking across the 3's row to 18 and 24 and then looking to the top of each column for the missing factor. We see that the missing factors are 6 and 8.

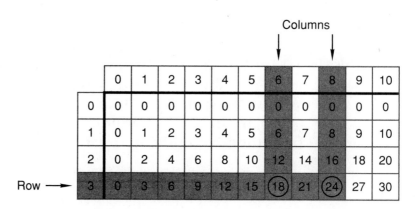

The fastest way to find the missing factors is to remember the multiplication facts. Since $3 \times 6 = 18$ and $3 \times 8 = 24$, the missing factors are (a) **6** and (b) **8**.

Practice*　For problems a–d, copy the problems down and multiply. Show which numbers you chose to multiply first.

a. $5 \times 7 \times 6$　　　　　　　**b.** $10 \times 9 \times 8$

c. $3 \times 4 \times 25$　　　　　　　**d.** $4 \times 3 \times 2 \times 1 \times 0$

Find the missing factor:

e.　$\begin{array}{r} M \\ \times\ 5 \\ \hline 30 \end{array}$　　**f.**　$\begin{array}{r} 3 \\ \times\ B \\ \hline 21 \end{array}$　　**g.**　$\begin{array}{r} P \\ \times\ 4 \\ \hline 24 \end{array}$　　**h.**　$\begin{array}{r} 9 \\ \times\ Q \\ \hline 81 \end{array}$

Problem set
18

1. Draw a horizontal line and a vertical line. Then write
(16)　the words *horizontal* and *vertical* to label each line.

2. Use tally marks to show the number 14.
(12)

3. In one class there are 33 students. Fourteen of the
(11)　students are boys. How many girls are in the class?

4. In another class there are 17 boys and 14 girls. How
(11)　many students are in the class?

For problems 5–8, try to find the product mentally before using pencil and paper:

5. 6 × 4 × 5
(18)

6. 5 × 6 × 12
(18)

7. 5 × 10 × 6
(18)

8. 9 × 7 × 10
(18)

9. $407
(17)   ×   8

10.   375
(17)   ×   6

11. $4.86
(17)   ×   9

12.   308
(17)   ×   7

13.   *G*
(18)   ×   9
──────
       36

14. $573
(17)   ×   9
──────

15.   8
(18)   × *H*
──────
       48

16. $7.68
(17)   ×   4
──────

17. 456 + 78 + *F* = 904
(10)

18. 34 + 75 + 123 + 9
(6)

19. $36.70 − $7.93
(13)

20. *H* − 354 = 46
(14)

21. 37 + 37 + 37 + 37 + 37 + 37
(17)

22. Think of a one-digit odd number and a one-digit even
(2)   number. Multiply them. Is the product odd or even?

23. Find the missing factor: 6 × 4 = 8 × *N*
(18)

24. Use digits and symbols to write the following:
(4)   *Eight times eight is greater than nine times
         seven.*

25. For the fact family 7, 8, 15, write two addition facts
(8)   and two subtraction facts.

LESSON
19

Learning Division Facts

Facts Practice: 100 Multiplication Facts (Test C in Test Masters)

Mental Math: Count up and down by 5's between 2 and 52.
(2, 7, 12, 17, ...)

a. 2 × 5 × 6   b. 6 × 5 × 3
c. 6 × 30 plus 6 × 2   d. 4 × 60 plus 4 × 5
e. 1000 − 800   f. 640 + 24
g. $5.00 − $0.50   h. 9 × 9 − 1 + 10 + 10

Problem Solving: For breakfast, lunch, and dinner Sam ate soup and eggs and ham, one for each meal, but not necessarily in that order. (a) List all the possible arrangements of meals Sam could have eaten. (b) If Sam never ate eggs for lunch, how many arrangements of meals are possible?

Searching for a missing factor is called **division.** A division problem is like a miniature multiplication table. The product is inside the box. The two factors are outside the box. One factor is in front and the other is on top.

$$3\overline{)12}^{\,?}$$

The factor on top is missing. We need to know what number times 3 equals 12. Since 3 × 4 = 12, we know that the missing factor is 4. We write our answer this way.

$$3\overline{)12}^{\,4}$$

Example 1   What is the missing number in this problem? $$4\overline{)20}^{\,?}$$

Solution   The symbol $\overline{)\quad}$ is a division box. When we find the missing number, we write the answer above the box. To find the missing number we may think, "Four times what number equals 20?" We find that the missing number is **5.**

Example 2 $3\overline{)18}$

Solution   This is the way division problems are
often written. We are to search for the
number which goes above the box. We
think, "Three times what number equals 18?" We
remember that $3 \times 6 = 18$, so the answer to the division
problem is **6**.

$$\begin{array}{r} 6 \\ 3\overline{)18} \end{array}$$

Example 3 $10\overline{)80}$

Solution   How many 10's make 80? Since $8 \times 10 = 80$, the answer
is **8**.

The three numbers that make a division fact also make
a multiplication fact.

Example 4   Write two multiplication facts and two division facts for
the fact family 5, 6, 30.

Solution

$$\begin{array}{r} 6 \\ \times\ 5 \\ \hline 30 \end{array} \qquad \begin{array}{r} 5 \\ \times\ 6 \\ \hline 30 \end{array} \qquad \begin{array}{r} 6 \\ 5\overline{)30} \end{array} \qquad \begin{array}{r} 5 \\ 6\overline{)30} \end{array}$$

Practice   Find the missing number in each of these division facts:

     a. $2\overline{)16}$ **b.** $4\overline{)24}$ **c.** $6\overline{)30}$ **d.** $8\overline{)56}$

     e. $3\overline{)21}$ **f.** $10\overline{)30}$ **g.** $7\overline{)28}$ **h.** $9\overline{)36}$

     i. Write two multiplication facts and two division facts
for the fact family 3, 8, 24.

Problem set 19   **1.** The $45 dress was marked down to $29. By how much
(16)   had the dress been marked down? Use the "some went
away" pattern.

     2. Room 15 collected 243 aluminum cans. Room 16
(11)   collected 487 cans. Room 17 collected 608 cans. How
many cans did they collect in all?

3. There are 5 rows of desks with 6 desks in each row.
(17) How many desks are there in all? Find the answer
once by adding and again by multiplying.

4. Use words to name $4,587.20.
(7,5)

5. For the fact family 7, 8, 56, write two multiplication
(19) facts and two division facts.

6. $3\overline{)24}$ **7.** $6\overline{)18}$ **8.** $4\overline{)32}$ **9.** $10\overline{)40}$
(19)   (19)   (19)   (19)

| **10.** (17) $4.83 $\times$ 7 | **11.** (17) 659 $\times$ 8 | **12.** (17) $706 $\times$ 4 | **13.** (18) M $\times$ 9 ‾‾‾ 54 |

use
calculator

14. 8 × 10 × 7   **15.** 9 × 8 × 5
(18)   (18)

| **16.** (13) $65.40 − $19.18 | **17.** (14) 4000 − T ‾‾‾ 1357 | **18.** (14) R − 1915 ‾‾‾ 269 |

19. (6) 907
           415
        + 653

20. (13) $3.67
            $4.25
          + $7.40

21. (10) 427
          + K
           ‾‾‾
           813

22. 356 + L + 67 = 500   **23.** 86 + w = 250
(10)   (10)

24. Find the missing factor: 6 × 6 = N × 4
(18)

25. Use digits and symbols to write the following:
(4)   *Eight times six is less than seven times seven.*

**LESSON
20**

Three Ways to Show Division

Facts Practice: 90 Division Facts (Test E or F in Test Masters)

Mental Math: Count up and down by 5's between 2 and 52.

  a. 5 × 8 × 3   **b.** 4 × 5 × 6
  c. 4 × 32 equals 4 × 30 plus 4 × 2. Find 4 × 32.
  d. 4 × 23   **e.** 4 × 54   **f.** 1000 − 990
  g. 7 × 7 + 1 + 25 + 25

Problem Solving: Copy this addition problem and fill in the missing digits.

$$\begin{array}{r} \_3\_ \\ + \quad\_1 \\ \hline \_\_3\_ \end{array}$$

We use different ways to show division. Here are three ways to show "twelve divided by four."

$$4\overline{)12} \qquad 12 \div 4 \qquad \frac{12}{4}$$

In the first we use a division box. In the second we use a division sign. In the third we use a division bar. To solve longer division problems, we usually use the first form. In later math courses we will use the third form more often. We should be able to solve problems in any form, to read a problem in any form, and to change from one form to another.

Example 1 Use words to show how these problems are read:

  (a) 12 ÷ 6   (b) $\dfrac{12}{6}$ (c) $6\overline{)12}$

Solution Every division symbol is read by saying "divided by." We read problem (a) from left to right: "Twelve divided by six."

    We read problem (b) from top to bottom: "Twelve divided by six." (This is sometimes read "Twelve over six.")

Problem (c) is written with a division box. To read a problem written with a division box, we begin by reading the number inside the box: "Twelve divided by six."

We see that all three parts are read the same way. The parts are three different ways to show the same division, **"Twelve divided by six."**

Example 2   Write this problem in the other two division forms. $15 \div 3$

Solution   We read this problem, "Fifteen divided by three." Fifteen is the number being divided.

To show division with a division bar, we write the number being divided on top. $\dfrac{15}{3}$

To show division with a division box, we write the number being divided inside the box. $3\overline{)15}$

Example 3   Divide: $\dfrac{15}{5}$

Solution   The bar is a way to show division: Five times what number is 15? The answer is **3.**

Practice   **a.** Show 10 divided by 2 in three different forms.

b. Use three different division forms to show 24 divided by 6.

Use words to show how these division problems are read:

c. $3\overline{)21}$ **d.** $12 \div 6$

e. $\dfrac{30}{5}$

Rewrite these division problems with a division box:

f. $63 \div 7$ **g.** $\dfrac{42}{6}$ **h.** 30 divided by 6

Find the answer to the following division problems:

i. $\dfrac{60}{10}$ **j.** $\dfrac{42}{7}$ **k.** $28 \div 4$ **l.** $36 \div 6$

Problem set 20

1. Draw a horizontal number line with even numbers
(12) marked and numbered from 0 to 12.

2. Write two multiplication facts and two division facts
(19) for the fact family 4, 9, 36.

3. Use tally marks to show the number 16.
(12)

4. Jim reads 40 pages per day. How many pages does Jim
(17) read in 4 days? Find the answer once by adding and
again by multiplying.

5. There are 806 students at Gidley School. If there are
(11) 397 girls, how many boys are there? Draw a "some and
some more" pattern.

6. What is the sum of five hundred twenty-six and six
(6) hundred eighty-four?

7. Use words to show how this problem is read: $6\overline{)24}$
(20)

8. Use words to show how this problem is read: $15 \div 3$
(20)

9. Divide: $\dfrac{15}{3}$
(20)

10. $24 \div 8$ **11.** $10\overline{)90}$ **12.** $\dfrac{27}{3}$
(20)   (20)   (20)

13. $\begin{array}{r} \$23.18 \\ \times 6 \\ \hline \end{array}$ **14.** $\begin{array}{r} 4726 \\ \times 8 \\ \hline \end{array}$ **15.** $\begin{array}{r} \$34.09 \\ \times 7 \\ \hline \end{array}$
(17)   (17)   (17)

16. Compare: $5 \times 6 \times 7 \bigcirc 7 \times 6 \times 5$
(4)

17. $352 + 352 + 352 + 352 + 352$
(17)

18. $40.00
(13) − $24.68

19.   1207
(14) −   R
         943

20.   Z
(14) − 1358
         4444

21.   3426
(6)   1547
      + 2684

22.   4318
(10) +   M
         4343

23. $13.06
(13) $4.90
      + $60.75

24. Use digits and symbols to write the following:
(4)   *Ten times two is greater than ten plus two.*

25. What is the next number in this sequence?
(1)   ..., 24, 18, 12, 6, _____

LESSON 21

"Equal Groups" Stories

Facts Practice: 90 Division Facts (Test E or F in Test Masters)

Mental Math: Count up and down by 25's between 0 and 200. Count up and down by 250's between 0 and 2000.

a. 3 × 40 plus 3 × 5
b. 4 × 50 plus 4 × 4
c. 4 × 45
d. 4 × 54
e. 120 + 70
f. 560 − 200
g. 210 + 35
h. 5 × 6, + 2, ÷ 4, + 1, ÷ 3*

Problem Solving: The upper case letter A encloses one area, B encloses two areas, and C does not enclose an area. List all the upper case and lowercase letters that enclose at least one area.

*This statement implies that the operations separated by commas be performed sequentially, from left to right. In this case, 5 × 6 = 30, then 30 + 2 = 32, then 32 ÷ 4 = 8, then 8 + 1 = 9, and then 9 ÷ 3 = 3. The answer is 3.

"Some and some more" stories have an addition pattern. "Some went away" stories have a subtraction pattern. **"Equal groups"** stories have a multiplication pattern.

Number of objects in each group
× Number of groups
_____
Total number of objects in all groups

In an "equal groups" story problem, one of the numbers is missing. If the missing number is the total, we multiply to find the missing number. If the missing number is the number of objects or the number of groups, we divide.

Example 1   At Lincoln School there are 4 classes of fifth graders with 30 students in each class. Altogether, how many fifth graders are in the 4 classes?

Solution   This story is about equal groups. We fit the story into an "equal groups" pattern. The objects are students. The groups are classes.

30 students in each class
×   4 classes
_____
120 students in all 4 classes

The missing number is the total in all 4 classes. We find the total by multiplying.

Example 2   The coach separated 48 players into 6 teams with the same number of players on each team. How many players were on each team?

Solution   In this "equal groups" story, the objects are players and the groups are teams. The missing number is the number of players on each team.

N players on each team
×   6 teams
_____
48 players on all 6 teams

The missing number is a factor which we find by dividing.

$$6\overline{)48}^{\,8}$$

There were 8 players on each team.

Example 3 Stan raked up 28 bags of leaves. On each trip he could carry away 4 bags. How many trips did it take Stan to carry away all the bags?

Solution The objects are bags, and the groups are trips. The missing number is the number of trips.

$$\begin{array}{r} 4\text{ bags in each trip} \\ \times\ N\text{ trips} \\ \hline 28\text{ bags in all the trips} \end{array}$$

The missing number is a factor which we find by dividing.

$$28 \div 4 = 7$$

Stan took 7 trips to carry away all 28 bags.

Practice Draw an "equal groups" pattern for each problem:

a. Thirty desks are arranged in 6 equal rows. How many desks are in each row?

b. Twenty-one books are stacked in piles with 7 books in each pile. How many piles are there?

c. If 56 zebus were separated into 7 equal herds, then how many zebus would be in each herd?

d. Alex used a pay phone to call his friend. Each minute he must put 3 nickels into the phone. If he began with 18 nickels, how many minutes can he talk on the phone?

Problem set 21

1. The coach separated the PE class into 8 teams with the
(21) same number of players on each team. If there are 56 students in the class, how many are on each team? Draw an "equal groups" pattern.

2. Draw an oblique line.
(16)

3. Write two multiplication facts and two division facts
(19) for the fact family 6, 7, 42.

4. Use words to show how this problem is read: $\dfrac{10}{2}$
(20)

5. The set of drums cost eight hundred dollars. The band
(11) has earned four hundred eighty-seven dollars. How much more does the band need to earn to have enough money to buy the drums? Use a "some and some more" pattern.

6. $8\overline{)72}$ **7.** $6 \times N = 42$ **8.** $9\overline{)36}$
(20)   *(18)*   *(20)*

9. $6\overline{)48}$ **10.** $56 \div 7$ **11.** $\dfrac{70}{10}$
(20)   *(20)*   *(20)*

12. Compare: $24 \div 4 \bigcirc 30 \div 6$
(4)

13.   367   **14.** $5.04   **15.**   837
(17) $\times\ \ \ 8$ *(17)* $\times\ \ \ \ 7$ *(17)* $\times\ \ \ 9$

16. $6 \times 8 \times 10$ **17.** $7 \times 20 \times 4$
(18)   *(18)*

18. $37.05   **19.** R **20.**   5003
(13) $-\ 29.34 *(14)* $-\ 4568$ *(14)* $-\ \ \ \ W$
                              $\overline{6318}$ $\overline{\ \ \ 876}$

21.   268   **22.** $9.65   **23.**   382
(10) $+\ \ \ M$ *(13)* $2.43   *(6)*   96
        $\overline{687}$ $+\ 1.45 $+\ 182$

24. If a dozen items are divided into two equal groups,
(21) how many will be in each group?

25. What are the next three numbers in this sequence?
(1)
        …, 50, 60, 70, 80, 90, _____, _____, _____, …

LESSON 22

Dividing and Writing a Remainder

Facts Practice: 64 Multiplication Facts (Test D in Test Masters)

Mental Math: Count up and down by 50's between 0 and 500. Count up and down by 500's between 0 and 5000.

a. 10×5 b. 10×25
c. 5×50 plus 7×5 d. 4×56
e. 3×56 f. $150 + 25$ g. $180 + 30$
h. $850 - 150$ i. $6 \times 6, -1, \div 5, +1, \div 2$

Problem Solving: Copy this subtraction problem and fill in the missing digits.

$$\begin{array}{r} 4\_6 \\ - \_1\_ \\ \hline 237 \end{array}$$

Division and multiplication are closely related. We can use division to find missing factors. Then we can use multiplication to check our division.

Here we use multiplication to check a division answer.

$$5\overline{)35} \qquad \begin{array}{r} 7 \\ \times\ 5 \\ \hline 35 \end{array} \quad \text{check}$$

$$\begin{array}{r} 7 \\ 5\overline{)35} \end{array}$$

Instead of showing a separate multiplication, we can show the multiplication as part of the division problem. After dividing to get 7, we multiply 7 by 5 and write the product under the 35. This shows that there are exactly 7 fives in 35.

$$\begin{array}{r} 7 \\ 5\overline{)35} \\ 35 \end{array}$$

Not all division problems have an exact whole number answer. Look at this question:

If 5 children share 16 pennies, how many pennies will each child receive?

If we try to divide 16 into 5 equal groups, we find there is no whole number which is an exact answer.

$$5\overline{)16}^{\,?}$$

To answer this question we think, "How many fives are closest to but are not more than 16?" We answer that question with the number 3 and multiply to show that 3 fives is 15. Each child will get 3 pennies.

$$\begin{array}{r} 3 \\ 5\overline{)16} \\ 15 \end{array}$$

Now we subtract 15 from 16 to show how many pennies are left over. The amount left over is called the **remainder.** Here the remainder is 1.

$$\begin{array}{r} 3 \\ 5\overline{)16} \\ -15 \\ \hline 1 \end{array}$$

How we deal with a remainder depends upon the question we are asked to answer. For now, when we answer problems written with digits and division symbols, we will write the remainder at the end of our answer with the letter "r" in front, as we show here.

$$\begin{array}{r} 3\text{ r }1 \\ 5\overline{)16} \\ -15 \\ \hline 1 \end{array}$$

Example $50 \div 8$

Solution   We rewrite the problem with a division box. How many eights are closest to but are not more than 50? We answer 6 and multiply 6×8 to get 48. We subtract to show the amount left over and write this remainder at the end of the answer.

$$\begin{array}{r} \mathbf{6\text{ r }2} \\ 8\overline{)50} \\ -48 \\ \hline 2 \end{array}$$

Practice*   Divide and write the answer with a remainder:

a. $5\overline{)23}$ b. $6\overline{)50}$ c. $37 \div 8$

d. $4\overline{)23}$ e. $7\overline{)50}$ f. $40 \div 6$

g. $10\overline{)42}$ h. $9\overline{)50}$ i. $34 \div 9$

**Problem set
22**

1. Draw two horizontal lines, one above the other.
(16)

2. Huck collected 32 night crawlers for fishing. If he put
(21) an equal number in each of his 4 pockets, how many did he put in each pocket? Draw an "equal groups" pattern.

3. Grandpa has 10 quarters. If he gives each of his 3
(21) grandchildren 3 quarters, how many quarters will he have left?

4. Eight hundred forty mice came in the front door. Four
(11) hundred eighteen mice came in the back door. Altogether, how many came in through the front and back doors? Use a "some and some more" pattern.

5. $56 \div 10$ **6.** $20 \div 3$ **7.** $7\overline{)30}$
(22)   (22)   (22)

8. $3 \times 7 \times 10$ **9.** $2 \times 3 \times 4 \times 5$
(18)   (18)

10. $394   **11.**   678   **12.** $6.49
(17) $\times$ 8   (17) $\times$ 4   (17) $\times$ 9

13. $\dfrac{63}{7}$ **14.** $\dfrac{56}{8}$ **15.** $\dfrac{42}{6}$
(20)   (20)   (20)

16. $4.08   **17.**   3645   **18.**   3904
(17) $\times$ 7   (17) $\times$ 6   (17) $\times$ 4

19. $387 + 426 + q = 950$ **20.** $C - 462 = 548$
(10)   (14)

21. $\$36.15 - \$29.81$ **22.** $963 + a = 6000$
(13)   (10)

23. Use words to show how this problem is read: $4\overline{)12}$
(20)

24. Think of an odd number. Multiply it by 2. Is the
(2) product odd or even?

25. What is the next number in this sequence?
(1)
        $\ldots, 50, 40, 30, 20, 10, \underline{\quad\quad}$

LESSON
23

Halves, Fourths, Tenths

Facts Practice: 90 Division Facts (Test E or F in Test Masters)

Mental Math: Count up by 5's from 1 to 51. (1, 6, 11, 16, ...)
Count up and down by 3's between 0 and 36.

a. 10×7 **b.** 10×750
c. 7×30 plus 7×5 **d.** 5×35
e. 6×35 **f.** $280 + 14$ **g.** $240 + 12$
h. $960 - 140$ **i.** $6 \times 4, + 1, \div 5, + 1, \div 2$

Problem Solving: Behind curtains A, B, and C were three prizes: a car, a boat, and a pogo stick, one behind each curtain. List all the possible arrangements of prizes behind the curtains.

A fraction is part of a whole. The "whole" may be a single thing like a whole pie or a whole inch, or the "whole" may be a group such as a whole class or a whole bag of marbles.

It takes two numbers to write a fraction. The bottom number, the **denominator,** shows the number of *equal* parts in the whole. The top number, the **numerator,** shows how many of the parts are counted.

$$\frac{1}{2} \begin{array}{l} \leftarrow \text{Numerator} \\ \leftarrow \text{Denominator} \end{array}$$

We read a fraction from top to bottom.

$\dfrac{1}{2}$ one half (Sometimes we just say "half.")

$\dfrac{1}{4}$ one fourth or one quarter

$\dfrac{3}{4}$ three fourths or three quarters

$\dfrac{1}{10}$ one tenth

$\dfrac{9}{10}$ nine tenths

Many fraction problems are "equal groups" stories. The denominator of the fraction shows the number of equal groups.

Example 1   Half of the 18 students in the class are girls. How many girls are in the class?

Solution   The word *half* means one of two equal groups. In this story, one group is girls and the other is boys. We need to find the number in each group.

$$
\begin{array}{r}
N \text{ students in each group} \\
\times\ 2 \text{ groups} \\
\hline
18 \text{ students in all groups}
\end{array}
$$

We find the number in each group by dividing 18 by 2.

$$
\begin{array}{r}
9 \\
2\overline{)18} \\
18
\end{array}
$$

In each group there are 9 students. This means there are **9 girls in the class.**

Example 2   (a) How many cents is one fourth of a dollar?

(b) How many cents is three fourths of a dollar?

Solution   The denominator *fourths* means that the whole dollar is divided into four equal parts. Since four quarters equal a dollar, one fourth of a dollar equals a quarter, which is twenty-five cents. Three fourths of a dollar—three quarters—equals seventy-five cents.

(a) **One fourth of a dollar is twenty-five cents.**

(b) **Three fourths of a dollar is seventy-five cents.**

Example 3   One tenth of the 30 students earned an A on the test. How many students earned an A?

Solution   One tenth means one of ten equal parts. We can find one tenth of 30 by dividing 30 by 10.

$$
\begin{array}{r}
3 \\
10\overline{)30} \\
30
\end{array}
$$

One tenth of 30 is 3. So **3 students earned an A.**

Practice   How many cents is:

    a. $\frac{1}{2}$ of a dollar?   **b.** $\frac{1}{4}$ of a dollar?   **c.** $\frac{1}{10}$ of a dollar?

Use the following story to answer questions d–g:

> *There were 20 pumpkins in the garden. One fourth of the pumpkins were too small, one tenth were too large, and one half were just the right size. The rest of the pumpkins were not ripe yet.*

    d. How many pumpkins were too small? 5

    e. How many pumpkins were too large? 2

    f. How many pumpkins were just the right size? 10

    g. How many pumpkins were not ripe yet? 3

Problem set 23

1. It cost $3.48 to rent a movie. Leo gave the clerk $5.00.
(16) How much money should Leo get back? Use a "some went away" pattern.

2. The burger cost $1.45, and the fries cost $0.95. What
(11) was the cost of the burger and fries together? Use a "some and some more" pattern.

3. A week is 7 days. How many days is 52 weeks? Use an
(21) "equal groups" pattern.

4. Jim, Hector, and Julie divided the money equally. If
(21) there was $24 to start with, how much money did each receive? Use an "equal groups" pattern.

5. One half of the 20 students had finished the book. One
(23) fourth had not started the book yet.

    (a) How many students had finished the book?

    (b) How many students had not started the book?

6. Compare: $36 \div 4 \ominus 45 \div 5$
(4)

$60 = \underline{\quad} \times 10$

7. $40 \div 6$ 4
(22)

8. $3\overline{)20}$ 6 R2
(22)

9. $60 = N \times 10$
(18)

10. $\$3.08$
(17) $\times \quad 7$
2156

11. 2514
(17) $\times \quad 3$

12. 697
(17) $\times \quad 8$

13. Use words to show how this problem is read: $7\overline{)35}$
(20)

14. $4 \times 3 \times 10$
(18)

15. $12 \times 2 \times 10$
(18)

16. 4035
(14) $- \quad 8$
$\overline{3587}$

17. M
(14) $- 1056$
$\overline{5694}$

18. $\$70.00$
(13) $- \quad \$7.53$

19. $\$5.00 + \$8.75 + \$10.00 + \$0.35$
(13)

20. $\$6.25 + \$0.85 + \$4.00 + D = \$20.00$
(10)

21. Write two multiplication facts and two division facts
(19) for the fact family 7, 9, 63.

22. Write the numbers 48, 16, and 52 in order from
(4) greatest to least.

23. Draw two vertical lines side by side.
(16)

24. Use words to name the number 212,500.
(7)

25. Write two addition facts and two subtraction facts for
(8) the fact family 7, 9, 16.

LESSON 24

Dollars • Parentheses

Facts Practice: 64 Multiplication Facts (Test D in Test Masters)

Mental Math: Count up by 5's from 2 to 52. Count up and down by 3's between 0 and 36.

a. 10 × 12   **b.** 10 × 20
c. 8 × 40 plus 8 × 2   **d.** 7 × 42
e. 6 × 42   **f.** $\frac{1}{2}$ of 12   **g.** $\frac{1}{4}$ of 12
h. $\frac{1}{10}$ of 30   **i.** 1000 − 100
j. 6 × 3, + 2, ÷ 2, − 2, ÷ 2

Problem Solving: Copy this subtraction problem and fill in the missing digits.

$$\begin{array}{r} 4\_ \\ -\ 3\_2 \\ \hline 58 \end{array}$$

Dollars   A number of dollars may be written either with or without a decimal point. Both of these numbers mean five dollars.

$$\$5 \qquad \$5.00$$

When we add or subtract dollars and cents, it is a good idea to use a decimal point and two zeros to write whole dollar amounts.

Example 1   Add: $5 + $8.75 + $10 + $0.35

Solution   We will rewrite the problem so that whole dollars are written with a decimal point and two zeros.

$$\$5.00 + \$8.75 + \$10.00 + \$0.35$$

Next, we set up the problem so that the decimal points line up vertically. Then we add and place the decimal point in the answer in line with the decimal points in the problem.

$$\begin{array}{r} \$\ 5.00 \\ 8.75 \\ 10.00 \\ +\ \ 0.35 \\ \hline \$24.10 \end{array}$$

Parentheses   The **operations** of arithmetic are addition, subtraction, multiplication, and division. When there is more than one operation in a problem, **parentheses** can show us the order for doing the operations. Parentheses separate a problem into parts. We do the part in the parentheses first. In the problem below, the parentheses tell us to add 5 + 4 before we multiply by 6.

First we do the work inside the parentheses. Then we multiply.

$$6 \times \underbrace{(5 + 4)}_{9} =$$
$$6 \times \quad 9 \quad = 54$$

Example 2 8 − (4 + 2)

Solution It takes two steps to find the answer to this problem. The parentheses show us which step to take first. We add 4 and 2 to get 6. Then we subtract 6 from 8 and get **2**.

$$8 - \underbrace{(4 + 2)}_{6} =$$
$$8 - \quad 6 \quad = 2$$

Example 3 Compare: 2 × (3 + 4) ◯ (2 × 3) + 4

Solution The numbers and operations on both sides are the same, but the order for doing the operations is different. We do the operations on both sides in the proper order and find that the left-hand side is greater than the right-hand side. The correct comparison symbol is **>**.

$$2 \times \underbrace{(3 + 4)}_{7} \bigcirc \underbrace{(2 \times 3)}_{6} + 4$$
$$2 \times \quad 7 \quad \bigcirc \quad 6 \quad + 4$$
$$14 \quad > \quad 10$$

Practice* Solve these problems by doing the operations in the proper order:

a. 6 − (4 − 2)

b. (8 ÷ 4) ÷ 2

c. (6 − 4) − 2

d. 12 ÷ (4 − 1)

e. 8 ÷ (4 ÷ 2)

f. (12 ÷ 4) − 1

g. Name the four operations of arithmetic.

h. $10 + $2 + $6.25

i. $10 − $6.87

Problem set
24

1. How much money is one half of a dollar plus one
(23) fourth of a dollar?

2. How many horseshoes are needed to shoe 25 horses?
(21) Use an "equal groups" pattern.

3. Write two multiplication facts and two division facts
(19) for the fact family 5, 10, 50.

4. Draw two vertical lines.
(16)

5. The auditorium had nine hundred fifty-six seats. Only
(11) ninety-eight seats were occupied. How many seats
were not occupied? Which pattern did you use?

6. Compare: $3 \times (4 + 5) \bigcirc (3 \times 4) + 5$
(24)

7. $30 - (20 + 10)$ **8.** $(30 - 20) + 10$
(24)   (24)

9. Compare: $4 \times (6 \times 5) \bigcirc (4 \times 6) \times 5$
(24)

10. $60 \div 7$ **11.** $50 \div 6$ **12.** $10\overline{)44}$
(22)   (22)   (22)

13. $\$50.36$ **14.** 7408 **15.** 4637
(17) $\times \quad 4$ (17) $\times \quad 6$ (17) $\times \quad 9$

16. W **17.** 4730 **18.** $\$30.00$
(14) $- \$9.62$ (14) $- \quad J$ (13) $- \$0.56$
    $\overline{\$14.08}$ $\overline{2712}$

19. $\$3.54 + \$12 + \$1.66$ **20.** $\$20 - \$16.45$
(24)   (24)

21. Write two addition facts and two subtraction facts for
(8) the fact family 9, 5, 14.

22. Which digit shows the number of hundreds in 256?
(3)

23. Change this addition problem to a multiplication
(13) problem:

$$10 + 10 + 10 + 10 + 10 + 10 + 10$$

24. What is the tenth number of this sequence?
(1)

$$3, 6, 9, 12, 15, \ldots$$

25. The first three odd numbers are 1, 3, and 5. What is
(2)   the eighth odd number?

1, 3, 5, 7, 9, 11, 13, (15) 17

LESSON 25

Listing the Factors of Whole Numbers

Facts Practice: 90 Division Facts (Test E or F in Test Masters)

Mental Math: Count up by 5's from 3 to 53. (3, 8, 13, 18, ...)
Count by 7's from 0 to 77. (A calendar can help you start.)

a. 10×10	**b.** 10×100	**c.** 6×24
d. 6×42	**e.** 7×42	**f.** $\frac{1}{2}$ of 40
g. $\frac{1}{4}$ of 40	**h.** $\frac{1}{10}$ of 40	**i.** $365 - 100$
j. $6 \times 2, -2, \times 2, +1, \div 3$		

Problem Solving: Tom was thinking of a two-digit even number. Tom hinted that you say the number when counting by 3's and when counting by 7's, but not when counting by 4's. Of what number was Tom thinking?

The factors of a number are all the whole numbers which can divide it without leaving a remainder. The factors of 6 are 1, 2, 3, and 6 because any of these can divide 6 without leaving a remainder.

Example 1   List the factors of 20.

Solution   We are looking for all the numbers which divide 20 without leaving a remainder. What numbers can be put in this box which will give an answer without a remainder?

$$\boxed{}\,)\overline{20}$$

One way to find out is to start with 1 and to try every number up to 20. If we do this, we find that the numbers which divide 20 evenly are **1, 2, 4, 5, 10**, and **20**. These numbers are the factors of 20. These are the only numbers which divide 20 evenly. All other numbers leave a remainder.

Example 2   List the factors of 23.

Solution   The only factors of 23 are **1** and **23**. Every number greater than 1 has at least two factors: the number 1 and the number itself.

Practice   List the factors of each of these numbers:

    a. 4   **b.** 3   **c.** 6   **d.** 5

    e. 8   **f.** 11   **g.** 9   **h.** 12

    i. 1   **j.** 14   **k.** 2   **l.** 15

Problem set 25

1. The Christmas tree farm planted 9 rows of trees with
(21) 24 trees in each row. How many trees were planted? Use an "equal groups" pattern.

2. The haircut cost $6.75. Tony paid for it with a $10 bill.
(16) How much money should he get back? Use a "some went away" pattern.

3. Donna bought two cartons of milk for $1.12 each and a
(11) loaf of bread for $0.89. How much did she spend? Use a "some and some more" pattern.

4. List the factors of 30.   **5.** List the factors of 13.
(25)   (25)

6. Compare: $4 \times (6 \times 10) \bigcirc (4 \times 6) \times 10$
(24)

7. $6 \times (7 + 8)$ **8.** $(6 \times 7) + 8$
(24)   (24)

9. Write two multiplication facts and two division facts
(19) for the fact family 10, 12, 120.

10. 55 ÷ 9
(22)

11. 10$\overline{)55}$
(22)

12. 55 ÷ 8
(22)

13.   1234
(17)   ×   5

14. $5.67
(17)   ×   8

15.   987
(17)   ×   6

16. W − $13.55 = $5
(14)

17. 2001 − R = 1002
(14)

18. 4387 + 124 + 96
(6)

19. 3715 + 987 + 850
(6)

20. $6.75 + $8 + $1.36 + P = $20
(10)

21. How much money is $\frac{1}{2}$ of a dollar plus $\frac{1}{4}$ of a dollar
(23) plus $\frac{1}{10}$ of a dollar?

22. Use words to name the number 894,201.
(7)

23. 60 = 6 × W
(18)

24. What is the tenth number in this sequence?
(1)
$$5, 10, 15, 20, \ldots$$

25. Think of a whole number. Multiply it by 2. Is the
(2) answer odd or even?

LESSON
26

Practicing the Division Algorithm

Facts Practice: 64 Multiplication Facts (Test D in Test Masters)

Mental Math: Count up by 5's from 4 to 54. Count by 7's from 0 to 77.

    a. How many cents is 1 quarter? 2 quarters? 3 quarters?
    b. 10 × 34   **c.** 5 × 34   **d.** $\frac{1}{2}$ of 8
    e. $\frac{1}{4}$ of 8   **f.** $\frac{3}{4}$ of 8   **g.** 640 + 32
    h. 5 × 8, + 2, ÷ 6, × 3, − 1, ÷ 2

Problem Solving: Use the digits 5, 6, 7, 8, and 9 in this addition problem.

$$\begin{array}{r} \_\_ \\ + \ \_ \\ \hline \_\_ \end{array}$$

A **division algorithm** is a method for dividing number combinations which have not been memorized. The division algorithm breaks down large divisions into a series of smaller divisions that are easier to do. In each of the smaller problems we follow four steps. The four steps are **divide, multiply, subtract,** and **bring down.** As we do each step we write a number. Drawing this division chart a few times will help us remember the steps.

Division Chart

Step 1. Divide and write a number.

Step 2. Multiply and write a number.

Step 3. Subtract and write a number.

Step 4. Bring down the next digit.

Every time we bring down a digit we divide again, even if the answer when we divide is zero. We continue to divide, multiply, subtract, and bring down until there are no digits left to bring down.

Example 1   Divide: $3\overline{)\$8.52}$

Solution   We begin by breaking the division problem into a smaller problem. We first divide $8 by 3. So our first division in this example is $3\overline{)\$8}$.

$$3\overline{)\$8.52}$$

We divide and write "$2" above the $8. Then we multiply $2 by 3, which is $6. We write "6" below the $8. We subtract and get $2. Then we bring down the next digit, which is 5.

$$\begin{array}{r} \$2 \\ 3\overline{)\$8.52} \\ -6\downarrow \\ \hline 2\,5 \end{array}$$

Now we begin the new division, $3\overline{)25}$. The 2 of 25 is in the dollars' place and the 5 is in the dimes' place. So this division is like dividing 25 dimes by 3. The answer is 8 dimes, which we write on top. We multiply 8 dimes by 3, which is 24 dimes. We write "24" below the 25. Then we subtract and get 1 dime and bring down the 2 cents.

$$\begin{array}{r} \$2\;8 \\ 3\overline{)\$8.52} \\ -6\downarrow \\ \hline 2\,5 \\ -2\,4\downarrow \\ \hline 12 \end{array}$$

We are ready to begin the last division, $3\overline{)12}$. The "12" is 12¢. We divide and write "4" for 4¢ above the line. Then we multiply and subtract. There are no digits to bring down. There is no remainder. We write the decimal point in the answer above the decimal point in the division box to get an answer of **$2.84.**

$$\begin{array}{r} \$2.84 \\ 3\overline{)\$8.52} \\ -6 \\ \hline 2\,5 \\ -2\,4 \\ \hline 12 \\ -12 \\ \hline 0 \end{array}$$

We can check a division answer by multiplying. We multiply $2.84 by 3 and get $8.52. The three numbers of the multiplication answer should match the three numbers in the division box.

$$\begin{array}{r} {\scriptstyle 2\;1} \\ \$2.84 \\ \times\qquad 3 \\ \hline \$8.52 \quad \text{check} \end{array}$$

Example 2 Divide: $5\overline{)234}$

Solution Since we cannot divide $5\overline{)2}$, we begin with the division $5\overline{)23}$. We divide and write "4" above the 3 of 23. Then we multiply, subtract, and bring down.

$$\begin{array}{r} 4 \\ 5\overline{)234} \\ -20\downarrow \\ \hline 34 \end{array}$$

Now we begin the new division, $5\overline{)34}$. We divide and write "6" on top. Then we multiply and subtract. Since there is no number to bring down, we are finished. The remainder is 4. Thus the answer is **46 r 4**. The answer means that 234 is 46 fives plus 4.

$$\begin{array}{r} 46\ r\ 4 \\ 5\overline{)234} \\ -20\downarrow \\ \overline{)34} \\ -30 \\ \hline 4 \end{array}$$

To check a division answer with a remainder takes two steps. First we multiply. Then we add the remainder to that answer. To check this problem, we multiply 46 and 5. Then we add 4 to the answer.

$$\begin{array}{r} 46 \\ \times\ \ 5 \\ \hline 230 \\ +\ \ \ 4 \quad \text{remainder} \\ \hline 234 \quad \text{check} \end{array}$$

Practice* **a.** $4\overline{)\$5.56}$ **b.** $9\overline{)375}$ **c.** $3\overline{)\$4.65}$ **d.** $5\overline{)645}$

e. $7\overline{)\$3.64}$ **f.** $7\overline{)365}$ **g.** $10\overline{)546}$ **h.** $4\overline{)\$4.56}$

Problem set 26

1. The bike tire cost $2.98. Jenna paid for the tire with a $5 bill. How much should she get back in change? Use a "some went away" pattern.
(16)

2. Sheila sent 3 dozen cupcakes to school for a party. How many cupcakes did she send? Use an "equal groups" pattern.
(21)

3. What is the sum of three hundred forty-seven and eight hundred nine?
(6)

4. Draw two oblique line segments.
(16)

5. List the factors of 16.
(25)

6. $5\overline{)\$3.75}$
(26)

7. $4\overline{)365}$
(26)

8. 234 ÷ 6
(26)

9. $4.32 ÷ 6
(26)

10. $\dfrac{123}{3}$
(26)

11. $\dfrac{576}{6}$
(26)

12. $7.48 × 4
(17)

13. 609 × 8
(17)

14. 7 × 8 × 10
(18)

15. 7 × 8 × 11
(18)

16. 9374 − M = 4938
(14)

17. $10 − $6.24
(24)

18. L + 427 + 85 = 2010
(10)

19. $12.43 + $0.68 + $10
(24)

20. 365 + 365 + 365 + 365 + 365 + 365
(17)

21. 8 × 90 = 8 × 9 × N
(18)

22. Write two multiplication facts and two division facts
(19) for the fact family 8, 9, 72.

23. A checkerboard has 64 squares. The squares are in 8
(21) rows. How many squares are in each row? Use an "equal groups" pattern.

24. How much money is $\frac{3}{4}$ of a dollar plus $\frac{3}{10}$ of a dollar?
(23)

25. What number is halfway between 400 and 600?
(12)

LESSON 27

Solving Problems About Divisions of Time

Facts Practice: 90 Division Facts (Test E or F in Test Masters)

Mental Math: Name the months of the year in order. Count up and down by 25's between 0 and 200.

a. How many days are in 1 week? 2 weeks? 3 weeks?

b. 5×42
c. 5×24
d. $\frac{1}{2}$ of 20

e. $\frac{1}{4}$ of 20
f. $\frac{3}{4}$ of 20
g. $\frac{1}{10}$ of 20

h. $\frac{3}{10}$ of 20
i. $3 \times 8, \div 4, \times 3, \div 9$

Problem Solving: The dog, the cat, and the turtle won the first, second, and third prizes in the pet show. However, the dog was not first, the cat was not second, and the turtle was not third. List the remaining possible orders of awards.

We measure time by the movement of the earth. A **day** is the length of time it takes the earth to spin around on its axis once. We divide a day into 24 equal parts called **hours.** Each hour is divided into 60 equal lengths of time called **minutes,** and each minute is divided into 60 **seconds.**

Besides spinning on its axis, the earth also moves on a long journey around the sun. The time it takes to travel around the sun is a **year.** It takes the earth a little more than 365 days to travel around the sun, so every 4 years we add an extra day to our calendar and call that year a **leap year.** Common years have 365 days. Leap years have 366 days with the additional day added to February.

A **decade** consists of ten years in a row, and a **century** consists of 100 years in a row. The days of the year have been divided into 12 groups called **months.** We call seven days in a row a **week.** A calendar lists the days of a month with the days of the week.

Example 1 A century is how many decades?

Solution A century is 100 years. A decade is 10 years. Since 10 tens equals 100, a century is **10 decades.**

Example 2 According to this calendar, June 8, 2014, is what day of the week?

JUNE 2014						
S	M	T	W	T	F	S
1	2	3	4	5	6	7
8	9	10	11	12	13	14
15	16	17	18	19	20	21
22	23	24	25	26	27	28
29	30					

Solution Many calendars are designed so that the first day of the week is Sunday. On this calendar the letters at the top stand for *Sunday, Monday, Tuesday, Wednesday, Thursday, Friday,* and *Saturday,* respectively. Thus, June 8, 2014, is a **Sunday,** the second Sunday of the month of June.

Example 3 How many years were there from 1492 to 1620?

Solution To find the number of years from one date to another, we may subtract.[†] We subtract the earlier date from the later date. In this problem we subtract 1492 from 1620 and find that there were **128 years** from 1492 to 1620.

Practice **a.** Four centuries is how many years?

b. According to the calendar in Example 2, what is the date of the third Thursday in June?

c. How many years were there from 1066 to 1776?

d. A leap year lasts how many days?

e. What is the name for $\frac{1}{10}$ of a century?

[†]Years have been numbered forward (A.D.) and backward (B.C.) from the birth of Jesus of Nazareth. In this book, all year dates should be considered years A.D.

Problem set 27 [24]

1. When $0.60 is subtracted from $6, what is the difference?

2. [21] There are 12 inches in a foot. How many inches are in 3 feet? Use an "equal groups" pattern.

3. [27,23] Use the "equal groups" pattern. Nathan read his book for half an hour in the morning and for a quarter of an hour in the evening. How many minutes is $\frac{1}{2}$ of an hour plus $\frac{1}{4}$ of an hour?

4. [23] In John's class there are half as many girls as boys. There are 14 boys. How many girls are there?

5. [25] List the factors of 21.

6. [26] $9\overline{)\$2.34}$

7. [26] $4.32 ÷ 9

8. [26] $8\overline{)304}$

9. [26] 500 ÷ 10

10. [27] According to this calendar, June 26, 2014, is what day of the week?

JUNE 2014
S M T W T F S
1 2 3 4 5 6 7
8 9 10 11 12 13 14
15 16 17 18 19 20 21
22 23 24 25 26 27 28
29 30

11. [18] 8 × 7 × 6

12. [17] 397 × 4

13. [17] $8.79 × 6

14. [17] 8 × 1437

15. [9] 6175 − 5817

16. [13] $20.00 − $6.84

17. [24] 456 ÷ (54 ÷ 9)

18. [24] $3.48 + $24.95 + $8

19. [10] 3746 + 3625 + 529 + W = 8000

20. [7] Use words to name 68,200.

21. The number 387 is between which of these pairs of
(4) numbers?

   A. 200 and 300   B. 300 and 400   C. 400 and 500

22. $6 \times 70 = 6 \times 7 \times N$
(18)

23. What are the next three numbers in this sequence?
(1)
   ..., 200, 250, 300, 350, _____, _____, _____, ...

24. How many years were there from 1517 to 1620?
(27)

25. What number is halfway between 500 and 600?
(12)

**LESSON
28**

Reading and Drawing
Number Lines, Part 2

Facts Practice: 64 Multiplication Facts (Test D in Test Masters)

Mental Math: How many days are in a common year? in a
leap year? Count by 12's from 12 to 60.

a. How many days are in 2 weeks? 3 weeks? 4 weeks?

b. 10×24 **c.** 6×24 **d.** $\frac{1}{2}$ of 100

e. $\frac{1}{4}$ of 100   **f.** $\frac{3}{4}$ of 100   **g.** $\frac{1}{10}$ of 100

h. $\frac{7}{10}$ of 100   **i.** $6 \times 6, -1, \div 5$

Problem Solving: Use the digits 5, 6, 7, 8, and 9 in
this subtraction problem.

$$\begin{array}{r} \underline{} \\ -\ \underline{} \\ \hline \underline{} \end{array}$$

We have drawn horizontal number lines, but number lines
may also be vertical or even curved. We have marked and
labeled whole numbers on number lines, but it is not
necessary to mark every whole number. Number lines may

mark only some of the whole numbers. The location of the rest of the numbers must be figured out. In this lesson we will practice reading different kinds of number lines.

Example 1   What temperature is shown by this thermometer?

Solution   This thermometer indicates the temperature in degrees Fahrenheit, which is abbreviated °F. On the scale, only every 10° is labeled. There are five spaces between every 10°. That means every space equals 2°. Counting up from 70°, we count 72°, 74°, 76°. The thermometer shows a temperature of **76°F.**

Example 2   To what mark on this scale is the arrow pointing?

Solution   As we move toward the right around the curve, we see that the numbers grow larger. The arrow is past the 400 mark and near the 600 mark. Halfway between the 400 and 600 marks is a long mark which marks 500. The arrow points halfway between the 500 and 600 marks, so it points to the **550 mark.**

Example 3   Draw a horizontal number line from zero to 500 with only zero and hundreds marked and labeled.

Solution   A horizontal number line is drawn. Only the hundreds will be marked, so we will mark zero and 100, 200, 300, 400, and 500. These marks should be evenly spaced. The number line should look like this.

Practice   Draw a number line from 0 to 100 with only zero and tens marked and labeled.

Problem set 28

1. On the first 3 days of their trip, the Smiths drove 408 miles, 347 miles, and 419 miles, respectively. Altogether, how far did they drive in 3 days? Use a "some and some more" pattern.
(11)

2. Tom is 5 feet tall. There are 12 inches in 1 foot. How many inches tall is Tom? Use an "equal groups" pattern.
(21)

3. How much money is $\frac{3}{4}$ of a dollar and $\frac{7}{10}$ of a dollar?
(23)

4. Andrew's age is half of David's age. If David is 12 years old, then how old is Andrew?
(23)

5. List the factors of 30.
(25)

6. 864 ÷ 5
(26)

7. $2.72 ÷ 4
(26)

8. 608 ÷ 9
(26)

9. 378 ÷ (18 ÷ 3)
(24)

10. What temperature is shown by this thermometer?
(28)

11. $52.60
(17)   ×   7

12.   3874
(17)   ×   6

13.   9063
(17)   ×   8

14. To what mark on this scale is the arrow pointing?
(28)

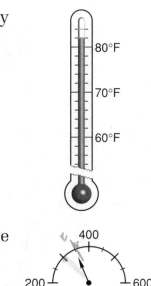

15. $386 + 4287 + 672 + M = 5350$
(10)

16. Draw a horizontal number line from zero to 50 with
(28) only zero and tens marked and labeled.

17. The number 78 is between which of these pairs of
(4) numbers?

A. 60 and 70   B. 70 and 80   C. 80 and 90

18. Compare: five decades ◯ one half of a century
(27,4)

19. When three hundred ninety-seven is subtracted from
(9) four hundred five, what is the difference?

20. In Joshua's class there is one more boy than there are
(2) girls. Which could not be the number of students in
Joshua's class?

A. 25   B. 27   C. 28   D. 29

21. How many years were there from 1776 to 1789?
(27)

22. What are the next three numbers in this sequence?
(1)
    ..., 160, 170, 180, _____, _____, _____, ...

23. Which digit shows the number of hundreds in 537?
(3)

24. Use words to name 327,040.
(7)

25. The arrow is pointing to what number on this number
(28) line?

LESSON
29

Reading and Writing Time from a Clock

Facts Practice: 90 Division Facts (Test E or F in Test Masters)

Mental Math: How many years are in a century? in a decade? Count by 12's from 12 to 60.

  a. How many months are in 1 year? 2 years? 3 years?

  b. 100×25 **c.** 7×25 **d.** $\frac{1}{2}$ of 40

  e. $\frac{1}{4}$ of 40   **f.** $\frac{3}{4}$ of 40   **g.** $\frac{1}{10}$ of 40

  h. $\frac{9}{10}$ of 40   **i.** $7 \times 7, + 1, \div 5, \div 5$

Problem Solving: Half of the students in the room were girls. Half of the girls had brown hair. Half the brown-haired girls wore pony tails. If 4 brown-haired girls were wearing pony tails, how many students were in the room?

The time of day can be shown by a clock with the hands pointing to places on a circular number line. The number line of a clock is actually two number lines in one. One number line is the hour scale. It has 12 marks, usually numbered, to show the hour of the day. The other number line is the minute scale. It has 60 smaller marks. These marks are not numbered. These marks show the minutes of the hour. These two scales are formed into one line and wrapped into a circle so that the ends are joined.

The two hands of the clock point to places on the number line to indicate the time of day. We "tell time" by reading the location on the number line to which the hands are pointing. With the shorter hand, we read from the hour scale, and with the longer hand we read from the minute scale.

When writing the time of day, we write the hour, a colon, and two digits to show the number of minutes after the hour. We write the time shown by the clock on the previous page as 1:45.

A full day is 24 hours long, but most clocks show only 12 hours. Noon is the midpoint of the day. The 12 hours before noon are known as **a.m.** The 12 hours after noon are known as **p.m.** When stating the time of day, the labels "a.m." and "p.m." should be used. Noon is written as "12:00 p.m." and midnight is written as "12:00 a.m."[†]

Example   If it is morning, what time is shown by this clock?

Solution   The clock shows 5 minutes after the ninth hour. The proper form is hour, colon, two digits for the minutes, and then a.m. or p.m. The time indicated is **9:05 a.m.**

Practice*   **a.** Write the time that is 2 minutes after eight in the evening.

b. Write the time that is a quarter to nine in the morning.

c. Write the time that is 20 minutes after noon.

d. Write the time that is 30 minutes after midnight.

e. Write the time that is a quarter after nine in the morning.

f. If it is morning, what time is shown by the clock?

g. What time would be shown by the clock 2 hours later?

[†]The use of p.m. and a.m. to designate 12:00 is unclear. To avoid confusion, we refer to these times as *noon* and *midnight*.

**Problem set
29**

1. How many years were there from 1620 to 1776?
(27)

2. Jenny had $1873. She earned $200 more for passing
(11) GO. Then how much money did she have? Use a "some and some more" pattern.

3. One half of a decade is how many years?
(27)

4. Dan separated 52 cards into 4 equal piles. How many
(21) cards were in each pile? Use an "equal groups" pattern.

5. Which factors of 18 are also factors of 24?
(25)

6. $\dfrac{\$5.43}{3}$ **7.** $\dfrac{\$6.00}{8}$
(26)   (26)

8. $528 \div (28 \div 7)$ **9.** $700 \div 6$
(24)   (26)

10. If it is evening, what time is
(29) shown by this clock?

11. Write the time that is half past
(29) noon.

12. How much money is $\frac{1}{2}$ of a dollar plus $\frac{5}{10}$ of a dollar?
(23)

13. According to this calendar, May 10,
(27) 2042, is what day of the week?

MAY 2042						
S	M	T	W	T	F	S
					1	2	3
4	5	6	7	8	9	10
11	12	13	14	15	16	17
18	19	20	21	22	23	24
25	26	27	28	29	30	31

14. What is the largest three-digit even number that has
(2) the digits 5, 6, and 7?

15. 4387
(6) 2965
    + 4943
   ——————

16. $63.75
(13) − $46.88
   ——————

17. 4010
(14) −   F
   ——————
    563

18. 3408
(17) ×   7
   ——————

19. $3.56
(17) ×   8
   ——————

20. 487
(17) ×   9
   ——————

21. What time is 5 minutes before nine in the morning?
(29)

22. Write two multiplication facts and two division facts
(19) for the fact family 10, 2, 20.

23. How many years were there from 1776 to 1787?
(27)

24. What are the next three numbers in this sequence?
(1)   ..., 400, 500, 600, 700, _____, _____, _____, ...

25. The arrow is pointing to what number on this number
(28) line?

LESSON 30

Multiplying by Multiples of 10 and 100

Facts Practice: 64 Multiplication Facts (Test D in Test Masters)

Mental Math: How many months are in a year? How many weeks are in a year? Name the months of the year in order.

a. How many months are in 2 years? 3 years? 4 years?

b. 10×50 c. 6×43 d. $\frac{1}{2}$ of 50

e. $\frac{1}{10}$ of 50   f. $\frac{5}{10}$ of 50   g. $750 - 250$

h. $9 \times 9, -1, \div 2, +2, \div 6$

Problem Solving: Copy this multiplication problem and fill in the missing digits.

$$\begin{array}{r} 36 \\ \times\ \underline{} \\ \hline \underline{}2 \end{array}$$

Whole numbers that end with zero are **multiples of 10.** These numbers are multiples of 10.

$$10, 20, 30, 40, 50, 60, \ldots$$

Any multiple of 10 can be written as a number times 10, as we show here.

$$20 = 2 \times 10$$

$$30 = 3 \times 10$$

$$40 = 4 \times 10$$

and so on

When we multiply another number by a multiple of 10, we may multiply by the digit(s) in front of the zero and then multiply by 10. We will show this by multiplying 25×30.

The problem: $25 \times \quad 30 \quad =$

We think: $25 \times 3 \times 10 =$

We multiply 25×3: $75 \quad \times 10 =$

Then we multiply 75×10: $75 \quad \times 10 = 750$

The last multiplication placed a zero after the 75. So when we multiply by a multiple of 10, we may multiply by the digit(s) in front of the zero and then place a zero on the end of that answer.

When we write a problem vertically, we may show this by writing the numbers so that the multiple of 10 is on the bottom and the zero "hangs out" to the right. Here we write 25 times 30 vertically. We multiply 25 times 3. Then we bring down the zero (multiply by 10) and find that 25 × 30 is 750.

$$\begin{array}{r} 1 \\ 25 \\ \times\ \ 30 \\ \hline 750 \end{array}$$

We may use a similar method to multiply by **multiples of 100.** Multiples of 100 end with two zeros. When we multiply by multiples of 100, we write the problems so that two zeros "hang out" to the right. We show this by multiplying 25 × 300.

We write the problem with 300 on the bottom with zeros out to the right. We multiply 25 times 3 hundreds and get 75 hundreds. We write 7500.

$$\begin{array}{r} 1 \\ 25 \\ \times\ \ 300 \\ \hline 7500 \end{array}$$

Example 1   37 × 40

Solution   We write the problem so that the number ending with zero is on the bottom. We let the zero hang out to the right. Then we multiply.

$$\begin{array}{r} 2 \\ 37 \\ \times\ \ 40 \\ \hline \mathbf{1480} \end{array}$$

Example 2 $3.75 × 10

Solution   When multiplying whole numbers by 10, we may simply attach a zero. The zero shifts all other digits one place to the left. However, when multiplying dollars and cents by 10, attaching a zero does not shift the other digits from their places.

$3.750 still equals $3.75

This is because the decimal point marks the place values, and the position of the decimal point was not changed. When multiplying dollars and cents by whole numbers, we position the decimal point in the answer so that there are two digits to the right of the decimal point.

$$\begin{array}{r} \$3.75 \\ \times \quad 10 \\ \hline \$37.50 \end{array}$$

Practice*   **a.** 34 × 20   **b.** 50 × 48

c. 34 × 200   **d.** 500 × 36

e. 55 × 30   **f.** $1.25 × 30

g. 55 × 300   **h.** $1.25 × 300

i. 60 × 45   **j.** $2.35 × 40

k. 400 × 37   **l.** $1.43 × 200

Problem set 30

1. Ruben, Martin, and James equally shared 1 dozen
(21) cookies. Each of the boys had how many cookies? Use the "equal groups" pattern.

2. Michael had $841 before he had to pay a $75 luxury
(16) tax. Then how much money did he have? Use the "some went away" pattern.

3. What year came one century after 1776?
(27)

4. The sheet of stamps had 10 rows of stamps with 10
(21) stamps in each row. How many stamps were on the sheet? Use the "equal groups" pattern.

5. List the factors of 10.
(25)

6. 37 × 60   **7.** 28 × 300
(30)   (30)

8. 50 × 46
(30)

9. 60 × $0.73
(30)

10. 50 × (1000 − 200)
(24)

11. What is the place value of the 5 in 356?
(7)

12. Write the time that is 30 minutes before noon.
(29)

13. How much money is $\frac{1}{2}$ of a dollar plus $\frac{3}{4}$ of a dollar
(23) plus $\frac{3}{10}$ of a dollar?

14. What is the product of thirty-eight and forty?
(30)

15. Use words to name 944,000.
(7)

16.   4637
(6)   2843
    + 6464

17.   4618
(9)   − 2728

18. $60.00
(13)   − $7.63

19. 364 ÷ 10
(26)

20. 5)364
(26)

21. $\frac{364}{7}$
(26)

22. Think of a whole number. Multiply it by 2. Now add
(2) 1. Is the final answer odd or even?

23. According to this calendar, what
(27) is the date of the third Sunday in
May 1957?

MAY 1957						
S	M	T	W	T	F	S
			1	2	3	4
5	6	7	8	9	10	11
12	13	14	15	16	17	18
19	20	21	22	23	24	25
26	27	28	29	30	31	

24. The number 356 is between which pair of numbers?
(4)   A. 340 and 350   B. 350 and 360   C. 360 and 370

25. What are the next three numbers in this sequence?
(1)
    ..., 600, 700, 800, _____, _____, _____, ...

LESSON 31

Picturing Fractions, Part 1 • Cents and Percents

Facts Practice: 90 Division Facts (Test E or F in Test Masters)

Mental Math: Count by 12's from 12 to 72. Count by 5's from 2 to 52.

  a. How many days is 2 weeks? 3 weeks? 4 weeks?
  b. 35 + 47   **c.** 370 + 50   **d.** 100 × 40
  e. 4 × 36   **f.** $\frac{1}{2}$ of 12   **g.** $\frac{1}{4}$ of 12
  h. 4 × 7, − 1, ÷ 3, + 1, × 10

Problem Solving: Bob flipped a coin three times. It landed heads up twice and tails up once, but not necessarily in that order. List the possible orders of the three coin flips.

Picturing fractions, part 1

A picture can help us understand the meaning of a fraction. This circle is divided into six equal parts. One of the parts is shaded. So $\frac{1}{6}$ of the circle is shaded.

Five of the six parts are not shaded. So $\frac{5}{6}$ of the circle is not shaded.

Example 1   What fraction of this group of circles is shaded?

Solution   We see a group of five circles. Three of the five circles are shaded. So $\frac{3}{5}$ of the group is shaded.

Example 2   What fraction of this circle is not shaded?

Solution   The circle is divided into four equal parts. One part is shaded, and three parts are not shaded. The fraction that is not shaded is $\frac{3}{4}$.

Cents and percents
Fractions and percents are two ways to describe part of a whole. A whole is 100 percent, which we abbreviate 100%. So half of a whole is half of 100%, which is 50%.

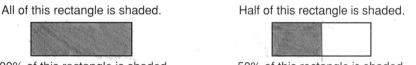

All of this rectangle is shaded.

100% of this rectangle is shaded.

Half of this rectangle is shaded.

50% of this rectangle is shaded.

Thinking about cents as part of a dollar can help us understand percents.

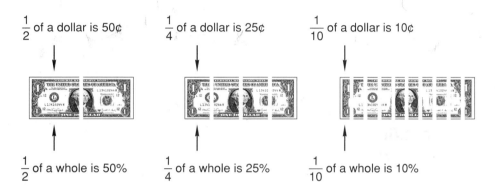

$\frac{1}{2}$ of a dollar is 50¢ $\frac{1}{4}$ of a dollar is 25¢ $\frac{1}{10}$ of a dollar is 10¢

$\frac{1}{2}$ of a whole is 50% $\frac{1}{4}$ of a whole is 25% $\frac{1}{10}$ of a whole is 10%

Example 3 What percent of this square is shaded?

Solution One half of the square is shaded. The whole square is 100%, so one half of the square is **50%.**

Example 4 Three quarters plus a dime is what percent of a dollar?

Solution Three quarters plus a dime is 85¢, which is 85 hundredths of a dollar. This is **85%** of one dollar.

Practice **a.** What fraction of this triangle is shaded?

b. What percent of this triangle is shaded?

c. What fraction of this triangle is not shaded?

d. What percent of this triangle is not shaded?

e. What two fractions name the shaded part of this circle?

f. What percent of the circle is shaded?

g. What fraction of this rectangle is shaded?

h. What percent of this rectangle is shaded?

i. A quarter plus a nickel is what percent of a dollar?

Problem set 31

1. Draw two oblique lines that stay the same distance apart.
(16)

2. There were 100 stamps on the sheet. Thai has used 36 of them. How many stamps are left? Use a "some went away" pattern.
(16)

3. What year came one decade after 1802?
(27)

4. A quarter plus a dime is what percent of a dollar?
(31)

5. List the factors of 25.
(25)

6. What fraction of this rectangle is not shaded?
(31)

7. What fraction of the triangle is shaded?
(31)

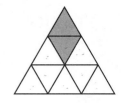

8. What number is the denominator in the fraction $\frac{2}{3}$?
(23)

9. Write the time that is a quarter to eight in the morning.
(29)

10. $\begin{array}{r} W \\ -\ \$19.46 \\ \hline \$28.93 \end{array}$
(14)

11. $\begin{array}{r} 3010 \\ -\ 1342 \\ \hline \end{array}$
(9)

12. $\begin{array}{r} 28 \\ 54 \\ 75 \\ 91 \\ +\ 26 \\ \hline \end{array}$
(6)

13. $\begin{array}{r} 764 \\ \times\quad 30 \\ \hline \end{array}$
(30)

14. $\begin{array}{r} \$9.08 \\ \times\qquad 60 \\ \hline \end{array}$
(30)

15. $6\overline{)\$7.44}$
(26)

16. $362 \div 10$
(26)

17. $4\overline{)898}$
(26)

18. $42.37 + \$7.58 + \$0.68 + \$15$
(24)

19. $(48 \times 6) - 9$
(24)

20. $6 \times 30 \times 12$
(18)

21. From February 1 to September 1 is how many months?
(27)

22. What is the sum of six hundred five and five hundred
(6) ninety-seven?

23. Which of these numbers is between 360 and 370?
(4)
 A. 356 B. 367 C. 373

24. What are the next three numbers in this sequence?
(1)
 ..., 250, 260, 270, 280, _____, _____, _____, ...

25. What temperature is shown by
(28) this thermometer?

LESSON 32

Drawing Pairs of Lines: Parallel, Intersecting, Perpendicular

---

Facts Practice: 64 Multiplication Facts (Test D in Test Masters)

Mental Math: How many days are in a leap year? in a common year? Count by 12's from 12 to 84. Count by 5's from 3 to 53.

  a. How many is 2 dozen? 3 dozen? 4 dozen?
  b. 48 + 25   **c.** 1200 + 340   **d.** 50% of 20
  e. 25% of 20   **f.** 10% of 20   **g.** 7 × 32
  h. 4 × 9, − 1, ÷ 5, + 1, × 4

Problem Solving: Copy this multiplication problem and fill in the missing digits.

$$\begin{array}{r} 45 \\ \times\ \underline{} \\ \hline \underline{0} \end{array}$$

Where lines "cross" we say that they **intersect.** If we draw two straight lines on the same flat surface, then either those lines will intersect or they will not intersect. Lines which go in the same directions and stay the same distance apart are called **parallel lines.** Thinking of train tracks can give us the idea of parallel lines. Here are pairs of parallel lines and parallel line segments.

    Lines on the same surface that are not parallel are **intersecting lines.** Here are pairs of intersecting lines and intersecting line segments.

As we look at the third pair, we see that the segments intersect in a special way. Where they intersect, "square corners" are formed. Intersecting lines and segments that form square corners are **perpendicular.**

Activity Pair off with a partner. Draw a line segment. Then have your partner draw one line segment parallel to your segment and another segment perpendicular to your segment. Repeat the activity with the roles reversed.

Example 1 Draw a pair of intersecting lines which are not perpendicular.

Solution We are to draw two lines which intersect but do not form square corners. Many arrangements are possible.

Example 2 Which of the following do *not* appear to be perpendicular segments?

A.   B.   C.   D.

Solution Segments that are perpendicular meet and form square corners. The segments in A appear to be perpendicular. (You may need to turn the page slightly to help you see this.) The segments in B and D also appear to be perpendicular. The segments that do not appear to be perpendicular are those in choice **C**.

Practice **a.** Draw two parallel segments.

b. Draw two perpendicular lines.

c. Draw two segments that intersect but are not perpendicular.

Problem set **1.** Draw a pair of intersecting lines that are
32 (32) perpendicular.

2. Lani bought a kaleidoscope for $4.19. If she paid for it
(16) with a $10 bill, how much money should she get back? Use a "some went away" pattern.

3. How many hours are there in 7 days? Use an "equal
(21) groups" pattern.   *168*

4. What fraction of the group is
(31) shaded?

5. List the factors of 19. *1, 19*
(25)

6. $16.38   **7.**   1000   **8.** $\dfrac{280}{5}$ **9.**   792
(13) − $9.47   (14)   − Q   (26)   (6)   488
                                                       42
                          576   96

10.   476   **11.** $9.68   **12.** 8)$19.44   5
(30)   × 80   (30)   × 60   (26)   28
                                                      + 49

13. Write the time that is thirty minutes before midnight.
(29)

14. Compare: $\frac{1}{10}$ of 100 $\gt$ $\frac{1}{2}$ of 20
(23,4)

15. 287 + 287 + 287 + 287 + 287
(17)

16. $96 + $128.13 + $27.49 + W = $300
(10)

17. 328 ÷ (32 ÷ 8)   **18.** 648 − (600 + 48)
(24)   (24)

19. Think of an odd number. Multiply it by 2. Now add 1.
(2)   Is the final answer odd or even?

20. The United States Constitution became effective in
(27)   1789. What year came one century after 1789?

21. If it is afternoon, what time is
(29)   shown by this clock?

22. What number is the numerator of
(23)   the fraction $\frac{2}{3}$?

23. Use words to name the number 123,400.
(7)

24. Three quarters plus a dime is what percent of a dollar?
(31)

25. Copy this number line and draw an arrow to show
(28) where 75 would be.

LESSON
33

Drawing Angles

Facts Practice: 90 Division Facts (Test E or F in Test Masters)

Mental Math: How many years are in a decade? in a century?
Count by 12's from 12 to 84. Count by 5's from
4 to 54.

a. How many hours are in 1 day? 2 days?
b. 39 + 45   **c.** 680 − 400   **d.** 10 × 60
e. 50% of 30   **f.** 10% of 30   **g.** 8 × 45
h. 6 × 7, − 2, ÷ 5, × 2, − 1, ÷ 5

Problem Solving: Jan flipped a coin three times. It landed
heads up once and tails up twice. List the
possible orders of the three coin flips.

When lines or segments intersect, angles are formed. Here
we show three angles.

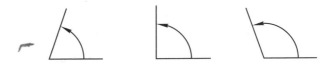

An **angle** is an "opening" between intersecting lines or
segments. We see by the drawings that the amount of the
opening may be small or large. We have different names
for angles depending upon how open they are.

An angle which is like the corner of a square is called a **right angle.** "Right angle" does not mean that the angle opens to the right. A right angle may open in any direction. "Right angle" simply means "square corner." Sometimes we draw a little square in the angle indicating that the angle is a right angle.

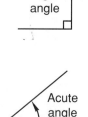
Right angle

Right angle

An angle which is open less than a right angle is called an **acute angle.** Some remember this as "a cute" little angle.

Acute angle

An angle which is open more than a right angle is called an **obtuse angle.**

Obtuse angle

Example Which of these angles appears to be a right angle?

A.   (B)   C.

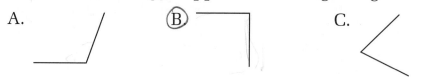

Solution A right angle matches the corner of a square. Angle A is open too wide, and angle C is not open wide enough. The only right angle is **angle B.**

Practice Draw an example of each angle:

  a. Acute angle   **b.** Obtuse angle   **c.** Right angle

Name each angle shown:

  d.   **e.**   **f.**

Problem set 33

1. Jean took $20 to the carnival. She spent $\frac{1}{2}$ of her money on rides, $\frac{1}{4}$ of her money on food, and $\frac{1}{10}$ of her money on parking. How much did Jean spend on rides, on food, and on parking?

2. Hank said that the horse trough holds 18 buckets of
(21) water. If a bucket holds 3 gallons, how many gallons
does the trough hold? Use an "equal groups" pattern.

15

3. Draw a horizontal line segment and a vertical line
(32) segment that intersect.

4. How many seconds are there in 1 hour?
(27)

5. Paul chopped a tree that was 52 feet tall into 4 logs of
(21) equal length. How many feet long was each log? Use
an "equal groups" pattern.

6. $56.37   **7.**   5286   **8.** $40.00   **9.**   67
(13) $34.28 (14) $-$ K   (13) $-$ $39.56 (10)   72
  $+$ $9.75   4319   43

                                        91

                                     48

10. $936 \div (36 \div 9)$ **11.**   596   19
(24)   (30) $\times$ 600   648

                                     $+$ M

12. $\dfrac{\$46.56}{8}$ **13.** 4.07×80 996
(26)   (30)

14. $9 \times 12 \times 20$ **15.** $936 \div 7$
(18)   (26)

16. Compare: $\frac{1}{4}$ of 80 $\bigcirc$ $\frac{1}{2}$ of 40
(23,4)

17. Which of these angles does not appear to be a right
(33) angle?

A.   B.   C.

18. List the factors of 18.
(25)

19. What fraction of the rectangle is
(31) shaded? What percent of the rectangle is shaded?

20. How many years were there from 1776 to 1976?
(27)

21. According to this calendar, July 17,
(27) 2025, is what day of the week?

JULY 2025
S M T W T F S
1 2 3 4 5
6 7 8 9 10 11 12
13 14 15 16 17 18 19
20 21 22 23 24 25 26
27 28 29 30 31

22. What is the name for the bottom number of a fraction?
(23)

23. Write two multiplication facts and two division facts
(19) for the fact family 9, 10, 90.

24. What are the next three numbers in this sequence?
(1)

..., 660, 670, 680, _____, _____, _____, ...

25. To what number on this scale is
(28) the arrow pointing?

LESSON 34

Rounding Numbers Using a Number Line

Facts Practice: 64 Multiplication Facts (Test D in Test Masters)

Mental Math: How many months are in half a year? in a year and a half? Count by 12's from 12 to 96. Count by 6's from 6 to 96.

a. How much money is 4 quarters? 5 quarters? 6 quarters?
b. 9 × 42   **c.** 25 × 10   **d.** 50% of 40
e. 25% of 40   **f.** 10% of 40   **g.** 840 − 140
h. 8 × 8, − 1, ÷ 9, × 3, − 1, ÷ 4

Problem Solving: Copy this multiplication problem and fill in the missing digits.

$$\begin{array}{r} \_\,\_ \\ \times\ \ 8 \\ \hline \_\,6 \end{array}$$

Two of the following statements use **exact numbers,** while the other two statements use **rounded numbers.** Can you tell which statements use rounded numbers?

- About 600 people attended the homecoming game.

- The attendance at the game was 614.

- The price of the shoes was $48.97.

- The shoes cost about $50.

The first statement and the last statement use rounded numbers. Rounded numbers are often used in place of exact numbers because rounded numbers are easy to understand and easy to work with. When we change an exact number into a rounded number, we **round** the number.

When we round a number, we find another number to which the number is **close.** We will use the number line below to round 67 to the nearest ten.

To round the number 67, we name the round number to which it is closest. **Round numbers end with one or more zeros.** On the number line we see that 67 falls between the round numbers 60 and 70. We pick the **closest** round number. Since 67 is closer to 70, we round to 70.

When the number we are rounding is halfway between two round numbers, we usually round up to the larger round number. Sixty-five is halfway between 60 and 70. We would round 65 to 70. Likewise, 450 is halfway between 400 and 500. We would round 450 to 500.

Example   Round 523 to the nearest hundred.

Solution   When we round a number to the nearest hundred, we name the "hundred number" to which it is closest. The hundred numbers are the numbers we say when we count by hundreds: 100, 200, 300, 400, and so on. We use a number line marked off with hundreds to picture this problem.

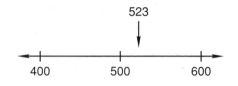

523

400   500   600

Placing 523 on the number line, we see that it falls between the hundred numbers 500 and 600. Since 523 is closer to 500 than it is to 600, we round 523 to **500**.

Practice*   For each problem below, sketch a number line to show your work. Round these numbers to the nearest ten:

a. 72   **b.** 87   **c.** 49   **d.** 95

Round these numbers to the nearest hundred:

e. 685   **f.** 420   **g.** 776   **h.** 350

Problem set 34

1. Draw a pair of vertical parallel lines.
(32)

2. Round 537 to the nearest hundred.
(34)

3. Round 78 to the nearest ten.
(34)

4. Forty animals were brought to the pet show. One half were mammals, one fourth were fish, one tenth were reptiles, and the rest were birds. How many mammals, fish, reptiles, and birds were brought to the pet show?
(23)

5. Sharon was standing in a line that had 10 people in it, including herself. If there were 5 people in front of her, how many people were behind her?
(7)

6. Draw an acute angle.
(33)

7. List the factors of 7.
(25)

8. At which of these times are the hands of a clock perpendicular?
(32)
A. 6:00   B. 12:30   C. 9:00

9. $34.28
(13) $9.76
   + $20.84

10.   3526
(14) −   V
    1617

11. $10.00
(13) − $0.86

12. 499
(6)   25
   43
  756
   67
   94
+   32

13.   563
(30) ×   90

14. $2.86
(30) ×   70

15.   479
(30) × 800

16. 3)1122
(26)

17. $5.76 ÷ 6
(26)

18. 10)2735
(26)

19. $64.23 + $5.96 + $17 + ($1 − $0.16)
(24)

20. From March 1 to December 1 is how many months?
(27)

21. What fraction of the circle is
(31) shaded? Is more or less than 50%
of the circle shaded?

22. Which word means "parallel to the horizon"?
(32)   A. vertical   B. oblique   C. horizontal

23. Write the time that is a quarter after one in the
(29) afternoon.

24. Draw a horizontal number line from zero to 50 with
(28) only zero and tens marked and labeled.

25. What is the tenth number of this sequence?
(1)   7, 14, 21, …

LESSON 35

Dividing with Zeros in the Quotient

Facts Practice: 90 Division Facts (Test E or F in Test Masters)

Mental Math: How many years is half a century? half a decade?
  a. Round 48 to the nearest ten.
  b. 50 + 80   **c.** 50 × 8   **d.** 4 × 27
  e. 50% of 50   **f.** 10% of 50   **g.** 1420 + 300
  h. 3 × 8, + 1, × 2, − 1, ÷ 7, ÷ 7

Problem Solving: If a coin is flipped twice, it may land heads then heads, or heads then tails, or tails then heads, or tails then tails. What are the possible orders if a coin is flipped three times?

The answer to a division problem is called a **quotient.** Sometimes when we divide, one or more of the digits in the quotient is a zero. When this happens, we continue to follow the four steps: divide, multiply, subtract, and bring down.

Example 1   Divide: $6\overline{)365}$

Solution   We begin by breaking the division problem into a smaller problem: $6\overline{)36}$.

$$6\overline{)365}$$

Then we divide, multiply, subtract, and bring down. When we subtract, we get zero, which we may or may not write, and we bring down the 5. Since there is a number to bring down, we divide again. The new division is $6\overline{)5}$.

$$\begin{array}{r} 6 \\ 6\overline{)365} \\ -36\downarrow \\ \hline 5 \end{array}$$

Since we cannot divide 5 by 6 even once, we write a zero in the answer, multiply by zero, and subtract. Since there is no other number to bring down, the division is finished and the remainder is 5. Our answer is **60 r 5.**

$$\begin{array}{r} 60\ \text{r}\ 5 \\ 6\overline{)365} \\ -36\downarrow \\ \hline 5 \\ -0 \\ \hline 5 \end{array}$$

Example 2   Divide: 6)635

Solution   We begin by breaking the division problem into a smaller problem. We can divide 6)6, so we divide, multiply, subtract, and bring down. The next division is 6)3.

$$\begin{array}{r} 1 \\ 6\overline{)635} \\ -6 \\ \overline{)3} \end{array}$$

Since the number we are dividing is less than the number we are dividing by, we write a zero in the quotient, then multiply, and then subtract and bring down. The next division is 6)35.

$$\begin{array}{r} 10 \\ 6\overline{)635} \\ -6 \\ \overline{)3} \\ -0 \\ \overline{)35} \end{array}$$

We divide 35 by 6, multiply, and subtract. Since there is no other number to bring down, the division is finished and the remainder is 5. When we divide 635 into 6 equal parts, there are 105 in each part with 5 "left over." Our answer is **105 r 5.**

$$\begin{array}{r} 105\ r\ 5 \\ 6\overline{)635} \\ -6 \\ \overline{)3} \\ -0 \\ \overline{)35} \\ -30 \\ \overline{5} \end{array}$$

Practice*   **a.** 3)61   **b.** 6)242   **c.** 3)121   **d.** 4)1628

e. 4)122   **f.** 5)$5.25   **g.** 2)$6.18   **h.** 6)4981

i. 10)301   **j.** 4)$8.24   **k.** 7)$5.60   **l.** 8)4818

**Problem set
35**

1. Draw a horizontal line. Draw another line which is
(32) perpendicular to the first line.

2. One hundred students named their favorite vegetable.
(23) One half named beans, one fourth named broccoli, one tenth named peas, and the rest named spinach. How many students named beans, broccoli, peas, and spinach?

3. How many minutes are in 1 day?
(27)

4. What year was one century after 1849?
(27)

5. In one year Henrietta laid 10 dozen eggs. How many
(21) eggs is that? Use an "equal groups" pattern.

6. When Morgan finished page 127 of a 300-page book,
(16) he still had how many pages to read? Use a "some
went away" pattern.

7. 6$\overline{)365}$ **8.** 6$\overline{)\$6.36}$ **9.** 5$\overline{)536}$
(35)   (35)   (35)

10. 10$\overline{)653}$ **11.** 4$\overline{)\$4.36}$ **12.** 95 × 500
(26)   (35)   (30)

13. Round 83 to the nearest ten.
(34)

14. 345 + 57 + 760 + 398 + 762 + 584 + W = 3000
(10)

15. 3004 − (3000 − 4)   **16.** $5.93 × 40
(24)   (30)

17. Compare: $\frac{1}{2}$ of 10 $\bigcirc$ $\frac{1}{4}$ of 24
(23,4)

18. $12 + $8.75 + $0.96   **19.** $20 − $12.46
(24)   (24)

20. 8 × 30 × 15   **21.** 6 × 7 × 8 × 9
(18)   (18)

22. What are the next three numbers in this sequence?
(1)
          ..., 460, 470, 480, _____, _____, _____, ...

23. What fraction of the square is
(31) shaded? What percent of the
square is shaded?

24. If two segments that intersect are perpendicular, then
(33) what kind of an angle do they form?

     A. acute   B. right   C. obtuse

25. If it is morning, what time is
(29) shown on this clock?

LESSON 36

"Larger-Smaller-Difference" Stories

Facts Practice: 64 Multiplication Facts (Test D in Test Masters)

Mental Math: Name the months of the year. How many months are in 3 years? 4 years? 5 years?

a. Round 285 to the nearest hundred.

b. 300 + 800   **c.** 300 × 8   **d.** 42 × 5

e. $\frac{1}{2}$ of 42   **f.** 50% of $8.00   **g.** 25% of $8.00

h. 3 × 9, + 1, ÷ 7, + 1, × 5, − 1, ÷ 4

Problem Solving: List the possible arrangements of the letters A, E, and R. What percent of the possible arrangements spell words?

Numbers are used to describe the quantity of objects.

There were 11 football players on the team.

Numbers are also used to describe the size of objects.

The biggest player weighed 245 pounds.

Stories that compare numbers of objects or sizes of objects are "larger-smaller-difference" stories.

The biggest player weighed 245 pounds. The smallest player weighed 160 pounds. The biggest player weighed how much more than the smallest player?

Drawing a sketch can help us understand "larger-smaller-difference" stories. We will draw two towers, one larger than the other. Then we will draw an arrow from the smaller tower that reaches as high as the larger tower. The two towers and the arrow each have a circle for a number. For this story the towers stand for the weights of the two players.

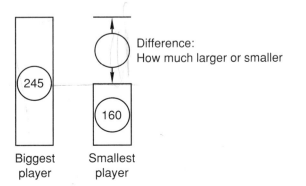

A "larger-smaller-difference" story has a subtraction pattern.

$$\begin{array}{r}
\text{Larger} \\
-\text{Smaller} \\
\hline
\text{Difference}
\end{array}
\qquad
\begin{array}{r}
245 \text{ pounds} \\
-160 \text{ pounds} \\
\hline
\rule{1cm}{0.4pt}
\end{array}$$

In this story the number missing is the difference, which we find by subtracting.

$$\begin{array}{r}
\overset{1}{2}\overset{1}{4}\,5 \text{ pounds} \\
-\ 1\ 6\ 0 \text{ pounds} \\
\hline
8\ 5 \text{ pounds}
\end{array}$$

We find that the biggest player weighs 85 pounds more than the smallest player.

Example Abe is 6 years younger than his brother Gabe. Abe is 11 years old. How old is Gabe?

Solution We will sketch two towers to illustrate the story. The towers stand for the boys' ages. Since Abe is younger, his tower is smaller.

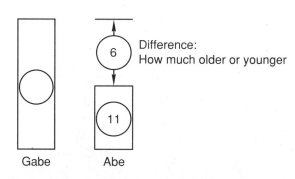

From the story we find that Abe is 11 and the difference between his age and his brother's age is 6 years. We write the numbers in the circles and use the "larger-smaller-difference" pattern.

$$\begin{array}{r}
\text{Larger} \\
-\text{Smaller} \\
\hline
\text{Difference}
\end{array}
\qquad
\begin{array}{r}
G \\
-11 \\
\hline
6
\end{array}$$

We find the first number of a subtraction by adding.

$$\begin{array}{r} 6 \\ + 11 \\ \hline 17 \end{array}$$

Gabe is 17 years old.

Practice

a. There were 4 more boys than girls in the class. If there were 17 boys in the class, how many girls were there?

b. The Mackinac Bridge spans 3800 feet, which is 400 feet less than the span of the Golden Gate Bridge. What is the span of the Golden Gate Bridge?

c. From Rome to Paris is 1098 kilometers. From Rome to London is 1427 kilometers. The distance to London from Rome is how much greater than the distance from Rome to Paris?

Problem set 36

1. Draw a pair of oblique parallel lines.
(32)

2. In three games Sherry's bowling scores were 109, 98, and 135, respectively. What was her total score for all three games? Use a "some and some more" pattern.
(11)

3. What is the product of nine hundred nineteen and ninety?
(30)

4. Draw a triangle that has an obtuse angle.
(33)

5. How many years were there from 1886 to 1986?
(27)

6. List the factors of 28.
(25)

7. Sal is 8 inches taller than Sammy. If Sal is 63 inches tall, how tall is Sammy? Use a "larger-smaller-difference" pattern.
(36)

8. 432 ÷ 4
(35)

9. 423 ÷ 6
(35)

10. 243 ÷ 8
(35)

11. 2001 ÷ 4
(35)

12. 1020 ÷ 10
(35)

13. 420 ÷ (42 ÷ 6)
(24)

14. Round 468 to the nearest hundred.
(34)

15.   4657
(6)   285
        + 1223

16.   3165
(9)   − 1635

17. $10.00
(13)   − $8.93

18.   24
(6)   56
        17
        73
        25
      + 19

19.   436
(30) ×   70

20. $8.57
(17) ×   7

21.   600
(30) ×   900

22. What fraction of the rectangle is shaded? Is more or less than 50%
(31) of the rectangle shaded?

23. What time is a quarter to three in the afternoon?
(29)

24. From November 1 of one year to March 1 of the next
(27) year is how many months?

25. What are the next three numbers in this sequence?
(1)
        …, 1900, 2000, 2100, _____, _____, _____, …

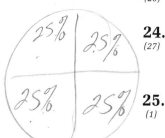

LESSON
37

Using Fraction Manipulatives, Part 1

Facts Practice: 90 Division Facts (Test E or F in Test Masters)

Mental Math: How many quarters are 1 dollar? 2 dollars? 3 dollars?

a. Round 86 to the nearest ten.   **b.** 90 + 80

c. 90 × 8   **d.** 62 × 7   **e.** 10 × 70

f. 50% of 24   **g.** 25% of 24   **h.** 1500 + 1500

i. 9 × 6, − 4, ÷ 2, − 1, ÷ 2, ÷ 2

Problem Solving: Use the digits 1, 2, 3, 4, and 5 in the blanks of this multiplication problem.

$$\begin{array}{r} \_\_ \\ \times\ \_ \\ \hline \_\_ \end{array}$$

Fraction manipulatives such as fractions of circles can help us understand fractions. In this lesson you will make your own set of fraction manipulatives. You may use the fraction manipulatives as you work future problem sets.

Activity   Materials needed:

- Each student needs a copy of "Fraction Master 1: Halves, Fourths, Tenths" (available in the *Math 65 Test Master*)
- scissors
- envelopes or locking plastic bags in which to store fraction pieces
- crayons (optional)

Preparation for activities:

- Distribute materials and have students separate the fraction slices by cutting along the lines.

Note: Some classes like to color-code their fraction manipulatives. If you wish to color the fractions, agree upon a different color for each fraction circle. Lightly color the front and back of each circle before cutting. Following the activity, store the fraction "slices" in an envelope or plastic bag for use in later lessons.

Use your fraction manipulatives to help you with these activities:

(a) Show that two quarters equal one half.

(b) Two quarters of a circle is what percent of a whole circle?

(c) How many tenths equal one half?

(d) Is one quarter plus two tenths more or less than one half?

(e) One fourth of a circle plus two tenths of a circle is what percent of a whole circle?

(f) One half of a circle plus four tenths of a circle is what percent of a whole circle?

(g) Two half circles can be put together to make a whole circle. This number sentence states that two halves equal a whole.

$$\frac{1}{2} + \frac{1}{2} = 1$$

Another way to write this is

$$\frac{2}{2} = 1$$

One half circle and two quarter circles can also be put together to make a whole circle.

$$\frac{1}{2} + \frac{1}{4} + \frac{1}{4} = 1$$

Another way to write this is

$$\frac{1}{2} + \frac{2}{4} = 1$$

Use the fraction manipulatives to find other ways to make a whole circle. Write a number sentence for each way you find.

Example   One fourth of a circle plus one tenth of a circle is what percent of a whole circle?

Solution   We select a $\frac{1}{4}$ fraction piece and a $\frac{1}{10}$ fraction piece from the fraction manipulatives. Fitting these pieces together, we see that they form less than half of a whole circle.

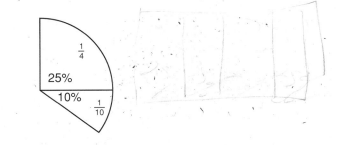

On the fraction pieces we see that $\frac{1}{4}$ is 25% and $\frac{1}{10}$ is 10%. We add 25% and 10% and find that the total is 35%. So one fourth of a circle plus one tenth of a circle is **35%** of a whole circle.

Problem set 37

1. *(37)* Use your fraction manipulatives to help you with this problem: One fourth of a circle plus three tenths of a circle is what percent of a whole circle?

2. *(36)* Del is 6 years older than his sister. If Del is 13 years old, then how old is his sister? Use a "larger-smaller-difference" pattern.

3. *(21)* How many days is a dozen weeks? Use an "equal groups" pattern.

4. *(33)* Draw a triangle that has three acute angles.

5. *(7)* Use words to name the number 305,300.

6. *(37)* Monica has $\frac{1}{2}$ of a circle and $\frac{1}{4}$ of a circle. How much more does she need to have a whole circle?

7. *(4)* Compare: $\dfrac{560}{8} \bigcirc \dfrac{480}{6}$

8. *(26)* $\dfrac{\$4.59}{9}$

9. *(35)* $876 \div 8$

10. 611 ÷ 3
(35)

11. $10.32 ÷ 4
(26)

12. 346 + 2875 + 74 + 458 + 932 + 45
(6)

13. 5386 − 4957
(9)

14. $75 + $1.24 + $0.76
(24)

15. $100 − $20.63
(24)

16. $4.38 × 60
(30)

17. 60 × 700
(30)

18. 828 ÷ (28 ÷ 7)
(24)

19. 7 × 40 × 14
(18)

20. What fraction of the group is
(31) shaded? What percent of the
group is shaded?

21. Round 586 to the nearest
(34) hundred.

22. What number is the numerator of the fraction $\frac{3}{8}$?
(23)

23. Think of a whole number. Multiply it by 2. Now add
(2) 1. Is the final answer odd or even?

24. According to this calendar, what
(27) is the date of the second Tuesday
in January 1929?

JANUARY 1929						
S	M	T	W	T	F	S
		1	2	3	4	5
6	7	8	9	10	11	12
13	14	15	16	17	18	19
20	21	22	23	24	25	26
27	28	29	30	31		

25. What are the next three numbers in this sequence?
(1)
..., 470, 480, 490, _____, _____, _____, ...

LESSON 38

Drawing Segments to Close in an Area

Facts Practice: 64 Multiplication Facts (Test D in Test Masters)

Mental Math: Count by 12's from 12 to 96. Count by 6's from 6 to 72.

a. Round 623 to the nearest hundred.

b. $600 + 900$

c. 600×10 d. 48×5 e. $\frac{1}{2}$ of 48

f. 25% of 48   g. 10% of 60   h. $480 \div 50$

i. $7 \times 7, + 1, \div 5, \times 3, + 2, \div 4$

Problem Solving: There are two lights between Jimmy's home and school. Sometimes Jimmy can walk through both lights; sometimes he has to wait for both lights. List the four possible patterns of lights for Jimmy's walk to school. Use the words "walk" and "wait."

Situation 1

Tom used some pencils to surround an ant which was crawling on his desk. What is the fewest number of pencils he could have used?

We see that one pencil could not surround an ant. If Tom put a pencil on one side, the ant could crawl the other way.

We see that two pencils also could not surround an ant. There is still an opening which would allow the ant to crawl away.

Tom must have used at least three pencils to surround the ant. He may have used more.

Activity 1   On a piece of paper, draw an ant—or just the letter A—and try to surround it by drawing straight line segments. Be sure you close in an area so that there is no

way of escape. Do this several times. Try to close in an area with three segments, with four segments, with five segments, and with six segments.

Situation 2 *Sharon found an ant crawling on her desk. She placed two pencils on her desk parallel to each other with the ant between. Altogether, how many pencils will she need to surround the ant?*

We see that this time three pencils will not surround the ant. Sharon will need four pencils.

Activity 2 For each activity, begin by drawing a pair of parallel horizontal line segments on a piece of paper and draw an ant—or the letter A—between the line segments. Then surround the ant with two more line segments, following the directions given below.

(a) Close in the area with two segments which get closer together at the top.

(b) Close in the area with two segments which get closer together at the bottom.

(c) Close in the area with two segments which are perpendicular to the first pair of line segments.

(d) Close in the area with a pair of parallel segments which intersect the first pair but are not perpendicular to the first pair.

Practice **a.** Is it possible to close in an area with two segments?

b. Is it possible to close in an area with eight segments?

c. Draw a pair of parallel segments; then close in an area by drawing another pair of segments perpendicular to the first pair.

d. Draw a pair of parallel segments; then close in an area with another pair of parallel segments which are not perpendicular to the first pair.

e. Draw a pair of parallel segments; then close in an area with two segments which are not parallel to each other.

Problem set 38

1. Draw a pair of horizontal parallel lines and write an A
(38) between them. Then surround the A by drawing a pair of oblique parallel lines.

2. The first flag of the United States had 13 stars. How
(36) many more stars does our present flag have? Use a "larger-smaller-difference" pattern.

3. Joe walked 488 feet going to the end of the pier and
(23) back. How long is the pier?

4. Eighty vehicles drove past Barbara's home. She found
(23) that one half were sedans, one fourth were vans, one tenth were motorcycles, and the rest were trucks. How many sedans, vans, motorcycles, and trucks drove past Barbara's house?

5. Round 67 to the nearest ten.
(34)

6. What year was one century before 1620?
(27)

7. The population of Tunaville was 340 less than the
(36) population of Thorton. The population of Tunaville was 4360. What was the population of Thorton?

8. Draw a triangle which has two perpendicular sides.
(32)

9.
(10)

$$
\begin{array}{r}
4207 \\
P \\
+\ 1863 \\
\hline
9999
\end{array}
$$

10.
(14)

$$
\begin{array}{r}
3615 \\
-\ R \\
\hline
2946
\end{array}
$$

11.
(13)

$$
\begin{array}{r}
\$10.00 \\
-\ \$9.81 \\
\hline
\end{array}
$$

12.
(6)

$$
\begin{array}{r}
76 \\
98 \\
15 \\
832 \\
46 \\
328 \\
64 \\
+\ 75 \\
\hline
\end{array}
$$

13.
(30)

$$
\begin{array}{r}
368 \\
\times\ 40 \\
\hline
\end{array}
$$

14.
(30)

$$
\begin{array}{r}
\$5.40 \\
\times\ 70 \\
\hline
\end{array}
$$

15.
(30)

$$
\begin{array}{r}
700 \\
\times\ 800 \\
\hline
\end{array}
$$

16. One half of a circle plus two tenths of a circle is what
(37) percent of a whole circle?

17. $\dfrac{420}{10}$
(26)

18. $\dfrac{624}{6}$
(35)

19. $\dfrac{\$28.35}{7}$
(35)

20. $\$10 - (\$3.65 + \$4 + \$0.97)$
(24)

21. $496 + 496 + 496 + 496 + 496 + 496 + 496$
(17)

22. What fraction of the large triangle
(31) is not shaded? What percent of
the triangle is not shaded?

23. What are the next three numbers in this sequence?
(1)
          ..., 1600, 1700, 1800, _____, _____, _____, ...

24. What part of a building is perpendicular to the floor?
(32)
    A. Wall   B. Ceiling   C. Roof

25. If it is morning now, what time
(29) will be shown by this clock in 2
hours?

LESSON
39

Polygons

Facts Practice: 90 Division Facts (Test E or F in Test Masters)

Mental Math: How many is half a dozen? one and a half dozen? two and a half dozen?

a. Round 73 to the nearest ten.   **b.** 70 + 80
c. 70 × 8   **d.** 8 × 73   **e.** $\frac{1}{2}$ of 24
f. 50% of $12   **g.** 25% of $12   **h.** 360 + 200
i. 9 × 6, + 2, ÷ 7, + 1, × 4, ÷ 6

Problem Solving: There are three lights between Julie's home and school. List the eight possible patterns of lights for Julie's walk to school. Use the words "walk" and "wait."

Tom's and Sharon's teacher told them that when they surrounded an ant with pencils, they had formed polygons. A **polygon** is a shape made by line segments which close in an area. Each of these shapes is a polygon.

The line segments which form a polygon are called **sides.** A polygon may have three or more sides. Polygons are named by the number of sides they have. The chart below names some common polygons.

Polygons

SHAPE	NUMBER OF SIDES	NAME OF POLYGON
	3	triangle
	4	quadrilateral
	5	pentagon
	6	hexagon
	8	octagon

Notice that a four-sided polygon is a **quadrilateral.** There are different kinds of quadrilaterals. Squares, rectangles, parallelograms, and trapezoids are names of certain kinds of quadrilaterals which we will study later.

Example 1   Which of these shapes is not a quadrilateral?

Solution   A quadrilateral is a polygon with four sides. The shape which does not have four sides is choice **C.**

Sometimes we close in areas by using smooth curves. A circle is one kind of smooth curve that we use to close in an area. Since a circle does not close in an area with straight lines, a circle is not a polygon.

Example 2   Which of these shapes is not a polygon?

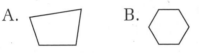

Solution   A polygon is formed by straight lines. A circle is a smooth curve. So the shape which is not a polygon is choice **C.**

Practice   **a.** Draw a triangle with two perpendicular sides.

b. A quadrilateral is a polygon with how many sides?

c. Draw a quadrilateral that has one pair of parallel sides.

d. Draw a quadrilateral with two pairs of parallel sides.

e. Draw a quadrilateral which has no parallel sides. (Begin by drawing two nonparallel segments; then connect those with two nonparallel segments.)

Name each shape:

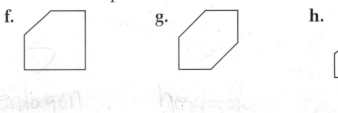

**Problem set
39**

1. Draw a pair of horizontal parallel line segments. Make
(32) both segments the same length.

2. Jason is reading a book that has 336 pages. Gilbert is
(36) reading a book that has 402 pages. Gilbert's book has
how many more pages than Jason's book? Use a
"larger-smaller-difference" pattern.

3. Jason has one week to read a 336-page book. How
(21) many pages should he read each day to finish the book
on time? Use an "equal groups" pattern.

4. A fortnight is 2 weeks. How many days is a fortnight?
(21) Use an "equal groups" pattern.

5. Round 780 to the nearest hundred.
(34)

6. Which triangle has one obtuse angle?
(33)

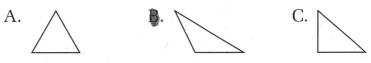

A.   B.   C.

7. How many years were there from 1776 to 1976?
(27)

8. When the students voted for president, Jeremy had
(36) 119 votes and Tina had 142 votes. Tina won by how
many votes? Use a "larger-smaller-difference" pattern.

9. What is the name for the top number of a fraction?
(23)

10. Which of these shapes is not a quadrilateral?
(39) A. □   B. ▱   C. ⬡   D. ▱

11. Cindy has two fourths of a circle and three tenths of a
(37) circle. What else does she need to have a whole circle?

12. ₍₃₀₎
$$763 \times 800$$

13. ₍₁₇₎
$$\$24.08 \times 6$$

14. ₍₃₀₎
$$976 \times 40$$

15. ₍₃₀₎
$$400 \times 50$$

16. ₍₁₃₎
$$\$98.98$$
$$\$36.25$$
$$\$4.97$$
$$+ \$87.64$$

17. ₍₁₄₎
$$5818 - M = 4747$$

18. ₍₉₎
$$1010 - 918$$

19. ₍₃₅₎
$$\frac{\$7.63}{7}$$

20. ₍₃₅₎ $368 \div 9$

21. ₍₃₅₎ $6\overline{)4248}$

22. ₍₂₆₎ $8\overline{)\$10.00}$

23. ₍₁₎ What are the next three numbers in this sequence?

..., 2700, 2800, 2900, _____, _____, _____, ...

24. ₍₃₁₎ What fraction of the hexagon is shaded? Is more or less than 25% of the hexagon shaded? Is more or less than 10% of the hexagon shaded?

25. ₍₂₈₎ To what number on this number line is the arrow pointing?

LESSON
40

Picturing Fractions, Part 2

Facts Practice: 64 Multiplication Facts (Test D in Test Masters)

Mental Math: Count by 12's from 12 to 96. How many months is 5 years? 6 years?

a. Round 890 to the nearest hundred.   **b.** 900 + 900

c. 900 × 4   **d.** 4 × 89

e. 4 × 90 minus 4 × 1   **f.** 9 × 9, − 9, ÷ 9

g. 50% of 60¢   **h.** 25% of 60¢   **i.** 10% of 60¢

Problem Solving: The license plates of a certain state have three letters followed by three digits. One license plate reads CAR 123. How many different license plates from the state could begin with the letters CAR and end with any arrangement of 1, 2, and 3?

In Lesson 31 we used pictures to represent fractions. A picture can help us to understand the meaning of a fraction. In this lesson we will practice drawing more pictures to represent fractions.

Example 1 Draw a square and shade $\frac{1}{2}$ of it three different ways.

Solution The denominator of this fraction tells us to cut the square into 2 equal parts. The numerator of the fraction tells us to shade 1 of the parts. There are many ways to do this. Here we show three different ways.

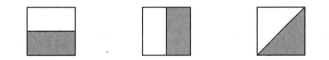

The important thing to remember when drawing pictures of fractions is to divide the pictures into **equal** parts. The square below has been cut into two parts, but the parts are not equal. Therefore, this picture does not represent $\frac{1}{2}$.

This does not represent $\frac{1}{2}$.

Example 2   Draw a rectangle and shade $\frac{1}{3}$ of it.

Solution   After we draw the rectangle, we must divide it into 3 equal parts. If we begin by dividing it in half, we will not be able to divide it into 3 equal parts.

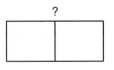

We must plan ahead. To form 3 parts, we draw 2 equally spaced segments. We show two different ways to shade $\frac{1}{3}$ of a rectangle.

Practice*   **a.** Draw a circle and shade $\frac{1}{4}$ of it.

b. Draw a rectangle and shade $\frac{2}{3}$ of it.

c. This square represents the fraction $\frac{3}{4}$. Show another way to shade $\frac{3}{4}$ of a square.

d. This circle represents the fraction $\frac{1}{3}$. Draw a circle and shade $\frac{2}{3}$ of it.

Problem set 40   **1.** Draw a pair of horizontal parallel line segments. Make
$^{(32)}$ the lower segment longer than the upper segment.

2. Draw a rectangle and shade $\frac{1}{2}$ of it three different ways.
$^{(40)}$ What percent of each rectangle is shaded?

3. When Bill cleaned his room, he found 39 marbles, 20
$^{(11)}$ baseball cards, a toothbrush, 4 pencils, and part of a peanut butter sandwich. How many items did he find?

4. Draw a rectangle and shade $\frac{1}{3}$ of it.
(40)

5. What year was one decade before 1932?
(27)

6. List the factors of 40.
(25)

7. What fraction of the octagon is **not**
(31) shaded? Is more or less than 50%
of the octagon not shaded?

8. From May 1 of one year to February 1 of the next year
(27) is how many months?

9. Round 45 to the nearest ten.
(34)

10. Draw an A on your paper. Surround it with three line
(38) segments. Make two of the segments perpendicular.

11. $36.51
(13) $74.15
         + $25.94

12.   3040
(14)   −   W
          2950

13. $90.00
(13)   − $20.30

14.   43
(10)   C
           29
          467
         + 94
          700

15.   592
(30)   ×   90

16. $4.75
(30)   ×   80

17.   720
(30)   ×   400

18. Compare: $\dfrac{840}{8} \bigcirc \dfrac{460}{4}$
(4)

19. $\dfrac{\$12.24}{6}$
(35)

20. 1000 ÷ (100 ÷ 10)
(24)

21. 60 × (235 ÷ 5)
(24)

22. 42 × 30 × 7
(18)

23. $20 − ($3.48 + $12 + $4.39)
(24)

24. Duncan fit one half of a circle, one fourth of a circle,
$^{(37)}$ and one tenth of a circle together. What percent of the
circle was missing?

25. Which of these shapes is not a polygon?
$^{(39)}$

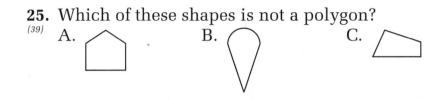

A.   B.   C.

LESSON
41

Half of an Odd Number •
Fractions on a Number Line

Facts Practice: 90 Division Facts (Test E or F in Test Masters)

Mental Math: Name the relationship: Diana's mother's father
is Diana's _____.
Count by 12's from 12 to 96. How many is 5
dozen? 6 dozen? 7 dozen?

a. Round 615 to the nearest hundred.   **b.** 700 + 800
c. 10 × 70   **d.** 5 × 24   **e.** $\frac{1}{2}$ of 44
f. 50% of 80¢   **g.** 25% of 80¢   **h.** 10% of 80¢
i. 6 × 6, − 6, ÷ 6, + 1, − 6

Problem Solving: Copy this addition problem and fill   __
in the missing digits.   + 1
                                              ___

Half of an odd number

We find half of a number by dividing the number by two.
Half of an even number is a whole number because an
even number of objects can be separated into two equal
groups. However, half of an odd number is not a whole
number. If an odd number of objects is divided into two
equal groups, then one of the objects will be broken in
half. These two stories illustrate dividing an even number
in half and dividing an odd number in half.

*Sherry had 6 cookies to share with her friend
Leticia. Each girl could have 3 cookies.*

*Herman had 5 cookies to share with Ivan. Each
boy could have $2\frac{1}{2}$ cookies.*

Activity We have listed the counting numbers 1 through 10. Below each counting number, we have recorded half of the number. Continue the list of counting numbers and their halves for the numbers 11 through 20.

Counting number	1	2	3	4	5	6	7	8	9	10
Half of number	$\frac{1}{2}$	1	$1\frac{1}{2}$	2	$2\frac{1}{2}$	3	$3\frac{1}{2}$	4	$4\frac{1}{2}$	5

Fractions on a number line A number line is made up of a series of points. The points on the line represent numbers. On this number line whole numbers are labeled. However, there are many other points on the line, some marked by arrows, that are not labeled.

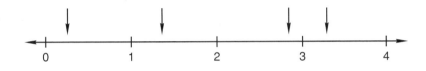

Many of the unlabeled points on a number line can be named with fractions and **mixed numbers.** Mixed numbers are numbers like $1\frac{1}{2}$ (one and one half) that are a whole number and a fraction together.

To identify a fraction or mixed number on a number line, we need to count the divisions between the whole numbers. On this number line, the distance between the whole numbers has been divided into three sections. (Be careful to count the *sections* of the number line and not the marks that separate the sections.)

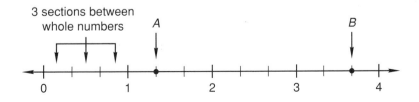

The distance between whole numbers has been divided into thirds. Each small section is one third $\left(\frac{1}{3}\right)$.

A point on a number line is named by its distance from zero. The point marked by arrow A is the whole number 1 plus one section. So the number for that point is $1\frac{1}{3}$. The point marked with arrow B is the whole number 3 plus two sections. The number of point B is $3\frac{2}{3}$.

When reading fraction number lines, follow these steps:

1. Find the whole number distance from zero up to but not past the point to be named. This is the whole number part of the answer.
2. Next, count the number of sections between whole numbers. This number is the denominator (bottom number) of the fraction.
3. Then count how many sections past the whole number there are to the point being named. This is the numerator (top number) of the fraction.

Example   Name each point marked by an arrow on these number lines:

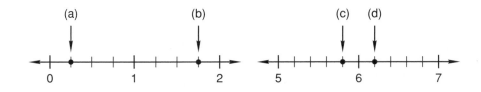

Solution   Point (a) is between 0 and 1, so it is named by a fraction and not by a mixed number. The distance between whole numbers on this number line is divided into four sections, fourths. Point (a) is one section from zero, which is $\frac{1}{4}$.

The distance from zero to point (b) is 1 plus three sections, which is $\mathbf{1\frac{3}{4}}$.

The distance from zero to point (c) is 5 plus a fraction. The distance between whole numbers on this number line has been divided into five sections, fifths. Point (c) is four sections from 5, which is $\mathbf{5\frac{4}{5}}$.

The distance from zero to point (d) is 6 plus one section, which is $\mathbf{6\frac{1}{5}}$.

Practice* Every odd number can be written as an even number plus 1. For example, 23 is 22 + 1. To find half of 23, we find half of 22, which is 11, and then find half of 1, which is $\frac{1}{2}$. So half of 23 is $11\frac{1}{2}$. Find half of each of these odd numbers:

    a. 15   **b.** 21   **c.** 25   **d.** 49

Name each point marked by an arrow on these number lines:

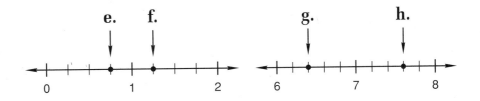

Problem set **1.** Draw a pair of horizontal parallel line segments. Make
41   (32)   the upper segment longer than the lower segment.

   2. What is the product of six hundred seventy and
   (30) eighty?

   3. Sam scored $\frac{1}{4}$ of the team's 28 points. How many
   (23) points did Sam score?

   4. The used-car salesman bought a car for $725 and sold
   (36) it for $1020. How much profit did he make on the car?
      Use a "larger-smaller-difference" pattern.

   5. Which triangle has three acute angles?
   (33)

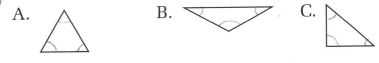

   6. Round 649 to the nearest hundred.
   (34)

   7. In 2 hours the 3 boys picked a total of 1347 cherries. If
   (21) they share the cherries evenly, then each boy will get
      how many cherries?

8. Draw a circle and shade $\frac{3}{4}$ of it. What percent of the circle is shaded?
(40)

9. How many days are in a "leap year"?
(27)

10. A stop sign has the shape of an octagon. An octagon has how many sides?
(39)

11. 3647 + 92 + 429
(6)

12. 3518 − 1853
(9)

13. 4 × 6 × 8 × 10
(18)

14. 3518 ÷ 10
(26)

15. $4.76 + $12 + $0.97 + W = $20
(10)

16. $100 − $87.23
(24)

17. 786 × 900
(30)

18. $63.18 ÷ 9
(35)

19. 375 × (640 ÷ 8)
(24)

20. What number is half of 51?
(41)

21. Every four-sided polygon is which of the following?
(39)
   A. Square   B. Rectangle   C. Quadrilateral

22. What are the next three numbers in this sequence?
(1)
       ..., 1800, 1900, 2000, _____, _____, _____, ...

23. Name the mixed number marked by an arrow on this number line.
(41)

24. Here is part of a number line. The arrow is pointing to what fraction on this number line?
(41)

25. If it is 9:45 a.m., what time will it be in 4 hours?
(29)

LESSON
42

Comparing Fractions by Drawing Pictures

Facts Practice: 64 Multiplication Facts (Test D in Test Masters)

Mental Math: Name the relationship: Gilbert's father's sister is Gilbert's _____.
Count by 7's from 7 to 84. How many days is 3 weeks? 4 weeks? 6 weeks?

a. Round 78 to the nearest ten.
b. 830 − 200
c. 600 × 4
d. 6 × 24
e. 10 × 100
f. $\frac{1}{2}$ of 21
g. 50% of $2.00
h. 25% of $2.00
i. 5 × 5, + 5, ÷ 5, − 5

Problem Solving: Which number do you say when you count by 6's from 6 to 36 that you also say when you count by 8's from 8 to 48?

One fourth of the circle on the left is shaded. One half of the circle on the right is shaded.

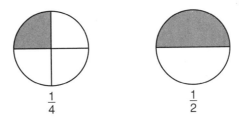

We see that less of the circle is shaded when $\frac{1}{4}$ is shaded than when $\frac{1}{2}$ is shaded because $\frac{1}{4}$ is a smaller fraction than $\frac{1}{2}$. We can write this comparison using a comparison symbol as

$$\frac{1}{4} < \frac{1}{2}$$

In this lesson we will begin **comparing** fractions. To compare fractions, we will draw **pictures** of the fractions and compare the pictures.

Example   Draw pictures to compare these fractions: $\frac{1}{2} \bigcirc \frac{1}{3}$

Solution   If we try to compare the fractions the way they are written, we might think that $\frac{1}{3}$ is greater than $\frac{1}{2}$ because 3 is greater than 2. By drawing pictures, we see that $\frac{1}{3}$ is actually less than $\frac{1}{2}$. If an object is divided into 3 parts, each part will be smaller than if the object is divided into 2 parts.

To begin, we draw two **identical** shapes. We choose to draw two equal-sized rectangles, and we label the rectangles $\frac{1}{2}$ and $\frac{1}{3}$. Next, we divide the rectangles into the number of parts shown by the denominator, and we shade in the number of parts shown by the numerator.

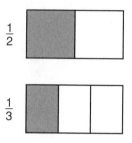

Then we compare the shaded areas. We see that more of the rectangle is shaded when $\frac{1}{2}$ is shaded than when $\frac{1}{3}$ is shaded. So our answer is

$$\frac{1}{2} > \frac{1}{3}$$

Practice   Compare each pair of fractions by first drawing pictures to represent each fraction. When drawing pictures of any two fractions, be sure to draw the shapes the same size.

a. $\frac{1}{2} \bigcirc \frac{2}{3}$ **b.** $\frac{1}{2} \bigcirc \frac{2}{4}$

c. $\frac{1}{3} \bigcirc \frac{1}{4}$ **d.** $\frac{2}{3} \bigcirc \frac{3}{4}$

Problem set 42   **1.** Draw a pair of horizontal parallel line segments of the
$^{(39,32)}$ same length. Make a quadrilateral by connecting the ends of the segments.

2. How many years is five centuries?
$^{(27)}$

3. The arrow is pointing to what mixed number on this
(41) number line?

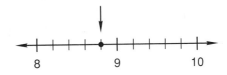

4. What is the product of four hundred sixteen and sixty?
(30)

5. Draw pictures to compare these fractions: $\frac{1}{4} \bigcirc \frac{1}{3}$
(42)

6. What number is half of 101?
(41)

7. Bill's cat ate $\frac{1}{4}$ of a dozen fish fillets. How many fish
(23) fillets did Bill's cat eat?

8. Round 84 to the nearest ten.
(34)

9. List the factors of 35.
(25)

10. $93.18
(13) $42.87
      + $67.95

11. $30.00
(13)   − $8.75

12.   4304
(14)   −   B
      3452

13.   46
(6)   23
    97
    15
    24
    55
  + 55

14. $6.38
(30) ×   60

15.   640
(30) ×   700

16. $\frac{640}{8}$
(35)

17. $\frac{720}{10}$
(26)

18. $\frac{$6.24}{6}$
(35)

19. $\frac{1236}{4}$
(35)

20. 563 ÷ 7
(35)

21. 4718 ÷ 9
(26)

22. 3000 ÷ 8
(26)

23. What time is 20 minutes before midnight?
(29)

24. A quarter of a circle plus a tenth of a circle is what
(37) percent of a circle?

25. According to this calendar, what
(27) is the date of the third Saturday in
April 1901?

| APRIL 1901 |
| S M T W T F S |
| 1 2 3 4 5 6 |
| 7 8 9 10 11 12 13 |
| 14 15 16 17 18 19 20 |
| 21 22 23 24 25 26 27 |
| 28 29 30 |

LESSON 43

Pictures of Mixed Numbers • Dividing Remainders, Part 1

Facts Practice: 90 Division Facts (Test E or F in Test Masters)

Problem Solving: Use the information in this paragraph to answer the questions that follow. Drawing a diagram may help you with the problem.

Alice and Bob are the mother and father of Carol and George. Carol and her husband Donald have a son, Edward. George and his wife Fiona have a daughter, Heather.

a. Alice is Edward's _____.
b. Heather is Bob's _____.
c. George is Edward's _____.
d. Heather is Carol's _____.
e. Donald is Bob's _____.
f. Alice is Fiona's _____.
g. Edward is Heather's _____.

Pictures of mixed numbers

The picture below shows some pies on a shelf.

We see two whole pies and one half of another pie. There are two and one half pies on the shelf. Using digits, we write two and one half this way.

$$2\frac{1}{2}$$

Example 1   Use a mixed number to name the number of shaded circles shown here.

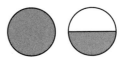

Solution   We see two circles. One circle is completely shaded and represents the whole number 1. Half of the second circle is shaded. It represents the fraction $\frac{1}{2}$. Together, the number of shaded circles is one and one half.

$$1\frac{1}{2}$$

Dividing remainders, part 1   Some story problems have answers that are mixed numbers, as we find in this story.

Example 2   Peter, Edmund, and Lucy will equally share seven chicken pot pies. How much pie is there for each person?

Solution   First we will use a diagram to explain the solution. We need to divide the pies into three equal groups. We can arrange six of the pies into three groups of two pies.

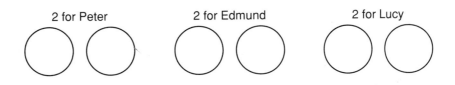

However, there are seven pies. So there is still a pie to be divided. We divide the remaining pie into thirds.

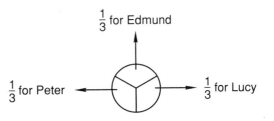

We find that **for each person there are $2\frac{1}{3}$ pies.**

Now we will show how to find the answer using a pencil-and-paper algorithm. To divide seven pies into three equal groups, we divide 7 by 3.

$$\begin{array}{r} 2 \\ 3\overline{)7} \\ \underline{6} \\ 1 \end{array}$$

The answer is 2, which means 2 whole pies. The remainder is 1, which means 1 pie has not been divided. Now we will divide the remainder. We show that we have divided the remainder by using a division bar. The remainder is 1, and we are dividing by 3. So we write

$$\frac{1}{3}$$

One divided by three is also the fraction one third. We write "$\frac{1}{3}$" after the whole number above the division box.

$$\begin{array}{r} 2\frac{1}{3} \\ 3\overline{)7} \\ \underline{6} \\ 1 \end{array}$$

This answer means that for each person there are $2\frac{1}{3}$ pies.

Practice   Write mixed numbers to name the number of shaded circles in the diagrams:

a. 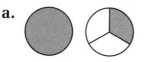   **b.**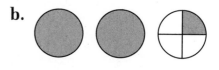

Draw and shade circles to represent the mixed numbers named:

c. Three and one half

d. One and three fourths

e. Draw a diagram to explain the answer to this story problem. Then show how to find the answer using pencil and paper. Follow the example in the lesson.

> *Peter, Susan, Edmund, and Lucy will equally share nine chicken pot pies. How many pies are there for each person?*

Problem set 43

1. ^(39,32) Draw a pair of horizontal parallel line segments. Make the lower segment longer than the upper segment. Connect the endpoints of the segments to form a quadrilateral.

2. ⁽⁴⁰⁾ If 1 pie is shared equally by 6 people, then each person will get what fraction of the pie?

3. ⁽⁴³⁾ Dan, Yesenia, and Hung are sharing 4 oranges. How many oranges are there for each person?

4. ⁽²¹⁾ One hundred forty students were divided equally into 5 classes. How many students were in each class?

5. ⁽⁴¹⁾ The arrow points to what fraction on this number line?

6. ⁽⁴²⁾ Draw two circles of the same size. Shade $\frac{1}{4}$ of one circle and $\frac{1}{3}$ of the other circle. Then compare these fractions:

$$\frac{1}{4} \bigcirc \frac{1}{3}$$

7. ⁽⁴¹⁾ What number is half of 25?

8. ⁽³⁹⁾ A hexagon has how many more sides than a pentagon?

9. One half of a circle plus one fourth of a circle is what
(37) percent of a whole circle?

10. The arrow points to what mixed number on this
(41) number line?

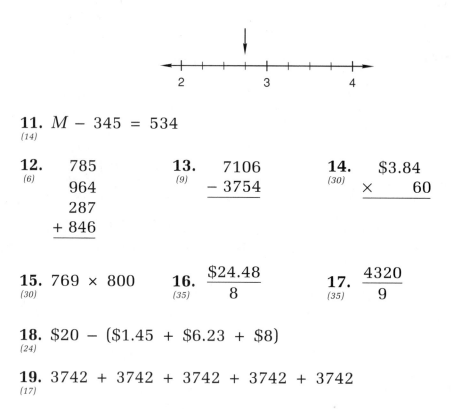

11. $M - 345 = 534$
(14)

12. 785
(6)   964
      287
    + 846

13.   7106
(9)   − 3754

14. $3.84
(30) ×   60

15. 769 × 800
(30)

16. $\dfrac{\$24.48}{8}$
(35)

17. $\dfrac{4320}{9}$
(35)

18. $20 − ($1.45 + $6.23 + $8)
(24)

19. 3742 + 3742 + 3742 + 3742 + 3742
(17)

20. How many circles are shaded?
(43)

21. Round 650 to the nearest hundred.
(34)

22. A year is what fraction of a decade? A year is what
(31,27) percent of a decade?

23. Which of these angles appears to be an obtuse angle?
(33)
A.   B.   C.

24. What are the next three numbers in this sequence?
(1)
　　　　…, 60, 70, 80, _____, _____, _____, …

25. To what number on this scale is the arrow pointing?
(28)

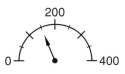

LESSON
44

Adding and Subtracting Fractions with Common Denominators

Facts Practice: 64 Multiplication Facts (Test D in Test Masters)

Mental Math: Name the relationship: Tony's mother's sister's son is Tony's _____.
How many is $\frac{1}{2}$ dozen? 2 dozen? $2\frac{1}{2}$ dozen?

  a. Round 380 to the nearest hundred.   **b.** 860 − 240
  c. 24 × 7   **d.** 8 × 800   **e.** 10 × 25
  f. $\frac{1}{2}$ of 15   **g.** 50% of 10¢   **h.** 10% of 10¢
  i. 6 × 7, − 2, ÷ 5, + 1, ÷ 3, − 3

Problem Solving: Copy this division problem and fill in the missing digits.
$$4\overline{)\underline{}}^{\,24}$$

Your fraction manipulatives can help you add and subtract fractions.

Example 1　Use your fraction manipulatives to illustrate this addition. Then write a number sentence for the addition.

$$\frac{2}{4} + \frac{1}{4}$$

Solution　We form the two fractions $\frac{2}{4}$ and $\frac{1}{4}$.

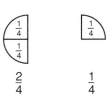

To add the two fractions, we move them together. We see that $\frac{2}{4}$ plus $\frac{1}{4}$ makes $\frac{3}{4}$.

$$\frac{2}{4} + \frac{1}{4} = \frac{3}{4}$$

Notice that the denominators of the fractions we added, $\frac{2}{4}$ and $\frac{1}{4}$, are the same. Fractions with the same denominators are said to have **common denominators.** When fractions have common denominators, we may add or subtract the fractions by simply adding or subtracting the numerators. We do not add or subtract the denominators.

$$\frac{2}{4} + \frac{1}{4} = \frac{3}{4}$$ Add the numerators.

    Leave the denominators unchanged.

Example 2   Use your fraction manipulatives to illustrate this subtraction. Then write a number sentence for the subtraction.

$$\frac{7}{10} - \frac{4}{10}$$

Solution   We form the fraction $\frac{7}{10}$.

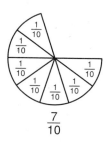

$$\frac{7}{10}$$

Then we remove $\frac{4}{10}$. We see that $\frac{3}{10}$ are left.

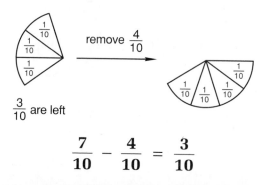

$$\frac{7}{10} - \frac{4}{10} = \frac{3}{10}$$

Example 3   Add: $1\frac{1}{4} + 1\frac{2}{4}$

Solution   To add mixed numbers, we add whole numbers to whole numbers and fractions to fractions. The whole numbers are 1 and 1. We add them and get 2. The fractions are $\frac{1}{4}$ and $\frac{2}{4}$. We add them and get $\frac{3}{4}$.

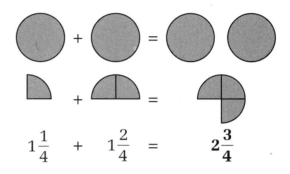

$$1\frac{1}{4} \quad + \quad 1\frac{2}{4} \quad = \quad 2\frac{3}{4}$$

Example 4   Subtract: $2\frac{1}{2} - 1\frac{1}{2}$

Solution   We start with $2\frac{1}{2}$.

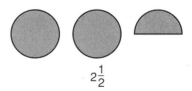

$2\frac{1}{2}$

We take away $1\frac{1}{2}$. What is left is 1.

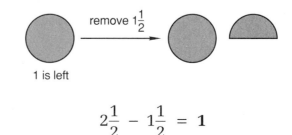

1 is left

$$2\frac{1}{2} - 1\frac{1}{2} = 1$$

Example 5 $2\frac{1}{2} + 1\frac{1}{2}$

Solution The sum is $3\frac{2}{2}$. The fraction $\frac{2}{2}$ is two halves, which is a whole. So $3\frac{2}{2}$ is $3 + 1$, which is 4.

$$\begin{array}{r} 2\frac{1}{2} \\ + 1\frac{1}{2} \\ \hline 3\frac{2}{2} = \mathbf{4} \end{array}$$

Practice Illustrate each addition and subtraction. Also, write a number sentence for each problem.

a. $\dfrac{1}{10} + \dfrac{2}{10}$

b. $\dfrac{3}{4} - \dfrac{2}{4}$

c. $1\dfrac{1}{2} + 1\dfrac{1}{2}$

d. $3\dfrac{4}{10} - 1\dfrac{1}{10}$

Problem set 44

1. Draw a pair of horizontal parallel line segments. Make the upper segment longer than the lower segment. Connect the ends of the segments to make a quadrilateral.
(39,32)

2. If a birthday cake is cut into 10 equal pieces, then each piece is what fraction of the whole cake? Each piece is what percent of the whole cake?
(37)

3. What year was two centuries after 1492?
(27)

4. What number is half of 75?
(41)

5. Draw two circles of the same size. Shade $\frac{1}{2}$ of one circle and $\frac{2}{3}$ of the other circle. Then compare these fractions:
(42)

$$\frac{1}{2} \bigcirc \frac{2}{3}$$

6. Four friends entered a nine-mile relay race. Each person ran one fourth of the distance. How many miles did each person run?
(43)

7. $3\frac{3}{10} - 1\frac{2}{10}$
(44)

8. $\frac{5}{10} + \frac{4}{10}$
(44)

9. $\frac{1}{2} - \frac{1}{2}$
(44)

10. $2\frac{1}{4} + 3\frac{2}{4}$
(44)

11. The arrow points to what mixed number on this
(41) number line?

12. 3784 + 2693 + 429 + 97 + 856 + 907
(6)

13. 3106 − 528
(9)

14. $80.00 − $77.56
(13)

15. 804 × 700
(30)

16. 60 × 43 × 8
(18)

17. 4008 ÷ 4
(35)

18. 4228 ÷ 7
(35)

19. 9635 ÷ 8
(35)

20. $7.98 ÷ 6
(26)

21. $10 − ($4.56 + $3 + $1.29)
(24)

22. Round 98 to the nearest ten.
(34)

23. Draw a triangle which has one obtuse angle.
(33)

24. One fifth of the 30 students in the class were left-
(23) handed. How many students were left-handed?

25. If it is evening, what time will be
(29) shown by this clock in 30 minutes?

LESSON 45

Short Division

We have learned a division algorithm in which we follow four steps: divide, multiply, subtract, and bring down. This algorithm is sometimes called "long division." In this lesson we will practice a shortened form of this algorithm. The shortened form is sometimes called "short division."

When we do short division, we follow four steps, but we do not write down every number. Instead we keep some of the numbers "in our head." We will show this by doing the same division problem both ways.

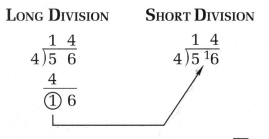

LONG DIVISION   SHORT DIVISION

We begin both divisions by dividing $4\overline{)5}$. We write "1" in the answer, and then we multiply. In short division we keep the multiplication answer in our head. Then we subtract. **In short division we write the subtraction answer in front of the next digit.** Here we write a small 1 in front of the 6 to make it 16. In short division we do not bring down this digit; instead we "bring up" the subtraction answer. Now we divide $4\overline{)^16}$ and write "4." We multiply and subtract in our head and find that there is no remainder.

Example $5\overline{)842}$

Solution   We will use short division to find the answer. First we divide and write "1" in the answer. Then we multiply and subtract in our head to get 3. We bring up the 3 and write it in front of the next digit. Next we divide $5\overline{)34}$. We continue to divide, multiply, subtract, and bring up. We bring up the last subtraction answer as the remainder to get an answer of **168 r 2.**

$$\begin{array}{r} 1\ \ 6\ \ 8\ \text{r}\ 2 \\ 5\overline{)8\ {}^34\ {}^42} \end{array}$$

Practice   Use short division to find the answers to these divisions:

a. $3\overline{)435}$ **b.** $6\overline{)500}$ **c.** $4\overline{)563}$

d. $4\overline{)500}$ **e.** $7\overline{)800}$ **f.** $10\overline{)836}$

g. $5\overline{)600}$ **h.** $3\overline{)616}$ **i.** $6\overline{)858}$

Problem set 45

1. Draw a pentagon.
(39)

2. A rattlesnake's rattle shakes about 50 times each second. How many times would it shake in 1 minute? Use an "equal groups" pattern.
(21)

3. Jim weighed 98 pounds before dinner and 101 pounds after dinner. How many pounds did Jim gain during dinner? Use a "larger-smaller-difference" pattern.
(36)

4. Sarah cut a 21-foot long ribbon into four equal lengths. How many feet long was each length of ribbon?
(43)

5. One foot is 12 inches. One fourth of a foot is how many inches?
(23)

6. Draw two rectangles of the same size. Shade $\frac{3}{4}$ of one
(42) rectangle and $\frac{3}{5}$ of the other rectangle. Then compare these fractions:

$$\frac{3}{4} \bigcirc \frac{3}{5}$$

7. $\dfrac{3}{10} + \dfrac{4}{10}$
(44)

8. $1\dfrac{1}{3} + 2\dfrac{1}{3}$
(44)

9. $\dfrac{7}{10} - \dfrac{4}{10}$
(44)

10. $5\dfrac{1}{4} - 2\dfrac{1}{4}$
(44)

11. Use a mixed number to name the number of shaded
(43) circles shown here.

12. Round 151 to the nearest hundred.
(34)

13. The arrow points to what fraction on this number
(41) line?

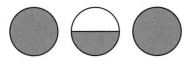

14. Compare: $\frac{1}{4}$ of 40 $\bigcirc$ $\frac{1}{5}$ of 50
(23,4)

15. Two fourths of a circle is what percent of a circle?
(37)

16. $18.73
(10) $34.26
       $+\qquad M$
        $79.33

17.   6010
(14) $-\qquad R$
        543

18.   936
(6)   47
         18
        493
         71
       $+\quad 82$

19.   346
(30)   ×   80

20. $7.25
(30)   ×   90

21.   670
(30)   ×   700

Practice short division:

22. $4\overline{)1736}$
(45)

23. $8\overline{)\$17.60}$
(45)

24. $3\overline{)100}$
(45)

25. Which word names an angle that is smaller than a
(33)   right angle?

    A. Acute   B. Right   C. Obtuse

LESSON
46

Using Fraction Manipulatives, Part 2

Facts Practice: 64 Multiplication Facts (Test D in Test Masters)

Mental Math: Name the relationship: Rodney is his mother's brother's _____.
A "score" is 20. How many is two score? three score?

a. Round 158 to the nearest ten.
b. 380 + 220
c. $\frac{1}{3} + \frac{1}{3}$
d. $\frac{1}{3} - \frac{1}{3}$
e. 9 × 24
f. 50% of a dozen
g. 25% of a dozen
h. 10 × 75
i. $\frac{1}{2}$ of 7
j. 6 × 4, + 1, ÷ 5, + 5, ÷ 2, + 1, ÷ 2

Problem Solving: Use the digits 1 through 9 in this "magic square" so that the sum of the digits in every row and every column is 15.

	5	

In this lesson we will make and use fraction manipulatives for thirds, fifths, and eighths.

Activity   Materials needed:

     • Each student needs a copy of "Fraction Master 2: Thirds, Fifths, and Eighths" (available in the *Math 65 Test Masters*)

     • scissors

- envelopes or locking plastic bags in which to store fraction pieces
- crayons (optional)
- fraction manipulatives for halves, fourths, and tenths (from Lesson 37)

Preparation for activities:

- Distribute materials. If fraction pieces are to be color-coded, we suggest agreeing upon different colors for each circle and lightly coloring the front and back of each circle before cutting. After the activities, store the manipulatives for later use.

Use all of your fraction manipulatives to help you with these activities:

(a) Show that four eighths equals one half.

(b) Show that a fifth equals two tenths.

(c) How many eighths equal a fourth?

(d) Is two fifths more or less than one half?

(e) Two thirds of a circle is what percent of a circle?

(f) Three fifths of a circle is what percent of a circle?

(g) Four eighths of a circle is what percent of a circle?

(h) Sarah has a half circle and a quarter circle and an eighth of a circle. How much more does she need to have a whole circle?

Use your fraction manipulatives to illustrate each of the following additions and subtractions. Write a complete number sentence for each.

(i) $\dfrac{1}{5} + \dfrac{2}{5}$ (j) $\dfrac{3}{8} + \dfrac{5}{8}$

(k) $\dfrac{2}{3} - \dfrac{1}{3}$ (l) $\dfrac{5}{8} - \dfrac{2}{8}$

Problem set 46

1. Draw a hexagon.
(39)

2. Captain Hook heard the alarm go off at 6 a.m. and got
(29) up quickly! If he had fallen asleep at 11 p.m., how
many hours of sleep did he get?

3. Joshua has $28.75. How much more money does he
(36) need to buy a $34.18 skateboard? Use a "larger-
smaller-difference" pattern.

4. Anita's grandfather has lived for seven decades. Seven
(27,21) decades is how many years? Use an "equal groups"
pattern.

5. Draw a rectangle. Shade one fourth of it. What percent
(40) of the rectangle is shaded?

6. List the factors of 30.
(25)

7. How many minutes is $\frac{1}{3}$ of an hour?
(27,23)

8. Use a mixed number to name the number of shaded
(43) circles shown here. Then use words to write the
mixed number.

9. What mixed number is marked by an arrow on this
(41) number line?

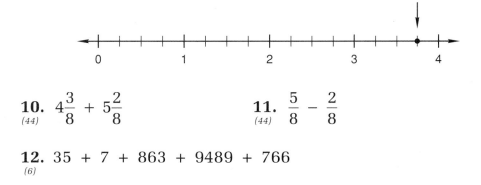

10. $4\frac{3}{8} + 5\frac{2}{8}$ 11. $\frac{5}{8} - \frac{2}{8}$
(44)   (44)

12. $35 + 7 + 863 + 9489 + 766$
(6)

13. 752 − (356 + 97)
(24)

14. 40 × (200 − 34)
(24)

15. 560 ÷ (56 ÷ 7)
(24)

16. $\dfrac{3}{5} + \left(\dfrac{2}{5} - \dfrac{1}{5} \right)$
(24)

17. 100 ÷ 7
(26)

18. 5760 ÷ 8
(35)

19. What number is half of the largest two-digit odd
(41) number?

20. Counting by tens, the number 158 is closest to which
(34) of the following?

A. 150   B. 160   C. 100   D. 200

21. Draw a triangle which has three acute angles.
(33)

22. What month is 10 months after June?
(27)

23. What time is 7 minutes before seven in the morning?
(29)

24. What are the next three numbers in this sequence?
(1)
    ..., 120, 130, 140, _____, _____, _____, ...

25. What temperature is shown on
(28) this thermometer?

**LESSON
47**

Dividing Remainders, Part 2 • Adding and Subtracting Whole Numbers, Fractions, and Mixed Numbers

---

Facts Practice: 90 Division Facts (Test E or F in Test Masters)

Mental Math: Name the relationship: Simon's brother's son is Simon's _____.
What coin is 10% of a dollar? 25% of a dollar?

a. Round 162 to the nearest ten.   **b.** $560 - 60$

c. $\frac{2}{3} + \frac{1}{3}$ **d.** $\frac{2}{3} - \frac{1}{3}$ **e.** 8×35

f. 10×24 **g.** $\frac{1}{2}$ of 9   **h.** 25% of 16

i. $2 \times 25, -1, \div 7, +1, \div 2, \times 5, +1, \div 3$ **j.** 50% of 50

Problem Solving: In the game tic-tac-toe, the goal is to get three X's or three O's in a row. How many ways are there to get three in a row?

X	O	X
X	O	O
X	O	O

Dividing remainders, part 2

In Lesson 43 we studied some story problems with answers that were mixed numbers. We found that the remainder of a division problem can be divided, resulting in a fraction. In this lesson we will continue our study.

Example 1   *Sir Pizza* donated 14 pizzas to the sixth-grade picnic. How many pizzas were there for each of the three classes of sixth graders?

Solution   We need to divide the 14 pizzas into three equal groups. We divide 14 by 3.

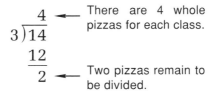

$$\begin{array}{r} 4 \\ 3\overline{)14} \\ \underline{12} \\ 2 \end{array}$$

There are 4 whole pizzas for each class.

Two pizzas remain to be divided.

Four pizzas for each class is 12 pizzas. There are still 2 pizzas to divide. If we divide each of the remaining pizzas into 3 parts, there will be 6 pieces to share. Each class will get two pieces.

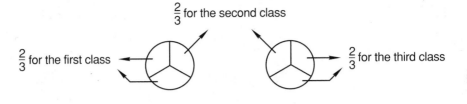

For each class there are $4\frac{2}{3}$ pizzas. Notice that the 2 of $\frac{2}{3}$ is the remainder, and the 3 of $\frac{2}{3}$ is the number by which we are dividing.

$$\begin{array}{r} 4\frac{2}{3} \\ 3\overline{\smash{)}14} \\ \underline{12} \\ 2 \end{array}$$

$4\frac{2}{3}$ ◄— The remainder is 2.
◄— We are dividing by 3.
We are dividing by 3. —►
2 ◄— remainder

Example 2   A whole circle is 100% of the circle. If a circle is divided into thirds, then each third is what percent of the whole circle?

100%

Solution   We divide 100% by 3 to find the percent for each third.

$$\begin{array}{r} 33 \\ 3\overline{\smash{)}100} \\ \underline{9} \\ 10 \\ \underline{9} \\ 1 \end{array}$$

33 ◄— 33% for each third

1 ◄— 1% remains to be divided.

If each third of the circle were 33%, then the total would be 99%. However, the total needs to be 100%. Therefore, we need to divide the remaining 1% by 3. One divided by three is $\frac{1}{3}$. We write "$\frac{1}{3}$" after the 33. **Each third of the circle is $33\frac{1}{3}$% of the circle.**

$$\begin{array}{r} 33\frac{1}{3} \\ 3\overline{\smash{)}100} \\ \underline{9} \\ 10 \\ \underline{9} \\ 1 \end{array}$$

Adding and subtracting whole numbers, fractions, and mixed numbers

We have studied whole numbers, fractions, and mixed numbers. When adding these numbers, we add whole numbers to whole numbers and fractions to fractions. When subtracting, we subtract whole numbers from whole numbers and fractions from fractions. Remember that order matters in subtraction.

Example 3 $5 + 1\frac{1}{2}$

Solution We add whole numbers to whole numbers and fractions to fractions. The sum of the whole numbers 5 and 1 is 6. There is no fraction to add to $\frac{1}{2}$. So 5 plus $1\frac{1}{2}$ is **$6\frac{1}{2}$**.

$$\begin{array}{r} 5 \\ + 1\frac{1}{2} \\ \hline 6\frac{1}{2} \end{array}$$

Example 4 $1 + \frac{1}{2}$

Solution We add whole numbers to whole numbers and fractions to fractions. There is no fraction to add to $\frac{1}{2}$ and no whole number to add to 1. We write the whole number and fraction together to make the mixed number **$1\frac{1}{2}$**.

Example 5 $3\frac{1}{2} - \frac{1}{2}$

Solution When we subtract the fractions, we find the answer is $\frac{0}{2}$, which is zero. So subtracting $\frac{1}{2}$ from $3\frac{1}{2}$ leaves **3**.

Practice* **a.** Draw a diagram to illustrate this story. Then find the answer using pencil and paper. Follow Example 1.

> *Sir Pizza donated 15 pizzas to the fifth-grade picnic. How many pizzas were there for each of the four classes of fifth graders?*

b. A whole circle is divided into sevenths. Each seventh is what percent of the whole circle?

100%

Add or subtract, as shown:

c. $3\frac{1}{2} + 2$

d. $3\frac{2}{4} - \frac{1}{4}$

e. $6\frac{2}{3} - 3$

f. $3\frac{2}{4} + \frac{1}{4}$

g. $2\frac{1}{2} - \frac{1}{2}$

h. $\frac{3}{4} + 2$

Problem set 47

1. Draw a pair of vertical parallel line segments of the same length. Connect the ends of the segments to make a quadrilateral.
(39,32)

2. Angela poured 32 ounces of juice equally into 4 cups. How many ounces of juice were in each cup?
(21)

3. A stick 100 centimeters long broke into two pieces. One of the pieces was 48 centimeters long. How long was the other piece?
(36)

4. Draw a square. Shade all but one fourth of it. What percent of the square is not shaded?
(40)

5. Round 158 to the nearest ten.
(34)

6. What mixed number names point y on this number line?
(41)

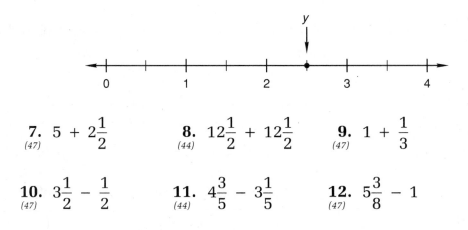

7. $5 + 2\frac{1}{2}$
(47)

8. $12\frac{1}{2} + 12\frac{1}{2}$
(44)

9. $1 + \frac{1}{3}$
(47)

10. $3\frac{1}{2} - \frac{1}{2}$
(47)

11. $4\frac{3}{5} - 3\frac{1}{5}$
(44)

12. $5\frac{3}{8} - 1$
(47)

13. A whole circle is divided into
(47) eighths. Each eighth is what percent of the whole circle?

14. How many eighths equal a half?
(46)

15. (30)	**16.** (30)	**17.** (30)
408 × 70	$9.67 × 60	970 × 900

18. $3.47
(13) $5.23
      $7.68
    + $2.42

19. R
(14) − 3977
       309

20. 9013
(14) − W
      3608

21. 7)890
(26)

22. 6)100
(26)

23. 4)8035
(35)

24. How many minutes is one tenth of an hour?
(27,23)

25. According to this calendar, Febru-
(27) ary 2047 would begin on what
day of the week?

JANUARY 2047						
S	M	T	W	T	F	S
			1	2	3	4	5
6	7	8	9	10	11	12
13	14	15	16	17	18	19
20	21	22	23	24	25	26
27	28	29	30	31		

LESSON
48

Reading Lengths on a
Metric Scale

Facts Practice: 64 Multiplication Facts (Test D in Test Masters)

Problem Solving: Use the information in this paragraph to answer the questions that follow. Drawing a diagram may help you with the problem.

Andrew's mother and father are Bernice and Charles. Andrew's mother's parents are Diana and Edmund. Bernice's brother is Fred. Fred and his spouse Gloria have a son, Harold.

a. Harold is Andrew's _____.   **b.** Fred is Andrew's _____.
c. Harold is Bernice's _____.   **d.** Charles is Fred's _____.
e. Bernice is Gloria's _____.   **f.** Diana is Andrew's _____.
g. Harold is Edmund's _____.

Inches, feet, yards, and miles are commonly used to measure distances in the United States. These words came to us from England. These units were used in the English system of units. But England does not use these units any more. No other big country in the world uses these units any more. All the other countries have changed to the units called the *Système International*, or SI for short. Some people call the **SI system** the **metric system.** In this system we use centimeters and millimeters to measure small distances.

Here we show a centimeter scale and a millimeter scale. The words "centimeter" and "millimeter" are abbreviated **cm** and **mm,** respectively.

The centimeter scale is divided into segments 1 centimeter long. The millimeter scale has been divided into smaller segments 1 millimeter long. A longer mark is used to mark every 10 millimeters. Notice that **10 millimeters equals 1 centimeter.** The arrow is 4 centimeters long. It is also 40 millimeters long.

Example 1   The distance across a nickel is about 2 centimeters. Two centimeters is how many millimeters?

Solution   We remember that 1 centimeter equals 10 millimeters, so 2 centimeters equals **20 millimeters.**

Example 2   What is the length of the rectangle?

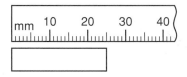

Solution   The millimeter scale marks each millimeter. Every 10 millimeters is marked with a longer mark. We count two longer marks plus five shorter marks and find the length is **25 mm.**

Practice   **a.** One centimeter is how many millimeters?

b. How many millimeters is 5 centimeters?

c. Write the abbreviations for centimeter and millimeter.

d. How many millimeters long is the nail?

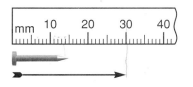

e. How many **centimeters** long is the arrow?

Problem set
48

1. Draw a quadrilateral that has four right angles.
(39)

2. In her pocket Sallie has 3 pennies, 2 nickels, a dime, 3 quarters, and a half dollar. How much money is in her pocket?
(13)

3. One hundred thirty-eight kindergartners climbed on three buses to go to the zoo. If there were the same number of children on each bus, how many children were on each bus?
(21)

4. The distance across a nickel is about 2 centimeters. Two centimeters is how many millimeters?
(48)

5. What year was two decades after 1620?
(27)

6. Three friends want to equally share five oranges. How many oranges are there for each of the friends?
(47)

7. What mixed number names point z on this number line?
(41)

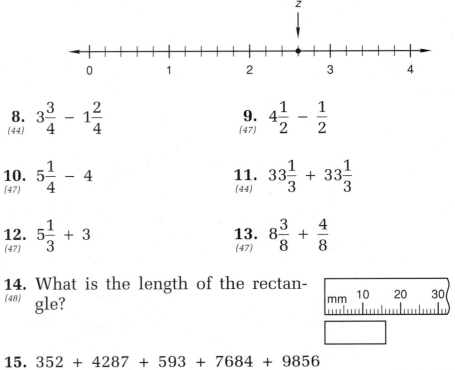

8. $3\frac{3}{4} - 1\frac{2}{4}$
(44)

9. $4\frac{1}{2} - \frac{1}{2}$
(47)

10. $5\frac{1}{4} - 4$
(47)

11. $33\frac{1}{3} + 33\frac{1}{3}$
(44)

12. $5\frac{1}{3} + 3$
(47)

13. $8\frac{3}{8} + \frac{4}{8}$
(47)

14. What is the length of the rectangle?
(48)

15. $352 + 4287 + 593 + 7684 + 9856$
(6)

16. 3627 − 429
(9)

17. 9104 − (2000 − 66)
(24)

18. 491 × 700
(30)

19. 60 × 8 × 37
(18)

20. 3175 ÷ 5
(26)

21. 2964 ÷ 10
(26)

22. Draw a circle. Shade all but one third of it. What
(46,40) percent of the circle is shaded?

23. Counting by tens, the number 256 is closest to which
(34) of the following?

A. 240 B. 250 C. 260 D. 300

24. If it is morning, what time will be
(29) shown by this clock in 30
minutes?

25. List the factors of 50.
(25)

LESSON
49

Reading an Inch Ruler to the Nearest Fourth of an Inch

Facts Practice: 90 Division Facts (Test E or F in Test Masters)

Mental Math: Name the relationship: Norma is her brother's daughter's _____.
Count by 25's from 25 to 300. How many cents is 3 quarters? 6 quarters?

a. Round 278 to the nearest ten.
b. 875 + 125
c. $\frac{3}{4} + \frac{1}{4}$
d. $\frac{3}{4} - \frac{1}{4}$
e. 7 × 42
f. 10 × 25¢
g. 50% of 10
h. 10% of 50
i. 6 × 4, ÷ 3, + 2, ÷ 5, × 7, + 1, ÷ 3

Problem Solving: Copy this division problem and fill in the missing digits.

$$3\overline{)}\,\,^{56}$$

To measure small lengths in the metric system, we use centimeters and millimeters. To measure small lengths in the U.S. Customary System, we use inches. We use the letters "in." to abbreviate the word *inch*. To avoid confusion with the word *in*, we write the abbreviation with a period.

An inch is a unit of length this long.

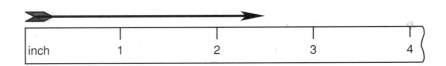

1 inch

When we measure the length of something, we count how many "inch units" it takes to reach across its length.

We often use a tape measure or ruler for measuring lengths. A ruler is usually 12 inch units placed next to each other, numbered, and marked into a board. Here we show part of a ruler.

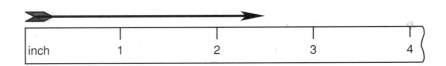

We notice that inch marks are farther apart than centimeter marks and much farther apart than millimeter marks. With this ruler we cannot measure as accurately as we can with a centimeter or millimeter ruler. The closer the marks are on a ruler, the more accurately we can measure. To make an inch ruler more accurate, we divide the inches into fractions. In this lesson we will practice reading from an inch ruler that has been divided into fourths.

Example   How many inches long is the arrow?

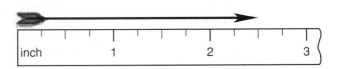

Solution   The marks on this ruler divide each inch into four smaller segments. Each small segment is one fourth of an inch long. Measuring the arrow, we see that its length is 2 full inches plus 2 small segments, that is, $2\frac{2}{4}$ inches. However, there is another way to name the fraction $\frac{2}{4}$. We see that the mark at the end of the arrow is **halfway** between 2 and 3. It is the two-and-one-half-inch mark. Notice on the ruler that the half-inch marks are slightly longer than the quarter-inch marks. The length of the arrow is $2\frac{1}{2}$ **inches,** or $2\frac{1}{2}$ **in.**

Practice Name the mark on the ruler to which each lettered arrow is pointing:

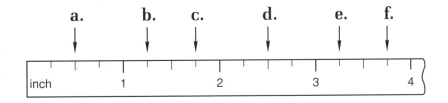

Problem set 49

1. Draw a rectangle with all sides the same length.
(39)

2. Julie paid $10 and got back $2.47. How much did she spend?
(16)

3. Draw two circles. Shade one and three fourths of them.
(43)

4. The *Phantom of the Opera* was a hit. The theater was filled all 4 nights. If 2500 attended in all, then how many attended each night?
(21)

5. There were 8 gallons of punch for the third-grade picnic. How many gallons of punch were there for each of the 3 third-grade classes?
(47)

6. Ten millimeters equals how many centimeters?
(48)

7. How many inches long is the arrow?
(49)

8. $3\frac{1}{3} + 1\frac{1}{3}$
(44)

9. $4\frac{1}{4} + 2$
(47)

10. $3 + \frac{3}{4}$
(47)

11. $5\frac{3}{8} - 2$
(47)

12. $6\frac{3}{4} - 1\frac{2}{4}$
(44)

13. $5\frac{1}{2} - 1\frac{1}{2}$
(44)

14. $87.93
(13) $35.16
          $42.97
        + $68.74
        ‾‾‾‾‾‾‾‾‾

15. $50.26
(13)   − $13.87
        ‾‾‾‾‾‾‾‾‾

16.   6109
(14)   −   A
        ‾‾‾‾‾‾‾‾‾
             4937

17. $\dfrac{9636}{9}$
(35)

18. $2.34
(30)   ×   600
        ‾‾‾‾‾‾‾‾‾

19.   4287
(17)   ×   5
        ‾‾‾‾‾‾‾‾‾

20.   9314
(30)   ×   70
        ‾‾‾‾‾‾‾‾‾

21. $\dfrac{\$34.16}{8}$
(26)

22. Draw a rectangle and shade $\frac{3}{5}$ of it. What percent of the
(40, 46) rectangle is shaded?

23. Round 256 to the nearest ten.
(34)

24. Which of these triangles appears to have one right
(33) angle?

A.   B.    C.

25. To what number on this number line is the arrow
(28) pointing?

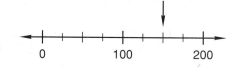

LESSON 50

Illustrating Fraction Stories

Facts Practice: 64 Multiplication Facts (Test D in Test Masters)

Mental Math: Name the relationship: Sal's sister's husband is Sal's _____.
What coin has a value of 50% of 50¢?

a. Round 271 to the nearest ten. **b.** $580 - 60$

c. $\frac{5}{10} + \frac{2}{10}$ **d.** $\frac{5}{10} - \frac{2}{10}$ **e.** 6×82

f. 10×75¢ **g.** $\frac{1}{2}$ of 51 **h.** 25% of 24

i. $10 \times 10, \div 2, -1, \div 7, -1, \div 3, -2$

Problem Solving: A "spare" in bowling is when all ten pins are knocked down in two rolls. Knocking down 3 pins on the first roll and 7 pins on the second roll is one way to bowl a spare. Make a table that lists all the possible ways to bowl a spare.

One type of "equal groups" story is the "fraction-of-a-group" story. Drawing diagrams of fraction stories can help us understand the story.

Example 1 The teacher was pleased that $\frac{1}{2}$ of her 30 students earned an A on the test. How many students earned an A on the test?

Solution We will draw a rectangle to stand for the whole group of 30 students. We will divide the rectangle into two equal parts. Half of 30 students is 15 students. So we write "15 students" in each half. We see that **15 students earned an A.**

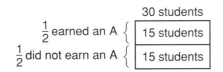

Example 2   Debbie scored $\frac{2}{3}$ of her team's 36 points. How many points did she score?

Solution   We draw a rectangle to stand for the team's 36 points. Debbie scored two thirds of the points, so we divide the rectangle into thirds. A third of 36 is 12. We write "12 points" in each third of the rectangle. Since Debbie scored **two** thirds of the points, she scored 12 plus 12 points. We see that **Debbie scored 24 points.**

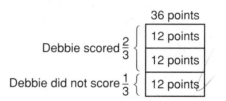

Example 3   Bill's cat ate $\frac{1}{4}$ of a dozen fish fillets. How many fish fillets were left for Bill and his family?

Solution   We draw a rectangle to stand for all 12 fish fillets. We divide the rectangle into four equal parts. A fourth of 12 is 3, so we write "3 fish fillets" in each fourth of the rectangle. Bill's cat ate 3 of the fish fillets. The rest were left for the family. So **9 fish fillets were left for Bill and his family.**

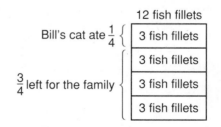

Practice   Illustrate these fraction stories:

   a. Two fifths of the 30 students in the class played in the band. How many students played in the band?

   b. Hugo practiced the trumpet for $\frac{3}{4}$ of an hour. For how many minutes did Hugo practice the trumpet?

Problem set
50

1. Walking at a steady rate, Mary walked 11 miles in 3
(47) hours. Write a mixed number that shows how far she
walked each hour.

2. The theater had 625 seats. If 139 seats were empty,
(16) how many seats were filled?

3. This line segment is 4 centimeters long. How many
(48) millimeters long is it?

_____

4. What year was two centuries before 1976?
(27)

5. Debbie was voted "Most Valuable Player of the Game"
(50) and she scored $\frac{2}{3}$ of her team's 48 points. How many
points did Debbie score?

6. Seven thousand passengers arrived on 8 ships. If each
(21) ship carried an equal number of passengers, how
many passengers were on each ship?

7. Compare: $\frac{1}{4}$ of 60 $\bigcirc$ $\frac{1}{3}$ of 60
(4)

8. Round 256 to the nearest hundred.
(34)

9. Draw a rectangle. Shade all but two fifths of it. What
(40, 46) percent of the rectangle is not shaded?

10. What month is 8 months after September?
(27)

11. How many inches long is the nail?
(49)

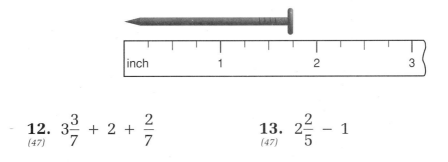

12. $3\frac{3}{7} + 2 + \frac{2}{7}$ **13.** $2\frac{2}{5} - 1$
(47)   *(47)*

14. $3\dfrac{2}{3} - \dfrac{1}{3}$
(47)

15. $6\dfrac{5}{12} - \left(4 + 1\dfrac{4}{12}\right)$
(24)

16. $1396 + 727 + 854 + 4685$
(6)

17. $97 + W = 512$
(10)

18. 938×800
(30)

19. $54 \times 7 \times 60$
(18)

20. $5445 \div 9$
(35)

21. $3205 \div 10$
(35)

22. $\$20 - (\$15.37 - \$12)$
(24)

23. $4826 + 4826 + 4826 + 4826$
(13)

24. A whole circle is divided into fifths. Each fifth is what percent of the whole circle?
(46)

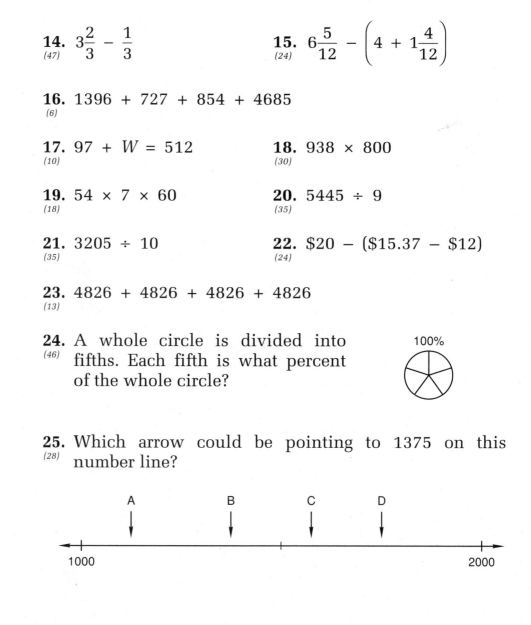

25. Which arrow could be pointing to 1375 on this number line?
(28)

LESSON
51

Practicing the Directions of the Compass

Facts Practice: 48 Uneven Divisions (Test G in Test Masters)

Mental Math: Name the relationship: Jorge is his sister's daughter's _____ .
Count up and down by 20's between 20 and 200.

a. Round 382 to the nearest hundred.
b. 640 + 300
c. $\frac{2}{5} + \frac{2}{5}$
d. $\frac{2}{5} - \frac{2}{5}$
e. 4 × 34
f. 50% of 30
g. Half of 31
h. 10% of 30
i. 60 + 3, ÷ 7, × 2, ÷ 3, × 4, ÷ 3

Problem Solving: Five dots need to be added to a 4-dot square pattern to make a 9-dot square pattern. How many dots need to be added to the 9-dot square pattern to make the next square pattern?

Four of the words used to name directions are **north, south, east,** and **west.** A good way to remember these directions is to think of a map of the United States. North is at the top. South is at the bottom.

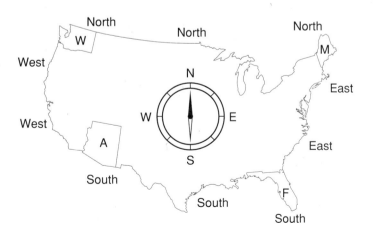

East is on the right, and west is on the left. Sometimes we combine the direction words. The M stands for Maine. We see that Maine is both north and east. So we say that

Maine is in the northeast. The letters W, A, and F on the map stand for the states of Washington, Arizona, and Florida, respectively. We see that Washington is in the northwest, Arizona is in the southwest, and Florida is in the southeast.

Example 1 If you are facing south and lift your left arm out to the side, in which direction will your arm be pointing?

Solution Until you get used to these questions, try thinking this way. Imagine yourself at the center of the United States facing south. As you lift your left arm, you should be able to "see" that it will point to the E for **east.**

Example 2 The original 13 colonies were located along which coast of the United States?

A. South   B. East   C. West

Solution The early colonists sailed west to reach this continent but did not travel far inland. Instead they settled along the east coast of this country. So our answer is **B. East.**

Activity Each student will sketch a map of the local area that can be used as a directional reference. On a blank piece of paper, sketch the school in the center. Label the top of the map north, the bottom south, the right-hand side east, and the left-hand side west.

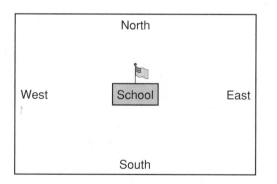

On the map, sketch familiar landmarks that lie to the north, east, south, and west of school. We suggest you sit facing north with your paper in front of you as you draw your landmark map.

Practice   **a.** Draw a sketch of a compass. Use the letters N, S, E, and W to stand for north, south, east, and west.

b. If the sun rises in the east and sets in the west and you face the rising sun, what direction is to your right?

c. Dan traveled north on Elm Street and turned left on Main Street. In what direction was he traveling on Main Street?

d. Sheila flew from Oklahoma to South Dakota. In what direction did she fly? (Look on a map.)

Problem set 51   **1.** Draw a pair of parallel oblique lines.
(32)

2. Matt has 30 cents worth of dimes and nickels in his
(21) hand. If he has the same number of dimes as nickels, how many coins does he have?

3. This screw is 60 millimeters long. How many
(48) centimeters long is it?

4. Draw a sketch for this fraction story:
(50)
Three fifths of the 30 students in the class were girls. How many girls were in the class?

5. Mike sliced five apples into quarters. If four children
(47) share the slices equally, then how many apples are there for each child?

6. If you are facing south and lift your right arm out to
(51) the side, in what direction will your arm be pointing?

7. Draw a circle. Shade all but one third of it. What
(47, 40) percent of the circle is not shaded?

8. $12\frac{1}{2} + 12\frac{1}{2}$
(44)

9. $5 + 1\frac{3}{8} + \frac{2}{8}$
(47)

10. $6\frac{2}{3} - \left(4\frac{2}{3} - 1\right)$
(24)

11. $(20 \times 4) + (3 \times 24)$
(24)

12. One foot is 12 inches. How many inches is 5 feet?
(21)

13. $\begin{array}{r} 860 \\ \times \quad 90 \\ \hline \end{array}$
(30)

14. $\begin{array}{r} 900 \\ \times \quad 70 \\ \hline \end{array}$
(30)

15. $\begin{array}{r} 36 \\ 47 \\ 28 \\ 49 \\ 53 \\ + 62 \\ \hline \end{array}$
(6)

16. $\begin{array}{r} T \\ - \$38.54 \\ \hline \$11.62 \end{array}$
(14)

17. $\begin{array}{r} \$29.01 \\ - \qquad N \\ \hline \$13.97 \end{array}$
(14)

18. $\dfrac{3663}{9}$
(35)

19. $\$20 - (\$4.36 + \$5 + \$1.29)$
(24)

20. $547 \div 10$
(26)

21. $3228 \div 4$
(35)

22. What number is $\frac{1}{2}$ of 61?
(41)

23. What are the next three numbers in this sequence?
(1)

      ..., 2800, 2900, 3000, _____, _____, _____, ...

24. To what mixed number on the number line is this
(41) arrow pointing?

25. According to this calendar, what
$^{(27)}$ would be the date of the first
Monday in September 2019?

AUGUST 2019						
S	M	T	W	T	F	S
				1	2	3
4	5	6	7	8	9	10
11	12	13	14	15	16	17
18	19	20	21	22	23	24
25	26	27	28	29	30	31

LESSON 52

Simplifying Mixed Measures

Facts Practice: 64 Multiplication Facts (Test D in Test Masters)

Mental Math: Name the relationship: Heidi is her husband's mother's _____.
A "score" is 20. How many is two score? three score? four score?

a. Round 381 to the nearest ten.   **b.** 760 − 400
c. $1\frac{1}{2} + \frac{1}{2}$ **d.** $1\frac{1}{2} - \frac{1}{2}$ **e.** Half of 3
f. 25% of 4   **g.** 9 × 8, − 2, ÷ 2, + 1, ÷ 4, + 1, ÷ 2
h. 3 × 34

Problem Solving: Copy this multiplication problem and fill in the missing digits.

$$\begin{array}{r} 7\_ \\ \times \ \_ \\ \hline 6\_5 \end{array}$$

Sometimes two units are used to name a measure. Here we show three examples.

John is **5 feet, 4 inches** tall.

Tracy ran a quarter mile in **1 minute, 15 seconds.**

The melon weighed **3 pounds, 8 ounces.**

In this lesson we will practice changing measures named with two units into measures named with one unit.

Example 1 John is 5 feet, 4 inches tall. How many inches tall is John?

Solution Five feet, 4 inches means 5 feet **plus** 4 inches. Before we can add, we first change 5 feet to inches. Since 1 foot equals 12 inches, we multiply 5 times 12 inches.

$$5 \text{ feet} = 5 \times 12 \text{ inches}$$

$$5 \text{ feet} = 60 \text{ inches}$$

Now we add 60 inches and 4 inches.

$$60 \text{ inches} + 4 \text{ inches} = 64 \text{ inches}$$

John is **64 inches** tall.

Example 2   Tracy ran a quarter mile in 1 minute, 15 seconds. What was her time in seconds?

Solution   One minute, 15 seconds means 1 minute **plus** 15 seconds. We first change 1 minute to seconds. Then we add.

$$1 \text{ minute} = 60 \text{ seconds}$$

$$60 \text{ seconds} + 15 \text{ seconds} = 75 \text{ seconds}$$

Tracy ran a quarter mile in **75 seconds.**

Example 3   One pound equals 16 ounces. The melon weighed 3 pounds, 8 ounces. How many ounces did the melon weigh?

Solution   Three pounds, 8 ounces means 3 pounds **plus** 8 ounces. We change pounds to ounces first.

$$3 \text{ pounds} = 3 \times 16 \text{ ounces}$$

$$3 \text{ pounds} = 48 \text{ ounces}$$

Now we add.

$$48 \text{ ounces} + 8 \text{ ounces} = 56 \text{ ounces}$$

The melon weighed **56 ounces.**

Practice   **a.** Change 6 feet, 2 inches to inches.

b. Change 3 minutes, 20 seconds to seconds.

c. Change 2 hours, 30 minutes to minutes.

d. Change 2 pounds, 12 ounces to ounces.
(1 pound = 16 ounces)

Problem set 52

1. When the students got on the buses to go to the picnic, there were 36 on one bus, 29 on another bus, and 73 on the third bus. Altogether, how many students were on the three buses?
(11)

2. What year was two decades before 1932?
(27)

3. Jenny was riding her bike east and made a left turn. Then in what direction was she going?
(51)

4. When Gabriel turned 12 years old, he was 5 feet, 6 inches tall. How many inches is 5 feet, 6 inches?
(52)

5. The 7 in 374,021 means which of the following?
(7)
A. 7 B. 70 C. 70,000

6. From March 1 of one year to May 1 of the next year is how many months?
(27)

7. Draw a rectangle. Shade three eighths of it. What percent of the rectangle is shaded?
(47, 40)

8. How long is the line segment?
(49)

9. $4 + 3\frac{3}{4}$
(47)

10. $3\frac{3}{5} + 1\frac{1}{5}$
(44)

11. $2\frac{3}{8} + \frac{2}{8}$
(47)

12. $5\frac{1}{3} - \left(5\frac{1}{3} - \frac{1}{3}\right)$
(24)

13. $2\frac{1}{2} - \frac{1}{2}$
(47)

14. $3\frac{5}{9} - 1\frac{1}{9}$
(44)

15. $\begin{array}{r} \$48,748 \\ \$37,145 \\ + \$26,498 \\ \hline \end{array}$
(6)

16. $\begin{array}{r} \$63,142 \\ - \$17,936 \\ \hline \end{array}$
(9)

17. $\begin{array}{r} \$5.63 \\ \times \quad 700 \\ \hline \end{array}$
(30)

18. 4729
(17) × 8

19. 9006
(30) × 80

20. $\frac{3456}{8}$
(26)

21. 1836 ÷ 9
(35)

22. 1405 ÷ 7
(35)

23. (20 × 25) + (5 × 25)
(24)

24. Draw a sketch for this fraction story:
(50)

In Andy's slice of watermelon there were 60 seeds. If he swallowed $\frac{2}{5}$ of the seeds, how many did he swallow?

25. If it is evening, what time will be
(29) shown by this clock in $3\frac{1}{2}$ hours?

LESSON 53

Reading and Writing Whole Numbers in Expanded Notation

Facts Practice: 48 Uneven Divisions (Test G in Test Masters)

Problem Solving: Use the information in this paragraph to answer the questions that follow. Drawing a diagram may help you with the problem.

Fred's spouse is Emily. Their daughter is Gloria. Fred's sister is Helen. Helen's husband is Ivan, and their son is James. Fred's mother and father are Carol and Dave.

a. James is Fred's _____.
b. Emily is Carol's _____.
c. Ivan is Dave's _____.
d. Carol is Gloria's _____.
e. James is Gloria's _____.
f. Ivan is Fred's _____.
g. James is Dave's _____.
h. Fred is Helen's _____.

One way to name numbers is to name the place value of each digit. The number 3256 could be named

3 thousands plus 2 hundreds plus 5 tens plus 6 ones

We could use numbers instead of words to name the same number if we write

$$(3 \times 1000) + (2 \times 100) + (5 \times 10) + (6 \times 1)$$

This method of naming numbers is called **expanded notation. When we write a number in expanded notation, we write a digit times its place value,** plus the next digit times its place value, and so on.

Example 1   Write the number 5600 in expanded notation.

Solution   The number 5600 is 5 thousands plus 6 hundreds plus no tens plus no ones. We write 5 times its place value plus 6 times its place value. Since there are no tens or ones, we write only

$$(5 \times 1000) + (6 \times 100)$$

Example 2   Write the standard form for $(3 \times 100) + (2 \times 1)$.

Solution   The "standard form" means the usual way of writing numbers. We are to write the number which has a 3 in the hundreds' place and a 2 in the ones' place.

100s'	10s'	1s'
3	0	2

Note that we use a zero to hold the tens' place and get **302**.

Practice*   Write in expanded notation:

   a. 56

   b. 5040

   c. 5280

Write the standard form for these expanded notations:

   d. $(6 \times 1000) + (4 \times 10)$

   e. $(5 \times 100) + (7 \times 10)$

   f. $(8 \times 10,000) + (4 \times 1000)$

   g. $(9 \times 1000) + (3 \times 100) + (2 \times 1)$

Problem set 53

1. Draw a square. Make each side $1\frac{1}{2}$ inches long.
(39)

2. Albert is 6 years older than Jorge. If Albert is 21, then how old is Jorge? Use a "larger-smaller-difference" pattern.
(36)

3. If you face the rising sun in the middle of the U.S., what direction is to your right?
(51)

4. The 6 in 356,287 means which of the following?
(7)

A. 6   B. 356   C. 6000   D. 6287

5. The new pencil was 19 centimeters long. How many
(48) millimeters long was it?

6. Draw a circle. Shade one sixth of it. What percent of
(47, 40) the circle is shaded?

7. Which digit is in the ten-thousands' place in 356,287?
(7)

8. Round 287 to the nearest ten.
(34)

9. Write the standard form for $(5 \times 100) + (2 \times 1)$.
(53)

10. Write the number 4700 in expanded notation.
(53)

11.   98,572
(6)
          42,156
          37,428
       + 16,984

12. W
(14)
       − 32,436
       ‾‾‾‾‾‾‾‾
         19,724

13.   10,000
(14)
       − Y
       ‾‾‾‾‾‾‾‾
          1,746

14. $34.78
(17)
       ×   6
       ‾‾‾‾‾‾‾‾

15.   6549
(30)
       ×   60
       ‾‾‾‾‾‾‾‾

16.   8037
(30)
       ×   90
       ‾‾‾‾‾‾‾‾

17. $3647 \div 6$
(35)

18. $5408 \div 9$
(35)

19. $1000 \div 10$
(35)

20. $3\frac{1}{3} + \left(4\frac{1}{3} - 2\right)$
(24)

21. $6 \times 800 = 6 \times 8 \times H$
(18)

22. $\$10 - (\$6 + \$1.47 + \$0.93)$
(24)

23. How many years is one fourth of a century?
(50)

24. What time is 1 minute before midnight?
(29)

25. To what number on this number line is the arrow
(28) pointing?

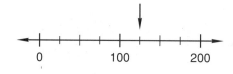

LESSON	**Finding Information to Solve**
54	**Problems**

Facts Practice: 64 Multiplication Facts (Test D in Test Masters)

Mental Math: Name the relationship: Anthony's father's brother's son is Anthony's _____ .
Count by 12's from 12 to 108. How many is 2 dozen? 4 dozen?

a. Round 528 to the nearest ten.   **b.** $590 - 60$
c. $\frac{1}{3} + \frac{2}{3}$ **d.** $1\frac{1}{3} + \frac{2}{3}$ **e.** 7×34
f. 50% of a dozen   **g.** 25% of a dozen
h. Start with a dozen, double it, $+ 1$, $\div 5$, $\times 6$, $+ 6$, $\div 3$

Problem Solving: Alba rolled two number cubes. The total was 5. Copy this table and write all the ways Alba could have rolled 5.

First Cube	Second Cube

Part of the process of solving problems is finding the information needed to solve the problem. We may find information in graphs, tables, books, or other places. In this lesson we will practice problems which require us to look for the information necessary to solve the problems.

Example 1   Read this information. Then answer the question.

> *In the first 6 games the Rio Vista football team won 4 games and lost 2 games. They won their next game by a score of 28 to 20. The team plays 10 games in all.*

In the first 7 games, how many games did the Rio Vista football team win?

Solution   More information is given than is needed to answer the question. We sort through the information until we find the information necessary to answer the question. We are asked to find how many of the first 7 games were won by the team. We are told that the team won 4 of the first 6 games. We are also told that the team won the next game (that is, the seventh game). Thus, the team **won 5** of their first 7 games.

Example 2   Use this graph to answer the question:

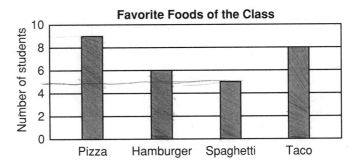

Pizza was the favorite food of how many students in the class?

Solution   This **bar graph** shows how many students in the class chose certain foods as their favorite food. The bar for pizza ends halfway between the line for 8 and the line for 10. Halfway between 8 and 10 is 9. Thus, pizza was the favorite food of **9 students.**

Example 3   Use this graph to answer the question:

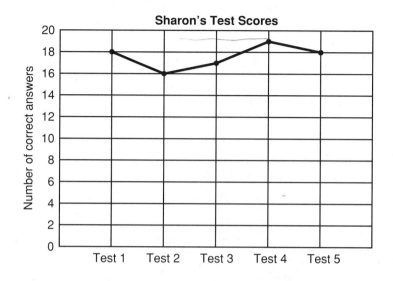

Sharon's Test Scores

There are 20 questions on each test. How many questions did Sharon miss on Test 3?

Solution   This **line graph** shows the number of answers Sharon had correct on each of her first 5 tests. We see that on Test 3 Sharon had 17 correct answers. We subtract 17 from 20 and find that Sharon missed **3 questions** on Test 3.

Problem set 54

1. Draw a pair of horizontal parallel lines. Make a
(32) quadrilateral by crossing the horizontal lines with a pair of oblique parallel lines. Shade the area closed in by the lines.

2. James was walking south and then he turned right. In
(51) what direction was he walking after he turned?

3. Draw a picture for this fraction story:
(50)

Jenny answered $\frac{4}{5}$ of the 20 questions correctly. How many questions did she answer correctly?

4. The 7 in 754,238 means which of the following?
(7)

A. 700,000   B. 700   C. 7   D. 754

5. Forty years is how many decades?
(27)

6. Write the standard form for (6 × 1000) + (4 × 100).
(53)

Use the graphs in this lesson to answer the next two questions:

7. Spaghetti was the favorite food of how many students in the class?
(54)

8. How many correct answers did Sharon have on Test 4?
(54)

9. Use words to name 63,250.
(7)

10. Draw a rectangle. Shade five eighths of it. What percent of the rectangle is shaded?
(47, 40)

11. Using digits, write one hundred forty-six thousand, two hundred thirty-four.
(7)

12. How long is the pin?
(48)

13.   342,579
(6)   + 416,919

14.   40,138
(9)   − 39,275

15.   3986
(30)   × 90

16. 30 × 400
(30)

17. $40.00 ÷ 8
(35)

18. 528 ÷ 7
(26)

19. $\frac{1}{2}$ of 25
(41)

20. $6\frac{3}{10} + 4\frac{4}{10} + 5$
(47)

21. $3\frac{9}{10} - \left(1\frac{1}{10} + \frac{7}{10}\right)$
(24)

22. 3675 + 3675 + 3675 + 3675
(13)

23. The three boys weigh 87 pounds, 121 pounds, and 103
(54) pounds, respectively. The boy who weighs most
weighs how many pounds more than the boy who
weighs least?

24. When Tina was born, she weighed 7 pounds, 2
(52) ounces. How many ounces did Tina weigh at birth? (1
pound = 16 ounces)

25. Use words to name the mixed number $3\frac{9}{10}$.
(43)

LESSON 55

Solving Two-Step Word Problems

Facts Practice: 48 Uneven Divisions (Test G in Test Masters)

Mental Math: Name the relationship: Gilberto's brother's wife
is Gilberto's _____.
Count up and down by 25's between 250 and 500.

a. Round 521 to the nearest hundred.

b. 740 + 60   **c.** $\frac{4}{10} + \frac{5}{10}$ **d.** $\frac{9}{10} + \frac{1}{10}$

e. 50% of 10   **f.** 10% of 10   **g.** $\frac{1}{3}$ of 12

h. 12 ÷ 2, + 2, ÷ 2, + 2, ÷ 2, + 2

Problem Solving: Six dots can make a triangle pattern with three dots on each side.
Ten dots can make a triangle pattern with four dots on each side.
How many dots are in a triangle
pattern that has seven dots on each
side?

Many of the problems we face in mathematics take more
than one step to solve. In an earlier lesson we solved two-
step problems which were written with parentheses. It
takes two steps to solve 10 − (6 − 3). We first find the
value within the parentheses. Then we subtract this value
from 10. In this lesson we will begin to solve **two-step
word problems.**

Example Bill is 5 years older than Robert. Robert is 3 years older than Sally. Sally is 15 years old. How old is Bill?

Solution This is a two-step problem. It is actually two "larger-smaller-difference" stories put together into one story. We are asked to find Bill's age. We cannot find his age in one step. We must first find Robert's age. Then we will be able to find Bill's age. We will draw two sets of towers for the two comparisons.

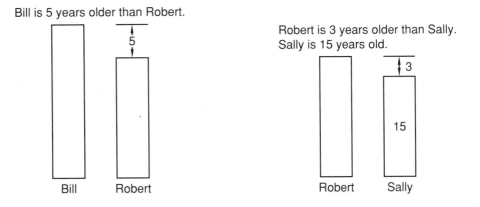

Sketching the towers helps us see that Robert is 18 years old. We write "18" in both towers that stand for Robert's age.

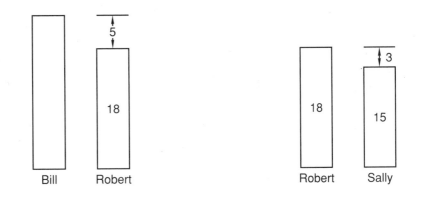

Since Bill is 5 years older than Robert, he is 18 years plus 5 years, which is **23 years old.**

Practice   **a.** The bus could carry 80 students. The 32 students from Room 8 and the 29 students from Room 12 got on the bus. How many more students can the bus carry? (*Note:* The first step is a "some and some more" story. What is the second step?)

b. Doreen collected 37 aluminum cans for school, and her brother collected 21. They decided to divide the cans evenly, so they put the cans into one big pile and from that they made two equal piles. How many cans were in each pile? (*Note:* What kind of story is the first step? What kind of story is the second step?)

Problem set 55

1. Draw a quadrilateral that has one pair of sides which
(39) are parallel and one pair of sides which are not parallel.

2. Kyle is 10 years older than Keith. Keith is 5 years
(55) older than Jill. Jill is 15 years old. How old is Kyle? (Draw two sets of towers to show the two "larger-smaller-difference" stories.)

3. Kerry's age is $\frac{1}{3}$ of her dad's age. If her dad is 36 years
(50) old, how old is Kerry?

4. On a map, north is usually toward the top. What
(51) direction is usually to the left side of a map?

5. Think of an odd number. Multiply it by 5. What is the
(2) last digit of the product?

6. Write the standard form for $(5 \times 100) + (6 \times 1)$.
(53)

7. Kathie and Kris were paid $5 for weeding the garden.
(21) If they shared the money equally, how much money did they each receive?

8. Round 234 to the nearest ten.
(34)

9. Use digits to write twenty-five thousand, three
(7) hundred.

10. Draw a circle. Shade five sixths of it. What percent of
(47, 40) the circle is not shaded?

11. $5\dfrac{2}{8} + 6 + \dfrac{3}{8}$ **12.** $8\dfrac{5}{6} - \left(3\dfrac{5}{6} - 3\right)$
(47)   (24)

13. $342 + 5874 + 63 + 285 + 8 + 96 + 87$
(6)

14. $\$42.01 - \$20.14$ **15.** $1000 - M = 1$
(13)   (14)

16. 800×50 **17.** $30 \times 8 \times 25$
(30)   (18)

18. $1205 \div 6$ **19.** $\$76.32 \div 8$
(35)   (26)

20. $\$20 - (\$12 + \$4.76 + \$2.89 + \$0.34)$
(24)

21. Use words to name the number 150,000.
(7)

22. What are the next three numbers in this sequence?
(1)
        ..., 900, 1000, 1100, _____, _____, _____, ...

23. Which place does the zero hold in 203,456?
(7)

24. To what number on the number line is the arrow
(28) pointing?

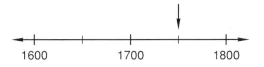

25. According to this calendar, what
(27) was the date of the first Sunday in
December 1941?

NOVEMBER 1941						
S	M	T	W	T	F	S
						1
2	3	4	5	6	7	8
9	10	11	12	13	14	15
16	17	18	19	20	21	22
23	24	25	26	27	28	29
30						

LESSON 56

Making Equal Groups to Find an Average

Facts Practice: 64 Multiplication Facts (Test D in Test Masters)

Mental Math: Count up and down by 3's between 3 and 36. A yard is 3 feet. How many feet are 2 yards? 5 yards? 10 yards?

a. Round 646 to the nearest hundred. **b.** 870 + 130

c. $1\frac{1}{2} + 1\frac{1}{2}$ **d.** $3\frac{1}{3} - 2$ **e.** $\frac{1}{3}$ of 15

f. 25% of 16   **g.** 10% of 50   **h.** 8 × 34

i. 6 × 5, + 3, ÷ 3, + 4, ÷ 3, + 1, ÷ 3

Problem Solving: Enrique rolled two number cubes. The total was 7. Copy this table and write all the ways Enrique could have rolled 7.

First Cube	Second Cube

Here are two stacks of nickels. In one stack there are 5 nickels and in the other stack there are 9 nickels. If some nickels were moved from the taller stack to the shorter stack so that the stacks were even, how many nickels would be in each stack?

One way to answer this question is to **find the total** number of nickels, and then divide the total into two **equal groups.** Since there are 5 nickels in one stack and 9 nickels in the other stack, there are 14 nickels in all. Dividing 14 nickels into 2 equal groups, we find that there would be 7 nickels in each stack.

When we even up the number of members in groups, we are finding the **average** number of members in the groups. Finding an average is a two-step problem.

Example If water is poured from glass to glass until the amount of water in each of these glasses is the same, how many ounces of water will be in each glass?

4 ounces   7 ounces   7 ounces

Solution The **total amount** of water will be **divided equally** in the three glasses. Finding the total amount of water is a "some and some more" problem. Adding, we find the total amount of water is 18 ounces. Finding the amount for each glass is an "equal groups" problem. We divide 18 ounces by 3 and find that **there will be 6 ounces of water in each glass.**

SOME AND SOME MORE	EQUAL GROUPS
4 ounces	
7 ounces	6 ounces in each glass
+ 7 ounces	× 3 glasses
18 ounces ⟶	18 ounces in all 3 glasses

Practice Each of these two-step problems is a "some and some more" and "equal groups" problem:

  a. The number of players on the four squads was 5, 6, 9, and 8, respectively. If the squads were changed so that there were the same number of players on each squad, how many players would each squad have?

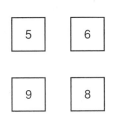

  b. When the class lined up, there were 11 students in one line and 17 students in the other line. If the lines were made even, how many students would be in each line?

  c. This picture shows three stacks of books. If the stacks were made even, how many books would be in each of the three stacks?

**Problem set
56**

1. Draw a quadrilateral so that the sides that intersect are
   (39) perpendicular.

2. Kim is 5 years older than Thi. Miguel is 2 years older
   (55) than Thi. Miguel is 13 years old. How old is Kim?
   Draw two sets of towers to show the two "larger-
   smaller-difference" stories.

3. If water is poured from glass to glass until the amount
   (56) of water in each glass is the same, how many ounces
   of water will be in each glass? (The first part is "some
   and some more" to find the total amount of water. The
   second part is "equal groups" to divide the total
   equally.)

5 ounces   8 ounces   8 ounces

4. Draw a sketch to illustrate this fraction question:
   (50)
   How many minutes is $\frac{3}{5}$ of an hour?

5. How many minutes are in 2 hours, 15 minutes?
   (52)

6. Four hundred years is how many centuries?
   (27)

7. Use digits to write fifty-four thousand, nine hundred
   (7) nineteen.

8. Draw a rectangle. Shade seven eighths of it. What
   (47) percent of the rectangle is not shaded?

9. At first there were 15 children in one line and 11
   (56) children in another line. Then some children moved
   from the longer line to the shorter line so that there
   were the same number of children in each line. Then
   how many children were in each line?

10. 342 + 67 + 918 + 897 + 42
(6)

11. $53.87 − $27.59
(13)

12. $34.28 × 60
(30)

13. 7 × 57 × 10
(18)

14. (4 + 7 + 7) ÷ 3
(24)

15. (5 + 6 + 9 + 8) ÷ 4
(24)

16. 4206 ÷ 7
(35)

17. $60.24 ÷ 6
(35)

18. 1000 ÷ 9
(26)

19. 6 × D = 18
(18)

20. $1\dfrac{1}{7} + 2\dfrac{2}{7} + 3\dfrac{3}{7}$
(44)

21. $9\dfrac{9}{10} - \left(7\dfrac{7}{10} - 5\dfrac{5}{10}\right)$
(24)

22. What month is 10 months after July?
(27)

23. Counting by hundreds, 1236 is closest to which of the
(34)   following numbers?

A. 1100   B. 1200   C. 1300   D. 1000

Read this information. Then answer questions 24 and 25.
Sketching a map may help.

> *From Sara's house, Arcadia Park is 4 miles north,
> Legg Lake is 5 miles south, the ocean is 32 miles
> west, and the mountain cabin is 98 miles east.*

24. Sara's family went to the ocean one Saturday. They
(54)   left home at 9 a.m. and returned home at 4 p.m.
Altogether, how far did they travel in going to the
ocean and back home?

25. How far is it from Arcadia Park to Legg Lake?
(54)

LESSON
57

Multiplying by Two-Digit Numbers

Facts Practice: 48 Uneven Divisions (Test G in Test Masters)

Mental Math: Count by 12's from 12 to 120. A foot is 12 inches. How many inches are 2 feet? 3 feet? 4 feet?

a. 2 feet, 2 inches is how many inches?   **b.** 650 − 250
c. $\frac{3}{4} + \frac{1}{4}$ **d.** $3\frac{1}{4} - 1\frac{1}{4}$ **e.** Half of 25
f. 25% of 24   **g.** 10% of 20   **h.** 8 × 34
i. Find $\frac{1}{2}$ of 20, + 2, ÷ 2, + 2, ÷ 2, + 2, ÷ 2

Problem Solving: The numbers 3, 6, and 10 may be called triangle numbers because 3, 6, and 10 objects can be arranged in a triangular pattern. What are the next three triangle numbers?

When we multiply by two digits, we really multiply twice. We multiply by the tens' digit, and we multiply by the ones' digit. Here we multiply 43 by 12. Since 12 is 10 + 2, we may multiply 43 by 2 and 43 by 10. Then we add the products.

$$
\begin{array}{c}
43 \\
\times\ 12 \\
\hline
\end{array}
\quad \text{is the same as} \quad
\begin{array}{c}
43 \\
\times\ 2 \\
\hline
86
\end{array}
\quad \text{plus} \quad
\begin{array}{c}
43 \\
\times\ 10 \\
\hline
430
\end{array}
= 516
$$

When we multiply by a two-digit number, we do not need to separate the problem into two problems before we start.

Example 1   Multiply: $\begin{array}{c} 43 \\ \times\ 12 \\ \hline \end{array}$

Solution   First we multiply 43 by the 2 of 12.

$$
\begin{array}{c}
43 \\
\times\ 12 \\
\hline
86
\end{array}
$$

We get 86, and we write the 86 so the 6 is in the ones' column under the 2. Next, we multiply 43 by the 10 of 12.

We get 430, which we write below the 86. Then we add 86 and 430 and find that 43 × 12 equals **516.** The numbers 86 and 430 are called *partial products.* The number 516 is the final product.

$$
\begin{array}{r}
43 \\
\times\,12 \\
\hline
86 \\
430 \\
\hline
516
\end{array}
\qquad \text{or} \qquad
\begin{array}{r}
43 \\
\times\,12 \\
\hline
86 \\
43 \\
\hline
516
\end{array}
\quad \longleftarrow \text{ The zero may be omitted.}
$$

Note: Some people do not write the 0 of 430 when they multiply. After multiplying by the 2 of 12, they move to the left one place and multiply by the 1 of 12. This reminds them to begin writing the product one place to the left. The 43 means 43 tens.

Example 2   Multiply: $0.35
  ×   25

Solution   We ignore the dollar sign and decimal point until we have a final product.

$$
\begin{array}{r}
\$0.35 \\
\times\quad 25 \\
\hline
1\,75 \\
7\,00 \\
\hline
\$8.75
\end{array}
\qquad \text{or} \qquad
\begin{array}{r}
\$0.35 \\
\times\quad 25 \\
\hline
1\,75 \\
7\,0 \\
\hline
\$8.75
\end{array}
$$

After multiplying, we place the decimal point. Since we multiplied cents, we show cents in the final product by placing the decimal point so that there are two digits to the right of the decimal point. We get an answer of **$8.75.**

Practice*   **a.**   32
              × 12

b. $0.62
        ×   23

c.   48
        × 64

d.   246
        × 22

e. $1.47
        ×   34

f.   87
        × 63

Problem set
57

1. Jayne is reading a 320-page book. She read 47 pages
(55) the first day, 76 pages the second day, and 68 pages
the third day. How many more pages does she have to
read?

2. To mail the letter Shannon used one 32-cent stamp
(11) and three 21-cent stamps. How many cents did it cost
to mail the letter?

3. Draw a diagram to illustrate this fraction story:
(50)

> John ate $\frac{3}{4}$ of the 60 raisins. How many raisins
> did he eat? What percent of the raisins did he
> eat?

4. Write $(1 \times 1000) + (1 \times 1)$ in standard form.
(53)

5. Compare: $\frac{1}{2}$ of $10 \bigcirc \frac{1}{3}$ of 12
(4)

6. Use words to name 1760.
(7)

7. Draw a circle. Shade all but one sixth of it. What
(47) percent of the circle is not shaded?

8. Use digits to write sixty-two thousand, four hundred
(7) ninety.

9. Counting by hundreds, 2376 is closest to which
(34) number?

   A. 2200   B. 2300   C. 2400   D. 2000

10. How long is the line segment?
(49)

11. Here are two stacks of coins. If some coins were taken
(56) from the taller stack and added to the shorter stack
until the stacks were even, how many coins would be
in each stack?

12.   43   **13.** $0.72   **14.**   248   **15.** $1.96
(57) × 12   *(57)* ×   31   *(57)* ×   24   *(57)* ×   53

16.   8762   **17.** $10.00 **18.**   600   **19.** $6.00
(6)   3624   *(13)* − $9.92 *(30)* ×   50   *(26)* ─────
          4795   8
        + 8473

20. $41.36 ÷ 4   **21.** 4275 ÷ 9
(35)   *(26)*

22. $3 + \dfrac{1}{4} + 2\dfrac{2}{4}$ **23.** $\left(5\dfrac{5}{8} - 3\dfrac{3}{8}\right) - 1\dfrac{1}{8}$
(47)   *(24)*

24. $(1 + 2 + 3 + 4 + 5) ÷ 5$
(24)

25. In the running long jump, Cynthia jumped 16 feet, 9
(52) inches. How many inches did she jump? (1 foot = 12
inches)

LESSON 58

Identifying Place Value Through Hundred-Millions'

Facts Practice: 64 Multiplication Facts (Test D in Test Masters)

Mental Math: Count by 6's from 6 to 60. Count by 60's from 60 to 300. A minute is 60 seconds. How many seconds are in 2 minutes? 3 minutes?

a. 2 minutes, 10 seconds is how many seconds?
b. $1.00 − $0.25   **c.** 50% of a minute   **d.** $1\frac{1}{8} + \frac{7}{8}$
e. 25% of a minute   **f.** 10% of a minute
g. $6 \times 6, -6, \div 6, +5, \div 5, \times 7, +1, \div 3$

Problem Solving: One man said of another man, "Brothers and sisters I have none, but that man's father is my mother's son." What was the relationship between the two men?

The table below shows the value of the first nine whole-number places.

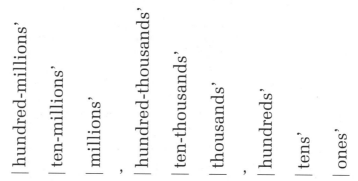

Drawing the place value chart another way emphasizes the repeating pattern of place values.

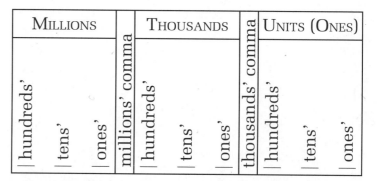

We see that the repeating pattern of **ones, tens, hundreds** continues through the thousands and millions.

Example 1 Which digit shows the number of hundred millions in 987,654,321?

Solution Moving from right to left, the pattern of ones, tens, hundreds continues through the thousands and millions. The digit in the hundred-millions' place is **9.**

Example 2 In the number 12,345,678 the 2 means what?

A. 2,000,000   B. 2000   C. 2

Solution The value of a digit depends upon its place in the number. Here the 2 means two **million.** The correct choice is **A.**

Practice* In problems (a)–(d) name the value of the place held by the zero in each number:

a. 345,052

b. 20,315,682

c. 1,057,628

d. 405,176,284

e. Which digit is in the ten-millions' place in 675,283,419?

f. In which of the following numbers does the 7 have a value of seventy thousand?

A. 370,123,429   B. 1,372,486   C. 4,703,241

g. Write the value of the 1 in 321,987,654.

Problem set 58

1. Debbie baked 5 dozen cookies and gave 24 to a friend. How many cookies did she have left?
(55)

2. Marco weighs 120 pounds. His little brother weighs one half as much. How much does his brother weigh?
(23)

3. On a map, north is usually toward the top. What direction is usually to the right side of the map?
(51)

4. From the year 1492 to the year 1992 is how many centuries?
(27)

5. Write the standard form for $(1 \times 100) + (4 \times 10) +$
(53) (8×1).

6. Draw a rectangle that is 2 inches long and 1 inch wide.
(47) Shade all but three eighths of it. What percent of the
rectangle is not shaded?

7. Use words to name 250,000.
(7)

8. This picture shows three stacks of
(56) books. If the stacks were made
even, how many books would
there be in each stack?

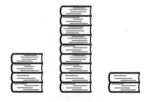

9. Which digit shows the number of hundred millions in
(58) 789,456,321?

10. Round 1236 to the nearest hundred.
(34)

11. Name the value of the place held by the zero in
(58) 102,345,678.

12.   57   **13.** $0.83   **14.**   167   **15.** $1.96
(57) $\times 22$ (57) $\times \quad 47$ (57) $\times \quad 89$ (57) $\times \quad 46$

16.   8437   **17.** $26.38   **18.**   3041
(6)   3429   (13) $- \$19.57$ (14) $- \quad W$
     5765   2975
  $+ 9841$

19. $\dfrac{4328}{4}$ **20.** $\dfrac{5670}{10}$ **21.** $\dfrac{\$78.40}{4}$
(35)   (26)   (35)

22. $\dfrac{3}{10} + 2 + 1\dfrac{4}{10}$ **23.** $5\dfrac{3}{4} - \left(2\dfrac{3}{4} - 2\right)$
(47)   (24)

24. $\$10 - (\$1.43 + \$2 + \$2.85 + \$0.79)$
(24)

25. Which arrow could be pointing to $3\frac{9}{10}$ on this number
(41) line?

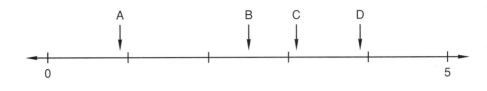

LESSON 59

Naming Numbers Through Hundred Millions

Facts Practice: 48 Uneven Divisions (Test G in Test Masters)

Mental Math: Count by 12's from 12 to 120. Count by 24's from 24 to 120. A day is 24 hours. How many hours are 2 days? 3 days?

a. 5 feet, 2 inches is how many inches?

b. $\frac{5}{8} + \frac{3}{8}$ **c.** $2\frac{3}{10} - 1\frac{2}{10}$ **d.** 9×34

e. How many hours is 50% of a day? 25% of a day?

f. $10 \times 10, -1, \div 9, \times 4, +1, \div 9, +4, \div 9$

Problem Solving: Copy this multiplication problem and fill in the missing digits.

$$\begin{array}{r} 6\_ \\ \times \quad\_ \\ \hline 5\_7 \end{array}$$

We have practiced naming whole numbers that have up to six digits. In this lesson we begin naming numbers that have up to nine digits. Again, we will use commas to help us name numbers.

To place commas, we count digits from the right-hand side of the whole number and write a comma after every three digits.

$$87{,}654{,}321$$

This places a comma after the millions' place and after the thousands' place. When reading a number with two commas, we say "million" when we come to the first comma and "thousand" when we come to the second comma.

$$8\ 7\ ,\ 6\ 5\ 4\ ,\ 3\ 2\ 1$$

"million"   "thousand"

Using words, we name this number:

Eighty-seven million, six hundred fifty-four thousand, three hundred twenty-one

Example 1   Use words to name 1345200.

Solution   We first put the commas in the number: 1,345,200. Then we name the number as **one million, three hundred forty-five thousand, two hundred.**

Example 2   Use digits to write one hundred thirty-four million, six hundred fifty-two thousand, seven hundred.

Solution   **134,652,700**

Practice*   Use words to name each number:

   a. 21462300

   b. 196500000

Use digits to write each number:

   c. Nineteen million, two hundred twenty-five thousand, five hundred

   d. Seven hundred fifty million, three hundred thousand

   e. Two hundred six million, seven hundred twelve thousand, nine hundred thirty-four

Problem set 59

   1. Mark bought a chain for $3.60 and a lock for $4. How
   ⁽⁵⁵⁾ much should he get back in change from a $10 bill?

   2. Draw a quadrilateral using two pairs of parallel line
   ⁽³⁹⁾ segments.

3. Draw a picture to illustrate this fraction story:
(50)

> *If $\frac{1}{3}$ of the 30 students earned A's on the test, how many students earned A's? What percent of the students earned A's?*

4. Use words to name 51698502.
(59)

5. In the number 123,456,789, the 2 means which of the
(58) following?

A. 2 million   B. 20 million   C. 200 million

6. Use digits to write two hundred forty-six million, six
(59) hundred fifty-two thousand, nine hundred.

7. Write the standard form for the following:
(53)

$(8 \times 1000) + (4 \times 100) + (6 \times 10) + (3 \times 1)$

8. Round 2376 to the nearest hundred.
(34)

9. It is 8 blocks from Beverlee's house to school. How
(55) many blocks does she ride her bike traveling to school and back for 5 days?

10. If water is poured from glass to glass until the amount
(56) of water in each glass is the same, how many ounces of water will be in each glass?

3 ounces   5 ounces   7 ounces

11. $3\frac{5}{8} + \left(2\frac{3}{8} - 1\frac{3}{8}\right)$ **12.** $3\frac{7}{8} - \left(2\frac{3}{8} + 1\frac{3}{8}\right)$
(24)   (24)

13.   382   **14.** $6.71   **15.**   790
(57) $\times$ 35   (57) $\times$ 73   (57) $\times$ 84

16. 8956
(6)   3428
      5916
    + 4684

17. $63.15
(13) − $41.26

18. M
(14)   − 173
         6837

19. 6)5405
(35)

20. 8)$76.56
(26)

21. 3)6000
(35)

22. What are the next three numbers in this sequence?
(1)   ..., 1210, 1220, 1230, _____, _____, _____, ...

23. Use words to name the mixed number $5\frac{3}{8}$.
(43)

24. From Marty's home to school and back is 5 miles. How
(47) far is it from Marty's home to school?

25. If it is evening now, what time
(29) will be shown by this clock in $3\frac{1}{2}$
      hours?

LESSON
60

Calculating the Perimeter of Polygons • Identifying the Measures of Circles

Facts Practice: 64 Multiplication Facts (Test D in Test Masters)

Mental Math: Count by 6's from 6 to 60. Count by 60's from 60 to 360. How many minutes are 2 hours? 3 hours? 4 hours? 10 hours?

a. 2 hours and 15 minutes is how many minutes?
b. $2000 - 500$ **c.** $2\frac{1}{2} + 2\frac{1}{2}$ **d.** $2\frac{1}{2} - 2\frac{1}{2}$
e. How many minutes is $1\frac{1}{2}$ hours? $2\frac{1}{2}$ hours?
f. Find half of 100, ÷ 2, ÷ 5, ÷ 5, × 10, ÷ 5

Problem Solving: The numbers 3, 6, 10, and 15 are triangle numbers. The numbers 4, 9, 16, and 25 are square numbers. Find a two-digit number that is both a triangle number and a square number.

Calculating the perimeter of polygons

When line segments close in an area, a polygon is formed. We can calculate the distance around a polygon. Since each of the line segments which form a polygon has a length, we can add these lengths together to find the distance around the polygon. The distance around a polygon is called the **perimeter.** We can find the perimeter of a polygon by adding the lengths of its sides.

We should note that the word *length* has more than one meaning. We have used length to mean the measure of a segment. But length may also mean the longer dimension of a rectangle. We use *width* to mean the shorter dimension of a rectangle.

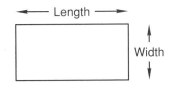

Example   What is the perimeter of this rectangle?

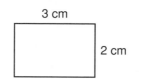

Solution   We see a rectangle with a length of 3 cm and a width of 2 cm. We are asked to find its perimeter. The perimeter is the distance around it. The four sides measure 2 cm, 3 cm, 2 cm, and 3 cm, respectively. We add these together and find that the perimeter is **10 cm.**

$$2 \text{ cm} + 3 \text{ cm} + 2 \text{ cm} + 3 \text{ cm} = 10 \text{ cm}$$

Identifying the measures of circles   A circle is a smooth curve. The length of the curve is its **circumference.** So the perimeter of a circle is called the circumference. The **center** is the "middle point" enclosed by the circle. The **radius** is the distance from the center to the curve. The **diameter** is the distance across the circle through the center. Thus **the diameter of a circle is twice the radius.**

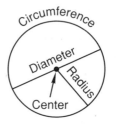

Practice   **a.** What is the *length* of this rectangle?

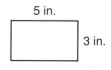

b. What is the *width* of this rectangle?

c. What is the perimeter of this rectangle?

d. What is the perimeter of this triangle?

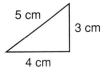

5 cm   3 cm   4 cm

e. What do we call the perimeter of a circle?

f. What do we call the distance across a circle?

g. If the radius of a circle is 6 inches, what is the diameter of the circle?

h. What is the perimeter of this square?

4 ft

Note: The drawings in this lesson and in the problem sets may not be the actual size indicated by the units used in the problem. In most cases the drawings will be smaller than the size indicated so that the drawings will fit on the page.

Problem set 60

1. Atop the beanstalk Jack was excited to discover that
(55) the goose had laid 3 dozen golden eggs. Jack took 15 eggs. How many golden eggs were left for the giant?

2. There are 13 players on one team and 9 players on the
(56) other team. If some of the players from one team join the other team so that there are the same number of players on each team, how many players will be on each team?

3. Name the value of the place held by the zero in
(58) 420,375,861.

4. From November 1 of one year to September 1 of the
(27) next year is how many months?

5. Draw a rectangle that is 3 inches long and 1 inch wide.
(47) Shade three sixths of it. What percent of the rectangle is shaded?

6. Which factors of 8 are also factors of 12?
(25)

7. From the year 1820 to 1890 was how many decades?
(27)

8. Use digits to write nineteen million, four hundred ninety thousand.
(59)

9. $6 + \left(4\frac{2}{3} - 2 \right)$ **10.** $4\frac{2}{3} - \left(2\frac{2}{3} + 2 \right)$
(24)   (24)

11. 300×200 **12.** 800×70 **13.** $50 \times T = 500$
(30)   (30)   (18)

14. $5.64   **15.**   865   **16.**   983
(57) $\times$ 78   (57) $\times$ 74   (57) $\times$ 76

17. $63.14   **18.**   3106   **19.** $68.09
(13) $-$ $42.87   (9) $-$ 875   (13) $43.56
                                                    $27.18
                                                  $+$ $14.97

20. $\dfrac{\$31.65}{5}$ **21.** $\dfrac{4218}{6}$ **22.** $5361 \div 10$
(26)   (35)   (26)

23. Counting by tens, 1236 is closest to which number?
(34)   A. 1230   B. 1240   C. 1200   D. 1300

24. What is the **length** of this rectangle?
(60)

2 cm

3 cm

25. What is the **perimeter** of this rectangle?
(60)

**LESSON
61**

Dividing by Multiples of 10

Facts Practice: 48 Uneven Divisions (Test G in Test Masters)

Mental Math: In Roman numerals, an X is ten and an I is one. When Roman numerals are arranged in order from largest to smallest, we add the values of the numerals. Find the value of the following:

    a. XII   **b.** XXI   **c.** XXIII   **d.** XXXIII

Problem Solving: Thirty-six dots are arranged in a square array of rows and columns. How many dots are in each row?

In this lesson we will begin to divide by two-digit numbers that are multiples of 10. We will divide by numbers such as 10, 20, 30, 40, 50, and so on. In later lessons we will practice dividing by other two-digit numbers.

We will continue to follow the four steps of the division algorithm: divide, multiply, subtract, and bring down. The divide step is more difficult when dividing by two-digit numbers because we have not memorized two-digit multiplication facts. To help us divide by a two-digit number, we may think of dividing by the first digit only.

To help us divide this, $\longrightarrow$ $30\overline{)75}$

we may think this: $\longrightarrow$ $3\overline{)7}$

We use the answer to the easier division for the answer to the more difficult division. Since $3\overline{)7}$ is 2, we use 2 as the division answer. We complete the division by doing the multiply and subtract steps.

$$\begin{array}{r} 2 \text{ r } 15 \\ 30\overline{)75} \\ -60 \\ \hline 15 \end{array}$$

Notice where we placed the 2 in our division answer.

$$30\overline{)7\overset{2}{5}}$$ A 2 above the 7 means there are two 30s in 7! **Incorrect!**

$$30\overline{)75}\overset{\;\;2}{}$$ The 2 above the 5 means there are two 30s in 75! This is the correct place.

It is important to place the digits in the quotient properly.

Example 1 $30\overline{)454}$

Solution   We follow the four steps: divide, multiply, subtract, and bring down. We begin by dividing $30\overline{)45}$. If we are unsure, we may think $3\overline{)4}$ to help us with the divide step. We divide and write "1" above the 5 of 454. Then we multiply, subtract, and bring down. Since we brought down a digit, we divide again. This time we divide $30\overline{)154}$. To help us divide **we may mentally remove the last digit from each number** and think $3\overline{)15}$.

$$
\begin{array}{r}
15\ \text{r}\ 4 \\
30\overline{)454} \\
-\ 30 \\
\hline
154 \\
-\ 150 \\
\hline
4
\end{array}
$$

Example 2 $20\overline{)\$4.60}$

Solution   When dividing money by a whole number, we place the decimal point in the answer directly above the decimal point in the division box. Then we ignore the decimal points and divide just as we would divide whole numbers. The answer is **$0.23.**

$$
\begin{array}{r}
\$\ .23 \\
20\overline{)\$4.60} \\
4\ 0 \\
\hline
60 \\
60 \\
\hline
0
\end{array}
$$

Practice*   **a.** $30\overline{)\$4.20}$ **b.** $60\overline{)725}$

     c. $40\overline{)\$4.80}$ **d.** $20\overline{)\$3.20}$

     e. $50\overline{)610}$ **f.** $10\overline{)345}$

Problem set 61

1. Betty went to the store with $5.25. She bought a box of cereal for $3.18 and a half gallon of milk for $1.02. How much money did Betty have left?
(55)

2. A yard is 36 inches. How many inches is $\frac{2}{3}$ of a yard? Draw a diagram to illustrate the problem.
(50)

3. Round 1236 to the nearest ten.
(34)

4. The 7 in 987,654,321 means which of the following?
(58)
  A. 700   B. 7,000,000   C. 700,000

5. Draw two circles. Shade $\frac{1}{2}$ of one and $\frac{2}{4}$ of the other.
(40) What percent of a circle is $\frac{2}{4}$ of a circle?

6. (a) How many cents is $\frac{1}{4}$ of a dollar?
(37)
  (b) How many cents is $\frac{2}{4}$ of a dollar?

7. Use words to name 3,150,000.
(59)

8. Which factors of 9 are also factors of 12?
(25)

9. $30\overline{)454}$ **10.** $40\overline{)\$5.60}$
(61)   (61)

11. $50\overline{)760}$ **12.** 500×400
(61)   (30)

13. 563×46 **14.** $68 \times \$4.32$
(57)   (57)

15. $25\frac{1}{4} + 8\frac{2}{4}$ **16.** $36\frac{2}{3} - 17\frac{2}{3}$
(44)   (44)

17. $2947 \div 8$ **18.** $7564 \div (90 \div 10)$
(26)   (24)

19.   12,345   **20.** $3.65
(9) $-\ 6,789$ (13) $2.47
                                   $4.83
                                 $+ \$2.79$

21. Thirty-six children were seated at tables with four
(21) children at each table. How many tables with children
   were there?

22. What is the perimeter of this
(60) triangle?

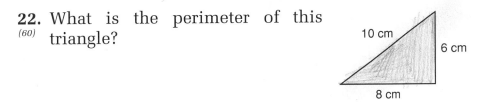
10 cm
6 cm
8 cm

23. What is the length of the rectangle?
(49)

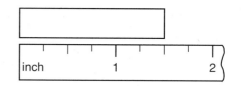

24. What year was five decades after 1896?
(27)

25. If the diameter of this circle is 30 millimeters, then what is the radius of the circle?
(60)

30 mm

LESSON 62

Multiplying by Three-Digit Numbers, Part 1

Facts Practice: 64 Multiplication Facts (Test D in Test Masters)

Mental Math: In Roman numerals, X is ten, V is five, and I is one. Find the value of the following:

  a. VII   **b.** XV   **c.** XVI   **d.** XXVIII

  e. Five feet four inches is how many inches?

  f. $1\frac{1}{2} + 1\frac{1}{2}$ **g.** 25% of 40

  h. $6 \times 8, + 1, \div 7, + 2, \div 3, + 1, \div 2$

Problem Solving: Two figures are **congruent** if they are the same shape and size. Draw a triangle that is congruent to this triangle.

When we multiply by a three-digit number, we actually multiply three times. We multiply by the number of hundreds, we multiply by the number of tens, and we multiply by the number of ones.

$$
\begin{array}{ccccccc}
234 & & 234 & & 234 & & 234 \\
\times\,123 & = & \times\,100 & \text{plus} & \times\,20 & \text{plus} & \times\,3 \\
\hline
& & 23{,}400 & + & 4680 & + & 702 = 28{,}782
\end{array}
$$

We do not need to separate a three-digit multiplication problem into three problems before we start. We may do all the multiplication within the same problem.

Example Multiply:
$$\begin{array}{r} 234 \\ \times\ 123 \\ \hline \end{array}$$

Solution
$$\begin{array}{r} 234 \\ \times\ 123 \\ \hline 702 \\ 4680 \\ 23400 \\ \hline 28782 \end{array}$$
702 ← We first multiply 234 by the 3 of 123.
4680 ← Then we multiply by the 20 of 123. ⎫
23400 ← Then we multiply by the 100 of 123. ⎬ The zeros need not be written.
28782 ← We add the three partial products to find the total product.

We place the thousands' comma and get an answer of **28,782.**

The multiplication problems in the problem sets are designed to provide frequent practice on basic multiplication combinations. Three-by-three multiplication provides valuable practice with basic facts in a convenient, compact form.

Practice Find each product:

a. $\begin{array}{r} 346 \\ \times\ 354 \\ \hline \end{array}$
b. $\begin{array}{r} 487 \\ \times\ 634 \\ \hline \end{array}$
c. $\begin{array}{r} 403 \\ \times\ 768 \\ \hline \end{array}$
d. $\begin{array}{r} 705 \\ \times\ 678 \\ \hline \end{array}$

Problem set 62

1. Carlos bought a hamburger for $1.65 and a drink for $0.70. He paid for the food with a $5 bill. How much should he get back in change?
(55)

2. Draw a diagram to illustrate this fraction story:
(50)

> There are 276 pages in the book. If Martin has read three fourths of the book, how many pages has he read?

3. Martin's 276-page book is 26 pages shorter than Jaime's book. How many pages long is Jaime's book?
(36)

4. Which digit in 98,765,432 is in the ten-millions'
(58) place?

5. Amanda can jump across a rug that is 2 yards, 3 inches
(52) long. How many inches is 2 yards, 3 inches? (A yard is
36 inches.)

6. Draw a circle. Shade all but one third of it. What
(47) percent of the circle is shaded?

7. Use digits to write six hundred seventy-nine million,
(59) five hundred forty-two thousand, five hundred.

8. $60\overline{)\$7.20}$ **9.** $70\overline{)850}$ **10.** $80\overline{)980}$
(61)   (61)   (61)

11.   234   **12.** $3.75   **13.**   604
(62) × 123   (57) ×   26   (62) × 789

14. Each side of this square is 10 mm
(60) long. What is the perimeter of this
square?   10 mm

Use mental math to answer questions 15–20:

15. 400 × 800   **16.** 60 × 500   **17.** 900 × 90
(30)   (30)   (30)

18.   300   **19.**   6000   **20.** $\dfrac{400}{20}$
(6)   400   (9)   − 2000   (61)
    + 500

21. $6\dfrac{5}{11} + 5\dfrac{4}{11}$ **22.** $3\dfrac{2}{3} - 3$ **23.** $7\dfrac{2}{3} - \left(3\dfrac{1}{3} - 3\right)$
(44)   (47)   (24)

Read this information. Then answer questions 24 and 25.

*The Arroyo High School stadium can seat 3000
fans. Two thousand, one hundred fifty fans came
to the first game. Arroyo won by a score of 35 to
28. Tickets to watch the game cost $2 each.*

24. Altogether, how much money was paid by the fans
(54) who came to the first game?

25. At the second game all but 227 seats were filled with
(54) fans. How many fans came to the second game?

**LESSON
63**

Multiplying by Three-Digit Numbers, Part 2

Facts Practice: 48 Uneven Divisions (Test G in Test Masters)

Mental Math:

  a. XVIII   **b.** XXV   **c.** XXXI   **d.** XXXVII
  e. How much is 600 divided by 10? $600 \div 20$? $600 \div 30$?
  f. 7×42 **g.** 50% of 42
  h. $6 \times 8, + 6, \div 9, \times 7, - 7, \div 5$

Problem Solving: Copy this multiplication problem and fill in the missing digits.

$$\begin{array}{r} 3\_ \\ \times \ \_ \\ \hline 333 \end{array}$$

When we multiply by a three-digit number that has a zero as one of its digits, we may find the product by doing two multiplications instead of three.

Example 1   Multiply: 243×120

Solution   When we multiply by a number that ends with a zero, we may write the problem so that the zero "hangs out" to the right.

$$\begin{array}{r} 243 \\ \times \ 120 \\ \hline 4860 \\ 24300 \\ \hline 29160 \end{array}$$

4860 ← We multiply by the 20 of 120.

24300 ← Then we multiply by the 100 of 120.

29160 ← We add the two partial products to find the total product.

We place the thousands' comma and get an answer of **29,160.**

Example 2   Multiply: 243 × 102

Solution   We may write the two factors in either order. Sometimes one order is easier than the other order. On the left we multiplied three times. On the right we used a shortcut and multiplied twice. Either way the product is **24,786.**

$$
\begin{array}{r}
102 \\
\times\,243 \\
\hline
306 \\
408 \\
204 \\
\hline
24786 \\
\end{array}
\qquad\qquad
\begin{array}{r}
243 \\
\times\,102 \\
\hline
486 \\
2430 \\
\hline
24786 \\
\end{array}
$$

On the right we used a shortcut. If we had not, then we would have written a row of zeros.

$$
\begin{array}{r}
243 \\
\times\,102 \\
\hline
486 \\
000 \\
243 \\
\hline
24786 \\
\end{array}
$$

← zero in bottom factor

← row of zeros

To use this pencil-and-paper shortcut, we write the number with the zero as the bottom factor.

Example 3 $3.25 × 120

Solution   We ignore the dollar sign and decimal point until we have finished multiplying. We place the dollar sign and decimal point in the final product to get **$390.00.**

$$
\begin{array}{r}
\$3.25 \\
\times\quad 120 \\
\hline
65\,00 \\
325 \\
\hline
\$390.00 \\
\end{array}
$$

Practice*

a.   234
      × 240

b. $1.25
      ×   240

c.   230
      × 120

d.   304
      × 120

e.   234
      × 204

f. $1.25
      ×   204

g.   230
      × 102

h.   304
      × 102

Problem set 63

1. Diana and her sister want to buy a radio for $30. Diana
(55) has $12, and her sister has $7. How much more money
do they need?

2. How many seconds equal three sixths of a minute?
(50) Draw a diagram to illustrate the problem.

3. The Smiths traveled from San Francisco to
(51) Washington, D.C. In what direction did they travel?

4. When the students got on the buses to go to the picnic,
(56) there were 36 on one bus, 29 on another bus, and 73
on the third bus. If students are moved so that there
are the same number on each bus, how many students
will be on each bus?

5. Which digit is in the ten-thousands' place in
(58) 123,456,789?

6. The radius of this circle is 5
(60) inches. What is the diameter of
the circle?

5 in.

7. Use digits to write the number three hundred forty-
(59) five million, six hundred fourteen thousand, seven
hundred eighty-four.

8. What is the perimeter of this
(60) rectangle?

20 mm

10 mm

9. 900 × 40
(30)

10. 700 × 400
(30)

11. 234 × 320
(63)

12. $3.45 × 203
(63)

13. 468 × 386
(62)

14. $W ÷ 5 = 6$
(19)

15. 4317 ÷ 6
(26)

16. 2703 ÷ 9
(35)

17. $86.08 ÷ 8
(35)

18. 79,089
(6)   37,865
        29,453
      + 16,257

19. 43,218
(9)   − 32,461

20. $100.00
(13) −   4.56

21. $3\dfrac{5}{6} - 1\dfrac{5}{6}$
(44)

22. $4\dfrac{1}{8} + 6$
(47)

23. Three weeks and three days is how many days?
(52)

24. Which arrow could be pointing to 1362?
(28)

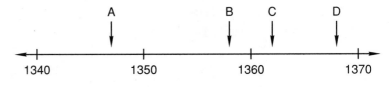

25. Use words to name the mixed number $7\dfrac{1}{10}$.
(43)

**LESSON
64**

Learning the Terms *Divisor, Dividend,* and *Quotient*

Facts Practice: 64 Multiplication Facts (Test D in Test Masters)

Mental Math: In Roman numerals, when an I comes before a V, we subtract one from five. So the value of IV is four. Likewise, when an I comes before an X, we subtract one from ten. So the value of IX is nine. Find the value of the following:

   a. XIX   **b.** XIV   **c.** XXIX   **d.** XXIV

Problem Solving: This is a Roman numeral addition problem. Add the numbers and express the sum as a Roman numeral.

                 XIII + XXII

There are three numbers involved in every division problem:

1. The number which is being divided:
   15 ÷ 3 = 5
2. The number by which it is divided:
   15 ÷ **3** = 5
3. The answer to the division: 15 ÷ 3 = **5**

These numbers are called the **dividend, divisor,** and **quotient.** In the example above, the dividend is 15, the divisor is 3, and the quotient is 5. The location of these numbers in a division problem is shown in the three forms below.

Position of Divisor, Dividend, and Quotient

FORM 1	$\dfrac{\text{quotient}}{\text{divisor }\overline{)\text{dividend}}}$
FORM 2	$\dfrac{\text{dividend}}{\text{divisor}} = \text{quotient}$
FORM 3	dividend ÷ divisor = quotient

If we know two numbers in a division problem, we can figure out the third number. We divide to find either the quotient or divisor. In both of these examples, we divide 30 by 5 to find the missing number.

$$5 \overline{)30} \qquad \overset{5}{?\,\overline{)30}}$$

We multiply to find the dividend. Here we multiply 5×6.

$$\overset{6}{5\,\overline{)?}}$$

Example 1   If 4 is the divisor and 8 is the quotient, what is the dividend?

Solution   We study the form and set up the problem. The missing number is **32.** $\qquad \overset{8}{4\,\overline{)?}}$

Example 2   Which number in this problem is the $\qquad 6 \div 3 = 2$ divisor?

Solution   The divisor is the number that we divide by. The divisor in this problem is **3.**

Practice   a. The divisor is 6; the quotient is 3. What is the dividend?

b. The dividend is 8; the quotient is 2. What is the divisor?

c. The dividend is 15; the divisor is 5. What is the quotient?

In each problem below, tell whether 12 is the divisor, the dividend, or the quotient:

d. $12 \div 4 = 3$ e. $24 \div 2 = 12$ f. $48 \div 12 = 4$

g. $\frac{12}{2} = 6$ h. $\frac{24}{12} = 2$ i. $\frac{36}{3} = 12$

j. $12\overline{)36}$ (3)   k. $6\overline{)12}$ (2)   l. $5\overline{)60}$ (12)

Problem set 64

1. There are 12 inches in a foot. A person 5 feet, 4 inches tall is how many inches tall?
(52)

2. How many years is 10 centuries?
(27)

3. What word is used to name the perimeter of a circle?
(60)

4. Use words to name the mixed number $10\frac{7}{10}$.
(43)

5. How many minutes is two thirds of an hour? Draw a diagram to illustrate the problem.
(50)

6. In the late afternoon, in what direction from an object is its shadow?
(51)

7. If 4 is the divisor and 12 is the quotient, what is the dividend?
(64)

8. What is the value of the place held by the zero in 321,098,765?
(58)

9. Which factors of 15 are also factors of 20?
(25)

10. What is the perimeter of this hexagon if each side is 3 cm long?
(60)

11. $3\frac{2}{3} - \left(2\frac{1}{3} + 1\frac{1}{3}\right)$
(24)

12. $3\frac{1}{3} + \left(2\frac{2}{3} - 1\frac{1}{3}\right)$
(24)

13. $40\overline{)\$5.20}$
(61)

14. $8\overline{)3161}$
(26)

15. Which number in this problem is the divisor?
(64)
$$6 \div 3 = 2$$

16. $43.15
(13) − $28.79

17.   423
(63) × 302

18.   99
(6)   36
       42
       75
       64
       98
     + 17

19. $3.45
(63) ×   360

20.   604
(63) × 598

21. $\dfrac{10}{10} - \dfrac{9}{10}$
(44)

22. $4\dfrac{2}{3} - \dfrac{1}{3}$
(47)

23. $5\dfrac{2}{2} - 1\dfrac{1}{2}$
(44)

24. From May 1 of one year to August 1 of the next year is
(27) how many months?

25. If it is morning, what time will be
(29) shown by this clock in 2 hours
       and 20 minutes?

**LESSON
65**

Dividing and Writing Quotients with Fractions

Facts Practice: 48 Uneven Divisions (Test G in Test Masters)

Mental Math:

   a. XVII   **b.** XXXIV   **c.** XXIII   **d.** XXIV
   e. How much is 800 ÷ 10?   800 ÷ 20?   800 ÷ 40?
   f. 50% of 800   **g.** $3\frac{1}{2} + 3\frac{1}{2}$ **h.** 8×24 **i.** $\frac{1}{3}$ of 24

Problem Solving: Two figures are similar if they are the same shape. These two triangles are similar. Draw a larger triangle that is similar to these two triangles.

Sometimes we need to write the answer to a division problem as a mixed number.

If two children share 5 cookies equally, how many cookies will each receive?

This is a division problem. We divide 5 into 2 equal parts. We find the answer is 2 with a remainder of 1. That is, each child will receive 2 cookies and there will be 1 extra cookie. Can that extra cookie be divided? We can take the extra cookie and divide it into 2 equal parts— halves. Then each child will receive $2\frac{1}{2}$ cookies.

$$\begin{array}{r} 2 \text{ r } 1 \\ 2\overline{)5} \\ \underline{4} \\ 1 \end{array}$$

$$1 \div 2 = \frac{1}{2}$$

To write a remainder as a fraction, we simply make the remainder the numerator of the fraction and make the divisor the denominator of the fraction.

Example 1 Divide and write the quotient with a fraction: $3\overline{)50}$

Solution We divide and find that the remainder is 2. We make the remainder the numerator of the fraction, and we make the divisor the denominator of the fraction. The quotient is **$16\frac{2}{3}$.**

$$\begin{array}{r} 16\frac{2}{3} \\ 3\overline{)50} \\ \underline{3} \\ 20 \\ \underline{18} \\ 2 \end{array}$$

Example 2 A 15-inch string of licorice is cut into 4 equal lengths. How long is each length?

Solution We divide 15 inches by 4 and find that the answer is not a whole number of inches. The answer is more than 3 inches but less than 4 inches. The answer is 3 inches plus a fraction. To find the fraction, we write the remainder as the numerator of the fraction and write the divisor as the denominator of the fraction. We find that the length of each piece of licorice is $3\frac{3}{4}$ **inches.**

$$4)\overline{15} \quad 3\frac{3}{4}$$
$$\underline{12}$$
$$3$$

In the problem sets that follow, we will continue to write division answers with remainders, unless a problem asks that an answer be written with a fraction.

Practice* Divide and write each answer with a fraction:

a. $4)\overline{17}$ **b.** $20 \div 3$ **c.** $\dfrac{16}{5}$

d. $5)\overline{49}$ **e.** $21 \div 4$ **f.** $\dfrac{49}{10}$

g. $6)\overline{77}$ **h.** $43 \div 10$ **i.** $\dfrac{31}{8}$

Problem set 65

1. (55) Martin bought 8 baseball cards for 15 cents each. If he paid $2, how much did he get back in change?

2. (65) Daphne bought a 21-inch-long string of licorice at the candy store. She cut it into 4 equal lengths to share with her friends. How long is each length of licorice?

3. (50) Draw a diagram to illustrate this fraction story:

Sarah used $\frac{3}{5}$ of a sheet of stamps to mail cards. If there are 100 stamps in a whole sheet, then how many stamps did Sarah use? What percent of the stamps did Sarah use?

4. (34) Round 1776 to the nearest hundred.

5. In which of these numbers does the 5 have a value of
(58) 500,000?

A. 186,542,039   B. 347,820,516   C. 584,371,269

6. What is the perimeter of this rectangle?
(60)

12 mm

8 mm

7. $30\overline{)640}$ **8.** $40\overline{)922}$ **9.** $50\overline{)800}$
(61)   (61)   (61)

10.   7200   **11.** $\$1.25 \times 80$ **12.** $700 \div 10$
(9) $-\ 1400$ (30)   (61)

13.   679   **14.**   8104   **15.** $\$2.86$
(62) $\times\ 489$ (9) $-\ 5647$ (13) $\$6.35$
                                                       $\$1.78$
                                                       $\$0.46$

16. $\dfrac{4228}{7}$ **17.** $\dfrac{4635}{9}$ $+\ \$0.62$
(35)   (26)

18. $\dfrac{5}{5} - \dfrac{1}{5}$ **19.** $3\dfrac{1}{3} - \dfrac{1}{3}$ **20.** $4\dfrac{6}{6} - 2\dfrac{5}{6}$
(44)   (47)   (44)

21. Divide and write the quotient with a fraction: $3\overline{)62}$
(65)

22. What is the denominator of the fraction in $6\frac{3}{4}$?
(23)

23. In a division problem, if the divisor is 3 and the
(64) quotient is 9, what is the dividend?

24. What year was five centuries before 1500?
(27)

25. If the radius of this circle is 12
(60) millimeters, then what is the
diameter of the circle?

12 mm

LESSON 66

Fractions Equal to 1 • Subtracting a Fraction from 1

Facts Practice: 64 Multiplication Facts (Test D in Test Masters)

Mental Math:

    a. XXIII   **b.** IV   **c.** XXVIII   **d.** XXIX

    e. How many days are 3 weeks and 3 days?

    f. Half of 101   **g.** 10% of 50

    h. $6 \times 6, -1, \div 7, \times 4, +1, \div 7$

Problem Solving: One hundred dots are arranged in a square array of rows and columns. How many dots are in each column?

Fractions equal to 1

We know that two halves make a whole. Similarly, it takes **three** thirds or **four** fourths or **five** fifths to make one whole.

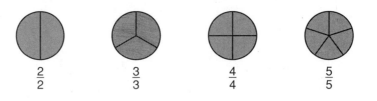

$$\frac{2}{2} \qquad \frac{3}{3} \qquad \frac{4}{4} \qquad \frac{5}{5}$$

We see that each of these is a "whole pie," yet we can use fractions to name each one. Notice that the numerator and the denominator are the same when we name a "whole pie." This is a very important idea in mathematics. Whenever the numerator and denominator are the same, the fraction is equal to 1.

Example 1 Write a fraction equal to 1 which has a denominator of 4.

Solution A fraction equal to 1 which has a denominator of 4 would also have a numerator of 4, so we write $\frac{4}{4}$.

Example 2 $\dfrac{1}{4} + \dfrac{3}{4}$

Solution   We add and find that the sum is $\frac{4}{4}$. We should always write our answers in simplest form. The simplest name for $\frac{4}{4}$ is **1**.

$$\frac{1}{4} + \frac{3}{4} = \frac{4}{4} = 1$$

Example 3   Compare: $4\frac{3}{3} \bigcirc 5$

Solution   The mixed number $4\frac{3}{3}$ means $4 + \frac{3}{3}$. But $\frac{3}{3}$ is equal to 1. So $4 + \frac{3}{3}$ equals $4 + 1$, which is 5.

$$4\frac{3}{3} = 5$$

Example 4 $1\frac{1}{2} + 1\frac{1}{2}$

Solution   We add and find that the sum is $2\frac{2}{2}$. The mixed number $2\frac{2}{2}$ means $2 + \frac{2}{2}$. Since $\frac{2}{2}$ is equal to 1, $2 + \frac{2}{2}$ equals $2 + 1$, which is **3**.

$$1\frac{1}{2} + 1\frac{1}{2} = 2\frac{2}{2} = 3$$

Subtracting a fraction from 1   To subtract a fraction from 1, we rewrite 1 as a fraction.

Example 5 $1 - \frac{1}{3}$

Solution   We can show this problem with a picture that represents a whole pie. If we remove one third of the pie, how much of the pie is still in the pan?

Before we can remove a third, we first slice the pie into three thirds. Then we can "subtract" one third. We see that two thirds of the pie is still in the pan. Using pencil and paper, we rewrite 1 as $\frac{3}{3}$. Then we subtract.

$$1 - \frac{1}{3}$$

$$\downarrow \qquad \downarrow$$

$$\frac{3}{3} - \frac{1}{3} = \frac{2}{3}$$

We could have chosen any name for 1, such as $\frac{2}{2}$ or $\frac{4}{4}$ or $\frac{3682}{3682}$, but we chose $\frac{3}{3}$ because it had the same denominator as the other fraction. Remember, we can only add and subtract fractions when their denominators are the same.

Practice   **a.** Write a fraction equal to 1 which has a denominator of 3.

b. Compare: $\frac{4}{4} \bigcirc 1$ **c.** $\frac{3}{10} + \frac{7}{10}$

d. Compare: $5\frac{4}{4} \bigcirc 6$ **e.** $3\frac{3}{5} + 2\frac{2}{5}$

f. $1 - \frac{1}{4}$ **g.** $1 - \frac{2}{3}$

h. How many fraction names for 1 are there?

Problem set 66

1. Cassandra jumped rope for three minutes and 24 seconds without stopping. How many seconds is three minutes and 24 seconds?
(52)

2. Brady's mom baked 5 dozen cookies, and Brady ate one tenth of them. How many cookies did he eat?
(55)

3. Draw a quadrilateral which has a pair of horizontal parallel line segments of different lengths.
(39)

4. Which factors of 8 are also factors of 20?
(25)

5. How many seconds is two fifths of a minute? Two fifths of a minute is what percent of a minute?
(50)

6. Maria stood on two scales at the same time. The scale
(56) under her right foot read 46 pounds, and the scale
under her left foot read 60 pounds. If she balances her
weight equally on both scales, how much will each
scale read?

7. $\dfrac{1}{4} + \dfrac{3}{4}$ **8.** $1\dfrac{1}{3} + 2\dfrac{2}{3}$ **9.** $2\dfrac{5}{8} + \dfrac{3}{8}$
(66)   (66)   (66)

10. $1 - \dfrac{1}{4}$ **11.** $1 - \dfrac{3}{8}$ **12.** $2\dfrac{8}{8} - \dfrac{3}{8}$
(66)   (66)   (47)

13.   98,789   **14.**   47,150   **15.**   368
(6)   41,286   (9)   − 36,247   (62)   × 479
        + 18,175

16. Use words to name the mixed number $8\dfrac{9}{10}$.
(43)

17. Divide and write the quotient with a fraction: $\dfrac{15}{4}$
(65)

In problems 18–20, write the answer with a remainder:

18. $30\overline{)\$5.40}$ **19.** $40\overline{)687}$ **20.** $60\overline{)850}$
(61)   (61)   (61)

21. $507 \times \$3.60$ **22.** $(900 - 300) \div 30$
(63)   (24)

23. Which of these mixed numbers is not equal to 3?
(66)   A. $2\dfrac{3}{3}$ B. $3\dfrac{2}{2}$ C. $2\dfrac{4}{4}$ D. $2\dfrac{8}{8}$

24. Write a fraction equal to 1 which has a denominator
(66) of 5.

25. Each side of this triangle is the same length. What is
(60) the perimeter of the triangle?

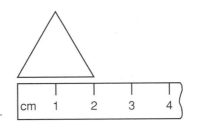

LESSON
67

Finding a Fraction to Complete a Whole

Facts Practice: 48 Uneven Divisions (Test G in Test Masters)

Mental Math:

   a. VII   **b.** XXXV   **c.** IX   **d.** XIV

   e. How much is $900 \div 10$? $900 \div 30$? $900 \div 90$?

   f. 9×25 **g.** 25% of a dozen   **h.** $9 \times 9, -1, \div 2, -1, \div 3$

Problem Solving: Two figures are congruent if they are the same shape and size. Draw a rectangle that is congruent to this rectangle.

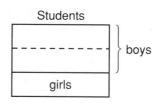

Sometimes we are given one part of a whole and need to know the other part of the whole. For example,

> *One third of the students are girls. What fraction of the students are boys?*

We begin to answer questions like this by thinking of the entire group as a whole. We draw the rectangle below to represent the whole group of students. The problem states that $\frac{1}{3}$ of the students are girls, so we divide the rectangle into three parts and label one of the parts "girls."

Students

```
┌─────────────────┐ ┐
│                 │ │
├ ─ ─ ─ ─ ─ ─ ─ ─ ┤ ├ boys
│                 │ │
├─────────────────┤ ┘
│      girls      │
└─────────────────┘
```

The fraction of the students that is not girls must be boys. Since the girls take up 1 of the 3 parts, the boys must take up 2 of the 3 parts. Thus, two thirds of the students are boys.

Example Bob found that commercials take up one sixth of TV time. What fraction of TV time is not taken up by commercials?

Solution   We begin by thinking of TV time as a whole. We draw a rectangle to show this. The problem uses the fraction $\frac{1}{6}$, so we divide the rectangle into six equal parts. We label one part "commercials." We see that the fraction of TV time that is not commercials is $\frac{5}{6}$.

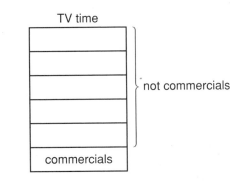

Practice   **a.** Kent has read one fourth of his book. What fraction of his book is left to read?

b. Five eighths of the gymnasts were able to do a back handspring. What fraction of the gymnasts were unable to do a back handspring?

c. If three fifths of the spectators were rooting for the home team, then what fraction of the spectators were not rooting for the home team?

Problem set 67   **1.** In one class there are three more girls than boys. There are 14 boys. How many students are in the class?
$^{(55)}$

2. Calvin bought two bicycle tubes for $2.39 each and a tire for $4.49. The tax was $0.56. If he paid $10, how much money should he get back?
$^{(55)}$

3. From the years 1800 to 1900 was how many decades?
$^{(27)}$

4. The diameter of Kitty's bicycle wheel is 24 inches. What is the radius of the wheel?
$^{(60)}$

5. Round 487 and 326 to the nearest hundred. Then add
(34) the rounded numbers together. What is their sum?

6. Find each missing numerator:
(66)

(a) $\dfrac{\square}{7} = 1$ (b) $4 = 3\dfrac{\square}{4}$

7. Find one half of each of these numbers:
(50)

(a) 6 (b) 8 (c) 12

8. What is the perimeter of this
(60) square field?

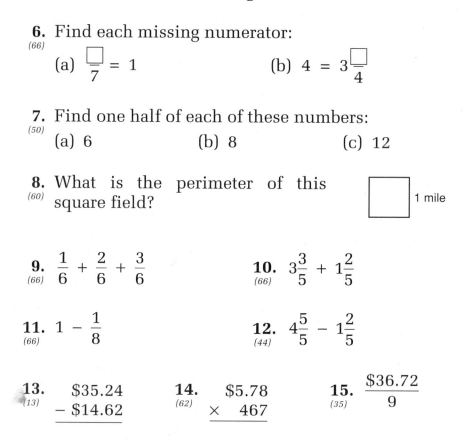
1 mile

9. $\dfrac{1}{6} + \dfrac{2}{6} + \dfrac{3}{6}$
(66)

10. $3\dfrac{3}{5} + 1\dfrac{2}{5}$
(66)

11. $1 - \dfrac{1}{8}$
(66)

12. $4\dfrac{5}{5} - 1\dfrac{2}{5}$
(44)

13. $\begin{array}{r} \$35.24 \\ - \$14.62 \end{array}$
(13)

14. $\begin{array}{r} \$5.78 \\ \times \quad 467 \end{array}$
(62)

15. $\dfrac{\$36.72}{9}$
(35)

16. Divide and write the quotient with a fraction: $\dfrac{23}{10}$
(65)

17. Selby found that commercials took up one eighth of
(67) TV time. What fraction of TV time was not taken up by
commercials? What percent of TV time was taken up
by commercials?

18. 374 × 360
(63)

19. 643 ÷ 40
(61)

20. 60 × (800 ÷ 40)
(24)

21. $20\overline{)1340}$
(61)

22. Compare: $\dfrac{4}{4} \bigcirc \dfrac{5}{5}$
(66)

23. Write a fraction equal to 1 which has a denominator
(66) of 8.

24. The arrow points to what fraction on the number line?
(41)

25. If the time is 11:35 a.m., how many minutes is it until
(29) noon?

LESSON
68

Recognizing Halves

Facts Practice: 64 Multiplication Facts (Test D in Test Masters)

Mental Math: Say these fractions equal to $\frac{1}{2}$:

$$\frac{1}{2}, \frac{2}{4}, \frac{3}{6}, \frac{4}{8}, \frac{5}{10}, \frac{6}{12}, \frac{7}{14}, \frac{8}{16}, \frac{9}{18}, \frac{10}{20}$$

a. XXXVII   **b.** XIX
c. How much is half of 5?   half of 9?   half of 15?
d. $1 - \frac{1}{3}$ **e.** $1 - \frac{1}{4}$ **f.** 10% of 500

Problem Solving: If an $8\frac{1}{2}$" × 11" sheet of paper is folded in half across its length, two congruent rectangles are formed. What are the dimensions (length and width) of each rectangle?

A fraction can be named many different ways. One half of each of these circles has been shaded, but the shaded part is named by four different fractions.

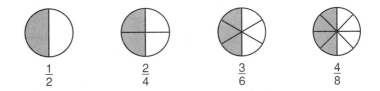

Notice that the numerator of each of these fractions is half of the denominator. Any fraction whose numerator is half of the denominator is equal to one half.

Example 1   Which of these fractions equal one half?

A. $\frac{4}{10}$ B. $\frac{8}{14}$ C. $\frac{9}{18}$

Solution   We will consider each choice.

A. The denominator of $\frac{4}{10}$ is 10. Half of 10 is 5. So $\frac{5}{10}$ equals $\frac{1}{2}$ and $\frac{4}{10}$ is less than $\frac{1}{2}$.

B. The denominator of $\frac{8}{14}$ is 14. Half of 14 is 7. So $\frac{7}{14}$ equals $\frac{1}{2}$ and $\frac{8}{14}$ is greater than $\frac{1}{2}$.

C. The denominator of $\frac{9}{18}$ is 18. Half of 18 is 9. So $\frac{9}{18}$ equals $\frac{1}{2}$.

The answer to the question is choice **C**.

Example 2   Write two fractions equal to $\frac{1}{2}$. Make 10 the denominator of the first fraction and the numerator of the second fraction.

Solution   We write 10 as the denominator of the first fraction and as the numerator of the second fraction.

$$\frac{?}{10} \qquad\qquad \frac{10}{?}$$

For each fraction to equal $\frac{1}{2}$, the numerator should be half of the denominator. The two fractions are

$$\frac{5}{10} \qquad\qquad \frac{10}{20}$$

Practice   a. Which of these fractions does not equal $\frac{1}{2}$?

A. $\frac{5}{10}$ B. $\frac{10}{20}$ C. $\frac{24}{50}$ D. $\frac{50}{100}$

b. Write two fractions equal to $\frac{1}{2}$. Make 8 the numerator of the first fraction and the denominator of the second fraction.

Problem set 68   1. The tallest teacher at Lincoln School is 6 feet, 3 inches
(52)   tall. A person 6 feet, 3 inches tall is how many inches tall?

2. One sixth of the class was absent. What percent of the
(67,47) class was absent? What fraction of the class was
present?

3. How many years were there from 1056 to 1215?
(27)

4. Write the standard number for $(7 \times 1000) + (4 \times 10)$.
(53)

5. Round 56 and 23 to the nearest ten. Multiply the
(34) rounded numbers. What is their product?

6. Which of these fractions does not equal $\frac{1}{2}$?
(68)
A. $\frac{6}{12}$ B. $\frac{12}{24}$ C. $\frac{24}{48}$ D. $\frac{48}{98}$

7. Which factors of 12 are also factors of 16?
(25)

8. If each side of an octagon is 10 inches long, then what
(60) is the perimeter of the octagon?

9. $1 - \dfrac{1}{5}$ **10.** $1 - \dfrac{3}{4}$ **11.** $3\dfrac{3}{3} - 1\dfrac{2}{3}$
(66)   (66)   (44)

12. $\dfrac{1}{10} + \dfrac{2}{10} + \dfrac{3}{10} + \dfrac{4}{10}$ **13.** $5\dfrac{3}{4} + 4\dfrac{1}{4}$
(66)   (66)

14. $\begin{array}{r} 4263 \\ -\quad Q \\ \hline 1784 \end{array}$ **15.** $\begin{array}{r} \$50.00 \\ -\$19.34 \\ \hline \end{array}$ **16.** $\begin{array}{r} 58 \\ 39 \\ 24 \\ 16 \\ 52 \\ +\ 11 \\ \hline \end{array}$
(14)   (13)   (6)

17. $\begin{array}{r} 389 \\ \times\ 470 \\ \hline \end{array}$ **18.** $\dfrac{5445}{9}$
(63)   (35)

19. Divide and write the quotient with a fraction: $\frac{25}{6}$
(65)

20. $894 \div 40$ **21.** $943 \div 30$
(61)   (61)

22. $(800 - 300) \times 20$
(24)

23. On this number line, the arrow is pointing to what
(41) mixed number?

24. Write two fractions equal to $\frac{1}{2}$. Make 20 the
(68) denominator of the first fraction and the numerator of
the second fraction.

25. What month is 15 months after November?
(27)

LESSON
69

Estimating Arithmetic Answers

Facts Practice: 48 Uneven Divisions (Test G in Test Masters)

Mental Math: Say these fractions equal to $\frac{1}{2}$: $\frac{1}{2}, \frac{2}{4}, \frac{3}{6}, \frac{4}{8}, \dots$
Continue the pattern to $\frac{10}{20}$.

a. XVIII   **b.** XXIV
c. One third of 7 is $2\frac{1}{3}$. How much is $\frac{1}{3}$ of 8? $\frac{1}{3}$ of 10?
d. $1 - \frac{1}{5}$ **e.** $1 - \frac{4}{5}$
f. 25% of 200   **g.** $100 \div 10, -2, \div 2, -2, \div 2$

Problem Solving: Two figures are similar if
they are the same shape.
Draw a rectangle that is $\frac{1}{2}$ in.
similar to this rectangle.
Make the rectangle 2 inches long. How wide
should you make the rectangle?

We have used arithmetic to find exact answers. For some
problems, finding an exact answer takes many steps and
may take a long time. In this lesson we will practice a way
to "get close" to an exact answer quickly. Trying to get
close to an exact answer is called **estimating.** To **estimate**
we use rounded numbers to make the arithmetic easier.

We may even do the arithmetic mentally ("in our head"). If we estimate the answer before we calculate, we can tell if our calculated answer "makes sense." Estimating first will cut down on our errors by helping us discover when our calculated answers are far from the correct answer. Since we use rounded numbers when we estimate, an estimated answer is not the exact answer, but it is close to the exact answer.

Example 1   Estimate the product of 29 and 21.

Solution   We estimate to find out **about** how much an answer will be. Estimating is a quick way to get close to an exact answer. To estimate, we round the numbers **before** we do the work. The numbers 29 and 21 round to 30 and 20, which we can multiply mentally. So our answer is **600.**

Practice*   Estimate each answer by rounding the numbers before doing the arithmetic. **Often you will be able to do the work mentally, but for this practice show how you rounded the numbers.**

a. 89 + 72   **b.** 58 × 23
90 + 70 = 160 (example)

c. 585 + 312   **d.** 38 × 19

e. 91 − 28   **f.** 29 × 312

g. 685 − 391   **h.** 59 ÷ 29

i. 703 − 497   **j.** 89 ÷ 31

Problem set 69

1. Mrs. Smith baked 6 dozen cookies for the party. There were 20 cookies left over. How many cookies were eaten?
   (55)

2. A millennium is 1000 years. A millennium is how many centuries?
   (27)

3. If the amount of water in each glass is made the same,
(56) how many ounces of water will be in each glass?

4 ounces   7 ounces   7 ounces   2 ounces

4. Draw and shade one third of a circle. What fraction of
(47) the circle is not shaded? What percent of the circle is
not shaded?

5. Estimate the product of 39 and 41.
(69)

6. $1 - \dfrac{1}{10}$ **7.** $1 - \dfrac{3}{8}$ **8.** $4\dfrac{4}{4} - 2\dfrac{3}{4}$
(66)   (66)   (44)

9. $3\dfrac{1}{3} + 1\dfrac{2}{3}$ **10.** $6\dfrac{10}{10} - \dfrac{1}{10}$ **11.** $8 = 7\dfrac{\square}{6}$
(66)   (47)   (66)

12. Estimate the sum of 586 and 317 by rounding the
(69) numbers to the nearest hundred before adding.

13.   89,786   **14.** $35,042   **15.**   428
(6)   26,428   (9)   − $17,651   (62)   × 396
         57,814
      + 91,875

16. $4735 \div 5$ **17.** $8 \times 43 \times 602$
(26)   (18)

18. Divide and write the quotient with a fraction: $\dfrac{15}{8}$
(65)

19. $967 \div 60$ **20.** $875 \div 40$
(61)   (61)

21. (a) Which of these fractions equals $\frac{1}{2}$?
(68)   (b) Which of these fractions is less than $\frac{1}{2}$?
       (c) Which of these fractions is greater than $\frac{1}{2}$?
           A. $\frac{4}{7}$ B. $\frac{7}{15}$ C. $\frac{15}{30}$

22. $100 − ($24 + $43.89 + $8.67 + $0.98)
(24)

23. The perimeter of this square is
(60) how many millimeters?

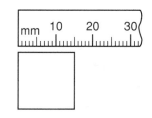

24. Think of an even number. Multiply it by 5. What
(2) number is the last digit of the product?

25. If it is morning, what time will be
(29) shown by this clock in 3 hours
and 20 minutes?

**LESSON
70**

Subtracting a Fraction from a Whole Number Greater than 1

Facts Practice: 64 Multiplication Facts (Test D in Test Masters)

Mental Math: Say these fractions equal to $\frac{1}{2}$: $\frac{1}{2}$, $\frac{2}{4}$, $\frac{3}{6}$, $\frac{4}{8}$, ...
Continue the pattern to $\frac{12}{24}$.

  a. XIV   **b.** XXXVI
  c. One fifth of 6 is $1\frac{1}{5}$. How much is $\frac{1}{5}$ of 7? $\frac{1}{5}$ of 8?
  d. $1 − \frac{1}{6}$ **e.** $1 − \frac{1}{10}$
  f. 10% of 200   **g.** 500 ÷ 10, ÷ 2, + 5, ÷ 5, + 3, ÷ 3

Problem Solving: Copy this multiplication problem and
fill in the missing digits.

$$
\begin{array}{r}
4\_ \\
\times \quad \_ \\
\hline
4\_4
\end{array}
$$

Recall that when we subtract a fraction from 1, we change
the 1 to a fraction name for 1. Then we can subtract. If the
problem is $1 − \frac{1}{3}$, we change the 1 to $\frac{3}{3}$ so that the
denominators will be the same; then we subtract.

We change from this form: $\quad 1 - \dfrac{1}{3}$

to this form: $\quad \dfrac{3}{3} - \dfrac{1}{3} = \dfrac{2}{3}$

In this lesson we will subtract fractions from whole numbers greater than 1.

Imagine you are a baker with 4 whole pies on the shelf. If someone asked for half a pie, you would have to cut one of the pies into 2 halves. While both halves were still in the pan, you would have 4 pies, but you could call those pies $3\frac{2}{2}$ pies.

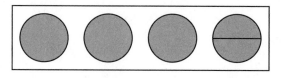

We use this idea to subtract a fraction from a whole number. We take 1 from the whole number and write it as a fraction with the same denominator as the fraction being subtracted. We will answer the problem $4 - \frac{1}{2}$ to show this.

We change from this form: $\quad 4 - \dfrac{1}{2}$

to this form: $\quad 3\dfrac{2}{2} - \dfrac{1}{2} = 3\dfrac{1}{2}$

Example 1 Name the number of shaded circles (a) as a whole number and (b) as a mixed number.

Solution (a) We see **3** circles.

(b) Since one of the circles is divided in fourths, we can also say that there are two whole circles and four fourths of a circle, which we write as the mixed number $2\frac{4}{4}$.

Example 2 $5 - \dfrac{1}{3}$

Solution   We think of 5 as being $4 + 1$, which we can write as $4\frac{3}{3}$. Now we can subtract.

$$5 - \dfrac{1}{3}$$

$$\downarrow$$

$$4\dfrac{3}{3} - \dfrac{1}{3} = \mathbf{4\dfrac{2}{3}}$$

Practice*   **a.** $4 - \dfrac{1}{4}$ **b.** $3 - \dfrac{3}{4}$ **c.** $4 - 2\dfrac{1}{4}$

d. $2 - \dfrac{1}{4}$ **e.** $4 - 1\dfrac{1}{2}$ **f.** $6 - 1\dfrac{2}{3}$

**Problem set
70**

1. A 100-centimeter stick broke into 3 pieces. One piece
$^{(55)}$ was 7 centimeters long, and another was 34 centimeters long. How long was the third piece?

2. Bill's pencil was 6 inches long. While doing his
$^{(70)}$ homework, Bill used up $1\frac{1}{2}$ inches of his pencil. Then how long was his pencil?

3. Isabel can make 4 hamburgers from 1 pound of meat.
$^{(21)}$ How many hamburgers can she make from 5 pounds of meat?

4. In the 4 stacks of math books there were 18, 19, 24,
$^{(56)}$ and 23 books, respectively. If the stacks were made even, how many books would be in each stack?

5. Estimate the sum of 398 and 487 by rounding to the
$^{(69)}$ nearest hundred before adding.

6. Which factors of 14 are also factors of 21?
$^{(25)}$

7. The distance around the earth at the equator is like
(60) what measurement of a circle?

A. Radius   B. Diameter   C. Circumference

8. What is the sum of five million, two hundred eighty-
(59) four thousand and six million, nine hundred eighteen
thousand, five hundred?

9. $7 - \dfrac{1}{3}$ **10.** $6 - 2\dfrac{1}{2}$ **11.** $8 - 3\dfrac{3}{4}$
(70)   (70)   (70)

12. $\dfrac{8}{9} + \left(\dfrac{2}{9} - \dfrac{1}{9}\right)$ **13.** $5\dfrac{3}{4} - \left(3\dfrac{2}{4} + 1\dfrac{1}{4}\right)$
(24)   (24)

14. $\begin{array}{r} 43{,}716 \\ -\ 19{,}537 \\ \hline \end{array}$ **15.** $\begin{array}{r} \$6.87 \\ \times\quad 794 \\ \hline \end{array}$ **16.** $\dfrac{\$14.72}{8}$
(9)   (62)   (26)

17. Divide and write the quotient with a fraction: $\dfrac{20}{9}$
(65)

18. $20\overline{)951}$ **19.** $50\overline{)2560}$
(61)   (61)

20. $50 \times (400 + 400)$ **21.** $(400 + 400) \div 40$
(24)   (24)

22. $4736 + 2849 + 351 + 78$
(6)

23. If three eighths of the class was absent, what fraction
(67) of the class was present? What percent of the class was
present?

24. Rearrange these fractions in order from least to
(68) greatest. (*Hint*: Decide if each fraction is less than,
equal to, or greater than $\frac{1}{2}$.)

$$\frac{5}{10}, \frac{5}{8}, \frac{5}{12}$$

25. Each side of this triangle is the same length. What is
(60) the perimeter of this triangle?

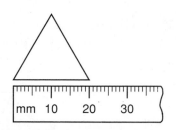

**LESSON
71**

Decimal Place Value Through Hundredths'

Facts Practice: 64 Multiplication Facts (Test D in Test Masters)

Mental Math: Say these fractions equal to $\frac{1}{2}$: $\frac{1}{2}$, $\frac{2}{4}$, $\frac{3}{6}$, ...
Continue the pattern to $\frac{12}{24}$.

  a. XVIII   **b.** XXXIX   **c.** XIX
  d. Two days and two hours are how many hours?
  e. 250 ÷ 10   **f.** 50% of 60, + 10, ÷ 5, + 2, × 10

Problem Solving: The symbol $\sqrt{}$ is a square root symbol. We read $\sqrt{25}$ as "the square root of 25." The expression $\sqrt{25}$ equals 5 because 5 × 5 = 25. What does $\sqrt{49}$ equal?

To name parts of a whole, we have used **common fractions.** Common fractions are written with a numerator and a denominator, like this.

$$\frac{1}{2}$$

Fractions may also be written as decimal numbers. For example, we use decimal numbers to write fractions of a dollar. To write half of a dollar, we do not write a common fraction.

We do not write half a dollar this way: $\$\frac{1}{2}$

Instead, we write half a dollar as a decimal number.

Half a dollar is $0.50.

We usually use two places to the right of the decimal point to name parts of a dollar. The first place to the right of the decimal point is the tenths' place. The second place to the right of the decimal point is the hundredths' place.

Place Value Chart

PLACE NAME	tens'	ones'		tenths'	hundredths'
PLACE VALUE	10	1		$\frac{1}{10}$	$\frac{1}{100}$
PLACE	___	___	.	___	___
MONEY VALUE OF PLACE	$10 bills	$1 bills		dimes	pennies

The last row of the chart gives the money value of the place. The first place to the right of the decimal point is the tenths' place. Since a dime is one tenth of a dollar, we may think of this as the dimes' place. The second place to the right of the decimal point is the hundredths' place. Since a penny is one hundredth of a dollar, we may think of this as the pennies' place. When using coins, think of a dime as a tenth of a dollar and a penny as a hundredth of a dollar.

Example 1   Use bills, dimes, and pennies to illustrate $6.25.

Solution   We use six whole dollar bills, two tenths of a dollar (dimes), and five hundredths of a dollar (pennies).

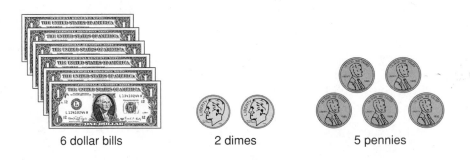

6 dollar bills   2 dimes   5 pennies

Example 2   Which digit in 12.3 is in the tenths' place?

Solution   Looking at the chart, we see that the tenths' place is one place to the right of the decimal point. The digit in the tenths' place is the **3**.

Example 3   Which digit in 3.125 is in the same place as the 7 in 48.67?

Solution   To find place values in decimal numbers, we must **pay attention to the decimal point,** not to the end of the number. The 7 is two places to the right of the decimal point. It is in the hundredths' place. In 3.125, the digit in the hundredths' place is the **2.**

Practice   Name the place occupied by the 5 in each number below:

    a. 25.34   **b.** 54.32   **c.** 23.54   **d.** 23.45

    e. Which of these numbers has a 3 in the same place as the 3 in 6.375?

      A. 23.47   B. 138.4   C. 42.35

    f. In which of these numbers does the 5 occupy the place with the greatest value?

      A. 15.67   B. 17.56   C. 14.75

Problem set 71

    1. What is the sum of one hundred sixteen thousand, five hundred twenty-one and two hundred fifty-three thousand, four hundred seventy-nine?
    (59)

    2. At the annual clearance sale, *Shutter Shop* lowered the price of all their cameras. Terry wants to buy a new camera that costs $30.63. She has $17.85. How much more money does she need?
    (11)

    3. In the auditorium there were 30 rows of seats with 16 seats in each row. If there were 21 empty seats, how many seats were filled?
    (55)

    4. Jeremy is reading a 324-page book. If he plans to finish the book in 6 days, how many pages should he read each day?
    (21)

    5. Estimate the product of 68 and 52.
    (69)

6. If three tenths of the bowling pins were up, what
(67) fraction of the bowling pins were down? What percent
of the bowling pins were down?

7. Which digit in 54.63 is in the hundredths' place?
(71)

8. In which of these numbers does the 3 occupy the place
(71) with the greatest value?

A. 3.25   B. 32.5   C. 2.53

9. Which digit in 45.32 is in the same place as the 6
(71) in 1.6?

10. Divide 25 by 8 and write the quotient with a fraction.
(65)

11. Which factors of 20 are also factors of 30?
(25)

12. What time is $1\frac{1}{2}$ hours before noon?
(29)

13. Think of an odd number. Divide it by 2. What is the
(2) remainder?

14.   36,012   **15.**   479   **16.** $\dfrac{8765}{5}$
(9) $-$ 15,365   (62) $\times$ 346   (26)

17. $4.34   **18.** $30.48 $\div$ 6   **19.** $60\overline{)1586}$
(13)   0.26   (35)   (61)
        5.58
        9.47
        6.23
      $+$ 0.65

20.   7   **21.** $1\frac{1}{3}$ **22.**   4
(70) $- 3\frac{2}{3}$ (66) $+ 2\frac{2}{3}$ (70) $- 3\frac{3}{4}$

23. 5 $\times$ 4 $\times$ 3 $\times$ 2 $\times$ 1 $\times$ 0
(18)

24. Draw a pentagon.
(39)

25. The sides of this triangle are equal in length. What is
(60) the perimeter of the triangle?

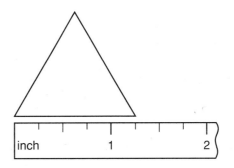

LESSON
72

Writing Tenths in Decimal Form

Facts Practice: 100 Multiplication Facts (Test C in Test Masters)

Mental Math: The Roman numeral L is 50 and C is 100. Find
the value of the following:

   a. CCL   **b.** CLXVI   **c.** CCXXXIV   **d.** LXIV

   e. One third of 11 is $3\frac{2}{3}$. How much is $\frac{1}{3}$ of 13? $\frac{1}{3}$ of 14?

   f. $\sqrt{36}$ **g.** $1 - \frac{2}{5}$ **h.** $8 \times 5, -10, \div 5, \times 7, -2, \div 5$

Problem Solving: Two figures are congruent if
they are the same shape and
size. These two angles are con-
gruent. They are both right angles. Draw a third
angle congruent to these two angles with a different orientation.

The first place to the right of a decimal point is the tenths'
place. A common fraction that has a denominator of 10
can be written as a decimal number. The numerator of the
common fraction is written in the tenths' place of the
decimal number.

    1. One tenth as a common fraction: $\frac{1}{10}$

    2. One tenth as a decimal number: 0.1

The common fraction $\frac{1}{10}$ and the decimal number 0.1 are both named "one tenth" and are equal in value. The zero to the left of the decimal point shows that the whole number part of the decimal number is zero.

Example 1 Write the fraction three tenths as a common fraction. Then write it as a decimal number.

Solution We write the common fraction three tenths this way: $\frac{3}{10}$. A fraction with a denominator of 10 can be written as a decimal number with one digit after the decimal point. The numerator of the fraction becomes the digit after the decimal point. We write the decimal number three tenths as **0.3.**

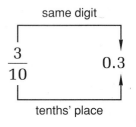

Example 2 A part of this shape is shaded. Name the part that is not shaded twice, once as a fraction and again as a decimal number.

Solution The rectangle is sliced into 10 equal parts. Three of the 10 parts are shaded, and seven parts are not shaded. We are told to name the part that is not shaded as a fraction and as a decimal number, which we write as $\frac{7}{10}$ and **0.7.**

Example 3 Name the number of shaded circles as a mixed number and as a decimal number.

Solution We see all of one circle is shaded and one tenth of another circle is shaded. We write one and one tenth as a mixed number as $1\frac{1}{10}$. We write one and one tenth as a decimal number by writing the whole number and then the decimal fraction, **1.1.**

Practice   Complete the chart of equivalent decimals and fractions:

Decimal form	a.	0.1	c.	0.2	e.	0.7	g.	0.9
Fraction form	$\frac{3}{10}$	b.	$\frac{4}{10}$	d.	$\frac{5}{10}$	f.	$\frac{6}{10}$	h.

Use this rectangle to do problems (i) and (j):

   i. Name the shaded part of the rectangle as a fraction and as a decimal number.

   j. Name the part of the rectangle that is not shaded both as a fraction and as a decimal number.

   k. Name the number of shaded circles both as a mixed number and as a decimal number.

Problem set 72

   1. Draw a quadrilateral with one pair of horizontal segments and one pair of vertical segments.
   (39)

   2. The players are divided into 10 teams with 12 players on each team. If all the players are divided into 8 equal teams instead of 10, then how many players will be on each team?
   (55)

   3. This is a drawing of a field that is 100 yards long and 40 yards wide. What is its perimeter?
   (60)

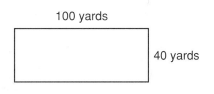

100 yards

40 yards

   4. A yard is 36 inches. How many inches is one fourth of a yard? One fourth of a yard is what percent of a yard?
   (50)

5. Tom's school starts at 8:30 a.m. If it is now 7:45 a.m.,
(29) how many minutes does he have until school starts?

6. Estimate the sum of 672 and 830 by rounding to
(69) hundreds before adding.

7. A part of this shape is shaded.
(72) Name the shaded part twice, once
as a fraction and once as a decimal number.

8. Write a decimal number equal to the fraction $\frac{4}{10}$.
(72)

9. Write a fraction equal to the decimal number 0.7.
(72)

10. Arrange these fractions in order from least to greatest.
(68) (*Hint*: Decide if each fraction is less than, equal to, or
greater than $\frac{1}{2}$.)

$$\frac{4}{4}, \frac{3}{8}, \frac{2}{3}, \frac{5}{10}$$

11. The number 9 has three different factors. The number
(25) 10 has how many different factors?

12. Divide and write the quotient as a mixed number: $\frac{15}{4}$
(65)

13. Write the largest odd number that uses each of the
(2) digits 3, 4, and 5 only once.

14. Five hundred is how much more than three hundred
(36) ninety-five?

15.   36,195   **16.**   41,026   **17.**   608
(6)   17,436   (9)   − 39,543   (63)   × 479
      + 42,374

18. 2637 ÷ 4   **19.** 40)$33.60   **20.** $\frac{3360}{20}$
(26)   (61)   (61)

21. $3\frac{3}{8} + 5\frac{5}{8}$ **22.** $5 - 3\frac{3}{8}$ **23.** $3\frac{3}{4} - 3$
(66)   *(70)*   *(47)*

24. $6 \times 42 \times 20$ **25.** $\$20 - (\$5.63 + \$12)$
(18)   *(24)*

LESSON 73

Naming Points on a Number Line with Decimal Numbers • Naming Line Segments

Facts Practice: 64 Multiplication Facts (Test D in Test Masters)

Mental Math: Say these fractions equal to $\frac{1}{2}$: $\frac{1}{2}, \frac{2}{4}, \frac{3}{6}, \ldots$
Continue the pattern to $\frac{12}{24}$.

   a. CCLX   **b.** CLIX   **c.** $\sqrt{16}$
   d. 6×29 **e.** Find $\frac{1}{2}$ of 30, + 3, ÷ 3, + 3, ÷ 3

Problem Solving: If an $8\frac{1}{2}$" × 11" sheet of paper is folded in half across its width, two congruent rectangles are formed. What are the dimensions of each rectangle?

Naming points on a number line with decimal numbers

Every point on the number line below can be "named" with a number. We see on this number line the points for the whole numbers 0, 1, and 2. The arrows mark points between the whole numbers. The distance between 0 and 1 has been divided into 10 equal lengths. The first arrow is pointing to a mark that is 3 of those lengths past the 0. It is pointing to a mark which is $\frac{3}{10}$ of the distance from 0 to 1. We may name that mark as the fraction $\frac{3}{10}$ or as the decimal number 0.3. The second arrow is pointing to a mark which is 7 of the 10 spaces past the 1. We may name that mark with the mixed number $1\frac{7}{10}$. To name this point as a decimal number, we write 1.7.

Example 1 Use a decimal number to name the point on the number line marked by the arrow.

Solution The distance between the whole numbers on the number line is divided into 10 small segments. Each segment represents one tenth. The arrow points five tenths past the 1 to **1.5.**

Naming line segments Recall that a line does not end. Part of a line is a line segment. A line segment has two ends. The points at which a segment ends are called the segment's **endpoints.** In mathematics we often label the endpoints of segments with letters. Then we name the segment by its endpoints. On this line we can name three line segments.

$$\underset{\text{●}}{A} \qquad \underset{\text{●}}{B} \qquad\qquad\qquad \underset{\text{●}}{C}$$

Segment AB is the part of the line between points A and B. This segment may also be named segment BA. Another segment is segment BC, which may also be named segment CB. The third segment we can name is segment AC, which is also segment CA. The length of segment AC is the length of segment AB plus the length of segment BC.

Example 2 The length of segment PQ is 3 cm. The length of segment PR is 8 cm. What is the length of segment QR?

$$\underset{\text{●}}{P} \qquad\qquad \underset{\text{●}}{Q} \qquad\qquad\qquad \underset{\text{●}}{R}$$

Solution The lengths of the two shorter segments added together equal the length of the longest segment.

The length of segment PQ	3 cm
+ The length of segment QR	+ L
The length of segment PR	8 cm

This is a missing addend problem. The missing addend is 5. **The length of segment QR is 5 cm.**

Practice Write a decimal number to name each point marked by an arrow on the number line below:

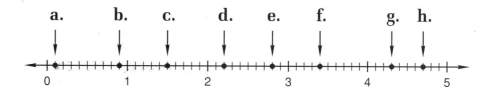

i. The length of segment *RT* is 9 cm. The length of segment *ST* is 3 cm. What is the length of segment *RS*?

R   S   T

Problem set 73

1. Draw a pair of parallel line segments that are neither
(32) horizontal nor vertical.

2. Nathan needs to buy grapes and bananas for the class
(55) picnic. What is the total cost of 3 pounds of grapes at $0.45 per pound and 2 pounds of bananas at $0.39 per pound?

3. Jason ran around the block. If the block is 200 yards
(60) long and 60 yards wide, how far did he run?

4. Jason ran 200 yards in three fifths of a minute. How
(50) many seconds did it take Jason to run 200 yards?

5. How many millimeters are in a centimeter?
(48)

6. One dozen records cost $72. At that rate, what would
(55) 4 records cost?

7. Name the fraction of the circles
(72) shaded as a fraction and as a decimal number.

8. What percent of these circles are
(31) shaded? What percent of the circles are not shaded?

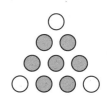

9. Use decimal numbers to name the points on the
(73) number line marked by the arrows.

10. Divide 12 by 5 and write the quotient as a mixed
(65) number.

11. List the factors of 18 that are also factors of 30.
(25)

12. Write the standard form for the following:
(53)
$$(6 \times 1000) + (5 \times 10) + (3 \times 1)$$

13. Points A, B, and C lie in order on a straight line. The
(73) line segment from point A to point B is 5 centimeters
long. The segment from point B to point C is 7 centimeters. How long is the segment from point A to
point C?

A B C

14.   10,000   **15.** $4.39   **16.** $\dfrac{\$36.54}{6}$
(9)   –   684   (62)   ×   648   (35)

17.   476   **18.** 46,528 ÷ 7   **19.** $60\overline{)7563}$
(6)   54   (26)   (61)
     823
     795
     227
  +   15

20. $8\frac{3}{4}$ **21.** $2\frac{3}{10}$ **22.**   4
(44) $-3\frac{3}{4}$ (66) $+4\frac{7}{10}$ (70) $-3\frac{1}{3}$

23. Compare: $12 \div 3 \bigcirc 120 \div 30$
(4)

Use this graph to answer questions 24 and 25. Notice that each ✗ stands for $10.

Money Earned in Fund Raiser

STUDENT	MONEY EARNED
Debbie	✗ ✗ ✗ ✗
Mark	✗ ✗ ✗
Vera	✗ ✗ ✗
John	✗ ✗ ✗ ✗
	✗ = $10

24. Altogether, how much money was earned by Vera and
(54) John?

25. Debbie earned how much more than Vera?
(54)

**LESSON
74**

Reading a Centimeter Scale to the Nearest Tenth

Facts Practice: 64 Multiplication Facts (Test D in Test Masters)

Mental Math:

  a. CCCLXXVI   **b.** LXXXIV   **c.** CXXIII   **d.** CIX
  e. One fifth of 11 is $2\frac{1}{5}$. How much is $\frac{1}{5}$ of 16? $\frac{1}{5}$ of 17?
  f. $\sqrt{9}$ **g.** $1 - \frac{3}{10}$ **h.** 6×23 **i.** $2 \times 2 \times 2 \times 2 \times 2$

Problem Solving: Copy this multiplication problem and
                    fill in the missing digits. Find two
                    different solutions.

$$\begin{array}{r} 2\_ \\ \times\ \_ \\ \hline 2\_2 \end{array}$$

Each centimeter on the following scale has been divided into 10 smaller segments. Each of these segments is one tenth of a centimeter. To find the length of the pin shown, we find the mark on the scale which is closest to the end of the pin. We see that the end of the pin is 3 small segments more than 2 centimeters. So, the length of the pin is $2\frac{3}{10}$ centimeters. When measuring in the metric system, we write fractions in decimal form. Using digits, the length of the pin is 2.3 cm.

Example　Find the length of the paper clip to the nearest tenth of a centimeter.

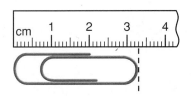

Solution　The paper clip is between 3 and 4 centimeters long. The marks on the scale divide each centimeter into fractions which are tenths of centimeters. The length of the paper clip is three tenths more than 3 centimeters. We write metric measures with decimal numbers. The length is **3.3 cm.**

Practice　The arrows point to which numbers on the centimeter scale?

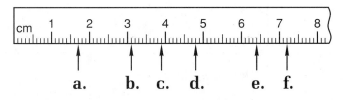

Problem set 74

1. How many tens are in 100?
   (61)

2. What number is next in this sequence?
   (1)
   　　　　2450, 2550, 2650, _____, ...

3. Estimate the difference of 794 and 312 by rounding to
   (69) the nearest hundred before you subtract.

4. Fernando could carry 6 containers at one time. If 4
(55) containers weigh 20 pounds, how much would 6
containers weigh?

5. When one end of the seesaw is 9
(56) inches above the ground, the
other end is 21 inches above the
ground. How far are the ends
above the ground when the seesaw is level?

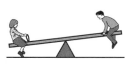

6. Compare: $\frac{3}{5} \bigcirc \frac{4}{9}$. (*Hint*: Is each fraction more than $\frac{1}{2}$ or
(42) less than $\frac{1}{2}$?)

7. Which digit in 4318 is in the same place as the 7 in
(58) 96,275?

8. Name the shaded part of the rect-
(72) angle as a fraction, as a decimal
number, and as a percent.

9. Find the length of this tack to the
(74) nearest tenth of a centimeter.

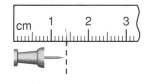

10. Write the fraction $\frac{8}{10}$ as a decimal
(72) number.

11. Divide 53 by 10 and write the quotient as a mixed
(65) number.

12. Four times a number n can be written $4n$. If $4n = 20$,
(18) then n equals what number?

13. Segment AB is 40 millimeters long. Segment BC is 35
(73) millimeters long. How long is segment AC?

A B C

14.
(6)
$$\begin{array}{r} 87,864 \\ 46,325 \\ + 39,784 \\ \hline \end{array}$$

15.
(9)
$$\begin{array}{r} 34,125 \\ - 16,086 \\ \hline \end{array}$$

16.
(13)
$$\begin{array}{r} \$400.00 \\ - \$398.57 \\ \hline \end{array}$$

17.
(26)
$$\dfrac{5628}{6}$$

18.
(63)
$$\begin{array}{r} 807 \\ \times 479 \\ \hline \end{array}$$

19.
(30)
$$\begin{array}{r} \$7.00 \\ \times \quad 800 \\ \hline \end{array}$$

20.
(24)
$3\dfrac{2}{3} - \left(2\dfrac{1}{3} + 1 \right)$

21.
(24)
$4 - \left(2 + 1\dfrac{1}{4} \right)$

22. $36 \times 60 \times 7$
(18)

23. $\$20 - (\$8 + \$2.07)$
(24)

Read this information. Then answer questions 24 and 25.

There are 16 players on the Norwood softball team. Ten players are in the game at one time. The rest of the players are substitutes. The team won 7 of its first 10 games.

24. The Norwood softball team has how many substitutes?
(54)

25. If the team played 12 games in all, what is the largest
(54) number of games the team could have won?

A. 12　　　B. 10　　　C. 9　　　D. 7

LESSON
75

Writing Hundredths in Decimal Form

Facts Practice: 48 Uneven Divisions (Test G in Test Masters)

Mental Math: Say these fractions equal to $\frac{1}{2}$: $\frac{1}{2}$, $\frac{2}{4}$, $\frac{3}{6}$, ...
Continue the pattern to $\frac{12}{24}$.

    a. CCLXXV   **b.** LIV   **c.** $\sqrt{64}$ **d.** 640 ÷ 20
    e. 6 × 8, − 3, ÷ 5, × 3, + 1, ÷ 4

Problem Solving: Two figures are similar if they are the same shape. These two triangles are not similar. Draw a triangle similar to the top triangle. Make the sides 2 cm long.

A common fraction with a denominator of 100 can be written as a decimal number with two digits after the decimal point. The digits of the numerator of the common fraction become the digits of the decimal number.

    1. One hundredth as a common fraction: $\frac{1}{100}$

    2. One hundredth as a decimal number: 0.01

Notice that in the decimal number, we placed the 1 **two places** to the right of the decimal point so that the 1 is in the **hundredths' place.** Study these examples.

$$\frac{3}{100} = 0.03 \qquad \frac{30}{100} = 0.30 \qquad \frac{97}{100} = 0.97$$

Notice that when the fraction has only one digit in the numerator, we still write two digits after the decimal point. In the first example above, we write the 3 in the second place and a 0 in the first place.

Example 1   Write twelve hundredths as a common fraction and again as a decimal number.

Solution   We write twelve hundredths as a common fraction this way, $\frac{12}{100}$. A common fraction with a denominator of 100 can be written as a decimal number with two digits after the decimal point, as **0.12**.

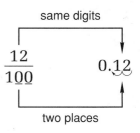

Example 2   Write the fraction $\frac{7}{100}$ as a decimal number.

Solution   A fraction with a denominator of 100 can be written as a decimal number with two digits after the decimal point. We may not write 0.7, because this is seven tenths. We may not write 0.70, because this is seventy hundredths. Instead, we write the 7 in the second place and put a zero in the first place. We write seven hundredths this way: **0.07**

Practice   Complete this chart:

Fraction form	$\frac{25}{100}$	a.	$\frac{5}{100}$	c.
Decimal form	0.25	0.09	b.	0.11

Problem set 75

1. The books are divided into 4 piles with 15 books in each pile. If the books are divided into 5 equal piles instead of 4, how many books will be in each pile?
   (55)

2. A loop of string 20 inches long is made into the shape of a square. How long is each side of the square?
   (60)

3. Sandy rented 2 movies for $2.13 each. She paid for them with a $10 bill. How much money did she get back?
   (55)

4. On the baseball field the bases are
(60) 90 feet apart. Hank hit a home run
and ran to first base, second base,
third base, and back to home.
How far did he run?

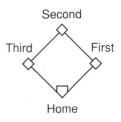

5. Write the fraction twenty-one hundredths as a
(75) common fraction and again as a decimal number.

6. Write the fraction $\frac{9}{100}$ as a decimal number.
(75)

7. Use a fraction, a decimal number,
(72) and a percent to name the part of
this rectangle that is **not** shaded.

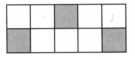

8. Write the length of this segment
(74) as a number of centimeters and
again as a number of millimeters.

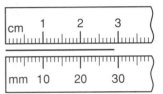

9. Write the decimal number 0.03 as a fraction.
(75)

10. Divide 81 by 10 and write the quotient as a mixed
(65) number.

11. Five times a number m can be written $5m$.
(18) If $5m = 30$, then m equals what number?

12. Segment AB is $1\frac{1}{2}$ inches long. Segment BC is 2 inches
(73) long. How long is segment AC?

A   B   C

13. $34.15   **14.**   20,101   **15.**   985   **16.**   488
(13) $78.09   (9)   − 19,191   (62) × 768   (6)   46
    + $87.76   797
                                                      49
                                                     666
                                                   + 54

17. $\dfrac{7848}{9}$ (26)

18. $\dfrac{3640}{70}$ (61)

19. $\dfrac{\$16.50}{30}$ (61)

20. $10 - \left(3 + 1\dfrac{1}{3}\right)$ (24)

21. $3\dfrac{1}{4} + \left(2 - 1\dfrac{1}{4}\right)$ (24)

22. $24 \times 8 \times 50$ (18)

23. Write two fractions equal to $\frac{1}{2}$. Make 30 the (68) denominator of the first fraction and make 25 the numerator of the second fraction.

Use this menu to answer questions 24 and 25:

24. What is the total cost of one taco, (54) two nachos, and one small drink?

25. Sam paid for 2 burritos with a $5 (54) bill. How much money should he get back?

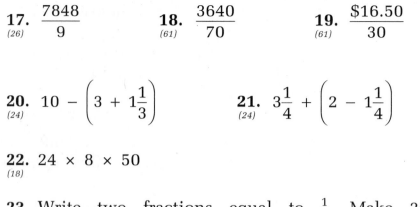

MENU	
Taco	$1.20
Nachos	$0.90
Burrito	$1.05
Drinks:	
Regular	$0.80
Small	$0.50
Prices include sales tax.	

LESSON 76

Naming Fractional Parts with Decimal Fractions–Hundredths

Facts Practice: 100 Multiplication Facts (Test C in Test Masters)

Mental Math: The numbers 1, 4, 9, 16, and 25 are square numbers. What are the next five square numbers in the sequence?

a. CXIV   **b.** CLXIX   **c.** $\sqrt{4}$ **d.** 750 ÷ 10

e. Find 25% of 80, + 1, ÷ 3, + 1, × 3, ÷ 2

Problem Solving: The "Old McDonald" code replaces the vowels A-E-I-O-U with the vowels E-I-E-I-O, in that order. For example, "on his farm" becomes "in hes ferm." Rewrite the sentence "Old McDonald had a farm" in Old McDonald code.

When a whole is divided into 10 equal parts, we can name the parts with a decimal number that has one place after the decimal point. When a whole is divided into **100 equal parts,** we can name the parts with a decimal number that has **two** places after the decimal point.

A decimal number with two places after the decimal point is like a fraction with a denominator of 100. Both mean that the whole has been divided into 100 parts. The shaded square below is a drawing that represents the fraction one hundredth.

The square is divided into 100 parts. One part is shaded, and this part is **one hundredth** of the square. We can write one hundredth as a common fraction or as a decimal number.

One hundredth as a common fraction is $\frac{1}{100}$.

One hundredth as a decimal number is 0.01.

We can also name one hundredth as a percent. The word *percent* means "of each hundred." So one out of 100 parts is one percent.

One hundredth as a percent is 1%.

Example   Name the fraction of the square that is shaded as a common fraction, as a decimal number, and as a percent.

Solution   Thirty-three of the hundred parts are shaded. As a common fraction, we write thirty-three hundredths as $\frac{33}{100}$. As a decimal number, we write it this way: **0.33.** As a percent, we write **33%.**

Practice   **a.** What common fraction names the shaded part of this square?

b. What decimal number names the shaded part of this square?

c. What percent names the shaded part of this square?

d. What common fraction names the unshaded part of this square?

e. What decimal number names the unshaded part of this square?

f. What percent names the unshaded part of this square?

Problem set 76   **1.** It takes Phil 20 minutes to walk to school. What time
(29)   should he leave for school if he wants to arrive at 8:10 a.m.?

2. To improve her physical condition, Donna swims,
(21)   bikes, and runs. Every day Donna swims 40 lengths of a pool that is 25 meters long. How far does Donna swim each day?

3. What is the next number in this sequence?
(1)

9876, 9866, 9856, _____, ...

4. Use words to name the mixed number $2\frac{3}{10}$.
(43)

5. If each side of a hexagon is 4 inches long, what is the
(60) perimeter of the hexagon?

6. William found $30,000 of misplaced money. The
(50) grateful owner gave William one tenth of the money as
a reward. How much money did William get?

7. Name the part of the square that is
(76) shaded as a fraction, as a decimal
number, and as a percent.

8. Divide and write the quotient of
(65) $\frac{35}{8}$ as a mixed number.

9. Use a common fraction and a decimal number to name
(73) the point marked by the arrow on this number line.

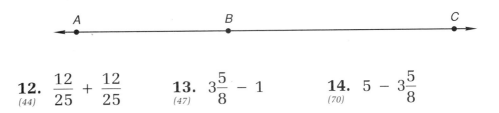

10. List the factors of 12 that are also factors of 20.
(25)

11. The length of segment *AC* is 10 centimeters. If the
(73) length of segment *AB* is 4 centimeters, how long is
segment *BC*?

A ———— B ———————————— C

12. $\frac{12}{25} + \frac{12}{25}$ **13.** $3\frac{5}{8} - 1$ **14.** $5 - 3\frac{5}{8}$
(44)   *(47)*   *(70)*

15. 68,085
(6)   42,357
        + 76,983

16.   31,060
(9)   − 19,363

17. $34.26
(57) ×   78

18. $\dfrac{36,012}{6}$
(35)

19. $40\overline{)\$9.60}$
(61)

20. 3989 ÷ 9
(26)

21. 17 × 30 × 9
(18)

22. $100 − ($90 + $9 + $0.01)
(24)

23. Write the following sentence using digits and math
(4) symbols:

"Five times one equals five plus zero."

Use the graph to answer questions 24 and 25:

24. Altogether, how many students liked either pizza or
(54) spaghetti best?

25. Which foods were the favorites of more than 6
(54) students?

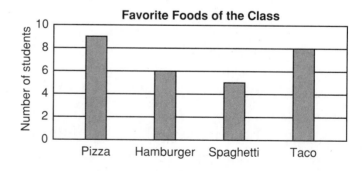

LESSON 77

Identifying Decimal Place Value Through Hundredths

Facts Practice: 90 Division Facts (Test E or F in Test Masters)

Mental Math:

a. CCCLXX   **b.** LXXVII   **c.** $\sqrt{81}$ **d.** $1 - \frac{5}{12}$

e. One tenth of 23 is $2\frac{3}{10}$. How much is $\frac{1}{10}$ of 43? $\frac{1}{10}$ of 51?

f. Find 25% of 40, + 1, × 3, − 1, ÷ 4

Problem Solving: Triangles A and B are congruent. Copy these triangles on your paper. If triangle A is "flipped" or reflected to the right, it will have the same orientation as triangle B. Imagine triangle B "flipped" down. Draw the triangle you imagine. Label the figure triangle C.

To name a decimal number that has digits on both sides of the decimal point, we mentally break the number into two parts: the whole-number part and the fraction part. The whole-number part is to the left of the decimal point. The fraction part is to the right of the decimal point.

To read this decimal number ⎯⎯⎯⎯⎯⎯⎯⎯→ 12.5

We mentally break it into two parts like this ⎯→ ⑫.⑤

We read the whole-number part first. We say "and" at the decimal point. Then we read the fraction part. To read the fraction part, we read the digits as though they named a whole number. Then we say the place value of the last digit. The last digit of 12.5 is 5. It is in the **tenths'** place.

$$\underset{\downarrow}{⑫} \quad \underset{\downarrow}{.} \quad \underset{\downarrow}{⑤}$$

twelve and five tenths

Example 1   Use words to name the decimal number 12.25.

Solution   We break the number into two parts. We name the whole-number part, then write "and," and then name the fraction part. **Then we write the place value of the last digit,** which in this case is hundredths. We write **twelve and twenty-five hundredths.**

⑫.㉕

Example 2   Use digits to write the decimal number ten and twelve hundredths.

Solution   The whole number part is ten. The decimal part is twelve hundredths. The word *hundredths* means there are two places to the right of the decimal point.

Ten and … hundredths

↓

10._ _

The twelve is written in the two decimal places.

10.12

Practice*   Use words to name each decimal number:

    a. 8.9

    b. 24.42

    c. 125.1

    d. 100.75

Use digits to write the decimal numbers:

    e. Twenty-five and fifty-two hundredths

    f. Thirty and one tenth

    g. Seven and eighty-nine hundredths

    h. Two hundred thirty-four and five tenths

**Problem set
77**

1. Draw a triangle that has an obtuse angle.
(33)

2. The years from 1401 to 1500 are known as the
(27) fifteenth century. What fifteenth-century year was five centuries before 1992?

3. Cordelia has read $\frac{1}{3}$ of a 240-page book. How many
(50) pages has she read? What percent of the book has she read?

4. If 3 tickets cost $12, how many tickets can be bought
(55) for $20?

5. Write these fractions in order from least to greatest:
(68)
$$\frac{5}{5}, \frac{3}{4}, \frac{2}{6}, \frac{1}{2}$$

6. A number is **divisible** by 4 if it can be divided by 4
(20) without a remainder. The numbers 8, 20, and 32 are all divisible by 4. What number between 10 and 20 is divisible by both 4 and 6?

7. Use a fraction, a decimal number,
(76) and a percent to name the shaded part of this square.

8. Which digit in 16.43 is in the
(71) tenths' place?

9. Which digit in 93.6 is in the same place as the 4 in
(71) 4.25?

10. Name the point on the number line marked by the
(73) arrow as a mixed number and as a decimal number.

11. The number 15 has how many different factors?
(25)

12. Six times a number y can be written $6y$. If $6y = 60$,
(18)   then y equals what number?

13. The length of segment RT is 100 millimeters. If the
(73)   length of segment RS is 30 millimeters, how long is
segment ST?

$$R \quad\quad\quad S \quad\quad\quad\quad\quad\quad\quad\quad T$$

14. 87,906
(6)
71,425
+ 57,342

15.   407
(63) × 819

16. $\dfrac{\$8.76}{6}$
(26)

17. $600 \div (60 \div 6)$
(24)

18. $40\overline{)5860}$
(61)

19. Divide and write the quotient with a fraction: $5\overline{)236}$
(65)

20. $341 + 5716 + 98 + 492 + 1375$
(6)

21. $7 \times 6 \times 5 \times 4$
(18)

22. $5\dfrac{1}{4} + \left(3 - 1\dfrac{1}{4}\right)$
(24)

23. $3\dfrac{1}{6} + 2\dfrac{2}{6} + 1\dfrac{3}{6}$
(66)

24. $20\overline{)300}$
(61)

25. Compare: $365 \times 1 \bigcirc 365 \div 1$
(4)

LESSON 78

Fractions of a Second · Comparing Decimal Numbers

Facts Practice: 64 Multiplication Facts (Test D in Test Masters)

Mental Math: Say these fractions equal to $\frac{1}{2}$: $\frac{1}{2}$, $\frac{2}{4}$, $\frac{3}{6}$, ...
Continue the pattern to $\frac{12}{24}$.

   a. CCIX   **b.** CLXIV   **c.** $\sqrt{100}$ **d.** $3\frac{1}{2} + 3\frac{1}{2}$
   e. Find $\frac{1}{3}$ of 12, × 5, − 2, ÷ 2, × 5, − 1, ÷ 4

Problem Solving: Some small cubes were stacked together to form this larger cube. How many small cubes were used?

Fractions of a second

Fractions of a second are usually expressed as decimals.

Cecilia ran 100 meters in 14.6 seconds.

Todd swam 50 meters in 28.43 seconds.

Athletes often state their race times in a shorter way. Cecilia's 100-meter time was fourteen and six tenths seconds. Cecilia might say she ran "fourteen point six" or even "fourteen six." If she runs 100 meters in 14.0 seconds, she might say she ran "fourteen flat." What is important to understand is that 14.6 seconds is a little more than 14 seconds but less than 15 seconds. A tenth of a second is a short period of time. A tenth of a second is about how long it takes to blink your eyes. A hundredth of a second is less than human reaction time. Races timed to a hundredth of a second are timed electronically rather than by a hand-held stopwatch.

A stopwatch can help us understand fractions of a second. Start a stopwatch. Then try to stop the watch exactly 5 seconds later. How close can you come to 5.00? Trying with your eyes closed tests your ability to estimate brief periods of time.

Comparing decimal numbers

To compare decimal numbers, we need to pay close attention to place value. The decimal point separates the whole number part of a decimal number from the fraction part.

Example 1   Compare: 12.3 ◯ 1.23

Solution   Although the same digits appear in both numbers in the same order, the numbers are not equal. The number 12.3 is a little more than 12 but is less than 13. The number 1.23 is more than 1 but less than 2. So 12.3 is greater than 1.23.

$$12.3 > 1.23$$

Example 2   Arrange these numbers in order from least to greatest:

$$1.02, 1.2, 1.12$$

Solution   The whole number part of each number is 1, so we need to compare the fraction part. The first digit to the right of the decimal point is in the tenths' place (in money, it is the dimes' place). The number 1.02 has a zero in the tenths' place. The number 1.12 has a one in the tenths' place, and the number 1.2 has a two in the tenths' place. This is enough information to place the numbers in order.

$$\textbf{1.02, 1.12, 1.2}$$

Practice   **a.** John ran 200 meters in 38.6 seconds. Mike ran 200 meters in 37.9 seconds. Which boy ran faster?

b. Compare: 3.21 ◯ 32.1

c. Write these numbers in order from least to greatest:

$$2.4, 2.04, 2.21$$

Problem set 78   **1.** The ceiling was covered with square tiles. There were
(21)   30 rows of tiles with 30 tiles in each row. How many tiles covered the ceiling?

2. Carlos gave the clerk $10 for a book that cost $6.95
(55)   plus $0.42 tax. How much money should he get back?

3. Silvia emptied a jar of 1000 pennies and put them into
(21)   rolls holding 50 pennies each. How many rolls did she fill?

4. The distance around the school track is $\frac{1}{4}$ mile. How
(23) many times must Steve run around the track to run 1
      mile?

5. A number is **divisible** by 3 if it can be divided by 3
(20) and not have a remainder. What even number greater
      than 20 and less than 30 is divisible by 3?

6. List the numbers that are factors of both 10 and 15.
(25)

7. Compare: 44.4 $\bigcirc$ 4.44
(78)

8. Which digit in 56,132 is in the same place as the 8 in
(58) 489,700?

9. Use a fraction, a decimal number,
(72) and a percent to name the part of
      this group of circles that is **not**
      shaded.

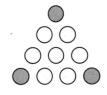

10. Give the length of this segment to the nearest tenth of
(74)   a centimeter.

11. Which digit in 67.89 is in the hundredths' place?
(71)

12. The length of segment *LN* is 4 inches. If segment *MN* is
(73) $1\frac{1}{2}$ inches, how long is segment *LM*?

13. Use words to name the decimal number 10.5.
(77)

14. Use digits to write the decimal number fifteen and
(77)   twelve hundredths.

15. $\dfrac{3744}{8}$
(26)

16. $\begin{array}{r} 30,000 \\ -\ 29,925 \\ \hline \end{array}$
(9)

17. $\begin{array}{r} 973 \\ \times\ 536 \\ \hline \end{array}$
(62)

18. $\begin{array}{r} 8746 \\ 954 \\ 6027 \\ 488 \\ 6517 \\ +\quad 79 \\ \hline \end{array}$
(6)

19. $\begin{array}{r} \$0.65 \\ \times\quad 10 \\ \hline \end{array}$
(30)

20. $5\overline{)\$9.60}$
(26)

21. $\dfrac{\$54.30}{30}$
(61)

22. $7 - \left(3 + 1\dfrac{1}{3} \right)$
(24)

23. $5\dfrac{2}{3} + \left(3\dfrac{1}{3} - 2 \right)$
(24)

Read this information. Then answer questions 24 and 25.

In the school election for president, Aaron received 239 votes, Bryce received 168 votes, and Sammie received 197 votes.

24. The winner received how many more votes than the
(54) person who came in second?

25. One other person ran for president and received 95
(54) votes. Altogether, how many votes were cast for president?

LESSON 79

Counting Decimal Places • Writing Equivalent Decimal Numbers

Facts Practice: 48 Uneven Divisions (Test G in Test Masters)

Mental Math: The Roman numerals XC mean 10 less than 100, which is 90. The Roman numerals XL mean 10 less than 50, which is 40. What is the value of each of these Roman numerals?

a. XCV   **b.** XLIV   **c.** XCIX   **d.** XLIX

(Notice we do not use an I and a C to make 99 or an I and an L to make 49.)

Problem Solving: Copy this multiplication problem and fill in the missing digits.

$$\begin{array}{r} \overline{}\overline{} \\ \times\ \ 7 \\ \hline 5\_6 \end{array}$$

Counting decimal places

When talking about decimal numbers, we may use the term "decimal places." **By decimal places we mean the number of digits to the right of the decimal point.** For example, the number 1.234 is written with three decimal places. The number 15.2 is written with one decimal place. Amounts of money are usually written with two decimal places.

Example 1 Which of these numbers is written with two decimal places?

24.5   8.56   0.765

Solution We pick the number that has two digits to the right of the decimal point, **8.56.**

Writing equivalent decimal numbers

We may add decimal places to a number without changing the value of the number by attaching one or more zeros to the right of the last decimal place. For example, we may write 0.3 as 0.30. The zero does not change the value of the number because it does not change the place value of the 3. In both numbers 3 is in the tenths' place. Thus, three tenths and thirty hundredths are equal in value.

Example 2 Write 12.6 with three decimal places.

Solution The number 12.6 is written with one decimal place. By attaching two zeros, we can write it with three decimal places, **12.600.**

Example 3 Compare: 12.6 ◯ 12.600

Solution When we compare decimal numbers, we must pay close attention to place value. We use the decimal point to locate places. We see that the whole-number parts of these two numbers are the same. The fraction parts look different, but both numbers have a 6 in the tenths' place. If we add two zeros to 12.6 so that 12.6 has three decimal places, we see that the numbers are the same.

$$12.600 \bigcirc 12.600$$

Since the numbers are equal, the correct comparison symbol is **=.**

Practice Write each of these numbers with three decimal places:

    a. 1.2   **b.** 4.08   **c.** 0.50000

Compare:

    d. 50 ◯ 500   **e.** 0.4 ◯ 0.04

    f. 0.50 ◯ 0.500   **g.** 0.2 ◯ 0.20000

Problem set 79

1. Each side of a 1-foot square is 1 foot long. What is the
_(60)_ perimeter of a 1-foot square?

2. Columbus landed in the Americas in 1492. The
_(27)_ Pilgrims landed in 1620. This was how many years after Columbus landed?

3. Estimate the product of 307 and 593 by rounding both
_(69)_ numbers to the nearest hundred before you multiply.

4. Three times a number n can be written $3n$. If n equals
_(17)_ the number 5, then what number does $3n$ equal?

5. Mike has read $\frac{1}{3}$ of his book. What fraction of his book
(67) does he still have to read? What percent of his book
does he still have to read?

6. Draw a circle. Shade one eighth of it. What percent of
(47) the circle is shaded?

7. Divide 100 by 7 and write the quotient as a mixed
(65) number.

8. Which digit in 12.3 is in the tenths' place?
(71)

9. Use a common fraction and a dec-
(76) imal number to name the part of
this square that is shaded. What
percent of the square is not
shaded?

10. Which digit in 98.765 is in the same place as the 2 in
(71) 1.23?

11. The length of segment QR is 3 centimeters. The length
(73) of segment RS is twice the length of segment QR. How
long is segment QS?

12. Use words to name the decimal number 16.21.
(77)

13. Write 1.5 with two decimal places.
(79)

14. Compare: 3.6 ◯ 3.60
(79)

15.   307   **16.** $\frac{765}{5}$ **17.** $60\overline{)\$87.00}$
(63) $\times\,593$ (26)   (61)

18. 3517 + 9636 + 48 + 921 + 8576 + 50,906
(6)

19. $2\frac{3}{10} + 1\frac{3}{10} + \frac{3}{10}$ **20.** $9\frac{4}{8} + \left(4 - 1\frac{7}{8}\right)$
(47)   (24)

21. $40 \times 50 \times 60$ **22.** $100 - (\$84.37 + \$12)$
(18)   (24)

23. Write the following sentence using digits and
(4)   symbols:

"Two thirds is less than three fourths."

Use the graph below to answer questions 24 and 25:

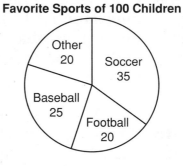

Favorite Sports of 100 Children

24. How many children liked either soccer or football
(54) best?

25. What was the second most favorite sport?
(54)

LESSON 80

Writing Money in Two Forms: As Cents and as Dollars

Facts Practice: 100 Multiplication Facts (Test C in Test Masters)

Mental Math: Say these fractions equal to $\frac{1}{2}$: $\frac{1}{2}$, $\frac{2}{4}$, $\frac{3}{6}$, ... Continue to $\frac{15}{30}$.

a. CXL   **b.** CXC   **c.** $\frac{1}{3}$ of 10
d. $\frac{1}{3}$ of 100   **e.** $\sqrt{25}$, + 3, × 4, + 1, ÷ 3

Problem Solving: All squares are similar. Each side of this square is $\frac{1}{2}$-inch long. Draw a square with sides half as long and another square with sides twice as long. Find the total perimeter of all three squares.

$\frac{1}{2}$ in.

There are two different ways to write amounts of money:

1. As a number of cents, such as 25¢.

2. As a number of dollars, such as $0.25.

When we write money as a number of cents, we write a cent sign, ¢, after the number. A penny is one cent and can be written 1¢. Thirty-five cents is written as 35¢. Fifty-eight cents is written as 58¢. We can also write these amounts of money with a dollar sign in front and then a decimal number. Remember that a penny is one hundredth of a dollar. We can write 1¢ as $0.01. We can write 35¢ as $0.35 and 58¢ as $0.58. We can use either the $ sign or the ¢ sign to write these values. We use one sign or the other sign.

Example 1 Write 5 cents in two forms: first as a number of cents and second as a fraction of a dollar.

Solution 5¢, $0.05

Example 2 $1.56 + 75¢

Solution   When the two forms of writing money are in the same problem, we usually rewrite the numbers so that all money amounts are in the same form

$$\begin{array}{r} \$1.56 \\ + \ \$0.75 \\ \hline \$2.31 \end{array}$$

before we solve the problem. Sums of money equal to a dollar or more are usually written with a dollar sign. To find the answer, we write 75¢ in dollar form, $0.75, and then we add to get **$2.31.**

Example 3   Olive bought 9 cans of spinach for 49¢ each. What was the cost of all 9 cans?

Solution   To find the cost of 9 cans, we may multiply 49¢ by 9. We will change 49¢ to dollar form, $0.49, before we multiply.

$$\begin{array}{r} \$0.49 \\ \times \ \ \ \ \ 9 \\ \hline \$4.41 \end{array}$$

Practice   Write the amount of money in two forms: first as a number of cents and second as a fraction of a dollar.

   a. Two cents   **b.** Fifty cents

   c. Twenty-five cents   **d.** Nine cents

Solve and write the answer in the form shown after each equal sign:

   e. 36¢ + 24¢ = $_____   **f.** $1.38 − 70¢ = _____ ¢

   g. $0.25 − 5¢ = $_____   **h.** $1 − 8¢ = _____ ¢

   i. 7 × 65¢   **j.** 20 × 18¢

Problem set 80

1. What is the total cost of a $7.98 notebook plus 49¢ tax?
(80)

2. In Room 7 there are 6 rows of desks with 5 desks in each row. There are 4 books in each desk. How many books are in all the desks?
(55)

3. This year Martin is "twice as old" as his sister. If
(55) Martin is 12 years old now, how old will his sister be
next year?

4. Silviano saves half dollars in a coin holder. How many
(50) half dollars does it take to total $5?

5. Louisa put her nickel collection into rolls that hold 40
(55) nickels each. She filled 15 rolls and had 7 nickels left
over. Altogether, how many nickels did Louisa have?

6. The number 7 has how many different factors?
(25)

7. Which of these fractions does not equal $\frac{1}{2}$?
(68)
$$\frac{6}{12}, \frac{7}{15}, \frac{8}{16}, \frac{9}{18}$$

8. Allison can swim 50 meters in half a minute. Amy can
(78) swim 50 meters in 28.72 seconds. Which of the two
girls can swim faster?

9. Use a mixed number and a decimal number to name
(73) the place on this number line marked by the arrow.

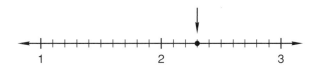

10. Which digit in 1.234 is in the same place as the 7 in
(71) 58.67?

11. Use digits to write the decimal number ten and one
(77) tenth.

12. How many cents is $\frac{4}{5}$ of a dollar?
(46)

13. Segment *AB* measures 50 millimeters. The length of
(73) segment *BC* is half the length of segment *AB*. How
long is segment *AC*?

14. Compare: 12.3 ◯ 12.30
(79)

15. $60.10   **16.** $9.84   **17.** $7.46
(13) − 48.37   (62) × 156   (13) $6.52
                                        $5.37
                                        $8.95
                                        $0.71
                                      + $0.39

18. $1.75 + 36¢ = $_____   **19.** $1.15 − $0.80 = _____ ¢
(80)   (80)

20. 40 × 76¢   **21.** $39.00 ÷ 50
(80)   (61)

22. $\dfrac{13}{100} + \dfrac{14}{100}$ **23.** $7 - \left(6\dfrac{3}{5} - 1\dfrac{1}{5}\right)$
(44)   (24)

Read this information. Then answer questions 24 and 25.

Matthew invented a machine to change numbers. When he puts a 7 into the machine, a 5 comes out. When he puts a 4 in the machine, a 2 comes out. When he puts a 3 in the machine, a 1 comes out.

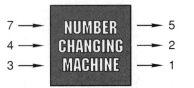

24. What does the machine do to the numbers Matthew
(54) puts into the machine?

    A. It adds 2.   B. It subtracts 2.

    C. It divides by 2.   D. It multiplies the number.

25. If Matthew puts in a 10, what number will come out?
(54)

LESSON 81

Using Fraction Manipulatives, Part 3 • More About Segments

Facts Practice: 90 Division Facts (Test E or F in Test Masters)

Mental Math: How many minutes is $2\frac{1}{2}$ hours?

   a. CCXC   **b.** XLVII   **c.** 60×70

   d. Find $\frac{1}{2}$ of 12, $\frac{1}{3}$ of 12, $\frac{1}{4}$ of 12   **e.** 10% of 250

   f. $\sqrt{36}$, $+ 1$, $\times 7$, $+ 1$, $\div 5$, $- 2$, $\div 2$

Problem Solving: Write the product of XII and XII as a Roman numeral.

Using fraction manipulatives, part 3

In this lesson we will make and use fraction manipulatives for sixths and twelfths.

Materials needed:

- Each student needs a copy of "Fraction Master 3—Sixths and Twelfths" (available in the *Math 65 Test Masters*)

- scissors

- envelopes or locking plastic bags to store fraction pieces in

- crayons (optional)

- fraction manipulatives for halves, fourths, and tenths (from Lesson 37) and for thirds, fifths, and eighths (from Lesson 46)

Preparation for activities:

- Distribute materials. If fraction manipulatives will be color-coded, we suggest agreeing on the color for each circle and lightly coloring the front and back of each circle before cutting. Students should save the manipulatives for later use.

Use your fraction manipulatives to help you with these activities:

(a) Show that two sixths equals one third.

(b) Show that one sixth is half of one third.

(c) Show that two twelfths equals one sixth.

(d) Show that one twelfth is half of one sixth.

(e) Compare: three sixths ◯ one half

(f) Compare: one twelfth ◯ one tenth

(g) How many twelfths equal one fourth?

(h) How many twelfths equal one third?

(i) What fraction is equal to one half of one half?

(j) What fraction is equal to one half of one fourth?

(k) What fraction is equal to one third of one fourth?

(l) One sixth of a circle is what percent of a circle?

(m) One twelfth of a circle is what percent of a circle?

More about segments   We may refer to segment *AB* by writing a bar over the *AB* like this, $\overline{AB}$. The bar takes the place of the word *segment*. We read $\overline{AB}$ as "segment *AB*." We may also write $\overline{BA}$ to refer to the same segment.

Segment *AB* has length. We may write that the length of $\overline{AB}$ is 5 cm. We may also write "*AB* is 5 cm." When we write *AB* without the bar, we mean the distance from *A* to *B*.

Practice   Segment *JK* is 2 cm long. *KL* is 3 cm. Find the length of $\overline{JL}$.

Problem set
81

1. Reggie bought a dozen candy bars for 20¢ each. What was the total cost of the candy bars?
(80)

2. What is the total price for 4 cartons of ice cream that cost $2.50 for each carton?
(21)

3. Four times a number m can be written $4m$. If m equals 7, then what does $4m$ equal?
(17)

4. Mary has read $\frac{1}{3}$ of a 240-page book. How many pages does she still have to read? What percent of the book does she still have to read?
(67)

5. One meter equals 100 centimeters. Five meters equals how many centimeters?
(21)

6. Use words to name the decimal number 12.25.
(77)

7. Use your fraction manipulatives to find how many twelfths equal one half.
(81)

8. List the factors of 16.
(25)

9. Leroy ran 100 meters in ten and twelve hundredths seconds. Use digits to write Leroy's race time.
(77)

10. Which digit in 436.2 is in the ones' place?
(71)

11. Divide and write the quotient with a fraction: $\frac{100}{3}$
(65)

12. Segment FH measures 90 millimeters. If GH is 35 millimeters, how long is $\overline{FG}$?
(81)

13. $10.35 + $5.18 + 8¢ + $11 + 97¢
(80)

14. $80.00
(13) − 72.47

15. $4.97
(17) ×   6

16.   375
(62) × 548

17. 7$\overline{)\$40.53}$ **18.** 60$\overline{)5340}$ **19.** 6000 ÷ 30
(26)   (61)   (61)

20. $3\frac{3}{8} + 1\frac{1}{8} + 4\frac{4}{8}$ **21.** $7\frac{3}{4} - \left(5 - 1\frac{1}{4}\right)$
(66)   (24)

22. Compare: $55.5 \bigcirc 5.55$
(78)

23. $4\frac{1}{10} + 5\frac{1}{10} + 10\frac{1}{10}$ **24.** $10 - \left(4 + 1\frac{1}{8}\right)$
(44)   (24)

25. This rectangle is half as wide as it is long. What is the
(60) perimeter of the rectangle?

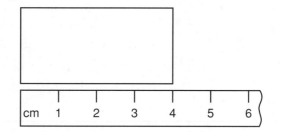

LESSON 82

Adding and Subtracting Decimal Numbers, Part 1

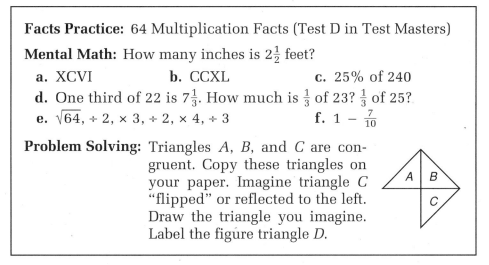

Facts Practice: 64 Multiplication Facts (Test D in Test Masters)

Mental Math: How many inches is $2\frac{1}{2}$ feet?

   a. XCVI   **b.** CCXL   **c.** 25% of 240

   d. One third of 22 is $7\frac{1}{3}$. How much is $\frac{1}{3}$ of 23? $\frac{1}{3}$ of 25?

   e. $\sqrt{64}$, ÷ 2, × 3, ÷ 2, × 4, ÷ 3   **f.** $1 - \frac{7}{10}$

Problem Solving: Triangles A, B, and C are congruent. Copy these triangles on your paper. Imagine triangle C "flipped" or reflected to the left. Draw the triangle you imagine. Label the figure triangle D.

Recall that when we add or subtract money, we write the numbers so that the decimal points are in a line vertically. The decimal point in the answer is placed in line below the other decimal points, as we show here.

$$
\begin{array}{r}
\$3.45 \\
+ \ 1.25 \\
\hline
\$4.70
\end{array}
\qquad
\begin{array}{r}
\$3.45 \\
- \ 1.25 \\
\hline
\$2.20
\end{array}
$$

We use the same rule when we add or subtract any decimal numbers. We keep the decimal points in line. This way we add and subtract digits with the same place value. See how the decimal points stay in a straight line.

$$
\begin{array}{r}
2\,.\,4 \\
+ 1\,.\,3 \\
\hline
3\,.\,7
\end{array}
\qquad
\begin{array}{r}
2\,.\,4 \\
- 1\,.\,3 \\
\hline
1\,.\,1
\end{array}
$$

Example 1
$$
\begin{array}{r}
4.3 \\
12.5 \\
+ \ 7.6 \\
\end{array}
$$

Solution We keep the decimal points in line in the problem and answer. We add the digits column by column, just as we would add whole numbers or money.

$$
\begin{array}{r}
4.3 \\
12.5 \\
+ \ 7.6 \\
\hline
\mathbf{24.4}
\end{array}
$$

Example 2   6.37
                − 4.2

Solution   As we saw in Lesson 79, we may
attach zeros to the end of a decimal
number without changing the value of
the number. We may attach a zero to
4.2 so that there are no empty places
in the problem. Then we subtract.

$$\begin{array}{r} 6.37 \\ -\ 4.20 \\ \hline \mathbf{2.17} \end{array}$$

Note: Attaching zeros may make the problem easier
to work. However, it is not necessary to
attach zeros as long as we remember that an
empty place has the same value as a zero in
that place.

Practice   Add:

a.	3.4	**b.**	4.63	**c.**	9.62
	6.7		2.5		12.5
	+ 11.3		+ 0.46		+ 3.7

Subtract:

d.	3.64	**e.**	5.37	**f.**	0.436
	− 1.46		− 1.6		− 0.2

**Problem set
82**

1. Ben bought a sheet of 35¢ stamps. The sheet had 5
(55) rows of stamps with 8 stamps in each row. How much
did the sheet of stamps cost?

2. Cynthia is half the age of her brother, but she is 2 years
(55) older than her sister. If Cynthia's brother is 18 years
old, how old is her sister?

3. Morten was asked to run to the fence and back. It took
(82) him 23.4 seconds to run to the fence and 50.9 seconds
to run back. How many seconds did the whole trip
take?

4. The classroom floor is covered with square tiles. There
(21) are 30 rows of tiles with 40 tiles in each row.
Altogether, how many tiles cover the floor?

5. Draw two circles. Shade $\frac{2}{8}$ of one circle and $\frac{1}{4}$ of the
(40) other circle. What percent of each circle is shaded?

6. What fraction is equal to one half of one third?
(81)

7. To the nearest tenth of a centimeter, what is the length
(74) of this rectangle? Use words to write your answer.

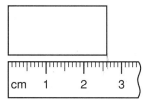

8. List the numbers that are factors of both 16 and 20.
(25)

9. Three times a number y can be written $3y$. If $3y = 12$,
(17) then what number does $2y$ equal?

10. The length of $\overline{AC}$ is 85 millimeters. If AB is 37
(81) millimeters, how long is $\overline{BC}$?

A   B   C

11. 12.0 ◯ 1.20
(78)

12.   53.46
(82) $-$ 5.7

13. $6.48
(17) $\times$ 9

14.   5.35
(82)   12.7
       3.64
       5.87
       9.42
       6.03
  $+$ 7.21

15. $5 − 5¢
(80)

16. 5)$8.60
(26)

17. 20)$8.60
(61)

18. 378
(62) × 296

19. 800
(30) × 500

20. $\frac{9870}{30}$
(61)

21. $12 + 1\frac{1}{2}$
(47)

22. $12 - 1\frac{1}{2}$
(70)

23. $\frac{49}{99} + \frac{49}{99}$
(44)

Read this information. Then answer questions 24 and 25.

Gilbert did yard work on Saturday. He worked for $2\frac{1}{2}$ hours in the morning and $1\frac{1}{2}$ hours in the afternoon. He was paid $3.50 for every hour he worked.

24. How many hours did Gilbert work in all?
(54)

25. How much money was Gilbert paid in all?
(54)

LESSON 83

Converting Units of Length

Facts Practice: 48 Uneven Divisions (Test G in Test Masters)

Mental Math: How many cents is two and a half dollars?

  a. CXIX   **b.** CCXLIV   **c.** 10% of 360

  d. $3\frac{1}{3} + 1\frac{2}{3}$ **e.** $1 - \frac{5}{8}$ **f.** $\frac{1}{3}$ of 360

  g. $\sqrt{49}$, + 3, × 10, − 1, ÷ 9, − 1, ÷ 10

Problem Solving: Some small cubes were stacked together to form this larger cube. How many small cubes were used?

The following chart lists some common units of length used in the metric system and in the U.S. Customary System. Units used in the metric system are millimeters (mm), centimeters (cm), meters (m), and kilometers (km). Units used in the U.S. Customary System† are inches (in.), feet (ft), yards (yd), and miles (mi). The chart also gives the number of units needed to equal larger units of length.

Equivalence Table for Units of Length

U.S. Customary System	Metric System
12 in. = 1 ft 3 ft = 1 yd 5280 ft = 1 mi 1760 yd = 1 mi	10 mm = 1 cm 1000 mm = 1 m 100 cm = 1 m 1000 m = 1 km
A meter is about 3 inches longer than a yard.	

Example 1 The star player on the basketball team is 197 centimeters tall. This is nearly how many meters tall?

Solution The chart shows that 100 centimeters equals 1 meter. The prefix *cent-* can help us remember this fact because there are **100 cents** in $1. Since 197 centimeters is nearly 200 centimeters, the height of the basketball player is nearly **2 meters.**

Example 2 Two yards is the same length as how many inches?

Solution The chart shows us that 1 yard equals 3 feet and that each foot equals 12 inches.

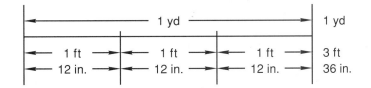

Thus, 1 yard equals 36 inches. Two yards is twice that much. Two yards equals **72 inches.**

---

†The units of the U.S. Customary System (USCS) originated in England. This system of measure was called the *English system* for many years. England has now converted to the metric system, and the United States is the only large country still using this system. Thus, the system is often called the *U.S. Customary System.*

Practice   **a.** How many yards are in one fourth of a mile?

b. Fifty millimeters is how many centimeters?

c. Tom's height is 5 feet, 1 inch. How many inches tall is he?

d. A 10K race is a 10-kilometer race. How many meters is 10 kilometers?

Problem set 83

1. Gizmos come in a carton. A carton holds 6 packages.
(55) Each package holds 10 small boxes. Each small box holds 12 gizmos. How many gizmos come in a carton?

2. When the decimal number two and three tenths is
(82) added to three and five tenths, what is the sum?

3. Bacchus bought 7 pounds of grapes for $3.43. What
(21) was the price for 1 pound of grapes?

4. Compare: $\frac{3}{6} \bigcirc \frac{6}{12}$
(68)

5. One of the players on the basketball team is 2 meters
(83) tall. Two meters is how many centimeters?

6. Use a fraction and a decimal number to name the
(73) point marked by the arrow on this number line.

7. Joanne ran the 100-meter dash in 11.02 seconds. Use
(77) words to name the decimal number 11.02.

8. Three yards is the same length as how many inches?
(83)

9. Segment RT measures 4 inches. If $\overline{RS}$ is $2\frac{1}{4}$ inches
(81) long, how long is $\overline{ST}$?

```
    R                        S                    T
◄───●────────────────────────●────────────────────●───►
```

10.   7
(47) $+\ 1\frac{3}{4}$ **11.** $3\frac{5}{12}$ **12.**   4
(44) $-\ 3\frac{5}{12}$ (70) $-\ 2\frac{1}{4}$

13.   16.2
(82) 27.35
    $+\ \ 9.4$ **14.**   30.1
(82) $-\ 14.2$ **15.**   \$12.98
(17) $\times\ \ \ \ \ \ 4$

16. $6\overline{)\$45.54}$ **17.** $\dfrac{4384}{8}$ **18.**   704
(26) (26) (63) $\times\ 987$

19. \$12 + 84¢ + \$6.85 + 9¢ + \$8 + \$98.42 + \$55.26
(80)

20. Divide and write the quotient with a fraction: $\frac{18}{5}$
(65)

21. Write a decimal number equal to 2.5 that has three
(79) decimal places.

22. The perimeter of a certain square is 24 inches. How
(60) long is each side of the square?

Look at this map. Then answer questions 23–25.

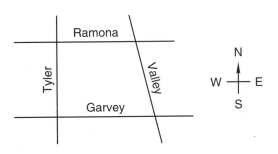

23. Which street runs north and south?
(54)

24. Which street is parallel to Ramona?
(54)

25. Which street is neither perpendicular nor parallel to
(54) Garvey?

LESSON 84

Changing Improper Fractions to Whole or Mixed Numbers

Facts Practice: 100 Multiplication Facts (Test C in Test Masters)

Mental Math: How many inches are in a foot? How many feet are in a yard? Hold your fingers an inch apart. Hold your hands a yard apart.

a. CCLXVI   **b.** CLXXIX   **c.** $\frac{1}{3}$ of 36
d. $360 \div 30$ **e.** $\sqrt{81}, -1, \times 10, +1, \div 9, -9$

Problem Solving: Sam takes about 600 steps when he walks around the block. In 6 steps Sam travels about 15 feet. About how many feet does Sam travel when he walks around the block?

A fraction may be less than 1, equal to 1, or greater than 1. A fraction that is equal to 1 or is greater than 1 is called an **improper fraction.** An improper fraction has a numerator equal to or greater than the denominator.

Less than 1	Equal to 1	Greater than 1
$\frac{3}{4}$	$\frac{4}{4}$	$\frac{5}{4}$

Improper fractions

Every improper fraction can be changed either to a whole number or to a mixed number. We convert an improper fraction into a whole number or mixed number by doing the division shown by the fraction line. A fraction line is the same as a division bar. The fraction $\frac{4}{4}$ may be thought of as 4 divided by 4. The fraction $\frac{5}{4}$ may be thought of as 5 divided by 4. If we actually divide an improper fraction, the answer will be a whole number or a mixed number.

$$\frac{4}{4} \longrightarrow 4)\overline{4} \qquad\qquad \frac{5}{4} \longrightarrow 4)\overline{5}^{1\frac{1}{4}}$$

$$\frac{4}{0} \qquad\qquad\qquad\qquad \frac{4}{1}$$

The fraction $\frac{4}{4}$ equals 1.   The fraction $\frac{5}{4}$ equals $1\frac{1}{4}$.

Example 1 Compare: Any improper fraction $\bigcirc$ $\dfrac{99}{100}$

Solution Any improper fraction is equal to or greater than 1. We know that the fraction $\frac{99}{100}$ is slightly less than 1. Thus, any improper fraction is greater than $\frac{99}{100}$. We replace the circle with the symbol **>**. Therefore, our answer is

$$\text{Any improper fraction} > \frac{99}{100}$$

Example 2 Write the fraction $\dfrac{8}{5}$ as a mixed number.

Solution If the numerator is equal to or greater than the denominator, the fraction is equal to or greater than 1. The fraction line is a division sign. We may read the fraction $\frac{8}{5}$ as 8 divided by 5. We divide and write the remainder as a fraction.

$$1\frac{3}{5}$$

Practice Convert each improper fraction into a whole number or a mixed number:

a. $\dfrac{2}{2}$ **b.** $\dfrac{5}{2}$ **c.** $\dfrac{5}{3}$ **d.** $\dfrac{9}{4}$

e. $\dfrac{3}{2}$ **f.** $\dfrac{3}{3}$ **g.** $\dfrac{6}{3}$ **h.** $\dfrac{10}{3}$

i. $\dfrac{4}{2}$ **j.** $\dfrac{4}{3}$ **k.** $\dfrac{7}{3}$ **l.** $\dfrac{15}{4}$

**Problem set
84**

1. Name the coin that is equal to half of a half dollar.
(80)

2. A number is divisible by 2 if it can be divided by 2
(2) without a remainder. Even numbers are divisible by 2.
What is the greatest two-digit number that is divisible
by 2?

3. In which of these numbers does the 5 have the greatest
(78) value?

A. 34.56   B. 35.64   C. 53.46   D. 64.35

4. Use the digits 2, 3, and 4 once each to make the
(2) greatest three-digit odd number possible.

5. When the decimal number two and twenty-five
(82) hundredths is added to six and seventeen hundredths,
what is the sum?

6. List the factors of 30.
(25)

7. Which digit in 16.34 is in the same place as the 2 in
(71) 2.875?

8. Name the number of shaded cir-
(72) cles as a mixed number and as a
decimal number.

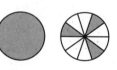

9. Three twelfths of a circle is what percent of a circle?
(81)

10. How many yards is one half of a mile?
(83)

11. Change the improper fraction $\frac{10}{3}$ to a mixed number.
(84)

12. Compare: Any improper fraction $\bigcirc$ $\frac{9}{10}$
(84)

13. Segment XY measures 3.2 centimeters. Segment YZ
(73) measures 4.7 centimeters. What is the length of
segment XZ?

X Y Z

14. $(345 + 57 + 219) \div 3$
(24)

15. $\$10 - (36¢ + \$1.42)$
(24)

16. 37.6
(82) 98.4
     + 76.8

17. 430.10
(82) $- 396.27$

18. $\$20.46
(17) $\times$ 5

19. $8\overline{)\$10.00}$
(26)

20. $\dfrac{3600}{50}$
(61)

21. 398
(62) $\times 746$

22. $9 + 1\dfrac{1}{3}$
(47)

23. $1 - \dfrac{3}{3}$
(66)

24. $10 - 1\dfrac{1}{10}$
(70)

25. If it is morning, what time will be
(29) shown by the clock in $6\frac{1}{2}$ hours?

LESSON 85

Changing Improper Mixed Numbers to Whole or Mixed Numbers

Facts Practice: Simplify 60 Improper Fractions (Test H in Test Masters)

Mental Math: How many feet are in a yard? How many inches are in a yard? Hold your fingers a foot apart. Hold your hands a yard apart.

   a. CXCIX   **b.** CCCXLV   **c.** $1 - \frac{3}{4}$

   d. 10% of 600   **e.** $\sqrt{100}$, × 2, + 5, × 2, − 1, ÷ 7

Problem Solving: Draw a rectangle that is similar to this rectangle with sides twice as long.

$\frac{3}{4}$ in.

$\frac{3}{8}$ in.

In Lesson 84 we practiced changing improper fractions to whole numbers or to mixed numbers. In arithmetic, we usually do not leave a fraction answer written as an improper fraction. When the answer to an arithmetic problem is an improper fraction, we usually convert it to a whole number or a mixed number.

Example 1 $\frac{3}{5} + \frac{4}{5}$

Solution   We add and find that the sum is the improper fraction $\frac{7}{5}$.

$$\frac{3}{5} + \frac{4}{5} = \frac{7}{5}$$

Then we convert the improper fraction to a mixed number by dividing.

$$\frac{7}{5} = 1\frac{2}{5}$$

When adding mixed numbers, the fraction part of the answer may be an improper fraction.

$$1\frac{2}{3} + 2\frac{2}{3} = 3\frac{4}{3} \longleftarrow \text{Improper fraction}$$

When an improper fraction is part of a mixed number, we call it an improper mixed number. To simplify an improper mixed number, we convert the improper fraction into a whole number or mixed number, and then we **add** it to the whole-number part of the answer.

$$3\frac{4}{3}$$

$$3 \,+\, 1\frac{1}{3} \,=\, 4\frac{1}{3}$$

Example 2 Simplify the improper mixed number $6\frac{3}{2}$.

Solution We simplify improper fractions by changing them to whole numbers or to mixed numbers. The fraction in $6\frac{3}{2}$ is an improper fraction. We divide and find that $\frac{3}{2}$ equals $1\frac{1}{2}$. We add this $1\frac{1}{2}$ to the 6 to get $7\frac{1}{2}$.

$$6\frac{3}{2}$$

$$6 \,+\, 1\frac{1}{2} \,=\, 7\frac{1}{2}$$

Practice* Convert each improper mixed number to a whole number or a mixed number:

a. $24\frac{2}{2}$ **b.** $7\frac{4}{2}$ **c.** $2\frac{5}{3}$ **d.** $9\frac{5}{4}$

e. $36\frac{3}{2}$ **f.** $32\frac{4}{3}$ **g.** $3\frac{3}{3}$ **h.** $10\frac{8}{8}$

Simplify each answer:

i. $\frac{4}{5} + \frac{4}{5}$ **j.** $8\frac{1}{3} + 8\frac{1}{3} + 8\frac{1}{3}$

k. $\frac{5}{8} + \frac{3}{8}$ **l.** $7\frac{4}{8} + 8\frac{7}{8}$

**Problem set
85**

1. Robin bought 10 arrows for 49¢ each and a package of
(80) bow wax for $2.39. How much did she spend in all?

2. On the shelf there are three stacks of books. In the
(56) three stacks there are 12, 13, and 17 books,
respectively. If the number of books in each stack were
made the same, how many books would be in each
stack?

3. Look at these four numbers. Find the difference
(78) between the smallest number and the largest number
by subtracting.

32.16   32.61   31.26   31.62

4. What is the largest four-digit even number that has the
(2). digits 1, 2, 3, and 4 used only once each?

5. You may use your fraction manipulatives to help you
(81) answer this question: What fraction is equal to one
third of one fourth?

6. Compare: $\dfrac{4}{3}$ ◯ $\dfrac{3}{4}$
(84)

7. Write 4.5 with the same number of decimal places
(79) as 6.25.

8. Name the point on the number line marked by the
(73) arrow with a mixed number and with a decimal
number.

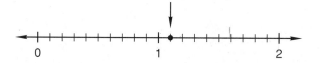

9. Daniel ran a 5-kilometer race in 15 minutes and 45
(83) seconds. How many meters did he run?

10. The length of $\overline{PQ}$ is $1\frac{1}{4}$ inches. The length of $\overline{QR}$ is $1\frac{3}{4}$
(81) inches. How long is $\overline{PR}$?

11. 600.4
(82) − 596.7

12. 9.275
(82) − 7.45

13. $30.75
(17) × 8

14. 75.2
(82) 84.3
962.6
41.7
12.4
89.2

15. 506
(63) × 478

16. $\dfrac{4690}{70}$
(61)

17. $\dfrac{\$20.01}{3}$
(26)

12.4
+ 89.2

18. 36 × 9 × 80
(18)

19. $10 + $8.16 + 49¢ + $2 + 5¢
(80)

20. $\dfrac{4}{5} + \dfrac{4}{5}$
(84)

21. $\dfrac{5}{9} + \dfrac{5}{9}$
(84)

22. $16\dfrac{2}{3} + 16\dfrac{2}{3}$
(85)

23. If each side of a square is 1 foot, then the perimeter of
(60) the square is how many inches? Each side of a square
is what percent of the square's perimeter?

Use this graph to answer questions 24 and 25:

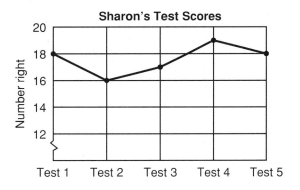

24. How many answers did Sharon get right on her best
(54) test?

25. There are 20 questions on each test. How many did
(54) Sharon miss on Test 2?

LESSON 86

Multiplying Fractions

Facts Practice: Simplify 60 Improper Fractions (Test H in Test Masters)

Mental Math: How many millimeters are in a centimeter? How many centimeters are in a meter? Hold two fingers one centimeter apart. Hold your hands one meter apart.

a. CLXVI **b.** CXLIV **c.** 50% of $5.00

d. $1 - \frac{7}{12}$ **e.** $\sqrt{9}$, × 9, + 1, ÷ 4, + 3, × 8, + 1, ÷ 9

Problem Solving: Copy this multiplication problem and fill in the missing digits.

$$\begin{array}{r} \_7 \\ \times\ \_\ \\ \hline 5\_6 \end{array}$$

We have added and subtracted fractions. In this lesson we will multiply fractions. When we add and subtract fractions, we count how many of the same size parts there are. When we multiply fractions, the sizes of the parts change. Consider this multiplication problem: How much is one half of one half?

Using our fraction manipulatives, we show one half of a circle. To find one half of one half, we divide the half in half. We see that the answer is one fourth.

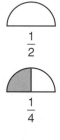

Written out, the problem looks like this.

$$\frac{1}{2} \times \frac{1}{2} = \frac{1}{4}$$

We find the answer to a fraction multiplication problem by multiplying the numerators to get the new numerator and multiplying the denominators to get the new denominator.

Example 1   What fraction is one half of three fourths?

Solution   First we show three fourths.

To find one half of three fourths, we may either divide each fourth in half or divide three fourths in half.

Since one half of one fourth is one eighth, one half of three fourths is three eighths. We may also find one half of three fourths by multiplying.

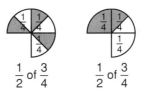

one half   of   three fourths

$$\frac{1}{2} \times \frac{3}{4} = \frac{3}{8}$$

We multiplied the numerators to find the numerator of the product, and we multiplied the denominators to find the denominator of the product.

Example 2   Multiply: $\frac{2}{3} \times \frac{4}{5}$

Solution   We find two thirds of four fifths by multiplying.

$$\frac{2}{3} \times \frac{4}{5} = \frac{8}{15}$$

Practice*   **a.** $\dfrac{1}{3} \times \dfrac{2}{3}$ **b.** $\dfrac{3}{5} \times \dfrac{1}{2}$

c. $\dfrac{2}{3} \times \dfrac{2}{3}$ **d.** $\dfrac{1}{2} \times \dfrac{2}{2}$

e. What fraction is three fourths of one half?

f. What fraction is one half of one third?

g. What fraction is two fifths of two thirds?

h. What fraction is one half of four fourths?

Note: Reducing fractions will be taught in Lesson 98. Until we get to that lesson, fraction answers will not be reduced.

Problem set 86

1. As the troop hiked, they kept the morning sun to their
(51) left. In what direction were they headed?

2. The troop hiked 57 miles in 3 days. The troop
(56) averaged how many miles per day?

3. When the decimal number six and thirty-four
(82) hundredths is subtracted from nine and twenty-six hundredths, what is the difference?

4. Which factors of 6 are also factors of 12?
(25)

5. If $3n = 18$, then what number does $4n$ equal?
(17)

6. When the largest two-digit even number is added to
(2) the smallest three-digit odd number, what is the sum?

7. Compare: $4.5 \bigcirc 4.500$
(79)

8. Arrange these fractions in order from least to greatest:
(68)
$$\dfrac{2}{3}, \dfrac{1}{2}, \dfrac{4}{3}, \dfrac{3}{8}, \dfrac{5}{5}$$

9. One half of the 64 squares on the board were black.
(54) One half of the black squares had checkers on them.

    (a) How many squares on the board were black?

    (b) How many squares had checkers on them?

    (c) What fraction of the squares had checkers on them?

    (d) What percent of the squares had checkers on them?

10. The length of segment *AC* is 78 millimeters. If *BC* is 29
(73) millimeters, what is the length of segment *AB*?

$$A \qquad\qquad\qquad\qquad\qquad B \qquad\qquad C$$
$$\longleftrightarrow\!\!\bullet\!\!\rule{8cm}{0.4pt}\!\!\bullet\!\!\rule{2cm}{0.4pt}\!\!\bullet$$

11. $\begin{array}{r} 87{,}437.8 \\ 5{,}696.4 \\ +\quad 275.9 \\ \hline \end{array}$
(82)

12. $\begin{array}{r} 6.003 \\ -\ 4.39 \\ \hline \end{array}$
(82)

13. $\begin{array}{r} \$16.08 \\ \times\qquad 9 \\ \hline \end{array}$
(17)

14. $8\overline{)\$36.00}$
(35)

15. $\dfrac{7600}{50}$
(61)

16. $\begin{array}{r} 638 \\ \times\ 517 \\ \hline \end{array}$
(62)

17. $\begin{array}{r} 3\frac{1}{3} \\ +\ 1\frac{2}{3} \\ \hline \end{array}$
(66)

18. $\begin{array}{r} 1\frac{2}{3} \\ +\ 1\frac{2}{3} \\ \hline \end{array}$
(85)

19. $\begin{array}{r} 4 \\ -\ 1\frac{2}{5} \\ \hline \end{array}$
(70)

20. $\dfrac{1}{2}$ of $\dfrac{3}{5}$
(86)

21. $\dfrac{1}{3} \times \dfrac{2}{3}$
(86)

22. $\dfrac{1}{2} \times \dfrac{6}{6}$
(86)

Read this information. Then answer questions 23–25.

Matthew has a machine that changes numbers. He fixed the machine so that when he puts in a 3, a 6 comes out. When he puts in a 4, an 8 comes out. When he puts in a 5, a 10 comes out.

$$\begin{array}{ccc}
3 \longrightarrow & \boxed{\begin{array}{c}\textbf{NUMBER}\\\textbf{CHANGING}\\\textbf{MACHINE}\end{array}} & \longrightarrow 6 \\
4 \longrightarrow & & \longrightarrow 8 \\
5 \longrightarrow & & \longrightarrow 10
\end{array}$$

23. What does the machine do to the numbers that are put
(54) into it?

A. It adds 3.   B. It doubles the number.

C. It divides by 2.   D. It multiplies by 3.

24. If Matthew puts in a 12, what number will come out?
(54)

25. Matthew put in a number and 20 came out. What
(54) number did Matthew put in the machine?

LESSON 87

Converting Units of Weight and Mass

Facts Practice: Simplify 60 Improper Fractions (Test H in Test Masters)

Mental Math: How many centimeters are in a meter? How many millimeters are in a meter? Hold your fingers a centimeter apart. Hold your hands a meter apart.

a. CC   **b.** CXCIX

Problem Solving: If rectangle I is rotated a quarter of a turn clockwise around point *A* it will be in the position of rectangle II. If it is rotated again, it will be in the position of rectangle III. If it is rotated again, it will be in the position of rectangle IV. Draw the congruent rectangles I, II, III, and IV.

As you grow, there is more and more "of you." How do you measure how much of you there is?

When you go to the doctor for a checkup, the doctor measures many things about you. The doctor measures your height. The doctor measures your temperature. The doctor measures your blood pressure. The doctor measures your heart rate. To measure how **much** of you there is, the doctor has you step up on a scale. Your weight[†] describes how much of you there is. To measure the weight of things, we often use units like ounces (oz), pounds (lb), and tons (ton). To measure the mass of objects in the metric system, we use grams (g) and kilograms (kg). The table below lists some common units of weight in the U.S. Customary System and units of mass in the metric system. The chart also gives the number of units needed to equal the next larger unit.

Equivalence Table for Units of Weight

U.S. CUSTOMARY SYSTEM	METRIC SYSTEM
16 oz = 1 lb 2000 lb = 1 ton	1000 g = 1 kg
On Earth, a kilogram weighs a little more than 2 pounds.	

Example 1 Most large elephants weigh about 4 tons. How many pounds is that?

Solution One ton is 2000 pounds. Four tons is 4 times 2000 pounds. A large elephant weighs about **8000 pounds.**

Example 2 The watermelon's mass was 6 kilograms. The mass of the watermelon was about how many grams?

Solution One kilogram is 1000 grams. Six kilograms is 6 times 1000 grams. The watermelon's mass was **6000 grams.**

Practice **a.** One half of a pound is how many ounces?

b. If a pair of tennis shoes is about 1 kilogram, then one tennis shoe is about how many grams?

c. Ten pounds of potatoes weighs how many ounces?

d. Sixteen tons is how many pounds?

[†]There is a technical difference between the terms *weight* and *mass* that will be clarified in other coursework. In this book we will use the word *weight* to include the meaning of both terms.

Problem set   **1.** Samuel Clemens wrote *Huckleberry Finn* using the
87   ⁽⁹⁾ pen name Mark Twain. Clemens turned 74 in 1909. In
what year was he born?

2. Add the decimal number sixteen and nine tenths to
⁽⁸²⁾ twenty-three and seven tenths. What is the sum?

3. Arrange these decimal numbers in order from least to
⁽⁷⁸⁾ greatest:

$$2.13, \ 1.32, \ 13.2, \ 1.23$$

4. One fourth of the 36 students earned an A on the test.
⁽⁵⁴⁾ One third of the students who earned an A scored
100%.

(a) How many students earned an A?

(b) How many students scored 100%?

(c) What fraction of the students scored 100%?

5. A VW Bug weighs about one ton. How many pounds is
⁽⁸⁷⁾ 1 ton?

6. Use a fraction, a decimal number,
⁽⁷⁶⁾ and a percent to name the shaded
part of this square.

7. A 2-pound box of cereal weighs
.⁽⁸⁷⁾ how many ounces?

8. Three kilograms is how many grams?
⁽⁸⁷⁾

9. *AB* is 3.5 centimeters. *BC* is 4.6 centimeters. Find *AC*.
⁽⁷³⁾

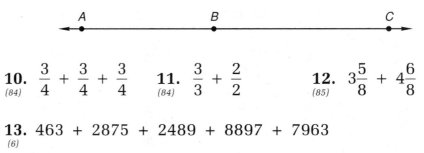

10. $\dfrac{3}{4} + \dfrac{3}{4} + \dfrac{3}{4}$ **11.** $\dfrac{3}{3} + \dfrac{2}{2}$ **12.** $3\dfrac{5}{8} + 4\dfrac{6}{8}$
⁽⁸⁴⁾   ⁽⁸⁴⁾   ⁽⁸⁵⁾

13. 463 + 2875 + 2489 + 8897 + 7963
⁽⁶⁾

14. $\dfrac{1}{2} \times \dfrac{5}{6}$
(86)

15. $\dfrac{2}{3} \times \dfrac{3}{4}$
(86)

16. $\dfrac{1}{2} \times \dfrac{2}{2}$
(86)

17. $\begin{array}{r} 401.3 \\ -\,264.7 \\ \hline \end{array}$
(82)

18. $\begin{array}{r} \$5.67 \\ \times\quad 8 \\ \hline \end{array}$
(17)

19. $\begin{array}{r} 347 \\ \times\,249 \\ \hline \end{array}$
(62)

20. $50 \times (500 \times 300)$
(24)

21. $(\$5 + 4¢) \div 6$
(24)

22. $64,275 \div 8$
(35)

23. $60\overline{)3780}$
(61)

Look at this drawing. Then answer questions 24 and 25:

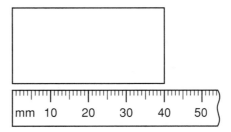

24. How long is this rectangle?
(48)

25. If this rectangle is half as wide as it is long, then what
(60) is the perimeter of the rectangle?

LESSON 88

Identifying Equivalent Fractions

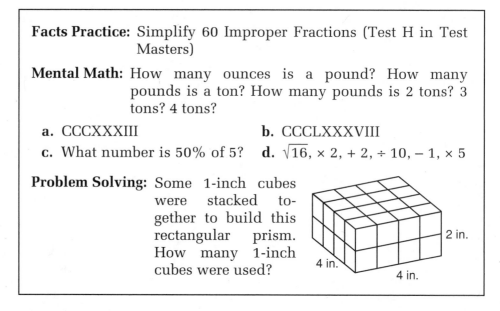

Facts Practice: Simplify 60 Improper Fractions (Test H in Test Masters)

Mental Math: How many ounces is a pound? How many pounds is a ton? How many pounds is 2 tons? 3 tons? 4 tons?

  a. CCCXXXIII   **b.** CCCLXXXVIII

  c. What number is 50% of 5?   **d.** $\sqrt{16}$, $\times 2$, $+ 2$, $\div 10$, $- 1$, $\times 5$

Problem Solving: Some 1-inch cubes were stacked together to build this rectangular prism. How many 1-inch cubes were used?

The same amount of each circle below is shaded. We can use different fractions to name the shaded part of each circle.

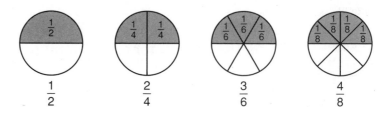

We can use $\frac{1}{2}$, $\frac{2}{4}$, $\frac{3}{6}$, and $\frac{4}{8}$. These fractions all name the same amount. Different fractions which name the same amount are called **equivalent fractions.** The word *equivalent* means "equal in value." The fractions $\frac{1}{2}$, $\frac{2}{4}$, $\frac{3}{6}$, and $\frac{4}{8}$ are all equivalent fractions because they all name the same amount.

Example 1   Which of these is equivalent to 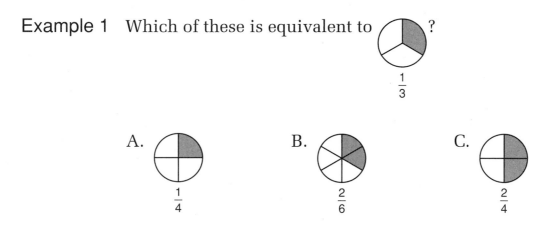 ?

Solution   Equivalent fractions name the same amount. By looking at the circles we see that the circle with the same amount shaded as the circle in the question is circle **B.** So $\frac{2}{6}$ is equivalent to $\frac{1}{3}$.

Example 2   Compare: $\frac{1}{2}$ ◯ $\frac{2}{4}$

Solution   We cannot compare these fractions by looking at the numerators because the denominators are different. Looking at the circles at the beginning of the lesson, we see that $\frac{1}{2}$ and $\frac{2}{4}$ are two ways to name the same number. The fractions are equivalent. We show that quantities are equal or equivalent by using an equal sign.

$$\frac{1}{2} = \frac{2}{4}$$

Practice   **a.** What do we call different fractions which name the same amount?

b. Which two fractions are equivalent? $\frac{2}{4}, \frac{3}{6}, \frac{1}{3}$

c. $\frac{1}{3} = \frac{2}{6}$ (true or false?)

d. Compare: $\frac{3}{6}$ ◯ $\frac{4}{8}$ **e.** Compare: $\frac{1}{2}$ ◯ $\frac{4}{6}$

Problem set
88

1. One half of the students are girls. One third of the girls
(86) have long hair. What fraction of the students are girls
with long hair? What percent of the students are girls
with long hair?

2. Friendly Fred bought a car for $860 and sold it for
(11) $1300. How much profit did he make?

3. Heather read a 316-page book in 4 days. She averaged
(56) reading how many pages per day?

4. The pickup truck could carry $\frac{1}{2}$ ton. How many
(87) pounds is $\frac{1}{2}$ ton?

5. The baby kitten weighed one half of a pound. How
(87) many ounces did it weigh?

6. Which shaded circle below is
(88) equivalent to this shaded circle?

A.   B.   C.

7. Which of these fractions is not equivalent to one half?
(68)
  A. $\frac{50}{100}$ B. $\frac{1000}{2000}$ C. $\frac{16}{30}$ D. $\frac{6}{12}$

8. Name the length of this segment twice: first as a
(74) number of millimeters and second as a number of
centimeters.

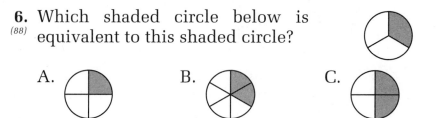

9. List the numbers that are factors of both 6 and 8.
(25)

10. *LN* is 64 millimeters. *LM* is 39 millimeters. Find *MN*.
(81)

11. $\frac{2}{3} + \frac{2}{3} + \frac{2}{3}$
(84)

12. $\frac{3}{3} - \frac{2}{2}$
(84)

13. $9\frac{4}{10} + 4\frac{9}{10}$
(85)

14.
(82)
$$43.625$$
$$5.78$$
$$+\ 16.942$$

15.
(13)
$$\$40.00$$
$$-\ \ 13.48$$

16.
(17)
$$\$20.50$$
$$\times\ \ \ \ \ \ 8$$

17. $9\overline{)\$56.70}$
(35)

18.
(62)
$$375$$
$$\times\ 842$$

19. $80\overline{)4650}$
(61)

20. Divide and write the quotient as a mixed number: $\frac{98}{5}$
(65)

21. $\frac{3}{4}$ of $\frac{1}{2}$
(86)

22. $\frac{3}{2} \times \frac{3}{4}$
(86)

23. $\frac{1}{3} \times \frac{2}{2}$
(86)

Read this information. Then answer questions 24 and 25.

It is 1.5 miles from Sandra's house to school. It takes Sandra 30 minutes to walk to school and 12 minutes if she rides her bike.

24. How far does Sandra travel going to school and back in 1 day?
(54)

25. If Sandra leaves her house at 7:55 a.m. and rides her bike, at what time will she get to school?
(54)

LESSON
89

Finding Equivalent Fractions by Multiplying by 1

Facts Practice: Simplify 60 Improper Fractions (Test H in Test Masters)

Mental Math: How many centimeters are in a meter? How many meters are in a kilometer? Hold two fingers one centimeter apart. Hold your hands a yard apart.

  a. CCL   **b.** CCXLIX   **c.** $\frac{1}{5}$ of 16
  d. 10% of $5.00   **e.** $\sqrt{49}, -2, \div 2, -2$

Problem Solving: Draw a triangle that is similar to this triangle with sides that are twice as long.

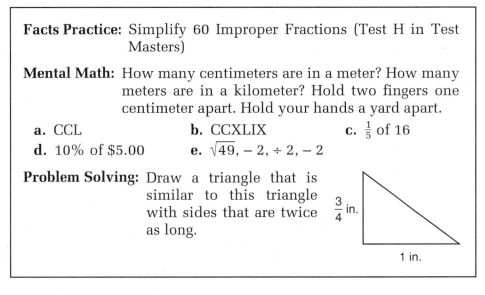

$\frac{3}{4}$ in.

1 in.

The same fraction may be named many different ways. The fractions $\frac{1}{2}$, $\frac{2}{4}$, $\frac{3}{6}$, and $\frac{4}{8}$ all name the same number. They are equivalent fractions.

In this lesson we will practice a method for making equivalent fractions. To make equivalent fractions we will use the name-changer machine.

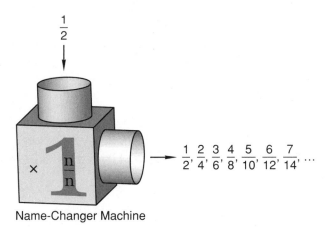

$\frac{1}{2}$

$\times \frac{n}{n}$

$\frac{1}{2}, \frac{2}{4}, \frac{3}{6}, \frac{4}{8}, \frac{5}{10}, \frac{6}{12}, \frac{7}{14}, \cdots$

Name-Changer Machine

The name-changer machine takes a fraction and multiplies it by a fraction name for 1. We know that when we multiply a number by 1, the size of the number is not changed. However, if we multiply a number by a fraction that is equal to 1, the answer will be a different name for the same number.

$$\frac{1}{2} \times \mathbf{1}\frac{2}{2} = \frac{2}{4} \quad \bigg| \quad \frac{1}{2} \times \mathbf{1}\frac{3}{3} = \frac{3}{6} \quad \bigg| \quad \frac{1}{2} \times \mathbf{1}\frac{4}{4} = \frac{4}{8}$$

The fractions $\frac{1}{2}$, $\frac{2}{4}$, $\frac{3}{6}$, and $\frac{4}{8}$ are equivalent fractions. They were formed by multiplying $\frac{1}{2}$ by different fraction names for 1.

Example 1 By what name for 1 should $\frac{3}{4}$ be multiplied to make $\frac{6}{8}$?

$$\frac{3}{4} \times \mathbf{1}\frac{?}{?} = \frac{6}{8}$$

Solution To change the name of $\frac{3}{4}$ to $\frac{6}{8}$, we multiply by $\frac{2}{2}$. The fraction $\frac{2}{2}$ is equal to 1, and when we multiply by 1 we do not change the value of the number. Therefore, $\frac{3}{4} = \frac{6}{8}$. The fractions are equivalent.

Example 2 Write a fraction equal to $\frac{2}{3}$ that has a denominator of 12.

$$\frac{2}{3} = \frac{?}{12}$$

Solution We may change the name of a fraction by multiplying by a fraction name for 1. To make the 3 a 12, we must multiply by 4. So the fraction name for 1 which we will use is $\frac{4}{4}$. We multiply $\frac{2}{3} \times \frac{4}{4}$ to make the equivalent fraction $\frac{8}{12}$.

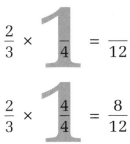

$$\frac{2}{3} \times \mathbf{1}\frac{}{4} = \frac{}{12}$$

$$\frac{2}{3} \times \mathbf{1}\frac{4}{4} = \frac{8}{12}$$

Example 3 Write a fraction equal to $\frac{1}{3}$ that has a denominator of 12. Also, write a fraction equal to $\frac{1}{4}$ that has a denominator of 12. Then add the two fractions you made. What is the sum?

Solution   We multiply $\frac{1}{3}$ by $\frac{4}{4}$ and $\frac{1}{4}$ by $\frac{3}{3}$.

$$\frac{1}{3} \times \frac{4}{4} = \frac{4}{12} \qquad \frac{1}{4} \times \frac{3}{3} = \frac{3}{12}$$

Then we add $\frac{4}{12}$ and $\frac{3}{12}$.

$$\frac{4}{12} + \frac{3}{12} = \frac{7}{12}$$

Practice*   What name for 1 is used to make these equivalent fractions?

a. $\frac{3}{4} \times \frac{?}{?} = \frac{9}{12}$ **b.** $\frac{2}{3} \times \frac{?}{?} = \frac{4}{6}$

c. $\frac{1}{3} \times \frac{?}{?} = \frac{4}{12}$

Find the numerator to complete the equivalent fractions:

d. $\frac{1}{3} = \frac{?}{9}$ **e.** $\frac{2}{3} = \frac{?}{15}$ **f.** $\frac{3}{5} = \frac{?}{10}$

g. Write a fraction equal to $\frac{1}{2}$ that has a denominator of 6. Also, write a fraction equal to $\frac{1}{3}$ that has a denominator of 6. Then add the two fractions. What is the sum?

Problem set 89

1. Mr. MacDonald bought 1 ton of hay for his cow, Geraldine. Every day Geraldine ate 50 pounds of hay. At this rate, 1 ton of hay will last how many days?
[87]

2. A platypus is a mammal with a ducklike bill and webbed feet. A platypus is about $1\frac{1}{2}$ feet long. One and one half feet is how many inches?
[83]

3. Sam bought 3 shovels for his hardware store for $6.30 each. He sold them for $10.95 each. How much profit did Sam make on all 3 shovels?
[55]

4. Add the decimal number ten and fifteen hundredths to twenty-nine and eighty-nine hundredths. Use words to name the sum.
(82)

5. By what name for 1 should $\frac{2}{3}$ be multiplied to make $\frac{6}{9}$?
(89)

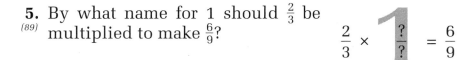

$$\frac{2}{3} \times \frac{?}{?} = \frac{6}{9}$$

6. Draw a rectangle that has all sides the same length.
(39)

7. List the numbers that are factors of both 9 and 12.
(25)

8. Write a fraction equal to $\frac{3}{4}$ that has a denominator of 12. Also, write a fraction equal to $\frac{2}{3}$ that has a denominator of 12. Then add the fractions you wrote. What is the sum?
(89)

9. *AC* is 9.1 centimeters. *BC* is 4.2 centimeters. Find *AB*.
(81)

$$\overset{A}{\underset{\bullet}{\longleftarrow}} \hspace{3cm} \overset{B}{\underset{\bullet}{}} \hspace{2cm} \overset{C}{\underset{\bullet}{\longrightarrow}}$$

10. $1\frac{1}{5} + 2\frac{2}{5} + 3\frac{3}{5}$
(85)

11. $5 - \left(3\frac{5}{8} - 3\right)$
(24)

12. $\$10 - 10\cent$
(80)

13. $\$10 \div 4$
(26)

14. $9 \times 64\cent = \$\_\_\_\_\_$
(80)

15.
(82)
$$\begin{array}{r} 9863.2 \\ 7775.46 \\ +\ \ 897.5 \\ \hline \end{array}$$

16.
(82)
$$\begin{array}{r} 30.10 \\ -\ 21.73 \\ \hline \end{array}$$

17.
(63)
$$\begin{array}{r} 408 \\ \times\ 748 \\ \hline \end{array}$$

18. $7\overline{)43,859}$
(26)

19. $\dfrac{6552}{9}$
(26)

20. $80\overline{)4137}$
(61)

21. $\frac{1}{2}$ of $\frac{1}{5}$
(86)

22. $\frac{3}{4} \times \frac{2}{2}$
(86)

23. $\frac{3}{5} \times \frac{5}{4}$
(86)

This graph shows the number of ice-cream cones sold at the snack bar. Use the information in the graph to answer questions 24 and 25.

Ice-Cream Cone Sales

MONTH	NUMBER OF CONES SOLD
June	
July	
August	

= 100 cones

24. The number of cones sold in July was how many?
(54)
    A. $3\frac{1}{2}$ B. 300   C. 305   D. 350

25. Altogether, how many cones were sold during June,
(54) July, and August?

LESSON 90

Identifying Prime Numbers

Facts Practice: Simplify 60 Improper Fractions (Test H in Test Masters)

Mental Math: How many grams equal a kilogram? A pair of shoes is about a kilogram. One shoe is about how many grams?

  a. CXC   **b.** CXCIV   **c.** $\frac{1}{3}$ of 16
  d. 25% of $20.00   **e.** $\sqrt{81}$, -2, $\div 2$, -1, $\times 2$, -5

Problem Solving: Find the next three numbers in this sequence.
              1, 1, 2, 3, 5, 8, 13, __ , __ , __ , ...

We have practiced listing the factors of whole numbers. Some whole numbers have many factors. Other whole numbers have only a few factors. In one special group of whole numbers, each number has exactly two factors. Here we list the first 10 counting numbers and their factors. Which of these numbers have exactly **two** factors?

NUMBER	FACTORS
1	1
2	1, 2
3	1, 3
4	1, 2, 4
5	1, 5
6	1, 2, 3, 6
7	1, 7
8	1, 2, 4, 8
9	1, 3, 9
10	1, 2, 5, 10

There are four numbers in this list which have exactly two factors. The four numbers are 2, 3, 5, and 7. These numbers are called **prime numbers. A prime number is a whole number which has exactly two factors.** We often think of a prime number as a number which is not divisible by any other number except itself and 1. Listing prime numbers will quickly give us a feel for which numbers are prime numbers.

Example The first three prime numbers are 2, 3, and 5. What are the next three prime numbers?

Solution A prime number is not divisible by any number except itself and 1. We will list the next several whole numbers and scratch out those which are divisible by some other number.

$$\not6, 7, \not8, \not9, \not{10}, 11, \not{12}, 13, \not{14}, \not{15}, \not{16}, 17, \not{18}$$

The numbers which are not scratched out are prime numbers. The next three prime numbers after 5 are **7, 11,** and **13.**

Practice   List all the prime numbers less than 50. (*Hint*: There are 15 of them.)

Problem set 90

1. *(55)* The student store buys one dozen pencils for 96¢ and sells them for 20¢ each. How much profit does the store make on a dozen pencils?

2. *(87)* A VW Bug weighs about 1 ton. If its 4 wheels carry the weight evenly, then each wheel carries about how many pounds?

3. *(25)* List the numbers that are factors of both 8 and 12.

4. *(90)* The first five prime numbers are 2, 3, 5, 7, and 11. What are the next three prime numbers?

5. *(89)* By what name for 1 should $\frac{3}{4}$ be multiplied to make $\frac{9}{12}$?

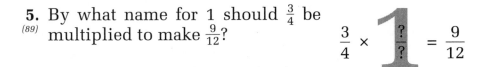

$$\frac{3}{4} \times \frac{?}{?} = \frac{9}{12}$$

6. *(89)* Write a fraction equal to $\frac{1}{2}$ that has a denominator of 6. Also, write a fraction equal to $\frac{2}{3}$ that has a denominator of 6. Then add the fractions you wrote. What is the sum?

7. *(90)* Think of a prime number. How many different factors does it have?

8. *(68)* Arrange these numbers in order from least to greatest:
$$\frac{3}{8}, \frac{4}{6}, \frac{5}{6}, \frac{6}{12}, \frac{7}{7}$$

9. *(83)* One mile is 1760 yards. How many yards is $\frac{1}{8}$ mile?

10. *(81)* *XZ* is 84 millimeters. *XY* equals *YZ*. Find *XY*.

11. *(80)* $8.43 + 68¢ + $15 + 5¢ + $12.87 + $0.05 + $0.15

12.   6.505
(82)   − 1.4

13. $12 − 12¢
(80)

14. $18.07
(17)   ×   6

15. 6)$76.32
(26)

16.   375
(62)   × 248

17. 70)4791
(61)

18. Divide 365 by 7 and write the quotient as a mixed
(65) number.

19. $\frac{3}{4}$ of $\frac{3}{4}$
(86)

20. $\frac{3}{2} \times \frac{3}{2}$
(86)

21. $\frac{6}{6} \times \frac{7}{7}$
(86)

22. $3\frac{2}{3} + 1\frac{2}{3}$
(85)

23. $5 − \frac{1}{5}$
(70)

24. $\frac{7}{10} − \frac{7}{10}$
(44)

25. If it is evening, what time will be
(29) shown by the clock in $6\frac{1}{2}$ hours?

LESSON 91

Finding Equivalent Fractions by Dividing by 1

Facts Practice: Simplify 60 Improper Fractions (Test H in Test Masters)

Mental Math: How many feet are in a yard? How many feet are in a mile? Hold your hands about a foot apart. Hold your hands about a yard apart.

a. XCIV   **b.** CCLXIX   **c.** 10% of $300

d. $\frac{1}{2}$ of 30 minutes   **e.** 30 × 30, + 100, ÷ 2, − 100, ÷ 4

Problem Solving: Triangles I, II, and III are congruent. If Triangle I is rotated a quarter turn in a clockwise direction around point *A*, it will be in the position of Triangle II. If it is rotated again it will be in the position of Triangle III. If it is rotated again it will be in the position of Triangle IV. Draw Triangles I, II, III, and IV.

In Lesson 89 we practiced making equivalent fractions by multiplying by a fraction form of 1. We changed the fraction $\frac{1}{2}$ to the equivalent fraction $\frac{3}{6}$ by multiplying by $\frac{3}{3}$.

$$\frac{1}{2} \times \boxed{\frac{3}{3}} = \frac{3}{6}$$

Multiplying by $\frac{3}{3}$ made the terms of the fraction greater. The terms of a fraction are the numerator and the denominator of the fraction. The terms of $\frac{1}{2}$ are 1 and 2. The terms of $\frac{3}{6}$ are 3 and 6.

Sometimes we can make the terms of a fraction smaller by dividing a fraction by a fraction form of 1. Here we change $\frac{3}{6}$ to $\frac{1}{2}$ by dividing by $\frac{3}{3}$.

$$\frac{3}{6} \div \frac{3}{3} = \frac{1}{2} \quad \begin{array}{l}(3 \div 3 = 1)\\(6 \div 3 = 2)\end{array}$$

Changing a fraction to an equivalent fraction with smaller terms is called **reducing.** We reduce a fraction by dividing the fraction by a fraction name for 1.

Example 1 Reduce the fraction $\frac{6}{8}$ by dividing $\frac{6}{8}$ by $\frac{2}{2}$.

Solution Dividing $\frac{6}{8}$ by $\frac{2}{2}$, we get $\frac{3}{4}$.

$$\frac{6}{8} \div \mathbf{1}\frac{2}{2} = \frac{3}{4}$$

The fractions $\frac{6}{8}$ and $\frac{3}{4}$ are equivalent fractions, but $\frac{3}{4}$ has smaller terms.

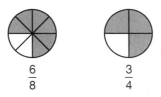

$$\frac{6}{8} \qquad \frac{3}{4}$$

Not all fractions can be reduced. Only fractions whose terms can be divided by the same number can be reduced.

Example 2 Which of these fractions cannot be reduced?

A. $\frac{2}{6}$ B. $\frac{3}{6}$ C. $\frac{4}{6}$ D. $\frac{5}{6}$

Solution We will consider each fraction:

A. The terms of $\frac{2}{6}$ are 2 and 6. Both 2 and 6 can be divided by 2, so $\frac{2}{6}$ can be reduced to $\frac{1}{3}$ by dividing by $\frac{2}{2}$.

B. The terms of $\frac{3}{6}$ are 3 and 6. Both 3 and 6 can be divided by 3, so $\frac{3}{6}$ can be reduced to $\frac{1}{2}$ by dividing by $\frac{3}{3}$.

C. The terms of $\frac{4}{6}$ are 4 and 6. Both 4 and 6 are even numbers, so they can be divided by 2. The fraction $\frac{4}{6}$ can be reduced to $\frac{2}{3}$ by dividing by $\frac{2}{2}$.

D. The terms of $\frac{5}{6}$ are 5 and 6. The only whole number that divides 5 and 6 is 1. Since dividing by 1 does not make the terms smaller, the fraction $\frac{5}{6}$ cannot be reduced. So the answer to the question is **D.**

Example 3   Reduce $\frac{9}{12}$.

Solution   We mentally search for a number that will divide both 9 and 12. We mentally try 2. Twelve is even but 9 is odd, so we cannot divide both terms by 2. Next we try 3. We find that both 9 and 12 can be divided by 3. So we reduce $\frac{9}{12}$ by dividing by $\frac{3}{3}$.

$$\frac{9}{12} \div \mathbf{1}\,\frac{3}{3} = \frac{3}{4}$$

We find that $\frac{9}{12}$ **reduces to** $\frac{3}{4}$.

Practice   **a.** Reduce $\frac{8}{12}$ by dividing $\frac{8}{12}$ by $\frac{4}{4}$.

b. Which of these fractions cannot be reduced?
   A. $\frac{2}{8}$ 　　　　　 B. $\frac{3}{8}$ 　　　　　 C. $\frac{4}{8}$

Reduce each of these fractions:
   c. $\frac{3}{9}$ 　　　　　 **d.** $\frac{6}{10}$ 　　　　　 **e.** $\frac{5}{10}$

Problem set 91

1. In 3 games, Sherry's bowling scores were 109, 98, and
   (36) 135, respectively. Her highest score was how much more than her lowest score?

2. The total price of 5 pounds of bananas was $1.95.
   (21) What was the price per pound?

3. Nathan is 5 feet, 4 inches tall. How many inches is 5
   (83) feet, 4 inches?

4. When twenty-six and five tenths is subtracted from
   (82) thirty-two and six tenths, what is the difference?

5. Write a fraction equal to $\frac{2}{3}$ that has a denominator of
   (89) 12. Also, write a fraction equal to $\frac{1}{4}$ that has a denominator of 12. Then add the two fractions. What is the sum?

6. List all the prime numbers between 20 and 30.
(90)

7. Reduce the fraction $\frac{10}{12}$ by dividing by $\frac{2}{2}$.
(91)

8. One fourth of the 24 students earned an A on the test.
(54) One half of the students who earned an A on the test were girls.

(a) How many students earned an A on the test?

(b) How many girls earned an A on the test?

(c) What fraction of the 24 students were girls who earned an A on the test?

9. If the width of this rectangle is
(60) half the length, then what is the perimeter of the rectangle?

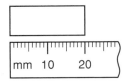

10. $\overline{QR}$ is 48 millimeters. Segment RS is one half as long
(81) as $\overline{QR}$. Find QS.

$$Q \qquad\qquad\qquad R \qquad\qquad S$$

11. $\$98.89$
(13) 46.37
    29.50
$+ \;\; 17.34$

12. 80.19
(82) $- \; 75.6$

13. $\$56.42$
(17) $\times \qquad 6$

14. $6)\overline{\$87.00}$
(35)

15. 706
(63) $\times\, 438$

16. $40)\overline{2438}$
(61)

17. Divide 5280 by 9 and write the quotient as a mixed
(65) number.

18. $\$10 - (\$5.80 + 28¢)$
(24)

19. $5\frac{3}{5} + \left(4 - 1\frac{3}{5}\right)$
(24)

20. Reduce $\frac{3}{6}$.
(91)

21. $\frac{4}{3} \times \frac{4}{3}$
(86)

22. $\frac{10}{7} \times \frac{7}{10}$
(86)

23. From September 1 of one year to June 1 of the next
$^{(27)}$ year is how many months?

Read this information. Then answer questions 24 and 25.

Jenny has a paper route. She delivers papers to 30 customers. At the end of the month she gets $6.50 from each customer. She pays the newspaper company $135 each month for the newspapers.

24. How much money does Jenny get each month from all
$^{(54)}$ of her customers?

25. How much profit does she make each month for her
$^{(54)}$ work?

LESSON 92

Finding the Greatest Common Factor of Two Numbers

Facts Practice: Simplify 60 Improper Fractions (Test H in Test Masters)

Mental Math: How many ounces is one pound? two pounds?
  a. CXCVII   **b.** CLXXIV   **c.** Reduce: $\frac{2}{4}, \frac{2}{6}, \frac{2}{8}, \frac{2}{10}$
  d. $\frac{1}{3}$ of 100   **e.** 25% of 60 minutes
  f. $\sqrt{81}, +1, \times 5, -2, \div 4$

Problem Solving: A pizza was cut into 10 slices. Brad ate four of the slices. What fraction of the pizza did Brad eat?

We have practiced finding the factors of whole numbers. In this lesson we will practice finding the **greatest common factor** of two numbers. **The greatest common factor of two numbers is the largest whole number which is a factor of both numbers.** The letters **GCF** are sometimes used to stand for the term **g**reatest **c**ommon **f**actor.

To find the greatest common factor of 12 and 18, we first list the factors of each. We have circled the common factors, that is, the numbers that are factors of both 12 and 18.

Number	Factors
12	①, ②, ③, 4, ⑥, 12
18	①, ②, ③, ⑥, 9, 18

The greatest of these common factors is 6.

Example 1   Find the greatest common factor (GCF) of 8 and 20.

Solution   We will first find the factors and identify the common factors. The factors of 8 and 20 are listed below with the common factors circled.

8	①, ②, ④, 8
20	①, ②, ④, 5, 10, 20

There are three common factors. The greatest of the three common factors is **4.**

We may use greatest common factors to help us reduce fractions.

Example 2   Use the GCF of 8 and 20 to reduce $\frac{8}{20}$.

Solution   In Example 1 we found that the GCF of 8 and 20 is 4. So we can use $\frac{4}{4}$ to reduce $\frac{8}{20}$.

$$\frac{8}{20} \div \frac{4}{4} = \frac{2}{5}$$

Practice* Find the greatest common factor (GCF) of each pair of numbers:

    a. 6 and 9   **b.** 6 and 12   **c.** 15 and 21

    d. 6 and 10   **e.** 12 and 15   **f.** 7 and 10

Reduce these fractions using the GCF of the terms of each fraction:

    g. $\frac{6}{9}$ **h.** $\frac{6}{12}$ **i.** $\frac{15}{21}$

Problem set 92

1. Javier was paid $22.50 for working on Saturday. He
(55) worked from 8 a.m. to 2 p.m. He earned how much money per hour?

2. Estimate the product of 396 and 507 by rounding to
(69) the nearest hundred before you multiply.

3. What is the next number in this sequence?
(1)
        ..., 3452, 3552, 3652, _____, ...

4. Most adults are between 5 and 6 feet tall. The height of
(83) most cars is about:

    A. 4 to 5 feet   B. 8 to 10 feet   C. 40 to 50 feet

5. When sixty-five and fourteen hundredths is subtracted
(82) from eighty and forty-eight hundredths, what is the difference?

6. If each side of an octagon is 12 inches, what is the
(39) perimeter of the octagon?

7. Which of these numbers is not a prime number?
(90)
    A. 11   B. 21   C. 31   D. 41

8. (a) Find the greatest common factor (GCF) of 20 and
(92)   30.

    (b) Use the GCF of 20 and 30 to reduce $\frac{20}{30}$.

9. How many inches is $\frac{3}{4}$ of a foot?
(83)

10. AC is 4 inches. BC is $\frac{3}{4}$ inch. Find AB.
(81)

A ————————————————————— B —— C

11. (a) What number is $\frac{1}{6}$ of 12?
(81)
(b) What number is $\frac{5}{6}$ of 12?

12. Reduce $\frac{6}{12}$ by dividing $\frac{6}{12}$ by $\frac{6}{6}$.
(91)

13. $\dfrac{5}{7} + \dfrac{3}{7}$ **14.** $\dfrac{4}{4} - \dfrac{2}{2}$ **15.** $\dfrac{2}{3} \times \square = \dfrac{6}{9}$
(84)   (84)   (89)

16. 976.5   **17.** $40.00   **18.** $8.47
(82)   470.4   (13) − 32.85   (17) ×   7
       436.7
     + 98.6

19. $6\overline{)43{,}715}$ **20.** $\dfrac{2640}{30}$ **21.** 367
(26)   (61)   (62) × 418

22. $6\dfrac{2}{3} + \left(5 - 3\dfrac{1}{3}\right)$ **23.** $18.64 ÷ 4
(24)   (26)

Use this graph to answer questions 24 and 25:

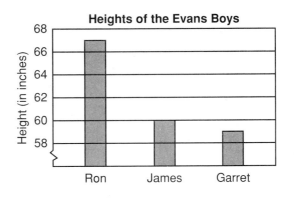

Heights of the Evans Boys

24. How many inches does Garret need to grow to be as
(54) tall as Ron?

25. Which boy is exactly 5 feet tall?
(54)

LESSON 93

Recognizing and Naming Geometric Solids

Facts Practice: Simplify 60 Improper Fractions (Test H in Test Masters)

Mental Math: How many inches are in a yard? How many feet are in a mile? Hold your hands about a yard apart. Hold your hands about an inch apart.

a. XCIII   **b.** XLVII   **c.** Reduce: $\frac{2}{8}, \frac{4}{8}, \frac{6}{8}$

d. $33\frac{1}{3} + 33\frac{1}{3}$ **e.** 50% of $\sqrt{36}, \times 4, \div 2, \times 6$

Problem Solving: Carlos, Bao, and Sherry drew straws. Carlos' $3\frac{3}{4}$-inch straw was a quarter inch longer than Bao's straw and half an inch shorter than Sherry's straw. How long were Bao's and Sherry's straws?

We have practiced identifying geometric shapes such as triangles, rectangles, and circles. These are "flat" shapes and are called **plane figures.** They take up a certain amount of area, but they do not take up space. Objects that take up space are things like baseball bats, houses, horses, and people. In this lesson we will identify some geometric shapes that take up space.

Geometric shapes that take up space are called **solids,** even though the objects we know that are similar to these shapes may not be "solid." We could make models of these shapes with clay, but we have difficulty drawing them because solids have **depth** and the surface of paper does not. To give a feeling of depth when drawing these shapes, we create **optical illusions** with the angles that we use or the extra lines we include.

Geometric Solids

SHAPE	NAME
	Cube
	Rectangular solid
	Pyramid
	Cylinder
	Sphere
	Cone

The flat surfaces of solids are called **faces.** A cube has six faces. A die (singular of dice) is a cube. The six faces of a die are numbered with one through six dots.

Example 1 (a) Name this shape.

(b) How many faces does it have?

Solution This shape is a **rectangular solid.** It has **six faces.**

Example 2 What is the shape of a basketball?

Solution A basketball is not a circle. A circle is a "flat" shape (a plane figure), but a basketball takes up space. A basketball is a **sphere.**

Practice Name the shape of the objects listed:

a. Brick

b. Soup can

c. Ice-cream cone

d. Shoebox

Problem set
93

1. Alicia left for school at a quarter to eight in the
(29) morning and arrived home $7\frac{1}{2}$ hours later. What time
was it when Alicia arrived home?

2. Mark has 5 coins in his pocket that total 47¢. How
(54) many dimes are in his pocket?

3. Use digits to write the number twenty-three million,
(59) two hundred eighty-seven thousand, four hundred
twenty.

4. (a) What number is $\frac{1}{3}$ of 24?
(50)
(b) What number is $\frac{2}{3}$ of 24?

5. List all the prime numbers between 10 and 20.
(90)

6. (a) What is the greatest common factor (GCF) of 4
(92)   and 8?

(b) Use the GCF of 4 and 8 to reduce $\frac{4}{8}$.

7. (a) Name this shape.
(93)
(b) How many faces does it have?

8. What is the shape of the earth?
(93)

9. Write a decimal number equal to the mixed
(72) number $1\frac{7}{10}$.

10. Which word names the distance across a circle?
(60)
A. Center   B. Circumference
C. Radius   D. Diameter

11.   3.625   **12.**   3704   **13.**   364
(82)   4.5   (9)   − 2918   (62)   × 478
+ 7.38

14. $6.25 × 4   **15.** 6)$14.58
(17)   (26)

16. Write a fraction equal to $\frac{1}{3}$ that has a denominator of
(89) 12. Also, write a fraction equal to $\frac{3}{4}$ that has a
denominator of 12. What is the sum of the two
fractions?

17. Reduce $\frac{6}{8}$.
(91)

18. $\frac{3}{4} = \frac{\square}{12}$
(89)

19. $\begin{array}{r} 4\frac{2}{5} \\ + \ \ \frac{1}{5} \\ \hline \end{array}$
(47)

20. $\begin{array}{r} 3\frac{3}{4} \\ + 1\frac{1}{4} \\ \hline \end{array}$
(66)

21. $\begin{array}{r} 5 \\ - 1\frac{1}{4} \\ \hline \end{array}$
(70)

22. Compare: $0.1 \bigcirc 0.01$
(78)

23. The multiplication $3 \times \frac{1}{2}$ means $\frac{1}{2} + \frac{1}{2} + \frac{1}{2}$. So $3 \times \frac{1}{2}$
(84) equals what mixed number?

Use the information given and the table to answer
questions 24 and 25:

Mr. and Mrs. Minick took their children, Samantha and Douglas, to a movie. Ticket prices are shown in the table.

Ticket Prices	
Adults	$5.00
Ages 9-12	$2.50
Under 9	$1.75

24. Samantha is 12 years old and Douglas is 8 years old.
(54) What is the total cost of all 4 tickets?

25. Before 5 p.m. adult tickets are half price. How much
(54) money would the Minicks save by going to the movie
before 5 p.m. instead of after 5 p.m.?

LESSON 94

Using Letters to Name Angles

The quadrilateral below is formed by four segments which intersect at four points and form four angles.

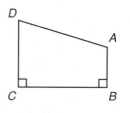

The letters A, B, C, and D are used in this drawing to name the points where the segments intersect. We may use all of these letters to name this polygon. This polygon is **quadrilateral *ABCD*.**

To name an angle, we may use a single letter, such as angle A, or we may use three letters. Angle DAB can be abbreviated $\angle DAB$ and is read "angle *D-A-B*." $\angle DAB$ names the angle that is formed by the segments which run from point A to point D and from point A to point B. If we trace the segments from D to A to B, it will help us see $\angle DAB$. This angle can also be named $\angle BAD$. So we have three ways to name the angle at A: $\angle A$, $\angle DAB$, and $\angle BAD$. We use three letters to name an angle when the use of a single letter would not be specific enough.

Notice the small squares in $\angle B$ and $\angle C$. We remember that the small square is a symbol that means the angle is a right angle.

Example 1 Which angle in this figure is an obtuse angle?

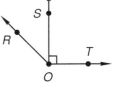

Solution An obtuse angle is larger than a right angle. The small square shows us that ∠*TOS* is a right angle. Angle *SOR* is an acute angle. Together, these two angles form ∠*TOR*. **Angle *TOR* is an obtuse angle.**

Example 2 Which angle in quadrilateral *ABCD* appears to be an acute angle?

Solution An acute angle is smaller than a right angle. The angle that is smaller than a right angle is ∠***CDA***, which can also be named ∠***ADC*** or ∠***D***.

Practice Use the diagram to answer these questions:

a. Name the acute angle.

b. Name the right angle.

c. Name the obtuse angle.

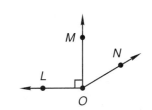

Use the drawing of quadrilateral *WXYZ* to answer these questions:

d. Which angle appears to be acute?

e. Which angle appears to be obtuse?

Problem set 94

1. Draw a circle and shade $\frac{1}{3}$ of it. What percent of the circle is shaded?
(47)

2. Tom and his two friends found $2418 of treasure buried in the cave. If they share the treasure equally, how much will each receive?
(21)

3. This math book is about 1 kilogram. A kilogram is how many grams?
(87)

4. Estimate the product of 732 and 480 by rounding the numbers to the nearest hundred before you multiply.
(69)

5. At which of these times do the hands of a clock form an acute angle?
(33)

   A. 3:00   B. 6:15   C. 9:00   D. 12:10

6. Arrange these decimal numbers in order from least to greatest:
(78)

$$0.1, 0.01, 1.0, 1.01$$

7. (a) Find the greatest common factor (GCF) of 8 and 12.
(92)
   (b) Use the GCF of 8 and 12 to reduce $\frac{8}{12}$.

8. (a) What number is $\frac{1}{4}$ of 80?
(50)
   (b) What number is $\frac{3}{4}$ of 80?

9. $\dfrac{1}{2} \times \square = \dfrac{3}{6}$ **10.** Reduce $\dfrac{4}{6}$.
(89)   (91)

11. Name the total number of shaded circles as a mixed number and as a decimal number.
(72)

12. 99,439 + 6148 + 751 + 8362
(6)

13. $10 − 59¢   **14.** 30$\overline{)672}$
(80)   (61)

15. 5 × 68¢ = $_____   **16.** $3.40 ÷ 5
(80)   (26)

17. $10 - 3\dfrac{1}{3}$ **18.** $\dfrac{3}{4} \times \dfrac{5}{4}$
(70)   (86)

19. What is the name of this solid?
(93)

20. In rectangle *MNOP,* which seg-
(32) ment is parallel to $\overline{MN}$?

A. $\overline{MP}$ B. $\overline{PO}$
C. $\overline{NO}$ D. $\overline{MO}$

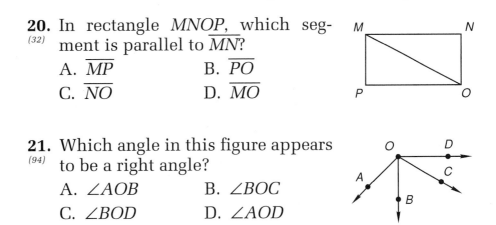

21. Which angle in this figure appears
(94) to be a right angle?

A. ∠*AOB* B. ∠*BOC*
C. ∠*BOD* D. ∠*AOD*

Use the grocery receipt to answer questions 22 and 23:

22. How much money was spent on
(54) eggs, juice, and cereal?

23. Each item labeled "Milk" is a half-
(54) gallon carton. What is the cost of 1
gallon of milk?

Milk	0.97
Milk	0.97
Milk	0.97
Milk	0.97
Apple juice	0.69
Apple juice	0.69
Eggs	1.51
Cereal	1.99
TOTAL	8.76

LESSON 95

Converting Units of Liquid Measure

Facts Practice: Simplify 60 Improper Fractions (Test H in Test Masters)

Mental Math: How many ounces is one pound? How many ounces is half a pound?

   a. CCLIX   **b.** CCXLVIII   **c.** Reduce: $\frac{2}{10}, \frac{4}{10}, \frac{6}{10}, \frac{8}{10}$

   d. 10% of $500   **e.** $33\frac{1}{3} + 66\frac{2}{3}$ **f.** $\frac{1}{2}$ of 5, × 2, × 5, × 4

Problem Solving: Draw pictures to show that $\frac{2}{3} < \frac{3}{4}$.

When we buy milk or soda pop or fruit juice at the store, we are buying a quantity of liquid. Liquid quantities are often measured in ounces (oz), pints (pt), quarts (qt), and gallons (gal). They are also measured in liters (L) and milliliters (mL).

$\frac{1}{2}$ gallon   2 liters   1 quart

The chart below lists some common units of liquid measure used in the U.S. Customary System and in the metric system. The chart also gives the number of units needed to equal the next larger unit of liquid measure.

Equivalence Table for Units of Liquid Measure

U.S. CUSTOMARY SYSTEM	METRIC SYSTEM
16 oz = 1 pt 2 pt = 1 qt 4 qt = 1 gal	1000 mL = 1 L
A liter is about 2 ounces more than a quart.	

Example 1　One quart of juice is how many ounces of juice?

Solution　The table tells us that a quart is 2 pints and that each pint is 16 ounces. Since 2 times 16 is 32, 1 quart is the same as **32 ounces.**

1 quart

pint = 16 ounces

pint = 16 ounces

Note: The word *ounce* is used to describe a weight as well as an amount of liquid. An ounce of liquid is often called a **fluid ounce.** Although ounce has two meanings, a fluid ounce of water does weigh about 1 ounce.

Example 2　A half gallon of milk is the same as how many quarts?

Solution　A whole gallon is equal to 4 quarts. A half gallon is equal to half as many quarts. A half gallon equals **2 quarts.** It can be helpful to remember that two pints equal a quart, two quarts equal a half gallon, and two half gallons equal a gallon.

Practice　**a.** One fourth of a dollar is a quarter. What is the name for one fourth of a gallon?

b. How many pints equal 1 gallon?

c. How many milliliters equal 2 liters?

d. A cup is one half of a pint. A cup is the same as how many ounces?

Problem set 95　**1.** Draw a rectangle. Shade all but two fifths of it. What
(47)　percent of the rectangle is shaded?

2. Write a three-digit prime number using the digits 4, 1,
(90)　and 0 once each.

3. Write the length of this segment as a number of
(74) centimeters and as a number of millimeters.

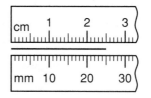

4. Tina counted her heartbeats. Her heart beat 20 times
(55) in 15 seconds. At that rate, how many times would it
beat in 1 minute?

5. In this quadrilateral, which seg-
(32) ment appears to be perpendicular
to $\overline{AB}$?

  A. $\overline{BC}$ B. $\overline{CD}$ C. $\overline{DA}$

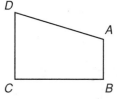

6. (a) Find the greatest common factor (GCF) of 6 and 9.
(92) (b) Use the GCF of 6 and 9 to reduce $\frac{6}{9}$.

7. (a) What number is $\frac{1}{5}$ of 60?
(50) (b) What number is $\frac{2}{5}$ of 60?

8. AB is $1\frac{1}{4}$ inches. BC is $2\frac{1}{4}$ inches. Find AC.
(81)

9. Arrange these numbers in order from least to greatest:
(78)
$$0.1, \; 0, \; 0.01, \; 1.0$$

10. Four quarts of water is how many pints of water?
(95)

11. Three liters equals how many milliliters?
(95)

12. Divide 100 by 6 and write the quotient as a mixed
(65) number. Then reduce the fraction part of the mixed
number.

13. $17.56 + $12 + 95¢
(80)

14. 4.324
(82) − 1.91

15. 396
(63) × 405

16. $1.25 × 20
(30)

17. $9\overline{)3605}$
(35)

18. $2.50 ÷ 10
(61)

19. Reduce $\dfrac{15}{20}$.
(91)

20. $3 - \left(2\dfrac{2}{3} - 1\right)$
(24)

21. Write a fraction equal to $\frac{3}{5}$ that has a denominator of
(89) 10. Also, write a fraction equal to $\frac{1}{2}$ that has a denominator of 10. What is the sum of the two fractions?

22. Find the sum when five and twelve hundredths is
(82) added to six and fifteen hundredths.

23. Since $\frac{1}{4} + \frac{1}{4} + \frac{1}{4} = \frac{3}{4}$, how many $\frac{1}{4}$s are in $\frac{3}{4}$?
(37)

Read this information. Then answer questions 24 and 25.

Stan is 6 inches taller than Roberta. Roberta is 4 inches shorter than Gilbert. Gilbert is 5 feet, 3 inches tall.

24. How tall is Roberta?
(54)

25. How tall is Stan?
(54)

LESSON 96

Multiplying Fractions and Whole Numbers

Facts Practice: Simplify 60 Improper Fractions (Test H in Test Masters)

Mental Math: How many quarters are in a dollar? How many quarts are in a gallon?

   a. CCXCVII   **b.** LIX   **c.** Reduce: $\frac{3}{6}, \frac{3}{9}, \frac{3}{12}, \frac{3}{15}$

   d. 25% of $60   **e.** $\frac{1}{3}$ of 90, + 3, ÷ 3, × 9

Problem Solving: Marissa is covering a 5-feet by 3-feet bulletin board with blue and gold construction paper squares, making a checker-board pattern. Each square is 1 foot by 1 foot. Copy this diagram on your paper and complete the patterns. How many squares of each color does Marissa need?

We have found fractions of whole numbers that have answers that are whole numbers.

$$\frac{1}{3} \text{ of 6 is 2.}$$

The answer to the following question is not a whole number.

$$\text{What number is } \frac{1}{3} \text{ of 2?}$$

We know that $\frac{1}{2}$ of 2 is 1. So $\frac{1}{3}$ of 2 is a fraction less than 1. We can find the answer by multiplying.

$$\frac{1}{3} \text{ of 2}$$
$$\downarrow \quad \downarrow \quad \downarrow$$
$$\frac{1}{3} \times \frac{2}{1}$$

Notice that we wrote the whole number 2 as a fraction, $\frac{2}{1}$. Since 2 divided by 1 is 2, the fraction $\frac{2}{1}$ equals 2. Writing the whole number as a fraction gives us a numerator and a denominator to multiply. The product is $\frac{2}{3}$.

$$\frac{1}{3} \times \frac{2}{1} = \frac{2}{3}$$

Remember that factors may be multiplied in reverse order. So another way to approach this problem is to reverse the factors.

$$\frac{1}{3} \times 2$$

We may reverse factors when we multiply.

$$2 \times \frac{1}{3}$$

Since $2 \times \frac{1}{3}$ means $\frac{1}{3} + \frac{1}{3}$, we again find that the product is $\frac{2}{3}$.

Example   What number is $\frac{2}{3}$ of 4?

Solution   Two thirds of 4 is less than 4 but more than 2. We know that it is more than 2 because $\frac{1}{2}$ of 4 is 2, and $\frac{2}{3}$ is more than $\frac{1}{2}$. We multiply to find the answer.

$$\frac{2}{3} \text{ of } 4$$
$$\downarrow \quad \downarrow \quad \downarrow$$
$$\frac{2}{3} \times \frac{4}{1} = \frac{8}{3}$$

Then we convert $\frac{8}{3}$ to the mixed number $2\frac{2}{3}$, which is less than 4 but more than 2. The answer is reasonable. We may check the answer by reversing the factors.

$$4 \times \frac{2}{3} \quad \text{means} \quad \frac{2}{3} + \frac{2}{3} + \frac{2}{3} + \frac{2}{3}$$

Again the answer is $\frac{8}{3}$, which equals **$2\frac{2}{3}$.**

Practice*   Multiply. Simplify answers when possible. Reverse the factors to check your answer.

a. $\frac{1}{3} \times 4$ **b.** $2 \times \frac{3}{5}$ **c.** $\frac{2}{3} \times 2$

d. What number is $\frac{1}{5}$ of 4?

e. What number is $\frac{1}{6}$ of 5?

f. What number is $\frac{2}{3}$ of 5?

Problem set 96

1. Draw a pair of horizontal parallel segments. Make the
(39) lower segment longer than the upper segment. Make a
quadrilateral by connecting the endpoints.

2. Estimate the difference when 3047 is subtracted from
(69) 6970 by rounding the numbers to the nearest thousand
before you subtract.

3. Write the following sentence using digits and symbols:
(4)
"The sum of six and four is ten."

4. A 2-liter bottle of soft drink contains how many
(95) milliliters of liquid?

5. Name the shaded part of the
(76) square as a fraction, as a decimal
number, and as a percent.

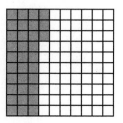

6. (a) What number is $\frac{1}{3}$ of 120?
(50)
(b) What number is $\frac{2}{3}$ of 120?

7. Which segment names a diameter
(60) of this circle?

    A. $\overline{RS}$ B. $\overline{RT}$

    C. $\overline{OS}$ D. $\overline{OT}$

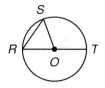

8. List these fractions in order from least to greatest:
(68)

$$\frac{9}{18}, \frac{8}{7}, \frac{7}{16}, \frac{6}{6}, \frac{5}{8}$$

9. The arrow is pointing to what mixed number on this
(41) number line?

Multiply to find each product. Then reverse the factors to check your answers.

10. $\dfrac{2}{3} \times 2$
(96)

11. $\dfrac{3}{4}$ of 4
(96)

12. $3 - \left(2\dfrac{3}{5} - 1\dfrac{1}{5}\right)$
(24)

13.
(82)
$$\begin{array}{r} 53.487 \\ 12.596 \\ + 18.427 \\ \hline \end{array}$$

14.
(82)
$$\begin{array}{r} 301.4 \\ - 143.5 \\ \hline \end{array}$$

15.
(63)
$$\begin{array}{r} 476 \\ \times 890 \\ \hline \end{array}$$

16. $4\overline{)348}$
(26)

17. $40\overline{)3480}$
(61)

18. $\$42.36 \div 6$
(35)

19. Reduce $\dfrac{8}{10}$.
(91)

20. (a) What is the greatest common factor (GCF) of 15,
(92)   21, and 6?

(b) Use the GCF of 15, 21, and 6 to reduce $\frac{15}{21}$.

21. Write a fraction equal to $\frac{3}{4}$ that has a denominator of
(89)   12. Next, write a fraction equal to $\frac{2}{3}$ that has a denominator of 12. Then subtract the second fraction from the first fraction.

22. Since $\frac{3}{4} + \frac{3}{4} + \frac{3}{4} = \frac{9}{4}$, how many $\frac{3}{4}$s are in $\frac{9}{4}$?
(37)

23. (a) What is the name of this solid?
(93)   (b) How many faces does it have?

Use this graph to answer questions 24 and 25:

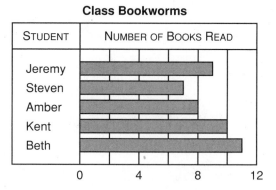

24. How many more books must Steven read to reach the
(54)   goal of 12?

25. Each book must be 180 pages or more. Kent has read at
(54)   least how many pages so far?

LESSON
97

Dividing Fractions, Part 1

Facts Practice: Simplify 60 Improper Fractions (Test H in Test
Masters)

Mental Math: How many quarts are in one gallon? two gallons?
three gallons?

  a. CIX   **b.** CCLXXVII   **c.** Reduce: $\frac{2}{10}, \frac{2}{12}, \frac{2}{14}, \frac{2}{16}$

  d. $\frac{1}{4}$ of 400, ÷ 2, − 5, ÷ 5, × 4, ÷ 6

Problem Solving: Write the sum of these Roman numerals as a
Roman numeral: CXCII + CLX

We may use our fraction manipulatives to help us divide
fractions. Before using the fraction manipulatives, let us
think about what dividing fractions means. The
expression

$$\frac{3}{4} \div \frac{1}{8}$$

means, "How many one eighths are in three fourths?" For example, how many one eighth slices of pizza are in three fourths of a pizza?

Using manipulatives, we may place three fourths on our desk.

If we cover the three fourths with eighths, we can see that there are six one eighths in three fourths.

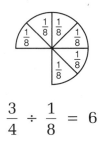

$$\frac{3}{4} \div \frac{1}{8} = 6$$

Example 1 How many one eighths are in one half?

Solution This is a division question. It could also be written this way:

$$\frac{1}{2} \div \frac{1}{8}$$

Using our fraction manipulatives, we place one half on our desk.

To find how many one eighths are in one half, we cover one half with one eighths and count how many one eighths we use.

The answer is **4**. There are four one eighths in one half.

Example 2 $\dfrac{3}{4} \div \dfrac{1}{4}$

Solution   The problem means, "How many one fourths are in three fourths?" This question is almost too easy. How many one fourths does it take to make three fourths? The answer is **3**.

There are three one fourths in three fourths.

Example 3 $1 \div \dfrac{1}{3}$

Solution   The problem means, "How many one thirds are in one?" Using our manipulatives, we want to find the number of one third pieces needed to make one whole circle.

The answer is 3. There are three one thirds in one.

$$1 \div \dfrac{1}{3} = \mathbf{3}$$

Practice Use your fraction manipulatives to help you with these division problems:

    a. How many one sixths are in one half?

    b. How many one twelfths are in one third?

Try answering these division problems mentally:

    c. $\dfrac{2}{3} \div \dfrac{2}{3}$ **d.** $1 \div \dfrac{1}{4}$

    e. $\dfrac{2}{3} \div \dfrac{1}{3}$ **f.** $1 \div \dfrac{1}{2}$

Problem set 97

1. Mary's rectangular garden is twice as long as it is
_(60)_ wide. Her garden is 10 feet wide. What is the perimeter of her garden?

2. In which of these numbers does the 1 mean $\frac{1}{10}$? Use
_(77)_ words to name the number.

    A. 12.34   B. 21.43   C. 34.12   D. 43.21

3. List these numbers in order of size from least to
_(78)_ greatest:

$$1, 0, \tfrac{1}{2}, 0.3$$

4. Two quarts of juice is how many ounces of juice?
_(95)_

5. (a) A quarter is what fraction of a dollar?
_(50)_
    (b) How many quarters equal 1 dollar?
    (c) How many quarters equal 3 dollars?

6. Name the shaded part of the rect-
_(72)_ angle as a fraction, as a decimal number, and as a percent.

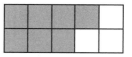

7. If $a = 3$, then $2a + 5$ equals:
_(17)_
    A. 10   B. 11   C. 16   D. 28

8. *AC* is 84 millimeters. *AB* is one fourth of *AC*. Find *BC*.
(81)

A   B   C

9. First write a fraction equal to $\frac{1}{2}$ that has a denominator
(89) of 6. Then write a fraction equal to $\frac{1}{3}$ that has a denominator of 6. Subtract the second fraction from the first fraction.

10. (a) Find the greatest common factor (GCF) of 10, 16,
(92)   and 6.

(b) Use the GCF of 10, 16, and 6 to reduce $\frac{10}{16}$.

11. $3 - \left(1\frac{3}{4} - 1\right)$ **12.** $\frac{3}{5}$ of 4
(24)   (96)

13. $20 − ($6.25 + 49¢)
(24)

14.   706   **15.** $12.75   **16.**   5365
(63) × 468   (17) ×   8   (6)   428
                                                         3997
                                                          659
                                                      7073
                                                + 342

17. $2250 \div 50$ **18.** $5\overline{)225}$ **19.** $4\overline{)\$8.20}$
(61)   (26)   (35)

20. Divide 100 by 8 and write the quotient as a mixed
(65) number. Then reduce the fraction part of the mixed number.

21. How many one eighths are in one fourth?
(97)

22. $\frac{1}{2} \div \frac{1}{12}$
(97)

23. Since $\frac{2}{3} + \frac{2}{3} + \frac{2}{3} = 2$, how many $\frac{2}{3}$s are in 2?
(97)

This map shows the number of miles it is between towns. Use this map to answer questions 24 and 25.

24. The distance from Marysville to
(54) Red Bluff is how many miles more than the distance from Marysville to Sacramento?

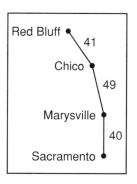

25. Allen was traveling from Sacra-
(54) mento to Chico. When he was halfway to Marysville, how far did he still have to go?

LESSON
98

Reducing Fraction Answers

Facts Practice: Simplify 60 Improper Fractions (Test H in Test Masters)

Mental Math: How many ounces are in a pound? How many ounces are in a pint? What is the meaning of the rhyme, "A pint's a pound the world around"?

  a. CXCVIII   **b.** CCCXLVI   **c.** Reduce: $\frac{3}{12}, \frac{10}{12}, \frac{9}{12}$

  d. 50% of 50, -1, $\div 3$, $+2$, $\times 10$

Problem Solving: Some 1-inch cubes were used to build this rectangular solid. How many 1-inch cubes were used?

2 in.   3 in.

2 in.

Remember that when we reduce fractions, we mentally search for a number that is a factor of both terms of the fraction. Then we divide both terms of the fraction by the common factor.

There is another number we may use to help us search for a common factor. That number is the difference of the two terms.

Terms $\Big\langle$ $\dfrac{12}{15}$ **The difference between the terms is 3.**

Notice that common factors of the terms are also common factors of the difference.

Factors of 12, 15, and 3

12	①, 2, ③, 4, 6, 12
15	①, ③, 5, 15
3	①, ③

Since the greatest common factor of all three numbers is 3, we reduce $\frac{12}{15}$ by dividing by $\frac{3}{3}$.

$$\frac{12}{15} \div \frac{3}{3} = \frac{4}{5}$$

The answers to fraction arithmetic problems should be reduced whenever possible.

Example $\dfrac{1}{8} + \dfrac{5}{8}$

Solution   We add $\frac{1}{8}$ and $\frac{5}{8}$.

$$\frac{1}{8} + \frac{5}{8} = \frac{6}{8}$$

The terms of $\frac{6}{8}$ are 6 and 8. Their difference is 2. We can reduce $\frac{6}{8}$ by dividing by $\frac{2}{2}$.

$$\frac{6}{8} \div \frac{2}{2} = \frac{3}{4}$$

The sum of $\frac{1}{8}$ and $\frac{5}{8}$ is $\frac{3}{4}$.

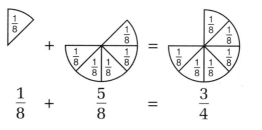

$$\frac{1}{8} + \frac{5}{8} = \frac{3}{4}$$

Practice Reduce each answer:

a. $\frac{5}{9} + \frac{1}{9}$

b. $\frac{5}{8} - \frac{1}{8}$

c. $\frac{2}{3} \times \frac{5}{4}$

Problem set 98

1. Pam lives $\frac{1}{4}$ mile from school. How far does she travel
$^{(54)}$ each day going to school and back?

2. According to this calendar, what
$^{(27)}$ is the date of the first Friday in
   April 2070?

MARCH 2070						
S	M	T	W	T	F	S
						1
2	3	4	5	6	7	8
9	10	11	12	13	14	15
16	17	18	19	20	21	22
23	24	25	26	27	28	29
30	31					

3. When the decimal number three and twelve
$^{(82)}$ hundredths is subtracted from four and twenty-five
   hundredths, what is the difference?

4. (a) How many dimes equal $1?
$^{(80)}$
   (b) How many dimes equal $5?

5. What number is $\frac{2}{3}$ of 150?
$^{(96)}$

6. A half gallon of milk is how many quarts of milk?
$^{(95)}$

7. Which part of a bicycle wheel is like a radius?
$^{(60)}$
   A. Rim   B. Spoke   C. Hub

8. Write a fraction equal to one third with a denominator
$^{(89)}$ of 6. Then subtract that fraction from five sixths.
   Remember to reduce the answer.

9. (a) What fraction of the rectangle
(98)   is shaded? (Reduce your
       answer.)

(b) What percent of the rectangle
    is shaded?

10. *RT* is 84 millimeters. *RS* is one third of *RT*. Find *ST*.
(81)

R ————•———————————— S ————————————————————— T →

11. Compare: $\frac{3}{5} + \frac{3}{5} + \frac{3}{5} \bigcirc 3 \times \frac{3}{5}$
(42)

12. In this drawing, which angle
(94)   appears to be obtuse?

A. ∠ABC   B. ∠ABD
C. ∠BDC   D. ∠DAB

13. $\frac{1}{8} \times 3$
(96)

14. $\frac{3}{8} \div \frac{1}{8}$
(97)

15. (a) How many one fourths are in one?
(97)

(b) $\frac{1}{6} \times 4$

16. $\frac{1}{4} + \frac{1}{4}$
(98)

17. $\frac{7}{8} - \frac{1}{8}$
(98)

18. $5 - 1\frac{3}{10}$
(70)

19. $6.57 + 38¢ + $16
(80)

20. 42,105 − 1,257
(9)

21. 7 × 35¢ = $_____
(80)

22. 340 × 607
(63)

23. 9)$7.65
(26)

Use this school schedule to answer questions 24 and 25.

School Schedule

Reading	8:00–8:50
Math	8:50–9:40
Recess	9:40–10:10
Language	10:10–10:50
Science	10:50–11:30
Lunch	11:30–12:30

24. How many total minutes are spent each morning in
(54) reading and language?

25. If students come back for 2 hours and 10 minutes after
(54) lunch, then at what time does school end?

LESSON 99

Reducing Mixed Numbers

Facts Practice: 64 Multiplication Facts (Test D in Test Masters)

Mental Math: How many ounces are in a pint? How many pints
are in a quart? How many ounces are in a quart?

  a. CCXVIII   **b.** CCCXLIX   **c.** Reduce: $\frac{4}{12}, \frac{6}{12}, \frac{8}{12}$

  d. $\frac{1}{10}$ of 1000, $- 1$, $\div 9$, $+ 1$, $\times 4$, $+ 1$, $\div 7$

Problem Solving: Two cups equal a pint. Two pints equal a
quart. Two quarts equal a half gallon. Two
half gallons equal a gallon. One pint and one
quart is a total of how many cups?

We reduce a mixed number by reducing its fraction. The
mixed number $4\frac{2}{4}$ is not in its simplest form because the
fraction can be reduced. When we reduce the fraction, the
whole number is not changed.

$$4\frac{2}{4} \text{ means } 4 + \frac{2}{4}$$

$$\frac{2}{4} \text{ reduces to } \frac{1}{2}$$

$$\text{So } 4\frac{2}{4} \text{ equals } 4\frac{1}{2}$$

Example 1 Reduce: $3\dfrac{4}{6}$

Solution We reduce a mixed number by reducing its fraction. Since the fraction $\frac{4}{6}$ reduces to $\frac{2}{3}$, the mixed number $3\frac{4}{6}$ reduces to **$3\frac{2}{3}$.**

Fraction answers which can be reduced should be. Be alert for fraction answers which can be reduced.

Example 2 $4\dfrac{5}{6} - 1\dfrac{1}{6}$

Solution We subtract and get the answer $3\frac{4}{6}$.

$$4\dfrac{5}{6} - 1\dfrac{1}{6} = 3\dfrac{4}{6}$$

However, the fraction can be reduced. We reduce $\frac{4}{6}$ to $\frac{2}{3}$ and write the answer as **$3\frac{2}{3}$.**

$$3\dfrac{4}{6} = 3\dfrac{2}{3}$$

Practice* Reduce each mixed number:

    a. $1\dfrac{2}{8}$ **b.** $2\dfrac{6}{9}$ **c.** $2\dfrac{5}{10}$

    d. $3\dfrac{2}{4}$ **e.** $3\dfrac{4}{6}$ **f.** $4\dfrac{3}{12}$

Add or subtract, as indicated. Reduce answers.

    g. $1\dfrac{1}{4} + 1\dfrac{1}{4}$ **h.** $4\dfrac{1}{10} + 2\dfrac{3}{10}$ **i.** $6\dfrac{9}{10} - 1\dfrac{1}{10}$

    j. $3\dfrac{1}{8} + \dfrac{5}{8}$ **k.** $5\dfrac{5}{8} - 1\dfrac{1}{8}$ **l.** $5\dfrac{5}{12} - \dfrac{1}{12}$

Problem set 99 **1.** Thomas Jefferson wrote the Declaration of Independence in 1776. He died exactly 50 years later. In what year did he die?

$^{(6)}$

2. Shannon won $10,000. She will be paid $20 a day
(21) until the money runs out. How many days will the money last?

3. A number is divisible by 4 if it can be divided by 4
(20) without leaving a remainder. Which of these numbers is divisible by both 4 and 5?

A. 15 B. 16 C. 20 D. 25

4. List these numbers in order from least to greatest:
(78)

$$0.5, \frac{3}{2}, 1, 0, 1.1$$

5. (a) How many half-gallon cartons of milk equal 1
(95) gallon?

(b) How many half-gallon cartons of milk equal 3 gallons?

6. Use digits to write the number one million, three
(59) hundred fifty-four thousand, seven hundred sixty.

7. Write a fraction equal to $\frac{1}{2}$ with a denominator of 6.
(98) Then subtract that fraction from $\frac{5}{6}$. Remember to reduce the answer.

8. (a) What fraction of the circles is shaded? (Reduce the fraction.)
(98)

(b) What percent of the circles is shaded?

9. (a) Name this shape.
(93) (b) How many faces does it have?

10. Write the length of the segment as a number of
(74) centimeters and as a number of millimeters.

11. $\frac{2}{5}$ of 3
(96)

12. $\frac{2}{5} + \frac{2}{5} + \frac{2}{5}$
(84)

13. $1\frac{1}{4} + 1\frac{1}{4}$
(99)

14. $3\frac{5}{6} - 1\frac{1}{6}$
(99)

15. 68,423 + 4976 + 2875 + 5318
(6)

16. $10 − (57¢ + $2.48)
(24)

17. 42 × 5 × 36
(18)

18. $6.15 × 10
(30)

19. $40\overline{)2760}$
(61)

20. $4\overline{)276}$
(26)

21. $\frac{1}{2} \div \frac{1}{10}$
(97)

22. $\frac{1}{2} \times \frac{6}{8}$
(98)

23. Divide 371 by 10 and write the answer with a
(61) remainder.

Read this information. Then answer questions 24 and 25.

When Jenny was born, her dad was 29 years old. Her brothers are Tom and Monty. Tom is 2 years older than Jenny and 2 years younger than Monty. Monty is 10 years old.

24. How old is Jenny?
(54)

25. How old is her dad?
(54)

**LESSON
100**

Reducing Fractions to Lowest Terms

Facts Practice: 64 Multiplication Facts (Test D in Test Masters)

Mental Math: How many milliliters are in a liter? Which U.S. Customary unit is nearly a liter?

    a. XLV   **b.** CCXIX   **c.** Reduce: $\frac{4}{8}$, $\frac{4}{12}$, $\frac{4}{16}$

Problem Solving: A **line of symmetry** divides a figure into mirror images. This rectangle has two lines of symmetry. Draw a different rectangle on your paper and show its lines of symmetry.

The equivalent fractions pictured below name the same amount. We see that $\frac{4}{8}$ is equivalent to $\frac{1}{2}$.

$$\frac{1}{2} \qquad\qquad \frac{4}{8}$$

We can reduce $\frac{4}{8}$ by dividing by $\frac{2}{2}$.

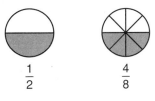

$$\frac{4}{8} \div \frac{2}{2} = \frac{2}{4}$$

If we reduce $\frac{4}{8}$ by dividing both terms by 2, we find that $\frac{4}{8}$ is equal to $\frac{2}{4}$. However, fractions should be reduced to lowest terms. The fraction $\frac{2}{4}$ can also be reduced, so we reduce again.

$$\frac{2}{4} \div \frac{2}{2} = \frac{1}{2}$$

The fraction $\frac{4}{8}$ reduces to $\frac{2}{4}$, which reduces to $\frac{1}{2}$. We reduce twice to find that $\frac{4}{8}$ equals $\frac{1}{2}$.

We can avoid the need to reduce more than once if we divide by the largest number which divides both terms evenly. The greatest common factor of 4 and 8 is 4. If we reduce $\frac{4}{8}$ by dividing both terms by 4, we reduce only once.

$$\frac{4}{8} \div \mathbf{1}\frac{4}{4} = \frac{1}{2}$$

Example Reduce: $\dfrac{8}{12}$

Solution The terms of $\frac{8}{12}$ are 8 and 12. Their difference is 4. Since 8, 12, and 4 are divisible by 2, we may reduce $\frac{8}{12}$ by dividing by $\frac{2}{2}$. This gives us $\frac{4}{6}$, which can also be reduced by dividing by $\frac{2}{2}$ again.

REDUCE TWICE:

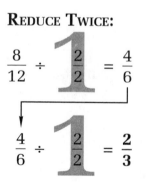

The GCF of 8, 12, and 4 is 4. If we divide $\frac{8}{12}$ by $\frac{4}{4}$, then we reduce only once.

REDUCE ONCE:

$$\frac{8}{12} \div \mathbf{1}\frac{4}{4} = \frac{2}{3}$$

Practice* Reduce each fraction to lowest terms:

a. $\dfrac{4}{12}$ b. $\dfrac{6}{18}$ c. $\dfrac{16}{24}$

d. $\dfrac{4}{16}$ e. $\dfrac{12}{16}$ f. $\dfrac{40}{100}$

Solve and reduce the answers to lowest terms:

g. $\dfrac{7}{16} + \dfrac{1}{16}$ h. $\dfrac{3}{4} \times \dfrac{4}{5}$ i. $\dfrac{19}{24} - \dfrac{1}{24}$

Problem set 100

1. This little poem is about what number?
(6)

> *I am a number, not 1, 2, or 3.*
> *Whenever I'm added, no difference you'll see.*

2. Write the following sentence using digits and symbols:
(4)

> "The product of nine and ten is ninety."

3. Write fractions equal to $\frac{1}{2}$ and $\frac{3}{5}$ with denominators of
(89) 10. Then add the fractions. Remember to convert the answer to a mixed number.

4. Write the greatest four-digit even number you can
(2) make using the four digits 1, 2, 3, and 4 one time each.

5. (a) How many quarts of milk equal a gallon?
(95)
(b) How many quarts of milk equal 6 gallons?

6. Find the sum when the decimal number fourteen and
(82) seven tenths is added to four and four tenths.

7. Name the shaded part of the rect-
(72) angle as a decimal number, as a reduced fraction, and as a percent.

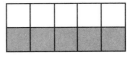

8. What is the shape of a basketball?
(93)

9. In this rectangle, which segment
(32) is parallel to $\overline{AB}$?

A. $\overline{BC}$ B. $\overline{CD}$

C. $\overline{BD}$ D. $\overline{DA}$

10. $\dfrac{5}{6} + \dfrac{5}{6}$
(84)

11. $\dfrac{5}{6} \times 2$
(96)

12. $\dfrac{2}{5} \div \dfrac{1}{10}$
(97)

13. $\dfrac{1}{12} + \dfrac{7}{12}$
(100)

14. $6\dfrac{2}{3} - \left(4 - \dfrac{1}{3}\right)$
(24)

15. $\dfrac{2}{3} \times \dfrac{3}{4}$
(100)

16.   8242.19
(82)   7657.36
      + 9414.87

17.   3015
(9)   − 2939

18.   487
(62)   × 396

19. $7.50 × 6
(17)

20. 480 ÷ 10
(61)

21. 240 ÷ 5
(26)

22. (a) $1 \div \dfrac{1}{3}$ (b) $\dfrac{3}{4} \times 3$
(97)

23. $\dfrac{3}{5} \times \boxed{} = \dfrac{60}{100}$
(89)

This table lists ways Brian can earn extra credit points in social studies. Use this table to answer questions 24 and 25.

Extra Credit Points

Magazine report	35 points
TV special	50 points
Book report	75 points
Museum report	100 points

24. Brian has done a book report, two magazine reports,
(54) and a TV special. How many points has he earned?

25. Brian needs to earn a total of 400 points. How many
(54) more points does he need?

LESSON 101

Converting and Reducing Improper Fractions

Facts Practice: Reduce 40 Fractions (Test I in Test Masters)

Problem Solving: This table lists the years from 2001 to 2006 and the day of the week which begins each year. Notice that each year begins one day of the week later than the first day of the previous year until 2005. Since 2004 is a leap year and has an additional day, the year 2005 begins an additional day later. Copy this table and continue it through the year 2015, which begins on a Thursday.

Year	First Day
2001	Monday
2002	Tuesday
2003	Wednesday
2004	Thursday
2005	Saturday
2006	Sunday

We have learned two ways to simplify fractions. We have converted improper fractions to whole numbers or mixed numbers, and we have reduced fractions. In some cases we should simplify a fraction answer **both** ways. To show this we will add $\frac{3}{4}$ and $\frac{3}{4}$.

$$\frac{3}{4} + \frac{3}{4} = \frac{6}{4}$$

We see that the answer is an improper fraction. To convert an improper fraction to a mixed number, we divide and write the remainder as a fraction.

$$\frac{6}{4} \longrightarrow 4\overline{)6} \begin{array}{c} 1\frac{2}{4} \\ \end{array} \qquad \text{so} \qquad \frac{6}{4} = 1\frac{2}{4}$$

$$\begin{array}{r} \underline{4} \\ 2 \end{array}$$

The improper fraction $\frac{6}{4}$ is equal to the mixed number $1\frac{2}{4}$. However, $1\frac{2}{4}$ can be reduced.

$$1\frac{2}{4} = 1\frac{1}{2}$$

The simplified answer to $\frac{3}{4} + \frac{3}{4}$ is $1\frac{1}{2}$.

Example 1   Write $\frac{8}{6}$ as a reduced mixed number.

Solution   To convert $\frac{8}{6}$ to a mixed number, we divide 8 by 6 and get $1\frac{2}{6}$. Then we reduce $1\frac{2}{6}$ by dividing both terms of the fraction by 2 and get $1\frac{1}{3}$.

$$\text{Convert:} \quad \frac{8}{6} = 1\frac{2}{6}$$

$$\text{Reduce:} \quad 1\frac{2}{6} = \mathbf{1\frac{1}{3}}$$

Example 2 $1\frac{7}{8} + 1\frac{3}{8}$

Solution   We add to get $2\frac{10}{8}$. We convert the improper fraction $\frac{10}{8}$ to $1\frac{2}{8}$ and add it to the 2 to get $3\frac{2}{8}$. Finally, we reduce the fraction to get $\mathbf{3\frac{1}{4}}$.

ADD	CONVERT ANSWER	REDUCE ANSWER

$$1\frac{7}{8} + 1\frac{3}{8} = 2\frac{10}{8} \quad \longrightarrow \quad 2\frac{10}{8} = 3\frac{2}{8} \quad \longrightarrow \quad 3\frac{2}{8} = 3\frac{1}{4}$$

Practice*   Simplify each fraction and mixed number:

a. $\frac{6}{4}$ b. $\frac{10}{6}$ c. $2\frac{8}{6}$ d. $3\frac{10}{4}$

e. $\frac{10}{4}$ f. $\frac{12}{8}$ g. $4\frac{14}{8}$ h. $1\frac{10}{8}$

Perform the operations. Then simplify the answers.

i. $1\frac{5}{6} + 1\frac{5}{6}$ j. $2\frac{3}{4} + 4\frac{3}{4}$ k. $\frac{5}{3} \times \frac{3}{2}$

Problem set 101

1. Two fathoms deep is 12 feet deep. How deep is 10 fathoms?
   (55)

2. When Jessica baby-sits, she is paid $1.50 per hour. If she baby-sits Saturday from 10:30 a.m. to 3:30 p.m., how much money will she be paid?
   (55)

3. Use digits to write the number one hundred fifty-four
(59) million, three hundred forty-three thousand, five
hundred fifteen.

4. (a) How many quarter-mile laps should Jim run to run
(97)   1 mile?

(b) How many quarter-mile laps should Jim run to run
5 miles?

5. Write a fraction equal to $\frac{3}{4}$ with a denominator of 8.
(89) Add that fraction to $\frac{5}{8}$. Remember to convert the
answer to a mixed number.

6. What mixed number names the
(43) number of shaded hexagons?

7. Which segment does **not** name a
(60) radius of this circle?

   A. $\overline{OR}$ B. $\overline{OS}$

   C. $\overline{RT}$ D. $\overline{OT}$

8. Compare: $\frac{1}{2}$ of 2 $\bigcirc$ $2 \times \frac{1}{2}$
(96)

9. What is the shape of a can of beans?
(93)

10. AB is 3.2 cm. BC is 1.8 cm. CD equals BC. Find AD.
(81)

11. $1\frac{3}{4} + 1\frac{3}{4}$ **12.** $5\frac{7}{8} - 1\frac{3}{8}$
(101)   (99)

13. $3 \times \frac{3}{8}$ **14.** $10 - (\$1.25 + 35¢)$
(101)   (24)

15. $4.32   **16.**   416   **17.**   9635
(17) $\times$ 5   (63) $\times$ 740   (6)   8247
                                                       7775
                                                       682
                                                       513
                                                     +   9

18. 960 ÷ 8
(35)

19. 80)‾9600‾
(61)

20. 5)‾$12.00‾
(35)

21. $\frac{5}{2} \times \frac{2}{3}$
(101)

22. $\frac{2}{3} \div \frac{1}{3}$
(97)

23. $\frac{2}{3} \div \frac{1}{6}$
(97)

Read this information. Then answer questions 24 and 25.

Matthew fixed his function machine so that when he puts in a 3, a 9 comes out. When he puts in a 6, an 18 comes out. When he puts in a 9, a 27 comes out.

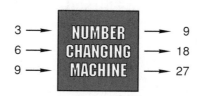

24. Which of the following does Matthew's function
(54) machine do to the numbers he puts into it?

A. It adds 3.

B. It multiplies by 3.

C. It adds 9.

D. It multiplies by 2 and 3.

25. Matthew put in a number and a 12 came out. What
(54) number did he put in?

LESSON 102

Dividing by Two-Digit Numbers, Part 1

Facts Practice: Reduce 40 Fractions (Test I in Test Masters)

Mental Math:

  a. Reduce: $\frac{6}{8}, \frac{6}{9}, \frac{6}{12}$ **b.** 10% of $5000   **c.** $\frac{1}{5}$ of $5000
  d. $\frac{1}{3}$ of 100   **e.** $\sqrt{100}$, × 2, × 50, − 1, ÷ 9

Problem Solving: Write the difference of these Roman numerals
as a Roman numeral.
CCCLXII − CXXIII

In this lesson we will begin dividing by two-digit numbers. When we can divide by two-digit numbers we will be able to solve problems like the following:

One hundred forty-four players signed up for soccer. If the players are separated into 12 equal teams, how many players will be on each team?

When we divide by a two-digit number, we continue to follow the four steps: divide, multiply, subtract, and bring down. When we divide by two-digit numbers, the "divide" step takes a little more thought, because we have not memorized the two-digit multiplication facts.

Example Divide: 150 ÷ 12

Solution We begin by breaking the division into a smaller division problem. Starting from the first digit in 150, we try to find a number that 12 will divide into at least once. Our first smaller division is $12\overline{)15}$. We see that there is **one** 12 in 15, so we write "1" above the 5 of 15. Then we multiply, subtract, and bring down.

$$\begin{array}{r} 1 \\ 12\overline{)150} \\ -12 \\ \hline 30 \end{array}$$

Now we begin a new division. This time we divide $12\overline{)30}$. If we are not sure of the division answer, we may need to try more than once to find the number of 12s in 30. We find that there are two 12s in 30. We write "2" above the 0 of 150, and then we multiply and subtract.

$$\begin{array}{r} \textbf{12 r 6} \\ 12\overline{)150} \\ -12 \\ \overline{)30} \\ -24 \\ \hline 6 \end{array}$$

Since there is no digit to bring down, we are finished. The remainder is 6.

To check our answer, we multiply 12×12, and then we add the remainder, which is 6.

$$12 \times 12 = 144 \qquad 144 + 6 = 150 \qquad \text{(check)}$$

Practice Divide.

a. $11\overline{)253}$ **b.** $21\overline{)253}$ **c.** $31\overline{)403}$

d. $12\overline{)253}$ **e.** $12\overline{)300}$ **f.** $23\overline{)510}$

g. One hundred forty-four players signed up for soccer. If the players are separated into 12 equal teams, how many players will be on each team?

Problem set 102

1. Draw a pair of horizontal line segments. Make them
(39) the same length. Then draw two more line segments to make a quadrilateral.

2. Nathan worked on his homework from 3:30 p.m. to
(55) 6 p.m. For how many **minutes** did he work on his homework?

3. Write a decimal number equal to the mixed number
(72) $3\frac{9}{10}$.

4. If 24 eggs exactly fill 2 cartons, how many eggs will it
(55) take to fill 3 cartons?

5. About $\frac{2}{3}$ of our body weight is water. Olivia weighs
(96) 105 pounds. Her body contains about how many pounds of water?

6. (a) How many apples weighing $\frac{1}{3}$ of a pound each
(97)   would it take to total 1 pound?

   (b) How many apples weighing $\frac{1}{3}$ of a pound each
   would it take to total 4 pounds?

7. Name this shape.
(93)

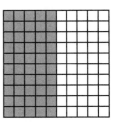

8. Name the shaded part of this
(76) square as a decimal number, as a
reduced fraction, and as a percent.

9. Which of these numbers does not equal $\frac{1}{2}$?
(68) A. 0.5   B. 50%   C. $\frac{6}{12}$ D. 0.05

10. AB is 40 millimeters. BC is half of AB. CD equals BC.
(81) Find AD.

$$\overset{\text{A}}{\bullet} \qquad\qquad\qquad \overset{\text{B}}{\bullet} \quad\quad \overset{\text{C}}{\bullet} \quad\quad \overset{\text{D}}{\bullet}$$

11. 905.363 **12.**   11,000 **13.**   640 **14.** $125
(82) 612.785   (9) $-$ 9,184 (63) $\times$ 806   (17) $\times$ 8
  + 66.547

15. $12\overline{)450}$ **16.** $293 \div 13$ **17.** $24\overline{)510}$
(102)   (102)   (102)

18. $3\frac{5}{8} + 1\frac{7}{8}$ **19.** $5 - 1\frac{2}{5}$ **20.** $\frac{1}{3}$ of 5
(101)   (70)   (96)

21. $\frac{3}{4} \times \frac{4}{3}$ **22.** $\frac{6}{10} \div \frac{1}{5}$
(86)   (97)

23. Write a fraction equal to $\frac{2}{5}$ with a denominator of 10.
(89) Add that fraction to $\frac{1}{10}$. Remember to reduce your
answer.

Read this information and study the table. Then answer questions 24 and 25.

Stephanie, Lupe, and Melanie bought treats for the party. Here is a list of the items they purchased.

Groceries

Nuts	$2.19
Mints	$1.19
Cake	$3.87
Ice cream	$1.39

24. What was the total cost of the treats?
(54)

25. If the girls share the cost evenly, how much will each girl pay?
(54)

LESSON 103

Dividing by Two-Digit Numbers, Part 2

Facts Practice: Reduce 40 Fractions (Test I in Test Masters)

Mental Math:

a. Reduce: $\frac{5}{20}, \frac{5}{15}, \frac{5}{10}$ **b.** CXLIV   **c.** CCXCVI

d. 50% of $100   **e.** 50% of $10   **f.** 50% of $1

g. $\frac{1}{3}$ of 6, × 2, + 1, × 5, − 1, ÷ 6

Problem Solving: Some 1-inch cubes were used to build this 4-inch cube. How many 1-inch cubes were used?

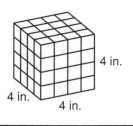

4 in.
4 in.
4 in.

We are practicing dividing by two-digit numbers. There are some "tricks" we can use to make dividing by two-digit numbers easier. One trick is to think of dividing by only the first digit.

Example   Divide: $32\overline{)987}$

Solution   We begin by breaking the division into the smaller division problem, $32\overline{)98}$. Instead of thinking, "How many 32s are in 98?" we may use the first-digit trick and think, "How many 3s are in 9?" We see $32\overline{)98}$ but we think $3\overline{)9}$. We answer "3." Since we are really dividing $32\overline{)98}$, we write the 3 above the 8 of 98. Then we multiply 3 × 32, subtract, and bring down.

$$\begin{array}{r} 30 \text{ r } 27 \\ 32\overline{)987} \\ 96 \\ \overline{27} \\ 0 \\ \overline{27} \end{array}$$

Now we begin the new division, $32\overline{)27}$. Since there is not even one 32 in 27, we write "0" in the answer; then we multiply and subtract. There are no digits to bring down. We are finished. The answer is **30 r 27.** We may check our answer by multiplying 30 × 32 and then adding the remainder, 27.

$$\begin{array}{r} 32 \\ \times \;\; 30 \\ \hline 960 \\ + \;\; 27 \quad \text{remainder} \\ \hline 987 \quad \text{(check)} \end{array}$$

Practice   Divide. Use the first-digit trick to help with the "divide" step.

a. $30\overline{)682}$ b. $32\overline{)709}$ c. $43\overline{)880}$

d. $22\overline{)924}$ e. $22\overline{)750}$ f. $21\overline{)126}$

g. $21\overline{)654}$ h. $41\overline{)910}$ i. $21\overline{)1290}$

Problem set 103

1. The saying "A pint's a pound, the world around" (95) means that a pint of water weighs about a pound. About how much does 2 quarts of water weigh?

2. If 3 of them cost $2.55, how much would 4 of them (55) cost?

3. If 300 marbles will fill a carton, how many marbles (50) will make the carton $\frac{1}{2}$ full?

4. Name the shaded part of this
(72) group as a decimal number, as a
reduced fraction, and as a percent.

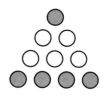

5. (a) How many plums weighing $\frac{1}{5}$ of a pound each
(97) would it take to total 1 pound?

(b) How many plums weighing $\frac{1}{5}$ of a pound each
would it take to total 3 pounds?

6. Write the following sentence using digits and
(4) symbols:

"When nine is subtracted from twelve, the
difference is three."

7. Compare: $\frac{2}{3}$ of 3 $\bigcirc$ 3 $\times$ $\frac{2}{3}$
(96)

8. If $3n = 18$, then $2n + 5$ equals:
(17)

A. 23 B. 17 C. 31 D. 14

9. Every face of this block is a
(93) square. This is a special type of
rectangular solid. What word
names this shape?

10. Which angle appears to be a right
(33) angle?

A. $\angle AOB$ B. $\angle BOC$

C. $\angle COD$ D. $\angle AOC$

11. $1\frac{3}{5}$
(101) $+\ 2\frac{4}{5}$
_____

12. $4\frac{5}{8}$
(99) $-\ \ \frac{1}{8}$
_____

13. $6\frac{5}{6}$
(44) $-\ 1\frac{5}{6}$
_____

14. $1 \div \dfrac{1}{8}$
(97)

15. $\dfrac{8}{10} \times \dfrac{5}{10}$
(101)

16. $\dfrac{1}{5} \div \dfrac{1}{10}$
(97)

17. 2657 + 484 + 93
(6)

18. ($20 − $6.55) ÷ 5
(24)

19. 10 × 56¢
(80)

20. 6 × 78 × 900
(18)

21. 31)‾970
(103)

22. 947 ÷ 22
(103)

23. Write fractions equal to $\frac{3}{4}$ and $\frac{1}{6}$ with denominators of
(89) 12. Then add the fractions.

Look at this picture. Then answer questions 24 and 25.

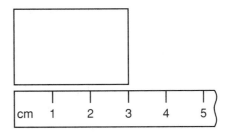

24. How long is the rectangle?
(48)

25. The rectangle is 1 centimeter longer than it is wide.
(60) What is the perimeter of the rectangle?

LESSON 104

Dividing by Two-Digit Numbers, Part 3

Facts Practice: Reduce 40 Fractions (Test I in Test Masters)

Mental Math:

a. Reduce: $\frac{3}{6}, \frac{3}{9}, \frac{3}{12}$ **b.** $\frac{1}{3}$ of 15   **c.** $\frac{2}{3}$ of 15

d. 50% of 15   **e.** $\sqrt{81}$, × 5, − 1, ÷ 4, + 1, ÷ 4, − 3

Problem Solving: Two cups equal a pint and two pints equal a quart. Two quarts equal a half gallon. Two half gallons equal one gallon. A quart of milk was poured out of a full gallon container. How many pints of milk were still in the container?

In Lesson 103 we learned a trick to help us divide by two-digit numbers. The problems in that lesson were chosen so that using the first digit to guess the division answer would work. However, often this method will not work. We need to learn more strategies for two-digit division.

We see.	We think.	We try the guess, but the guess is too large.

$$\frac{?}{19)\overline{59}} \qquad \frac{⑤}{1)\overline{5}} \longrightarrow \frac{5}{19)\overline{59}}$$
$$⑨⑤$$

If we use the first-digit trick here, we will guess 5. But this is not the right guess because there are not five 19s in 59. Our guess is too large. We will **estimate.** To estimate, we mentally round both numbers to the nearest 10. Then we use the first-digit trick with the rounded numbers.

We see.   We round.   We think.   We try.

$$19)\overline{59} \longrightarrow 20)\overline{60} \longrightarrow \frac{③}{2)\overline{6}} \longrightarrow \frac{3 \text{ r } 2}{19)\overline{59}}$$
$$\frac{57}{2}$$

Example   Divide: $19)\overline{595}$

Solution We begin by breaking the division into the smaller division problem $19\overline{)59}$. We round to $20\overline{)60}$ and focus on the first digits, $2\overline{)6}$. We guess "3." We write the 3 above the 9 of 59. Then we multiply 3×19, subtract, and bring down. The next division is $19\overline{)25}$. We may estimate to help us divide. We write "1" in the answer; then we multiply and subtract.

$$\begin{array}{r} 31 \text{ r } 6 \\ 19\overline{)595} \\ -\ 57 \\ \hline 25 \\ -\ 19 \\ \hline 6 \end{array}$$

The answer is **31 r 6.** To check our answer, we multiply 31×19 and add the remainder, which is 6.

Practice*   a. $19\overline{)792}$ b. $30\overline{)600}$ c. $29\overline{)121}$

d. $29\overline{)900}$ e. $48\overline{)829}$ f. $29\overline{)1210}$

g. $28\overline{)896}$ h. $18\overline{)782}$ i. $39\overline{)1200}$

Problem set 104

1. List all of the prime numbers less than 50 that end
(90) with the digit 1.

2. What number is missing in this division? $\square \div 8 = 24$
(64)

3. Cheryl ran 660 yards in 3 minutes. At this rate, how
(55) many yards would she run in 6 minutes?

4. Write a decimal number equal to the mixed number
(72) $4\frac{9}{10}$.

5. Seventy-six trombone players led the parade. If they
(21) marched in 4 rows, how many were in each row?

6. (a) A dime is what fraction of a dollar?
(80)
     (b) How many dimes are in \$1?

     (c) How many dimes are in \$4?

7. Which of these means, "How many 19s are there in
(104) 786?"

  A. 19 ÷ 786   B. 786 ÷ 19   C. 19 × 786

8. (a) How many $\frac{1}{4}$s are in 1?
(97)
  (b) How many $\frac{1}{3}$s are in 1?

9. What word names the shape?
(93)

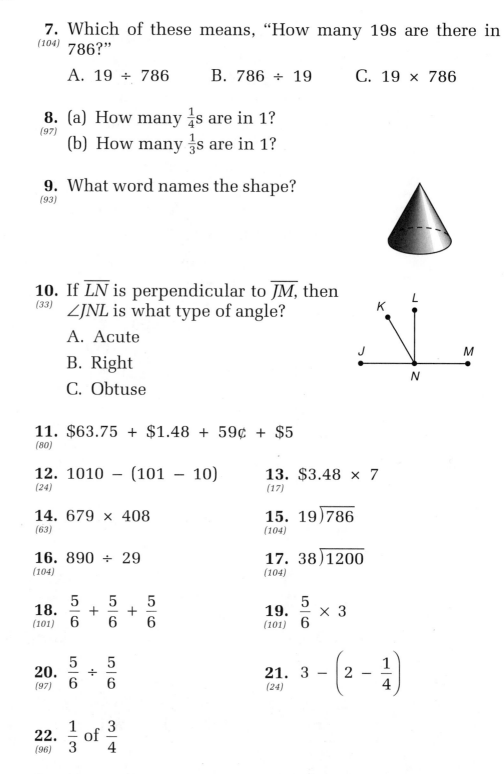

10. If $\overline{LN}$ is perpendicular to $\overline{JM}$, then
(33) $\angle JNL$ is what type of angle?

  A. Acute

  B. Right

  C. Obtuse

11. $63.75 + $1.48 + 59¢ + $5
(80)

12. 1010 − (101 − 10)   **13.** $3.48 × 7
(24)   (17)

14. 679 × 408   **15.** 19$\overline{)786}$
(63)   (104)

16. 890 ÷ 29   **17.** 38$\overline{)1200}$
(104)   (104)

18. $\dfrac{5}{6} + \dfrac{5}{6} + \dfrac{5}{6}$ **19.** $\dfrac{5}{6} × 3$
(101)   (101)

20. $\dfrac{5}{6} ÷ \dfrac{5}{6}$ **21.** $3 - \left(2 - \dfrac{1}{4}\right)$
(97)   (24)

22. $\dfrac{1}{3}$ of $\dfrac{3}{4}$
(96)

23. Write a fraction equal to $\frac{2}{3}$ with a denominator of 12.
(89) Subtract that fraction from $\frac{11}{12}$. Remember to reduce the
answer.

The graph shows Jeff's height on his birthday from ages 9 to 14. Use this graph to answer questions 24 and 25.

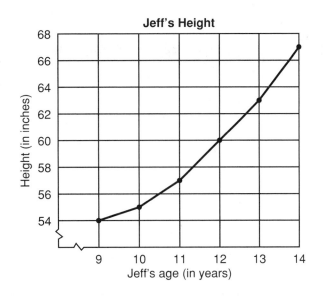

24. How many inches did Jeff grow between his twelfth
(54) and fourteenth birthdays?

25. On which birthday was Jeff 5 feet tall?
(54)

LESSON 105

Writing the Reciprocal of a Fraction

Facts Practice: Reduce 40 Fractions (Test I in Test Masters)

Mental Math:

  a. What is the reduced mixed number for $\frac{10}{4}$?   **b.** CCLX

  c. CXCIX   **d.** $\frac{1}{5}$ of 15   **e.** $\frac{2}{5}$ of 15   **f.** $\frac{3}{5}$ of 15

Problem Solving: A line of symmetry divides a figure into mirror images. A square has four lines of symmetry. We have shown two lines of symmetry. Draw a square and show all four lines of symmetry.

If we reverse the numerator and denominator of a fraction, the new fraction is the **reciprocal** of the first fraction. The reciprocal has the same digits, but the positions of the digits are reversed. When we reverse the position of the numerator and denominator, we say that we have *inverted* the fraction.

$$\text{The reciprocal of } \frac{2}{3} \text{ is } \frac{3}{2}.$$

$$\text{The reciprocal of } \frac{3}{2} \text{ is } \frac{2}{3}.$$

Whole numbers also have reciprocals. Recall that a whole number may be written as a fraction by writing a 1 under the whole number. So the whole number 2 may be written $\frac{2}{1}$. To find the reciprocal of $\frac{2}{1}$, we invert the fraction and get $\frac{1}{2}$.

$$\text{Since } 2 = \frac{2}{1}, \text{ the reciprocal of 2 is } \frac{1}{2}.$$

Notice that the product of $\frac{1}{2}$ and 2 is 1.

$$\frac{1}{2} \times 2 = 1$$

The product of a fraction and its reciprocal is 1. Since division finds a missing factor, when we divide 1 by any number (except 0), the answer is the reciprocal of the number.

$$\text{How many } \frac{2}{3}\text{s are in 1?}$$

The answer is the reciprocal of $\frac{2}{3}$, which is $\frac{3}{2}$. We can use reciprocals to help us divide fractions, as we will see in the next lesson.

Example 1 What is the reciprocal of $\frac{5}{6}$?

Solution The reciprocal of $\frac{5}{6}$ is $\frac{6}{5}$. We leave the answer as an improper fraction.

Example 2 What is the product of $\frac{1}{3}$ and its reciprocal?

Solution The reciprocal of $\frac{1}{3}$ is $\frac{3}{1}$. To find the product, we multiply.

$$\frac{1}{3} \times \frac{3}{1} = 1$$

The product of any fraction and its reciprocal is 1.

Example 3 What is the reciprocal of 4?

Solution To find the reciprocal of a whole number, we may first write the whole number as a fraction by writing a 1 under it. To write 4 as a fraction, we write $\frac{4}{1}$. The reciprocal of $\frac{4}{1}$ is $\frac{1}{4}$.

Practice Write the reciprocal of each of these numbers:

a. $\frac{4}{5}$ b. $\frac{6}{5}$ c. 3 d. $\frac{7}{8}$

e. $\frac{3}{8}$ f. 5 g. $\frac{3}{10}$ h. $\frac{5}{12}$

i. 2 j. $\frac{1}{5}$ k. 10 l. 1

Problem set
105

1. These three boxes of nails weigh
(56) 34, 35, and 42 pounds, respectively. If some nails are moved
from the heaviest box to the other
two boxes so that the boxes weigh
the same, how much will each
box weigh?

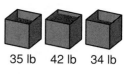

35 lb   42 lb   34 lb

2. Each finger of the human hand is formed by three
(54) bones except for the thumb, which is formed by two
bones. The palm contains five bones, one leading to
each finger. Not counting the wrist, the hand contains
how many bones?

3. Name the shaded part of this
(76) square as a decimal number, as a
reduced fraction, and as a percent.

4. What is the product of $\frac{2}{3}$ and its reciprocal?
(105)

5. (a) A quarter is what fraction of a dollar?
(80)
(b) How many quarters equal $1?
(c) How many quarters equal $5?

6. What is the reciprocal of $\frac{3}{4}$? What is the product of $\frac{3}{4}$
(105) and its reciprocal?

7. Which of these means, "How many 25s are there in
(104) 500?"

    A. 25 ÷ 500   B. 500 ÷ 25   C. 25 × 500

8. (a) What is the reciprocal of 6?
(105)
(b) What is the reciprocal of $\frac{1}{4}$?

9. If $\overline{LN}$ is perpendicular to $\overline{JM}$, then
(33) which of these angles is an acute
angle?

    A. ∠LNM   B. ∠JNL
    C. ∠KNL   D. ∠KNM

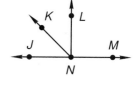

10. ($20 − $4.72) ÷ 8
(24)

11. 10 × $2.75
(30)

12.   742
(6)
        34,135
        6,947
        218
        7,865
     +   72
     ──────────

13. 36 × 10 × 42
(18)

14. 31)‾140‾
(104)

15. $\dfrac{567}{27}$
(104)

16. Reduce: $\dfrac{15}{25}$
(100)

17. $1\dfrac{5}{6} + 1\dfrac{5}{6}$
(101)

18. $4\dfrac{5}{6} - 1\dfrac{1}{6}$
(99)

19. $\dfrac{3}{8}$ of 24
(96)

20. $3 \times \dfrac{4}{5}$
(101)

21. $\dfrac{9}{10} \div \dfrac{1}{10}$
(97)

22. Write fractions equal to $\frac{3}{4}$ and $\frac{1}{6}$ that have denomina-
(89) tors of 12. Subtract the smaller fraction from the larger fraction.

23. Divide 123 by 10 and write the answer as a mixed
(65) number.

Diane used toothpicks to make this rectangle. Look at the rectangle. Then answer questions 24 and 25.

24. How many toothpicks form the
(60) perimeter of this rectangle?

25. The rectangle closes in an area
(38) covered with small squares. How many small squares cover the area of the rectangle?

LESSON
106

Dividing Fractions, Part 2

Facts Practice: Reduce 40 Fractions (Test I in Test Masters)

Mental Math:

   a. What is the reduced mixed number for $\frac{10}{6}$?

   b. What is the reciprocal of $\frac{5}{6}$?

   c. $\frac{1}{4}$ of 12   **d.** $\frac{2}{4}$ of 12   **e.** $\frac{3}{4}$ of 12

Problem Solving: Kerry is wearing a necklace with 30 beads strung in a red-white-blue-red-white-blue pattern. If she counts beads in the direction shown starting with red, what will be the color of the one hundredth bead?

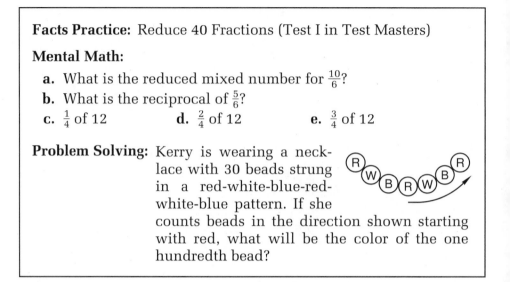

Reciprocals can help us solve division problems like the following:

$$\frac{1}{2} \div \frac{2}{3}$$

This problem means "How many $\frac{2}{3}$s are in $\frac{1}{2}$?" However, the answer is less than 1. So we change the question to

"How much of $\dfrac{2}{3}$ is in $\dfrac{1}{2}$?"

"How much of 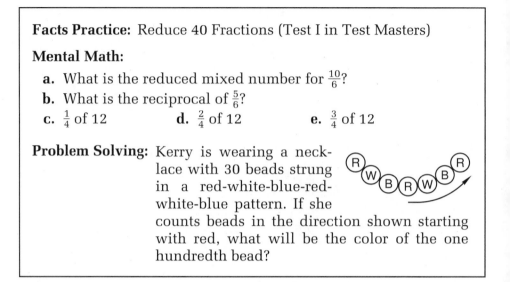 is in ?"

This problem is different from the problems we have been solving. To solve this problem, we will use another method. This method uses **reciprocals** to help us find the answer. We begin by asking a new question. We ask, "How many $\frac{2}{3}$s are in 1?" Once we know how many $\frac{2}{3}$s are in 1, then we can find how much of $\frac{2}{3}$ is in $\frac{1}{2}$.

Step 1. How many $\frac{2}{3}$s are in 1? (The answer is $\frac{3}{2}$, which is the reciprocal of $\frac{2}{3}$.)

Step 2.   The number of $\frac{2}{3}$s in $\frac{1}{2}$ is **half** the number of $\frac{2}{3}$s in 1. So we multiply $\frac{3}{2}$ by $\frac{1}{2}$.

$$\frac{1}{2} \times \frac{3}{2} = \frac{3}{4}$$

This method changes the division problem into a multiplication problem. Instead of dividing $\frac{1}{2}$ by $\frac{2}{3}$, we end up multiplying $\frac{1}{2}$ by the reciprocal of $\frac{2}{3}$.

$$\frac{1}{2} \div \frac{2}{3} = \text{?}$$

$$\frac{1}{2} \times \frac{3}{2} = \frac{3}{4}$$

Example 1 $\frac{2}{3} \div \frac{1}{2}$

Solution   We are finding the number of $\frac{1}{2}$s in $\frac{2}{3}$. The number of $\frac{1}{2}$s in 1 is $\frac{2}{1}$. So the number of $\frac{1}{2}$s in $\frac{2}{3}$ is $\frac{2}{3}$ of $\frac{2}{1}$. We multiply $\frac{2}{3}$ and the reciprocal of the second fraction. We simplify the answer $\frac{4}{3}$ to get **1$\frac{1}{3}$.**

$$\frac{2}{3} \div \frac{1}{2}$$

$$\frac{2}{3} \times \frac{2}{1} = \frac{4}{3}$$

$$= 1\frac{1}{3}$$

Example 2 $2 \div \frac{2}{3}$

Solution   We are finding the number of $\frac{2}{3}$s in 2. The number of $\frac{2}{3}$s in 1 is $\frac{3}{2}$. So the number of $\frac{2}{3}$s in 2 is twice that many. We begin by writing the whole number 2 as the fraction $\frac{2}{1}$. Then we multiply $\frac{2}{1}$ by the reciprocal of $\frac{2}{3}$. Finally, we simplify the answer and find that the number of $\frac{2}{3}$s in 2 is **3.**

$$\frac{2}{1} \div \frac{2}{3}$$

$$\frac{2}{1} \times \frac{3}{2} = \frac{6}{2}$$

$$= 3$$

Practice*   a. $\dfrac{1}{3} \div \dfrac{1}{2}$ b. $\dfrac{2}{3} \div \dfrac{3}{4}$ c. $\dfrac{2}{3} \div \dfrac{1}{4}$

d. $\dfrac{1}{2} \div \dfrac{1}{3}$ e. $\dfrac{3}{4} \div \dfrac{2}{3}$ f. $3 \div \dfrac{3}{4}$

g. $2 \div \dfrac{1}{3}$ h. $3 \div \dfrac{2}{3}$ i. $10 \div \dfrac{5}{6}$

Problem set 106

1. Draw two circles. Shade $\frac{1}{2}$ of one circle and $\frac{2}{3}$ of the other circle.
   (40)

2. James gave Robert half of a candy bar. Robert gave his sister half of what he had. What fraction of the whole candy bar did Robert's sister get? What percent of the whole candy bar did she get?
   (55)

3. How much is $\frac{2}{3}$ of one dozen?
   (96)

4. Estimate the product of 712 and 490 by rounding the numbers to the nearest hundred before you multiply.
   (69)

5. Use digits to write the number ninety-three million, eight hundred fourteen thousand, two hundred.
   (59)

6. Which of these means, "How many one tenths are there in three?"
   (97)

   A. $\dfrac{1}{10} \div 3$ B. $3 \div \dfrac{1}{10}$ C. $\dfrac{1}{10} \div \dfrac{3}{10}$

7. Write fractions equal to $\frac{1}{4}$ and $\frac{1}{5}$ with denominators of 20. Then add the fractions.
   (89)

8. (a) $1 \div \dfrac{1}{10}$ (b) $3 \div \dfrac{1}{10}$
   (106)

9. Recall that the **multiples** of a number are the numbers we say when counting by that number. The first four multiples of 2 are 2, 4, 6, and 8. What are the first four multiples of 3?
   (1)

10. Diane made this rectangle with toothpicks.
₍₆₀₎

    (a) How many toothpicks form the perimeter?

    (b) How many small squares cover the area?

11. *AB* is 3 cm. *BC* is 4 cm. *AD* is 10 cm. Find *CD*.
₍₈₁₎

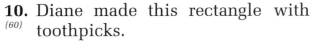

    A   B   C   D

12. Name the shaded part of the square as a decimal number, as a reduced fraction, and as a percent.
₍₇₆₎

13. $\dfrac{1}{3} \div \dfrac{1}{4}$
₍₁₀₆₎

14. $\dfrac{1}{4} \div \dfrac{1}{3}$
₍₁₀₆₎

15. $3 \div \dfrac{1}{2}$
₍₁₀₆₎

16.   793.459
₍₈₂₎
         827.8
     +   63.475

17.   30,103
₍₉₎
    −   7,457

18.   704
₍₆₃₎
    × 960

19. 20 × 47¢ = \$_____
₍₈₀₎

20. 568 ÷ 15
₍₁₀₄₎

21. 30$\overline{)427}$
₍₆₁₎

22. \$30.24 ÷ 6
₍₃₅₎

23. $\dfrac{1}{10} \times \square = \dfrac{10}{100}$
₍₈₉₎

24. $5 - \left(1\dfrac{1}{4} + 2\right)$
₍₂₄₎

25. $5 \times \left(\dfrac{2}{3} \times \dfrac{1}{2}\right)$
₍₂₄₎

LESSON 107

Ratios

A **ratio** is a way of describing a relationship between two numbers.

If there are 12 boys and 18 girls in a class, then the ratio of boys to girls in the class is 12 to 18.

We often write ratios as fractions. We write the terms of the ratio in order from top to bottom.

$$12 \text{ to } 18 \text{ is written } \frac{12}{18}.$$

We read the ratio $\frac{12}{18}$ by saying "twelve to eighteen."

We reduce ratios just like we reduce fractions. Since 12 and 18 are divisible by 6, we divide $\frac{12}{18}$ by $\frac{6}{6}$.

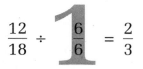

$$\frac{12}{18} \div \frac{6}{6} = \frac{2}{3}$$

So the ratio of boys to girls in the class is $\frac{2}{3}$ (two to three). This means that for every two boys in the class there are three girls.

Example There were 12 girls and 16 boys in the class. What was the ratio of boys to girls?

Solution First we place the numbers in the correct order. We are asked for the ratio of boys to girls. That order is boys first, girls second. We write the number of boys and the number of girls in the same order top to bottom.

$$\frac{\text{boys}}{\text{girls}} \qquad \frac{16}{12}$$

Unlike fractions, we do not write ratios as mixed numbers. The top number of a ratio may be greater than the bottom number. However, we do reduce ratios. The terms of the ratio, 16 and 12, are both divisible by 4.

$$\frac{16}{12} \div \frac{4}{4} = \frac{4}{3}$$

The ratio of boys to girls in the class was $\frac{4}{3}$.

Practice There were 20 prairie dogs and 30 jackrabbits in Henry's backyard. What was the ratio of jackrabbits to prairie dogs in Henry's backyard?

Problem set 107

1. There were 15 pennies and 10 nickels in Tom's drawer. What was the ratio of pennies to nickels in his drawer?
(107)

2. Write this sentence using digits and symbols:
(44)
   "The sum of one fourth and one fourth is one half."

3. Cynthia had 4 dollar bills, 3 quarters, 2 dimes, and 1 nickel. If she spent half of her money, how much money does she have left?
(80)

4. How many $\frac{1}{8}$s are there in $\frac{1}{2}$?
(97)

5. Name the number of shaded circles as a decimal number and as a reduced mixed number.
(72)

6. When the decimal number eleven and twelve
(82) hundredths is subtracted from twelve and eleven
hundredths, what is the difference?

7. (a) A quart is what fraction of a gallon?
(95) (b) How many quarts are in 1 gallon?
(c) How many quarts are in 4 gallons?

8. Write fractions equal to $\frac{2}{3}$ and $\frac{2}{5}$ with denominators of
(89) 15. Then subtract the smaller fraction from the larger
fraction.

9. Name the point marked by the arrow as a decimal
(73) number and as a fraction.

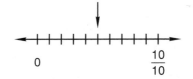

10. Compare: $\frac{1}{2} \div 2 \bigcirc 2 \div \frac{1}{2}$
(106)

11. *AB* is 30 millimeters. *CD* is 40 millimeters. *AD* is 90
(81) millimeters. Find *BC*.

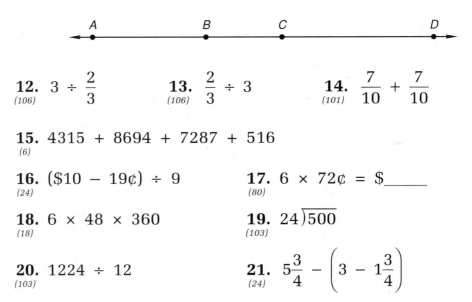

12. $3 \div \frac{2}{3}$ **13.** $\frac{2}{3} \div 3$ **14.** $\frac{7}{10} + \frac{7}{10}$
(106)   (106)   (101)

15. 4315 + 8694 + 7287 + 516
(6)

16. ($10 − 19¢) ÷ 9   **17.** 6 × 72¢ = $_____
(24)   (80)

18. 6 × 48 × 360   **19.** 24$\overline{)500}$
(18)   (103)

20. 1224 ÷ 12   **21.** $5\frac{3}{4} - \left(3 - 1\frac{3}{4}\right)$
(103)   (24)

22. $1\frac{1}{4} + 1\frac{1}{4} + 1\frac{1}{4} + 1\frac{1}{4}$ **23.** $\frac{3}{10} = \frac{\square}{100}$
(99)   (89)

24. Reduce: $\frac{50}{100}$
(100)

25. What is the perimeter of this square?
(60)

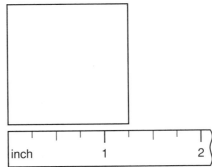

inch   1   2

LESSON 108

Adding and Subtracting Decimal Numbers, Part 2

Facts Practice: Reduce 40 Fractions (Test I in Test Masters)

Mental Math:
  a. Simplify: $\frac{6}{4}, \frac{7}{4}, \frac{8}{4}$ **b.** What is the reciprocal of $\frac{3}{4}$? of $\frac{1}{4}$?
  c. 50% of $20   **d.** 25% of $20   **e.** 10% of 100
  f. $\frac{1}{3}$ of 21, × 2, + 1, ÷ 3, × 6, + 2, ÷ 4

Problem Solving: Some 1-inch cubes were used to build this rectangular solid. How many 1-inch cubes were used?

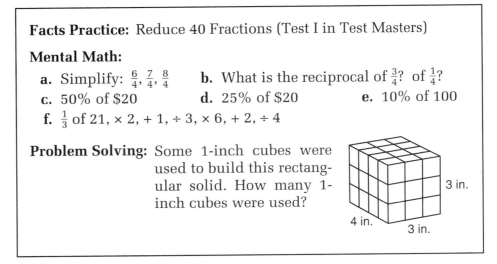

3 in.

4 in.   3 in.

Whenever we add and subtract, we must remember that we can only add and subtract **like things.** That means we must add and subtract digits with the same place value. When we add and subtract whole numbers, we line up the last digits so that digits with the same place value are in line. **In decimal arithmetic we line up the decimal points instead.** Lining up the decimal points automatically lines up digits with the same place value. The rule for adding and subtracting decimals is "Line up the decimal points."

Example 1   3.42 + 12.3

Solution   To add decimal numbers, we line up the decimal points. We find that 3.42 plus 12.3 is **15.72.**

$$\begin{array}{r} 3.42 \\ + \ 12.3 \\ \hline 15.72 \end{array}$$

Some people find it easier to add and subtract decimal numbers by using zeros as necessary to write every number with the same number of decimal places. We show this in the next example.

Example 2   23.45 − 1.2

Solution   This problem means to take 1.2 from 23.45, so we write "23.45" on top. We write "1.2" under 23.45 so that the decimal points are in line. This time we fill the empty decimal place with zero. Subtracting, we find that when we take 1.2 from 23.45, the number left is **22.25.**

$$\begin{array}{r} 23.45 \\ - \ \ 1.20 \\ \hline 22.25 \end{array}$$

Example 3   5.6 + 2.47 + 0.875

Solution   We write the problem vertically and line up the decimal points. We may fill in with zeros so that each number is written with the same number of decimal places. We add and find that the sum is **8.945.**

$$\begin{array}{r} 5.600 \\ 2.470 \\ + \ 0.875 \\ \hline 8.945 \end{array}$$

Practice   **a.** 9.87 + 12.4   **b.** 0.35 − 0.2

c. 0.4 + 0.428 + 0.12   **d.** 0.456 − 0.12

e. $3.6 + 0.63 + 4.75$

f. $4.25 - 1.7$

g. $5.6 + 4.0 + 1.38$

h. $26.48 - 9.5$

i. $42.8 + 5.2 + 0.95$

j. $1.000 - 0.375$

Problem set 108

1. There were 12 dogs and 8 cats at the class pet show. What was the ratio of cats to dogs at the show?
(107)

2. (a) What is the name of this solid?
(93)
    (b) How many faces does it have?

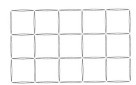

3. Juan lives 1.2 miles from school. How far does he travel going from home to school and back home?
(54)

4. Diane made this rectangle with toothpicks.
(60)

    (a) How many toothpicks form the perimeter?

    (b) How many small squares cover the area?

5. Which arrow could be pointing to $2\frac{1}{3}$ on the number line?
(41)

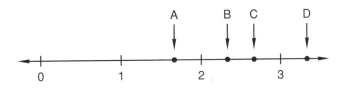

6. The first four multiples of 2 are 2, 4, 6, and 8. What are the first four multiples of 4?
(1)

7. If $\overline{LN}$ is perpendicular to $\overline{JM}$, then which of these angles is obtuse?
(33)

    A. $\angle JNK$ B. $\angle KNL$

    C. $\angle KNM$ D. $\angle LNM$

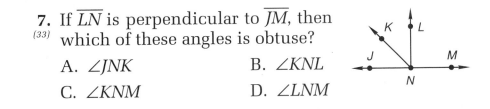

8. 6.5 + 2.47 + 0.875
(108)

9. 4.26 + 8.0 + 15.9
(108)

10. 23.45 − 1.2
(108)

11. 0.367 − 0.1
(108)

12. $1.25 × 7
(17)

13. 75 × 608
(57)

14. 364 ÷ 16
(104)

15. $7.20 ÷ 20
(61)

16. $3\frac{1}{2}$
(99) $+ 1\frac{1}{2}$

17. $5\frac{8}{15}$
(44) $- 4\frac{7}{15}$

18. 6
(70) $- 1\frac{1}{3}$

19. $1 \times \dfrac{5}{7}$
(96)

20. $\dfrac{4}{5}$ of 25
(96)

21. $\dfrac{3}{4} \div \dfrac{2}{3}$
(106)

22. $\dfrac{7}{10} = \dfrac{\square}{100}$
(89)

23. Reduce: $\dfrac{30}{100}$
(100)

This thermometer shows the temperature on a warm summer morning.

24. What temperature is shown on the
(28) thermometer?

25. What temperature would be
(28) shown if the temperature increased 10°?

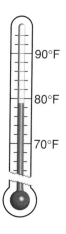

LESSON
109

Adding Whole Numbers and Decimal Numbers

Facts Practice: Reduce 40 Fractions (Test I in Test Masters)

Mental Math:

a. Simplify: $\frac{10}{8}, \frac{11}{8}, \frac{12}{8}$ **b.** What is the reciprocal of $\frac{1}{2}$? of 2?

c. $\frac{1}{8}$ of 100   **d.** $12\frac{1}{2} + 12\frac{1}{2} + 12\frac{1}{2}$

e. $\frac{3}{8}$ of 100   **f.** $\sqrt{64}$, × 6, ÷ 8, × 4, ÷ 3

Problem Solving: Two cups equal a pint. Two pints equal a quart. Two quarts equal a half gallon. Two half gallons equal a gallon. If a gallon container of water is used to fill a half gallon container, a quart container, a pint container, and a cup container, how much water will be left in the gallon container?

When decimal numbers are in an addition problem, we must line up the decimal points. Sometimes there are whole numbers in a decimal addition problem. The whole number might not be written with a decimal point. A decimal point marks the end of a whole number. We may write a decimal point on the back, or the right-hand side, of a whole number. We can write a whole number like 5 with a decimal point, 5., so that we can line up the decimal points and add.

It may help to remember the party game "Pin the Tail on the Donkey." The tail belongs on the back of the donkey, and the decimal point belongs on the back of the whole number. Remember this rule:

"Pin the decimal point on the back of the whole number."

Example   6.2 + 3 + 4.25

Solution   We use two rules: "Line up the decimal points" and "Pin the decimal point on the back of the whole number." We may also attach zeros. We add and find that the sum is **13.45.**

$$\begin{array}{r} 6.20 \\ 3.00 \\ + 4.25 \\ \hline 13.45 \end{array}$$

Practice*

a. 4.3 + 2

b. 12 + 1.2

c. 6.4 + 24

d. 4 + 1.3 + 0.6

e. 5.2 + 0.75 + 2

f. 56 + 75.4

g. 8 + 4.7 + 12.1

h. 9 + 4.8 + 12

Problem set 109

1. There were 50 boys and 60 girls on the playground.
(107) What was the ratio of girls to boys on the playground?

2. The pizza was sliced into 6 equal pieces. Martin ate 2
(31) pieces. What fraction of the pizza did he eat? What
percent of the pizza did he eat?

3. Artichokes were on sale. Five of them cost $1. At this
(55) rate, what would be the price for a dozen artichokes?

4. Maria ran 100 yards in 13.8 seconds. Mike ran 1
(78) second slower than Maria. How long did it take Mike
to run 100 yards?

5. Name the point on the number line marked with an x
(73) as a decimal number and as a reduced mixed number.

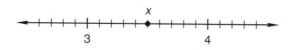

6. If $50n = 100$, then n equals what number?
(18)

7. Write the decimal number one thousand, six hundred
(77) twenty and three tenths.

8. Diana made this rectangle with
(60) toothpicks.

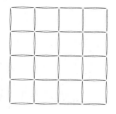

(a) How many toothpicks form
the perimeter?

(b) How many small squares
cover the area?

9. Write a fraction equal to $\frac{3}{4}$ with a denominator of 8.
(89) Then subtract that fraction from $\frac{7}{8}$.

10. Attach a zero to the number 8 without changing the
(79) value of the number.

11. QT is 100 mm. QR is 23 mm. RS equals QR. Find ST.
(81)

Q   R   S   T

12. 3.4 + 5   **13.** 7.25 − 7
(109)   (109)

14. 8 × 47¢ = $_____   **15.** 596 × 340
(80)   (63)

16. 28)952   **17.** $18.27 ÷ 9
(104)   (35)

18. $4\frac{5}{8} + 1\frac{7}{8}$ **19.** $5 - \left(2\frac{3}{5} - 1\right)$
(101)   (24)

20. $\frac{3}{4} \times \frac{1}{3}$ **21.** $\frac{3}{4} \div 3$
(100)   (106)

22. $\frac{9}{10} = \frac{\square}{100}$ **23.** Reduce: $\frac{20}{100}$
(89)   (100)

Read this information. Then answer questions 24 and 25.

*Matthew fixed his function machine so that
when he puts in a 12, a 6 comes out. When he puts
in a 10, a 4 comes out. When he puts in an 8, a 2
comes out.*

24. What rule does the machine use?
(54)
  A. It subtracts 2.   B. It divides by 2.
  C. It subtracts 6.   D. It adds 6.

25. If Matthew puts in a 6, what number will come out?
(54)

LESSON 110

Simplifying Decimal Numbers

Facts Practice: Reduce 40 Fractions (Test I in Test Masters)

Mental Math:

a. Simplify: $\frac{15}{10}, \frac{20}{10}, \frac{25}{10}$ **b.** What is the reciprocal of 3? of $\frac{3}{5}$?

c. 25% of $100   **d.** 25% of $10   **e.** 25% of $1

Problem Solving: The uppercase letter A has one line of symmetry. Write the first five letters of the alphabet in uppercase and show the line of symmetry for each letter.

When we write numbers, we should write them in simplest form. When we simplify a number, we change the form of the number, but we do not change the value of the number. We have learned how to simplify fractions by reducing. We can often simplify decimal numbers as well. We simplify decimal numbers by removing unnecessary zeros. We will explain this by simplifying 0.20.

The decimal number 0.20 has a 2 in the tenths' place and a 0 in the hundredths' place. The zero in the hundredths' place means "no hundredths." If we remove the zero from 0.20, we get 0.2. The number 0.2 also has a 2 in the tenths' place and "no hundredths." Thus, 0.20 equals 0.2. We say that 0.20 simplifies to 0.2.

We can remove zeros from the front of whole numbers and from the back of decimal numbers. We remove zeros until we come to a digit that is not a zero or until we come to a decimal point. Below we have simplified 02.0100, 20.0, and 0.200 by removing the unnecessary zeros.

02.0100	20.0	0.200
2.01	20. = 20	0.2 or .2

In the center example, we continue to simplify 20. by removing the decimal point. If there is no fraction part, the decimal point can be removed.

Notice the example on the right. Two simplified forms are shown, 0.2 and .2. We know that the decimal point separates the whole-number part of a decimal number from the fraction part. If there is no whole-number part, a zero may be written in the ones' place. The numbers 0.2 and .2 are equal to each other. Either form is correct. Calculators display a zero in the ones' place. We will continue to show a zero in the ones' place.

Practice   Simplify each decimal number:

a. 03.20   **b.** 0.320

c. 32.00   **d.** 3.020

Simplify each answer:

e.   3.65   **f.**   23.16   **g.**   4.23
   + 6.35   − 19.46   − 3.18

Problem set   **1.** James counted 60 peas and 20 carrot slices on his
110   *(107)* plate. What was the ratio of carrot slices to peas on his plate?

2. A package of 10 hot dogs costs $1.25. What would be
(55) the cost of 100 hot dogs?

3. Three fourths of the 28 students finished the test early.
(50) How many students finished the test early? What percent of the students finished the test early?

4. This rectangle was formed with
(60) pins 1 inch long.

(a) How many pins form the perimeter?

(b) How many small squares cover this rectangle?

5. Is $7.13 closer to $7 or $8?
(78)

6. Which arrow could be pointing to $7\frac{3}{4}$ on this number line?
(41)

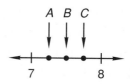

7. Write fractions equal to $\frac{5}{6}$ and $\frac{3}{4}$ with denominators of 12. Then subtract the smaller fraction from the larger fraction.
(89)

8. The giraffe stood 5 meters tall. Five meters is how many centimeters?
(83)

9. *AB* is 40 mm. *BC* is half of *AB*. *CD* equals *BC*. Find *AD*.
(81)

$$\overset{A}{\underset{\bullet}{\quad}} \qquad\qquad \overset{B}{\underset{\bullet}{\quad}} \quad \overset{C}{\underset{\bullet}{\quad}} \quad \overset{D}{\underset{\bullet}{\quad}}$$

10. 6.2 + 3 + 4.25
(109)

11. 0.62 + 4.2 + 412
(109)

12. 6.37 − 6
(109)

13. 234 × 506
(63)

14. 10 × $1.75
(30)

15. $17.50 ÷ 10
(61)

16. $32\overline{)832}$
(104)

17. 832 ÷ 16
(104)

18. $\frac{5}{9} + \frac{5}{9} + \frac{5}{9}$
(101)

19. $\frac{9}{10} \times \frac{9}{10}$
(86)

20. $\frac{2}{3} \div \frac{3}{4}$
(106)

21. $3 \div \frac{3}{4}$
(106)

22. $\frac{1}{50} = \frac{\square}{100}$
(89)

23. Reduce: $\frac{40}{100}$
(100)

24. The flagpole is 10 yards tall. The flagpole is how many feet tall?
(83)

25. How many months is it from May 1 of one year to January 1 of the next year?
(27)

LESSON
111

Rounding Mixed Numbers to the Nearest Whole Number

Facts Practice: Simplify 50 Fractions (Test J in Test Masters)

Mental Math: Describe how to estimate the sum of 29 and 19.

  a. Simplify: $\frac{10}{3}, \frac{10}{4}, \frac{10}{5}$ **b.** 50% of 50, + 50, + 2, ÷ 7, + 3, ÷ 7

Problem Solving: The multiples of 7 are 7, 14, 21, 28, 35, …. We can use multiples of 7 to help us count days of the week. Seven days after Monday is Monday. Fourteen days after Monday is Monday again. So 15 days after Monday is just 1 day after Monday. What day is 30 days after Monday? 50 days after Saturday? 78 days after Tuesday?

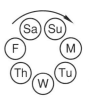

The mixed number $7\frac{3}{4}$ is between 7 and 8. To round $7\frac{3}{4}$ to the nearest whole number, we decide whether $7\frac{3}{4}$ is nearer 7 or nearer 8. To help us understand this question, we have drawn this number line.

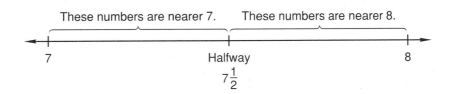

We see that $7\frac{1}{2}$ is halfway between 7 and 8. Since $7\frac{3}{4}$ is between $7\frac{1}{2}$ and 8, we know that $7\frac{3}{4}$ is nearer 8 than 7. So $7\frac{3}{4}$ rounds to 8.

Example 1 Round $6\frac{2}{5}$ to the nearest whole number.

Solution The mixed number $6\frac{2}{5}$ is between 6 and 7. We need to decide whether it is nearer 6 or nearer 7. The number $6\frac{1}{2}$ is halfway between 6 and 7. The number $6\frac{2}{5}$ is less than $6\frac{1}{2}$, so we round $6\frac{2}{5}$ down to **6**.

Example 2   Estimate the product of $8\frac{7}{8}$ and $5\frac{1}{4}$ by rounding each mixed number to the nearest whole number before multiplying.

Solution   We round $8\frac{7}{8}$ to 9, and we round $5\frac{1}{4}$ to 5. Then we multiply 9 and 5 and get 45. So the product of $8\frac{7}{8}$ and $5\frac{1}{4}$ is about **45.**

Practice   Round each mixed number to the nearest whole number:

a. $3\frac{2}{3}$ **b.** $7\frac{1}{8}$ **c.** $6\frac{3}{5}$

d. $6\frac{1}{4}$ **e.** $12\frac{5}{6}$ **f.** $25\frac{3}{10}$

g. Estimate the product of $9\frac{4}{5}$ and $5\frac{1}{3}$.

h. Estimate the sum of $36\frac{5}{8}$ and $10\frac{9}{10}$.

Problem set   **1.** There were 60 deer and 40 antelope playing on the
111   *(107)*   range. What was the ratio of deer to antelope playing on the range?

2. If each of the 8 sides of an octagon is 25 centimeters
(83)   long, then the perimeter of the octagon is how many **meters?**

3. What year was five decades before 1826?
(27)

4. What number is $\frac{3}{4}$ of 100?
(96)

5. Write the length of this line segment as a number of
(48)   millimeters and as a number of centimeters.

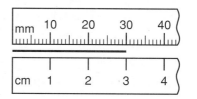

6. If the segment in problem 5 were cut in half, then each
(50)   small segment would be how many centimeters long?

7. Is $8.80 closer to $8 or $9?
(78)

8. Estimate the difference when $7\frac{3}{4}$ is subtracted from
(111) $18\frac{7}{8}$.

9. The kite was 240 feet away. How many yards of string
(83) had been let out?

10. *AB* is 60 mm. *BC* is half of *AB*. *CD* is one third of *AB*.
(81) Find *AD*.

$$A \qquad\qquad\qquad\qquad\qquad\qquad B \qquad\qquad C \qquad\qquad D$$

11. 43 + 8.57 + 12.3 + 0.09
(109)

12. 16.37 − 12
(109)

13. $3.58
(30) × ___ 10

14.   437
(62) × 648

15. $\dfrac{4300}{25}$
(104)

16. 14$\overline{)\$20.16}$
(104)

17. $20.16 ÷ 7
(26)

18. Write fractions equal to $\frac{5}{6}$ and $\frac{1}{4}$ with denominators of
(89) 12. Then subtract the smaller fraction from the larger
fraction.

19. $6\frac{3}{5} + 1\frac{3}{5}$
(101)

20. $8\frac{5}{6} - 1\frac{1}{6}$
(99)

21. $\dfrac{2}{10} \times \dfrac{5}{10}$
(100)

22. $2 \div \dfrac{4}{5}$
(106)

23. $\dfrac{9}{50} = \dfrac{\square}{100}$
(89)

Read this information; then answer questions 24 and 25.

*Becky ran two races at the track meet. She won the
100-meter race with a time of 13.8 seconds. In the
200-meter race, she came in second with a time of
29.2 seconds.*

24. In the 200-meter race, the girl who won ran 1 second
(78) faster than Becky. What was the winning time?

25. Becky earned points for her team. First place earns 5
(54) points. Second place earns 3 points, and third place
earns 1 point. How many points did Becky earn?

LESSON
112

Subtracting: Fill Empty Places
with Zero

Facts Practice: Simplify 50 Fractions (Test J in Test Masters)

Mental Math: Describe how to estimate the sum of $6\frac{7}{8}$ and $4\frac{5}{6}$.
 How many ounces is one pound? two pounds?
  a. Simplify: $\frac{4}{6}, \frac{8}{6}, \frac{9}{6}$ **b.** $\frac{1}{3}$ of 15, × 2, + 2, × 2, ÷ 3, + 1, ÷ 3, ÷ 3

Problem Solving: Write the product of these Roman numerals
 as a Roman numeral.
 XXIV times XII

The main rule for decimal subtraction is, "Line up the decimal points." For some subtraction problems we need to add decimal places to perform the subtraction. If we subtract 0.23 from 0.4, we find there is an "empty place" in the problem.

$$0.4\_ \longleftarrow \text{empty place}$$
$$-\,0.23$$

We fill the empty place with zero. Then we subtract.

$$
\begin{array}{r}
0 \,.\, \overset{3}{\cancel{4}}\,\overset{1}{0} \\
-\,0 \,.\, 2\ 3 \\
\hline
0 \,.\, 1\ 7
\end{array}
$$

Example 0.4 − 0.231

Solution We set up the problem by lining up the decimal points, remembering to write the first number on top. We fill empty places with zero. Then we subtract and get **0.169.**

$$
\begin{array}{r}
0 \,.\, \overset{3}{\cancel{4}}\,\overset{9}{\cancel{0}}\,\overset{1}{0} \\
-\,0 \,.\, 2\ 3\ 1 \\
\hline
0 \,.\, 1\ 6\ 9
\end{array}
$$

Practice*   **a.** 0.3 − 0.15   **b.** 0.3 − 0.25

  c. 4.2 − 0.42   **d.** 3.5 − 0.35

e. $0.4 - 0.123$ **f.** $0.4 - 0.321$

g. $5. - 0.5$ **h.** $5. - 4.1$

i. $1. - 0.25$ **j.** $1.2 - 0.123$

Problem set 112

1. Draw two parallel segments that are horizontal. Make
(39) the upper segment longer than the lower segment. Connect the endpoints of the segments to form a quadrilateral.

2. "A pint's a pound the world around" means that a pint
(95) of water weighs about a pound. About how much does a gallon of water weigh?

3. Estimate the sum of $7\frac{1}{5}$ and $3\frac{7}{8}$ by rounding both
(111) numbers to the nearest whole number before you add.

4. There are 43 people waiting in the first line and 27
(56) people waiting in the second line. If some of the people in the first line move to the second line so that there are the same number of people in each line, then how many people will be in each line?

5. If $25m = 100$, then m equals what number?
(18)

6. Name the shaded part of the
(76) square as a decimal number, as a reduced fraction, and as a percent.

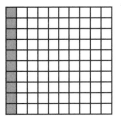

7. Write fractions equal to $\frac{1}{5}$ and $\frac{7}{8}$ that have
(89) denominators of 40. Then add the fractions. Remember to convert the answer to a mixed number.

8. Compare: one tenth $\bigcirc$ ten hundredths
(79)

9. The first four multiples of 2 are 2, 4, 6, and 8. What are
(1) the first four multiples of 6?

10. This rectangle was made with
(60) pins 1 inch long.

    (a) The length of the rectangle is
       how many inches?

    (b) The perimeter of the rectangle is how many
       inches?

11. *AB* is 60 mm. *BC* is half of *AB*. *CD* is half of *BC*. Find
(81) *AD*.

       A   B   C   D

12. $0.4 - 0.12$ **13.** $6.2 - 0.71$ **14.**   315
(112)   (112)   (6)   278
                                                     4197

15. $9 \times \$4.36$ 586
(17)   92

16. 540×780 + 3634
(63)

17. $\dfrac{432}{6}$
(26)

18. $\dfrac{864}{12}$ **19.** $5 - \left(1\dfrac{2}{3} + 1\dfrac{2}{3} \right)$
(104)   (24)

20. $\dfrac{5}{6} \times \left(3 \times \dfrac{2}{5} \right)$ **21.** $2 \div \dfrac{1}{3}$
(24)   (106)

22. $\dfrac{1}{3} \div 2$ **23.** $\dfrac{12}{50} = \dfrac{\square}{100}$
(106)   (89)

This graph shows how Darren spends his time each school day. Use the information in this graph to answer questions 24 and 25.

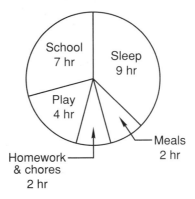

24. What is the total of all the hours listed in the graph?
(54)

25. What fraction of the day does Darren spend sleeping?
(54)

LESSON
113

Subtracting: Pin Decimal Point on Whole Number

Facts Practice: Simplify 50 Fractions (Test J in Test Masters)

Mental Math: Describe how to estimate the product of $7\frac{3}{4}$ and $6\frac{1}{3}$. How many feet is one yard? 100 yards?
  a. Simplify: $\frac{6}{8}, \frac{9}{8}, \frac{12}{8}$ **b.** $\sqrt{100}, \times 5, + 4, \div 9, \times 7, + 2, \div 4$

Problem Solving: How many 1-inch cubes would be needed to build a cube with edges 2 inches long?

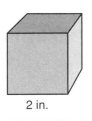

2 in.

When we add or subtract whole numbers and decimal numbers, we first "pin a decimal point" on the right-hand side of the whole numbers. Then we "line up the decimal points." We may also "fill empty places with zero." Then we add or subtract.

> When adding or subtracting decimal numbers:
> 1. Line up the decimal points.
> 2. Place a decimal point on whole numbers.
> 3. Fill empty places with zero.

Example $3 - 1.23$

Solution   We pin a decimal point on the back of the whole number 3. We line up the decimal points, remembering to write the first number on top. Then we fill all empty places with zeros and subtract.

$$\begin{array}{r} \overset{2}{\cancel{3}}.\overset{9}{\cancel{0}}\overset{1}{0} \\ -\,1\,.\,2\,3 \\ \hline \mathbf{1\,.\,7\,7} \end{array}$$

Practice*   **a.** $3 - 0.12$ **b.** $3 - 0.3$

c. $4.2 - 2$ **d.** $4 - 2.2$

e. $10 - 6.5$ **f.** $6.5 - 4$

g. $1 - 0.9$ **h.** $1 - 0.1$

i. $1 - 0.25$ **j.** $2.5 - 1$

Problem set 113   **1.** The room was cluttered with 15 magazines and 25 newspapers. What was the ratio of magazines to newspapers cluttering the room?
(107)

2. About $\frac{1}{3}$ of the weight of a banana is the weight of the peel. If a banana weighs 12 ounces, then the weight of the peel would be about how many ounces? About what percent of the weight of a banana is the weight of the peel?
(50)

3. As the "forty-niners" headed west, what direction was
(51) to their left?

4. Name the total number of
(72) shaded circles as a decimal number and as a reduced mixed
number.

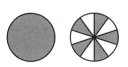

5. Which digit in 1.234 is in the same place as the 6 in
(71) 56.78?

6. If the radius of a wheel is 30 centimeters, then how
(60) many centimeters is its diameter?

7. Estimate the quotient when $9\frac{2}{3}$ is divided by $4\frac{5}{6}$.
(111)

8. Is $12.65 closer to $12 or to $13?
(78)

9. Which arrow could be pointing to 5.8 on this number
(73) line?

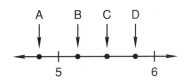

10. (a) The perimeter of this rectangle
(60)   is how many units?

(b) How many small squares
cover the area of this rectangle?

11. *QT* is 10 cm. *QR* is 4 cm. *RS* is half of *QR*. Find *ST*.
(81)

Q   R   S   T

12. $3 - 2.35$ **13.** $10 - 4.06$
(113)   (113)

14. $4.35 + 12.6 + 15$ **15.** $7 \times 47 \times 360$
(109)   (18)

16. $5 \times 68¢$
(17)

17. $\$47.00 \div 20$
(61)

18. $21\overline{)5292}$
(103)

19. $2112 \div 16$
(104)

20. $3\frac{2}{3} + \left(2 - \frac{2}{3}\right)$
(24)

21. $\frac{1}{2} \times \left(4 \times \frac{1}{4}\right)$
(24)

22. $1 \div \frac{7}{5}$
(106)

23. $\frac{3}{2} \div \frac{2}{3}$
(106)

24. $\frac{4}{10} \times \frac{5}{10}$
(100)

25. $\frac{1}{25} = \frac{\square}{100}$
(89)

LESSON 114

Rounding Dollars and Cents to the Nearest Dollar

Facts Practice: Simplify 50 Fractions (Test J in Test Masters)

Mental Math: Describe how to estimate the quotient when $9\frac{5}{8}$ is divided by $1\frac{9}{10}$.

　　a. What is the sum of XXIV and CLXVI?
　　b. Simplify: $\frac{12}{10}$, $\frac{15}{10}$, $\frac{25}{10}$

Problem Solving: If we multiply $2 \times 2 \times 2$, the product is the cube number 8. If we multiply $3 \times 3 \times 3$, the product is the cube number 27. What are the next two cube numbers?

In previous problem sets we have answered questions like the following:

Is $7.56 closer to $7 or $8?

When we answer this question, we are rounding $7.56 to the nearest dollar.

Example 1 Round $12.46 to the nearest dollar.

Solution The problem tells us to write the whole number of dollars to which $12.46 is closest. We know that $12.46 is more than $12 and less than $13. Halfway between $12 and $13 is $12.50. Since $12.46 is slightly less than halfway, we round $12.46 to **$12.**

Example 2 Round $99.95 to the nearest dollar.

Solution When we round money to the nearest dollar, we write dollars and no cents. Since $99.95 is between $99 and $100, our choice will be one of these two. Since $99.95 is much closer to $100, we round up to **$100.**

Example 3 Estimate the cost of 8 boxes of cereal at $3.95 for each box.

Solution We round $3.95 to $4. Then we multiply $4 by 8. Eight boxes of cereal would cost about **$32.**

Practice Round each amount of money to the nearest dollar:

    a. $6.24   **b.** $15.06   **c.** $118.59

    d. $9.75   **e.** $30.89   **f.** $198.47

    g. Estimate the sum of $12.89 and $6.95.

Problem set 114

1. Draw a quadrilateral that has four right angles.
(39)

2. In Michael's class there are twice as many boys as there are girls. There are 18 boys in the class.
(54)

    (a) How many girls are in the class?

    (b) How many children are in the class?

    (c) What is the ratio of boys to girls in the class?

3. Marcia's last seven test scores were 85, 90, 90, 80, 80,
(54) 80, and 75, respectively.

    (a) Arrange the seven scores in order from lowest to highest.

    (b) Which score is in the middle of the ordered list?

    (c) Which score did Marcia earn the most number of times?

4. Write the following sentence using digits and symbols:
(86)

    "The product of one half and one third is one sixth."

5. Which digit is in the tenths' place in 142.75?
(71)

6. Compare: $\dfrac{1}{2} \div \dfrac{1}{3} \bigcirc \dfrac{1}{3} \div \dfrac{1}{2}$
(106)

7. Draw four circles the same size. Shade 25% of the first
(40) circle, 50% of the second circle, 75% of the third circle, and 100% of the fourth circle.

8. Round $4\frac{3}{10}$ to the nearest whole number.
(111)

9. (a) Round $10.49 to the nearest dollar.
(114)
    (b) Round $9.51 to the nearest dollar.

10. The first five multiples of 2 are 2, 4, 6, 8, and 10. What
(1) are the first five multiples of 7?

11. Which arrow could be pointing to 7.2 on this number
(73) line?

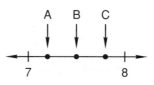

12. (a) What is the perimeter of this rectangle?
(60)

(b) How many squares cover the area of this rectangle?

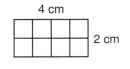
4 cm

2 cm

13. 6.4 + 2.87 + 4
(109)

14. ($16 − $5.74) ÷ 6
(24)

15. $5.64 × 10
(30)

16. 976 × 267
(62)

17. All of these ratios are equal. What is the quotient of each division?
(107)

$$\frac{888}{24}, \frac{444}{12}, \frac{222}{6}, \frac{111}{3}$$

18. Write a fraction equal to $\frac{2}{3}$ with a denominator of 9. Then add $\frac{7}{9}$ to the fraction you wrote. Remember to convert the sum to a mixed number.
(89)

19. $5\frac{2}{3} + \left(3 - \frac{1}{3}\right)$
(24)

20. $2 \times \left(\frac{1}{2} \times \frac{1}{3}\right)$
(24)

21. $\frac{3}{10}$ of 30
(96)

22. $\frac{4}{25} = \frac{\square}{100}$
(89)

This map has been divided into a grid to make towns easier to find. Use the map to answer questions 23–25.

23. We find Taft in region H2. In which region do we find Billings?
(54)

A. G4　　　　　　B. F4

C. H2　　　　　　D. F5

24. What town do we find in region J3?
(54)

25. What letter and number show where to find Evans?
(54)

LESSON 115

Rounding Decimal Numbers to the Nearest Whole Number

Facts Practice: Simplify 50 Fractions (Test J in Test Masters)

Mental Math: Describe how to estimate the cost of 8 yards of fabric if the price of the fabric is $6.95 per yard.

   a. $\frac{1}{5}$ of $20   **b.** $\frac{2}{5}$ of $20   **c.** $\frac{4}{5}$ of $20

   d. $\sqrt{49}, \times 8, -1, \div 5, -1, \times 4, +2, \div 6$

Problem Solving: Write the last three letters of the alphabet in uppercase. Which of the three letters has no lines of symmetry? Which of the letters has just one line of symmetry? Which of the letters has two lines of symmetry?

When a number is written with digits after the decimal point, the number is not a whole number but is between two whole numbers. We should be able to decide which of the two whole numbers it is nearer. The number line can help us understand this idea.

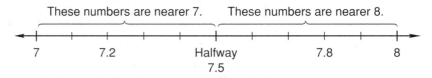

The decimal number which is halfway from 7 to 8 is 7.5. It is the same distance from 7 as it is from 8. The number 7.2 is less than halfway, so it is nearer 7. The number 7.8 is more than halfway, so it is nearer 8.

Example 1 Round 7.6 to the nearest whole number.

Solution The decimal number 7.6 is greater than 7 but is less than 8. Halfway from 7 to 8 is 7.5. Since 7.6 is more than halfway, we round up to the whole number **8**. We can see this if we use a number line.

We see that 7.6 is closer to 8 than it is to 7.

Example 2   Estimate the product of 8.78 and 6.12.

Solution   Rounding decimal numbers with two decimal places is similar to rounding money. The decimal number 8.78 rounds to the whole number 9 just as $8.78 rounds to $9. Likewise, 6.12 rounds to the whole number 6. We multiply the whole numbers 9 and 6 and find that the product of 8.78 and 6.12 is about **54**.

Practice*   Round each of these decimal numbers to the nearest whole number:

    a. 4.75   **b.** 12.3   **c.** 96.41

    d. 7.4   **e.** 45.7   **f.** 89.89

    g. Estimate the product of 9.8 and 6.97.

Problem set 115

1. *(107)* The ratio of boys to girls in the auditorium was 4 to 5. If there were 40 boys in the auditorium, how many girls were there? (*Hint*: In this problem, the ratio 4 to 5 means that for every 4 boys there were 5 girls.)

2. *(66)* This circle is divided into tenths. How many tenths does it take to equal one whole?

3. *(80)* Tony had six coins in his pockets totaling 43¢. How many of the coins were nickels?

4. *(77)* Carl finished the race in ten and twenty-three hundredths seconds. Write that number using digits.

5. *(55)* If 20 of them cost $50, how many of them could you buy with $100?

6. *(89)* The denominator of $\frac{9}{10}$ is 10. Write a fraction equal to $\frac{1}{2}$ that also has a denominator of 10. Then subtract that fraction from $\frac{9}{10}$. Remember to reduce the answer.

7. Sam and Felicia had three days to read a book. Sam
(56) read 40 pages the first day, 60 pages the second day, and 125 pages the third day. Felicia read the same book, but Felicia read an equal number of pages each of the three days. How many pages did Felicia read each day?

8. Round $18.68 to the nearest dollar.
(114)

9. Estimate the quotient when 20.8 is divided by 6.87 by
(115) rounding each decimal number to the nearest whole number before dividing.

10. (a) What is the perimeter of this
(60)   rectangle?

(b) How many squares cover its area?

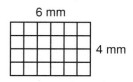

11. Recall that a right angle is some-
(33) times marked with a square in the corner. Both ∠CDA and ∠DCB are right angles. Which angle appears to be acute?

12. $\dfrac{1}{100} + \dfrac{9}{100}$
(100)

13. $\dfrac{63}{100} - \dfrac{13}{100}$
(100)

14. $\dfrac{5}{10} \times \dfrac{5}{10}$
(100)

15. $\dfrac{3}{5} \div \dfrac{3}{4}$
(106)

16. 3.76 + 12 + 6.8 + 14.6 + 907.61 + 413.5 + 0.05
(109)

17. 12 − 1.25
(113)

18. 8 × 63¢ = $_____
(80)

19. 804 × 740
(63)

20. 28$\overline{)5964}$
(104)

21. 5964 ÷ 14
(104)

22. $\dfrac{3}{20} \times \square = \dfrac{15}{100}$
(89)

23. $\dfrac{7}{25} = \dfrac{\square}{100}$
(89)

Read this information. Then answer questions 24 and 25.

Matthew fixed his function machine so that when he puts in a 24, an 8 comes out. When he puts in a 12, a 4 comes out. When he puts in a 6, a 2 comes out.

24. What rule does the function machine use?
(54)

A. It divides by 3.   B. It multiplies by 3.

C. It divides by 2.   D. It subtracts 8.

25. If Matthew puts in a 30, what number will come out?
(54)

LESSON 116

Decimal Place Value: Thousandths

Facts Practice: Simplify 50 Fractions (Test J in Test Masters)

Mental Math: Describe how you would estimate the cost of each pound of nails if a 50-pound box of nails costs $29.85.

How many pounds is one ton? two tons? half a ton?

a. $\frac{1}{3}$ of 100   **b.** $\frac{2}{3}$ of 100   **c.** $20 \times 30, + 40, \div 10$

Problem Solving: Fifty pennies fill a penny roll. Forty nickels fill a nickel roll. How many rolls of pennies are equal in value to two rolls of nickels?

We have used bills and coins to help us understand place value. As we move to the right, each place is one tenth of the value of the place to its left.

tens' place	ones' place		tenths' place	hundredths' place	thousandths' place
———	———	.	———	———	———
$10 bills	$1 bills		dimes	pennies	mills

The third place to the right of the decimal point is the thousandths' place. Its value is $\frac{1}{1000}$. We do not have a coin that is $\frac{1}{1000}$ of a dollar, but we do have a name for $\frac{1}{1000}$ of a dollar. A thousandth of a dollar is a **mill.** Ten mills equal one penny.

To name decimal numbers with three decimal places, we use the word *thousandths.*

Example 1   Use words to name 12.625.

Solution   **Twelve and six hundred twenty-five thousandths**

Example 2   Write 0.500 as a reduced fraction.

Solution   Five hundred thousandths may be written

$$\frac{500}{1000}$$

If we reduce by dividing by $\frac{100}{100}$, we get $\frac{5}{10}$.

$$\frac{500}{1000} \div \frac{100}{100} = \frac{5}{10}$$

We continue to reduce $\frac{5}{10}$ by dividing by $\frac{5}{5}$.

$$\frac{5}{10} \div \frac{5}{5} = \frac{1}{2}$$

So $\frac{500}{1000}$ reduces to $\frac{1}{2}$. We could have reduced mentally by noticing that 500 is half of 1000.

Since 0.500 equals $\frac{1}{2}$, halfway between two whole numbers can be named with a decimal number ending in .500.

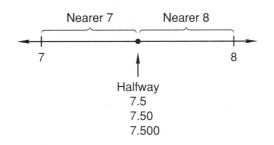

The halfway point may be named by using any number of decimal places. Halfway between 7 and 8 is 7.5, which is seven and **five tenths.** We may also name the halfway point seven and **fifty hundredths,** just as we do when we write $7.50. We may even name the halfway point seven and **five hundred thousandths.** Remember, zeros at the end of a decimal number do not change the value of the number. We will keep this idea in mind when rounding decimal numbers which have more than one digit after the decimal point.

Example 3   Round 6.345 to the nearest whole number.

Solution   The number 6.345 names a number which is **6 plus a fraction.** If the fraction part is less than 0.5 or 0.50 or 0.500, etc., we round down. If the fraction part is greater than 0.5 or 0.50 or 0.500, we round up. Since 0.345 is less than 0.500, we round 6.345 down to **6.**

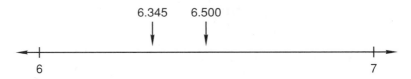

Practice   **a.** Use words to name 6.875.

b. Use digits to write one hundred twenty-five thousandths.

Round each of these decimal numbers to the nearest whole number:

c. 4.375   **d.** 2.625   **e.** 1.333

Problem set 116

1. Milton was given a $100 gift certificate for toys. If he
(55) could buy 6 games with $25, how many games could he buy with his $100 gift certificate?

2. Detective Brown found one thousand, three hundred
(50) sixty-eight clues. Only one ninth of the clues were helpful. How many helpful clues did he find?

3. Name the shaded part of the two squares as a decimal
(76) number and as a reduced mixed number.

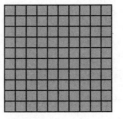

4. Estimate the product of 8.33 and 7.667 by rounding
(116) each decimal number to the nearest whole number
before multiplying.

5. What are the first five multiples of 8?
(1)

6. Three fifths of the 30 students in the class were girls.
(50)
(a) How many girls were in the class?

(b) How many boys were in the class?

(c) What was the ratio of boys to girls in the class?

7. Estimate the sum of $8.96, $12.14, and $4.88 by
(114) rounding each amount to the nearest dollar before
adding.

8. Use words to name 5.375.
(116)

9. (a) What is the perimeter of this
(60) rectangle?

(b) How many small squares
cover its area?

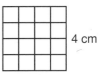

4 cm

10. What is the next number in this sequence?
(1)
..., 3465, 3475, 3485, _____, ...

11. $4\frac{3}{8}$ **12.** $3\frac{7}{10}$ **13.** 4
(99)   (99)   (70)
$+ 1\frac{3}{8}$ $+ \frac{3}{10}$ $- 1\frac{3}{10}$

14. 46.3 + 28.49 + 0.125 + 6 + 759.6 + 808.73 + 0.15
(109)

15. 4 − 1.3   **16.** 8 × 57 × 250
(113)   (18)

17. 5 × $7.25   **18.** 8)$26.00
(17)   (26)

19. 436 ÷ 21   **20.** 16)5040
(104)   (104)

21. $5 \times \dfrac{3}{10}$ **22.** $5 \div \dfrac{2}{3}$
(101)   (106)

23. Write fractions equal to $\frac{1}{6}$ and $\frac{1}{8}$ that have denomina-
(89)   tors of 24. Then add the fractions.

The graph below shows the fraction of students in a class who have hair of a certain color. Use this graph to answer questions 24 and 25.

24. There are 30 students in this
(54)   class. How many students have blonde hair? What percent of the students have blonde hair?

Hair Color of Students

25. Which two groups **taken together**
(54)   total one half of the class?

A. Black and brown

B. Brown and blonde

C. Blonde and black

**LESSON
117**

Using Percent to Name Part of a Group

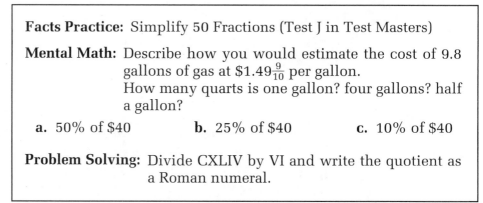

Facts Practice: Simplify 50 Fractions (Test J in Test Masters)

Mental Math: Describe how you would estimate the cost of 9.8 gallons of gas at 1.49\frac{9}{10}$ per gallon.
How many quarts is one gallon? four gallons? half a gallon?

a. 50% of $40   **b.** 25% of $40   **c.** 10% of $40

Problem Solving: Divide CXLIV by VI and write the quotient as a Roman numeral.

Percent is a word that means "out of 100." If we read that 50 percent of all Americans drive cars, we understand that 50 out of every 100 Americans drive cars. The statement, "Ten percent of the population is left-handed" means that 10 out of every 100 people are left-handed.

When we say "percent," we speak **as though there were 100** in the group. However, we may say "percent" even when there are more or less than 100 in the group. We have used fraction manipulatives to learn the percents that are equivalent to some fractions. We may also find the percent for some fractions by renaming the fraction with a denominator of 100.

Example 1 If 8 of the 20 students are boys, what percent of the students are boys?

Solution If we write the number of boys over the total number of students in the group, we get 8 boys over 20 total. If we multiply this fraction by a name for 1 so that the bottom number becomes 100, the top number will be the percent. So we will multiply by 5 over 5.

$$\frac{8 \text{ boys}}{20 \text{ total}} \times \frac{5}{5} = \frac{40 \text{ boys}}{100 \text{ total}}$$

This means that if there were 100 students there would be 40 boys. Thus **40 percent** of the students are boys.

Example 2 There were 400 pieces of candy in all. If 60 pieces were chocolate, what percent of the candy was chocolate?

Solution We have the fraction 60 chocolate over 400 total. We partially reduce the ratio to make the total equal 100 by dividing by 4 over 4.

$$\frac{60 \text{ chocolate}}{400 \text{ total}} \div \frac{4}{4} = \frac{15 \text{ chocolate}}{100 \text{ total}}$$

When we make the bottom number 100, the top number is the percent. Thus **15 percent** of the candy was chocolate.

Instead of using the word *percent*, we may use the percent sign (%). Using the percent sign, we write 15 percent as **15%**.

Practice **a.** If 120 of the 200 students are girls, then what percent of the students are girls?

b. If 10 of the 50 pieces of candy are green, then what percent of the pieces of candy are green?

c. Sixty out of 300 is like how many out of 100?

d. Forty-eight out of 200 is what percent?

e. Thirty out of 50 is what percent?

f. If half of the people came, then what percent of the people came?

Problem set 117

1. Estimate the product of $9\frac{7}{8}$ and $6\frac{3}{4}$.
₍₁₁₁₎

2. Gilbert swam 100 meters in 63.8 seconds. Julie swam 100 meters 1 second faster than Gilbert. How long did it take Julie to swim 100 meters?
₍₇₈₎

3. The camel could carry 245 kilograms. How many bundles of straw at 15 kilograms each could the camel carry?
₍₂₁₎

4. Estimate the total cost of 8 records priced at $6.98 each by rounding the cost per record to the nearest dollar before multiplying.
₍₁₁₄₎

5. If 60 of the 200 students are girls, then what percent of the students are girls?
₍₁₁₇₎

6. Compare: $\frac{1}{10} + \frac{1}{10} \bigcirc 0.1 + 0.1$
₍₇₂₎

7. Estimate the quotient when 19.8 is divided by 3.875.
₍₁₁₆₎

8. If a bag of M&M's contains 50 pieces of candy and 10 of the pieces are green, then what percent of the M&M's are green?
₍₁₁₇₎

9. Write a fraction equal to $\frac{1}{3}$ that has the same denominator as the fraction $\frac{1}{6}$. Then add the fraction to $\frac{1}{6}$. Remember to reduce your answer.
₍₈₉₎

10. (a) The perimeter of the darker
(60)   rectangle is how many units?

(b) How many small squares
    cover the area of the rectan-
    gle?

11. *QT* equals 9 centimeters. *QR* equals *RS* equals *ST*.
(81) Find *QR*.

$$Q \qquad\qquad R \qquad\qquad S \qquad\qquad T$$

12. $\dfrac{31}{100} + \dfrac{29}{100}$ **13.** $5 - 3\dfrac{7}{10}$
(100)   (70)

14. $10 + 7.45 + 8 + 32.5 + 946.8 + 78.64 + 423$
(109)

15. $5 - 3.7$ **16.** $10 \times \$3.65$
(113)   (30)

17. 468×579 **18.** $\$36.50 \div 10$
(62)   (61)

19. $5\overline{)8765}$ **20.** $800 \div 32$
(26)   (104)

21. $\dfrac{3}{5} \times 4$ **22.** $4 \div \dfrac{3}{5}$
(101)   (106)

The table below shows the number of votes students
received in a class election. Look at this table. Then
answer questions 23–25.

Election Results

Miguel	JHT JHT II
Debbie	JHT II
Patrick	JHT
Tina	JHT III

23. How many votes did Miguel receive?
(54)

24. What fraction of the votes did Tina get?
(54)

25. A student in the class noticed that there could have
(54) been a four-way tie in the election. If there had been a
four-way tie, then each of the four students would
have received how many votes?

LESSON
118

Writing a Percent as a Fraction

Facts Practice: Simplify 50 Fractions (Test J in Test Masters)

Mental Math: Describe how you would estimate the cost of 11.17 gallons of gas at 1.39\frac{9}{10}$ per gallon.
How many years is one century? ten centuries?

  a. $\frac{1}{4}$ of $80   **b.** $\frac{3}{4}$ of $80   **c.** 50% of $\frac{1}{2}$

Problem Solving: How many 1-inch cubes would be needed to build a cube with edges 3 inches long?

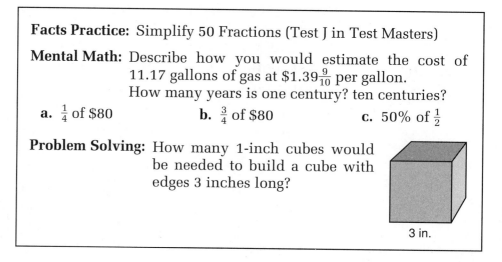

3 in.

Since *percent* means "out of 100," we may write a percent as a fraction by removing the percent sign and writing the number as the numerator of a fraction that has a denominator of 100. Look at these examples.

$$3\% = \frac{3}{100} \qquad 49\% = \frac{49}{100} \qquad 70\% = \frac{70}{100}$$

When we write a percent as a fraction, we should reduce the fraction if possible. In the examples above, 70% is written as the fraction $\frac{70}{100}$, which we reduce to $\frac{7}{10}$.

Example   Write 40% as a reduced fraction.

Solution   Forty percent may be written as the fraction $\frac{40}{100}$. Then we reduce to get $\frac{2}{5}$.

$$40\% = \frac{40}{100}$$

$$\frac{40}{100} = \frac{2}{5}$$

Practice*   Write each percent as a reduced fraction:

    a. 60%   **b.** 90%   **c.** 25%   **d.** 4%

Problem set
118

1. Bobby weighs forty-five million, four hundred fifty-
(59) four thousand, five hundred milligrams. Use digits to
write that number.

2. What is the total cost of 2 items at $1.26 each and 3
(55) items at 49¢ each plus a total tax of 24¢?

3. Flora rode her bike 2.5 miles from her house to the
(82) library. How far did she ride going to the library and
back home?

4. If $4y = 20$, then $2y - 1$ equals what number?
(17)

5. The arrow is pointing to what
(28) number on this scale?

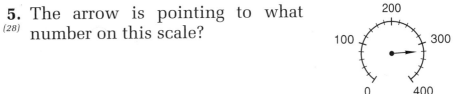

6. Fifteen of the 25 students in the class are boys.
(117)
　(a) What percent of the students are boys?
　(b) What is the ratio of boys to girls in the class?

7. Estimate the sum of 12.7 and 8.167 by rounding to the
(116) nearest whole number before adding.

8. Write the reduced fraction that equals 40%.
(118)

9. Compare: $50\% \bigcirc \dfrac{1}{2}$
(118)

10. Use words to name the number 76.345. Which digit is
(116) in the tenths' place?

11. A rectangle is drawn on this grid.
(60)
　(a) The perimeter of the rectangle
　　 is how many units?
　(b) How many small squares
　　 cover the area of the rectan-
　　 gle?

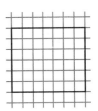

12. *WX* is 48 mm. *XY* is half of *WX*. *YZ* equals *XY*. Find
(81) *WZ*.

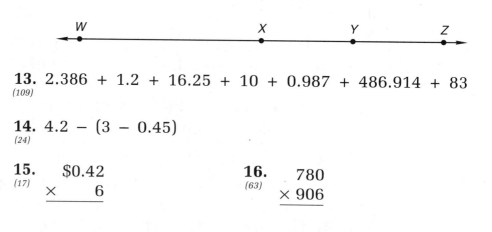

13. 2.386 + 1.2 + 16.25 + 10 + 0.987 + 486.914 + 83
(109)

14. 4.2 − (3 − 0.45)
(24)

15. $0.42
(17)   × ___6

16.   780
(63)   × 906

17. Write a fraction equal to $\frac{1}{2}$ that has the same
(89) denominator as $\frac{1}{6}$. Then add the fraction to $\frac{1}{6}$.
Remember to reduce your answer.

18. $\frac{1}{2} \div \frac{2}{3}$
(106)

19. $37.05 ÷ 15
(104)

20. $\frac{4}{11} + \frac{5}{11}$
(44)

21. $4\frac{5}{7} - \frac{1}{7}$
(47)

22. Five sixths of the two dozen juice bars were
(50) strawberry. How many of the juice bars were
strawberry?

The table shows the number of students who made certain
scores out of a possible 20 on the test. Look at this table.
Then answer questions 23–25.

Test Results

SCORE	NUMBER OF STUDENTS
20	4
19	4
18	5
17	6
16	3
15	2

23. Which score was made by the largest number of
(54) students?

24. If 25 students took the test, how many students got
(54) fewer than 15 correct?

25. If all 25 scores were listed in order like this:
(54)
$$20, 20, 20, 20, 19, 19, \ldots$$

which score would be in the middle of the list?

LESSON
119

Multiplying Decimal Numbers

Facts Practice: Simplify 50 Fractions (Test J in Test Masters)

Mental Math: Todd's car traveled 298 miles on 9.78 gallons of
gas. Describe how to estimate the number of
miles Todd's car traveled on each gallon of gas.

  a. CCCXCIX   **b.** CXLIV   **c.** $\frac{1}{8}$ of 80

  d. $\frac{3}{8}$ of 80   **e.** 25% of 80   **f.** $\sqrt{81}, \times 10, -2, \div 2, +1, \div 5$

Problem Solving: How many seconds long is one day?

What is one tenth of one tenth? We will use pictures to
answer this question.

    The first picture on the right is a
square. The square represents one
whole, and each column is one tenth
of the whole. We shaded one tenth of
the whole.

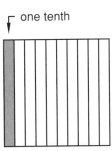

one tenth

To find one tenth of one tenth, we divide each tenth into 10 parts. The second picture shows the columns divided into 10 parts with one small square shaded. We shaded one tenth of one tenth of the square. The shaded part is **one hundredth** of the square. We see that one tenth of one tenth is one hundredth.

one tenth of one tenth

When we find one tenth of one tenth, we are multiplying. If we use arithmetic and multiply fractions, the work looks like this.

$$\frac{1}{10} \times \frac{1}{10} = \frac{1}{100}$$

If we use decimal numbers instead, the work looks like this.

$$\begin{array}{r} 0.1 \\ \times\ 0.1 \\ \hline 0.01 \end{array}$$

When we set up a decimal multiplication problem, we do not try to line up the decimal points. That rule is only for adding and subtracting. When we multiply, we just set up the problem as though it were a whole-number problem and multiply. To place the decimal point in the answer, we first count the total number of digits to the right of the decimal point in both factors. Then we place the decimal point in the answer so that there is the same total number of digits to the right of the decimal point in the answer.

Copy and **study** the following examples and solutions.

Examples,
Solutions

$$\begin{array}{r} 0.12 \\ \times\ \ \ \ 6 \\ \hline 0.72 \end{array}$$

2 digits to right of decimal point
0 digits to right of decimal point
2 digits to right of decimal point

$$\begin{array}{r} 25 \\ \times\ 0.3 \\ \hline 7.5 \end{array}$$

0 digits to right of decimal point
1 digit to right of decimal point
1 digit to right of decimal point

$$\begin{array}{r} 0.15 \\ \times\ \ 0.9 \\ \hline 0.135 \end{array}$$

2 digits to right of decimal point
1 digit to right of decimal point
3 digits to right of decimal point

The rule for multiplying decimal numbers is, **"Multiply, then count."** We **multiply** the digits; then we **count** the total number of decimal places in the factors. Then, starting from the right side of the answer, we count over that many digits to the left and mark the decimal point.

In this chart we have summarized the rules of decimal arithmetic for adding, subtracting, and multiplying.

Decimals Chart

+ −	×
Line up the decimal points.	Multiply. Then count decimal places.
Place a decimal point on whole numbers. Fill empty places with zero.	

The two rules at the bottom of the chart are sometimes used for adding, subtracting, multiplying, and dividing, as we shall see in later lessons.

Practice*

a.
$$\begin{array}{r} 0.3 \\ \times\ \ 4 \\ \hline \end{array}$$

b.
$$\begin{array}{r} 3 \\ \times\ 0.6 \\ \hline \end{array}$$

c.
$$\begin{array}{r} 0.12 \\ \times\ \ \ 4 \\ \hline \end{array}$$

d.
$$\begin{array}{r} 1.4 \\ \times\ 0.7 \\ \hline \end{array}$$

e. 0.3×0.5

f. 1.2×3

g. 1.5×0.5

h. 0.25×0.9

Problem set 119

1. Copy the decimals chart in this lesson.
(119)

2. Forty of Dan's 50 answers were correct. What percent of Dan's answers were correct?
(117)

3. Compare: $\dfrac{1}{10} \times \dfrac{1}{10} \bigcirc 0.1 \times 0.1$
(119)

4. What time is 35 minutes before midnight?
(29)

5. Use digits to write the decimal number one hundred one and one hundred one thousandths.
(116)

6. Three small blocks of wood are balanced on one side of a scale with a 100-gram weight and a 500-gram weight on the other side. If each block weighs the same, what is the weight of each block?
(56)

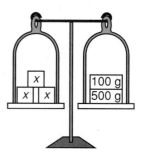

7. What are the first five multiples of 10?
(1)

8. Estimate the difference when $6.94 is subtracted from $23.07 by rounding to the nearest dollar before you subtract.
(114)

9. (a) How many units is the perimeter of the rectangle?
(60)
(b) How many small squares cover the area of the rectangle?

10. (a) Write the reduced fraction equal to 10%.
(118)
(b) Write the reduced fraction equal to 20%.

11. 32.3 + 4.96 + 7.5 + 11 + 478.6 + 94.372 + 462
(109)

12. 1 − (1.36 − 0.8)   **13.** 12 × 0.6
(24)   (119)

14. 0.15 × 0.9   **15.** 0.16 × 10
(119)   (119)

16. $\dfrac{3705}{13}$ **17.** $6)\overline{\$8.76}$ **18.** 980 ÷ 28
(104)   (26)   (104)

19. $1\frac{3}{5}$ **20.** $4\frac{3}{10}$ **21.** $4\frac{3}{10}$
(44) $+ 1\frac{1}{5}$ (99) $+ 1\frac{2}{10}$ (44) $- 1\frac{2}{10}$

22. Write fractions equal to $\frac{2}{3}$ and $\frac{1}{2}$ with denominators of 6. Then subtract the smaller fraction from the larger fraction.
(89)

23. $\dfrac{3}{10} \times \dfrac{1}{3}$ **24.** $\dfrac{3}{4} \div \dfrac{3}{5}$ **25.** $\dfrac{3}{10} \div 3$
(100)   (106)   (106)

LESSON
120

Multiplying Decimal Numbers: Fill Empty Places with Zero

Facts Practice: Simplify 50 Fractions (Test J in Test Masters)

Mental Math: Describe how to estimate the product of $8\frac{3}{4}$ and $5\frac{1}{4}$. How many centimeters is one meter? ten meters?

a. Simplify: $\frac{6}{9}, \frac{12}{9}, \frac{24}{9}$ **b.** $\frac{1}{6}$ of $30, \times 5, + 2, \div 3, \times 4, \div 6$

Problem Solving: Which uppercase letters of the alphabet have a vertical line of symmetry?

When we multiply decimal numbers, we follow the rule, "Multiply, then count." We count the total number of digits to the right of the decimal points in the factors. Then, starting from the right, we count over the same number of digits in the product to write the decimal point. Sometimes there are more digits to the right of the decimal point in the factors than there are digits in the product. Look at the problem below.

$$
\begin{array}{r}
0.3 \\
\times\, 0.3 \\
\hline
0.\underset{\smile}{\,\,9}
\end{array}
$$

There are two digits to the right of the decimal points in the factors. So we count over two places in the product, but there is only one digit.

To complete the multiplication, we use a rule from the bottom of the decimals chart. We "fill empty places with zero."

$$
\begin{array}{r}
0.3 \\
\times\, 0.3 \\
\hline
0.0\underline{9}
\end{array}
$$

Fill empty place with zero.

Changing the problem 0.3 × 0.3 to a fraction problem may help us understand why we use this rule. Since 0.3 equals $\frac{3}{10}$, we may write the problem the following way:

$$
\frac{3}{10} \times \frac{3}{10} = \frac{9}{100}
$$

The product $\frac{9}{100}$ may be written as the decimal number, 0.09.

Example 0.12×0.3

Solution   We set up the problem as though it were a whole-number problem. We follow the rule, "Multiply, then count." We "fill empty places with zero" and get the product **0.036**.

$$\begin{array}{r} 0.12 \\ \times\ \ 0.3 \\ \hline 36 \end{array}$$ Three digits to the right of the decimal points.

.036 Count over 3 places; fill empty place with zero.

Practice*   Multiply:

a. $\begin{array}{r} 0.25 \\ \times\ \ 0.3 \\ \hline \end{array}$ **b.** $\begin{array}{r} 0.12 \\ \times\ \ 0.4 \\ \hline \end{array}$ **c.** $\begin{array}{r} 0.125 \\ \times\ \ \ 0.3 \\ \hline \end{array}$ **d.** $\begin{array}{r} 0.05 \\ \times\ 0.03 \\ \hline \end{array}$

Set up and multiply:

e. 0.03×0.3 **f.** 3.2×0.03 **g.** 0.6×0.16

h. 0.12×0.2 **i.** 0.01×0.1 **j.** 0.07×0.12

Problem set 120

1. Estimate the product of 5.375 and 3.8 by rounding both numbers to the nearest whole number before you multiply.
(116)

2. The Jets played 10 games and won 5. What percent of their games did the Jets win?
(117)

3. (a) Write the reduced fraction that equals 30%.
(118)   (b) Write the reduced fraction that equals 40%.

4. Two fifths of the 100 passengers stayed in the subway cars until the last stop. How many of the 100 passengers got off the subway cars before the last stop?
(67)

5. Name the length of this segment as a number of centimeters and as a number of millimeters.
(74)

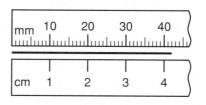

6. If the segment in problem 5 were cut in thirds, each third would be how many centimeters long?
(50)

7. Write fractions equal to $\frac{5}{6}$ and $\frac{3}{4}$ that have
(89) denominators of 12. Then add the fractions. Remember to convert the sum to a mixed number.

8. A hexagon is drawn on this grid.
(60)

(a) How many units is the perimeter of this hexagon?

(b) How many squares cover its area?

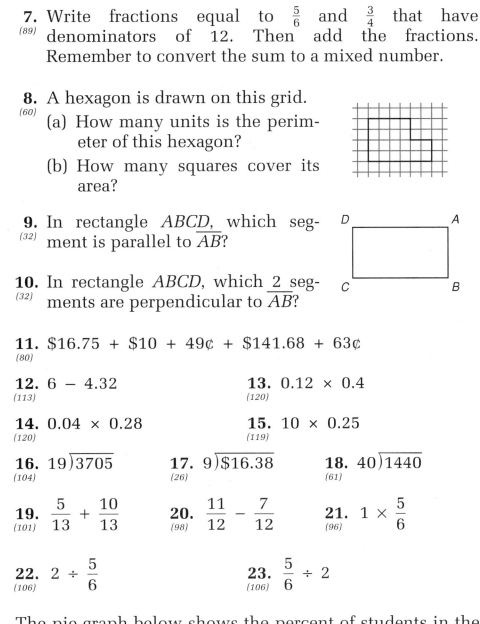

9. In rectangle *ABCD*, which segment is parallel to $\overline{AB}$?
(32)

10. In rectangle *ABCD*, which 2 segments are perpendicular to $\overline{AB}$?
(32)

11. $16.75 + $10 + 49¢ + $141.68 + 63¢
(80)

12. 6 − 4.32   **13.** 0.12 × 0.4
(113)   (120)

14. 0.04 × 0.28   **15.** 10 × 0.25
(120)   (119)

16. $19\overline{)3705}$ **17.** $9\overline{)\$16.38}$ **18.** $40\overline{)1440}$
(104)   (26)   (61)

19. $\frac{5}{13} + \frac{10}{13}$ **20.** $\frac{11}{12} - \frac{7}{12}$ **21.** $1 \times \frac{5}{6}$
(101)   (98)   (96)

22. $2 \div \frac{5}{6}$ **23.** $\frac{5}{6} \div 2$
(106)   (106)

The pie graph below shows the percent of students in the class who made certain grades in math. Use this graph to answer questions 24 and 25.

24. Add the percents shown on the
(54) graph. What is the total?

25. What grade was made by $\frac{1}{4}$ of the
(54) students?

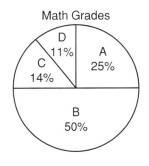

Math Grades

LESSON
121

Multiplying Decimal Numbers by 10, 100, and 1000

In our number system the places have value. The value of each place is 10 times greater each time we move one place to the left. When we multiply a number by 10, the digits all shift one place to the left. When we multiply 34 by 10, the 3 shifts from the tens' place to the hundreds' place, and the 4 shifts from the ones' place to the tens' place.

$$3 \quad 4 \,.$$
$$3 \quad 4 \quad 0 \,. \quad (10 \times 34 = 340)$$

This fact can help us multiply decimal numbers quickly when we multiply by 10 or 100 or 1000. When we multiply by 10, each digit shifts one place to the left.

$$0 \,. \, 3 \quad 4$$
$$3 \,. \, 4 \quad\quad (10 \times 0.34 = 3.4)$$

We see that the digit 3 moved to the other side of the decimal point when it shifted one place. The decimal point holds steady while the digits move. Although it is the digits which change places when the number is multiplied by 10, we can produce the same result by moving the decimal point in the opposite direction.

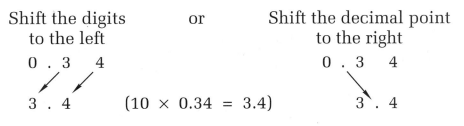

Shift the digits to the left   or   Shift the decimal point to the right

0 . 3   4   0 . 3   4

3 . 4   (10 × 0.34 = 3.4)   3 . 4

When we multiply by 10, we may simply shift the decimal point one place to the right.

Since 100 is 10 × 10, multiplying by 100 is like multiplying by 10 **twice.** When we multiply by 100, we may shift the decimal point **two** places to the right.

Since 1000 is 10 × 10 × 10, we may shift the decimal point **three** places to the right when we multiply by 1000.

The number of places we shift the decimal point is the same as the number of zeros we see in 10 or 100 or 1000.

Example   1.234 × 100

Solution   We may multiply by 100 mentally by shifting the decimal point two places to the right. The product is **123.4.**

$$1.234 \times 100 = 123.4$$

Practice   **a.** 1.234 × 10   **b.** 1.234 × 1000   **c.** 0.1234 × 100

d. 0.345 × 10   **e.** 0.345 × 100   **f.** 0.345 × 1000

g. 5.67 × 10   **h.** 5.67 × 1000   **i.** 5.67 × 100

Problem set 121   **1.** In three classrooms there were 23 students, 25 students, and 30 students, respectively. If the students in the three classrooms were rearranged so that there were an equal number of students in each room, how many students would there be in each classroom?

(56)

2. Genghis Khan was born in 1167. In 1211 he invaded
(27) China. How old was he then?

3. (a) Write the reduced fraction equal to 25%.
(118) (b) Write the reduced fraction equal to 50%.

4. (a) List the first six multiples of 6.
(1) (b) List the first four multiples of 9.

(c) Which two numbers appear in both lists?

5. Name the shaded part of the
(76) square as a percent, as a decimal
number, and as a reduced
fraction.

6. Name the shape of a basketball.
(93)

7. How many months are in $1\frac{1}{2}$ years?
(27)

8. (a) How many units long is the
(60) perimeter of this shape?

(b) How many squares cover the
area of this shape?

9. *QR* is 45 mm. *RS* is one third of *QR*. *QT* is 90 mm.
(81) Find *ST*.

Perform the multiplications in problems 10 and 11 by
shifting the decimal point:

10. 1.23 × 10   **11.** 3.42 × 1000
(121)   (121)

12. Use words to name this sum:
(116)
$$15 + 9.67 + 3.292 + 5.5$$

13. 4.3 − 1.21
(112)

14. 0.14 × 0.6
(120)

15. 48 × 0.7
(119)

16. 0.735 × 100
(121)

17. Write a fraction equal to $\frac{3}{4}$ that has the same
(89) denominator as $\frac{3}{8}$. Then add the fraction to $\frac{3}{8}$.

18. $16\overline{)4000}$
(104)

19. \$18.00 ÷ 10
(61)

20. $\frac{7}{11}$
(101) $+\ \frac{8}{11}$
        ———

21. $3\frac{7}{12}$
(99) $+\ \frac{1}{12}$
        ———

22. $5\frac{9}{10}$
(99) $-\ 5\frac{3}{10}$
        ———

23. $\frac{7}{2} \times \frac{1}{2}$
(101)

24. $\frac{2}{3} \div \frac{1}{4}$
(106)

25. $3 \div \frac{3}{4}$
(106)

**LESSON
122**

Finding the Least Common Multiple of Two Numbers

Facts Practice: Write 30 Percents as Fractions (Test K in Test Masters)

Mental Math: Describe how to estimate the cost of 98 tickets at $2.50 each.

How many ounces equal one pound? two pounds? half a pound?

a. $\frac{1}{10}$ of 30   **b.** $\frac{3}{10}$ of 30   **c.** $\frac{9}{10}$ of 30

d. $\sqrt{100}, \div 2, \times 7, + 1, \div 6, \times 4, \div 2$

Problem Solving: Victor dropped a rubber ball and found that each bounce was half as high as the previous bounce. He dropped the ball from 8 feet, measured the height of each bounce, and recorded the results in a table. Copy this table and complete it through the fifth bounce.

Heights of Bounces	
First	4 ft
Second	
Third	
Fourth	
Fifth	

Here we list some of the multiples of 4 and of 6.

Multiples of 4	4, 8, ⑫, 16, 20, ㉔, 28, 32, ㊱, ...
Multiples of 6	6, ⑫, 18, ㉔, 30, ㊱, ...

We have circled those multiples that 4 and 6 have in common that are multiples of both numbers. The smallest number that is a multiple of both 4 and 6 is 12.

The smallest number that is a multiple of two or more numbers is called the **least common multiple** of the numbers. The letters **LCM** are sometimes used to stand for least **c**ommon **m**ultiple.

Example   Find the least common multiple (LCM) of 6 and 8.

Solution We begin by listing some of the **multiples** of 6 and 8.

Multiples of 6	6, 12, 18, ⟨24⟩, 30, 36, 42, ⟨48⟩, ...
Multiples of 8	8, 16, ⟨24⟩, 32, 40, ⟨48⟩, ...

We now circle the multiples which 6 and 8 have in **common.** The **least** of the common multiples is **24.**

Practice* Find the least common multiple (LCM) of each pair of numbers:

    a. 2 and 3 6   **b.** 3 and 5 15   **c.** 5 and 10 10

    d. 2 and 4 4   **e.** 3 and 6 6   **f.** 6 and 10

    g. The denominators of $\frac{5}{8}$ and $\frac{3}{10}$ are 8 and 10. What is the least common multiple of 8 and 10?

Problem set 122

1. A VW Bug weighs about one ton. Most large elephants
(87) weigh 4 times that much. About how many pounds would a large elephant weigh?

2. The Arctic Ocean is almost completely covered with
(83) the polar ice cap, which averages about 10 feet thick. About how many inches thick is the polar ice cap?

3. What is the total cost of 10 movie tickets priced at
(21) $2.25 each?

4. Which digit in 375.246 is in the hundredths' place?
(71)

5. Draw a pentagon.
(39)

6. Write 12.5 as a mixed number.
(72)

7. Name the shaded part of the
(76) square as a percent, as a decimal number, and as a reduced fraction.

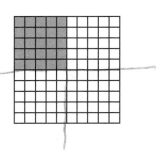

8. Name the shape of a can of pop.
(93)

9. All three sides of this triangle are equal in length.
_(60)_ What is the perimeter of this triangle?

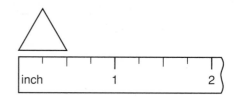

10. Find the least common multiple (LCM) of 6 and 9.
_(121)_

11. If $\overline{OM}$ measures 15 mm, then what
_(60)_ is the measure of $\overline{LN}$?

12. WX is 4.2 cm. XY is 3 cm. WZ is 9.2 cm. Find YZ.
_(81)_

```
        W                    X              Y          Z
  ←─────●────────────────────●──────────────●──────────●────→
```

13. 4.38 + 7.525 + 23.7 + 9 + 788.4 + 936.5 + 14
_(109)_

14. 5 − (4.3 − 0.21)   **15.** 3.6 × 4
_(24)_   _(119)_

16. 0.15 × 0.5   **17.** 10 × 0.125
_(120)_   _(121)_

18. $4\overline{)300}$ **19.** $40\overline{)3000}$ **20.** $25\overline{)3300}$
_(26)_   _(61)_   _(103)_

21. $3\dfrac{3}{7} + \left(5 - 1\dfrac{2}{7}\right)$ **22.** $1\dfrac{1}{2} - \left(3 \times \dfrac{1}{2}\right)$
_(24)_   _(24)_

23. Write fractions equal to $\frac{1}{4}$ and $\frac{2}{3}$ that have
_(89)_ denominators of 12. Then subtract the smaller fraction
from the larger fraction.

On this grid different shapes are centered at certain points where the grid lines intersect. For example, there is a circle at point B1 where the grid lines labeled "B" and "1" intersect. Use this grid to answer questions 24 and 25.

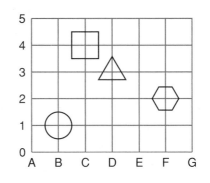

24. Name the shape at point D3.
(54)

25. What letter and number names the point where there
(54)   is a hexagon?

LESSON
123

Writing Mixed Numbers as Improper Fractions

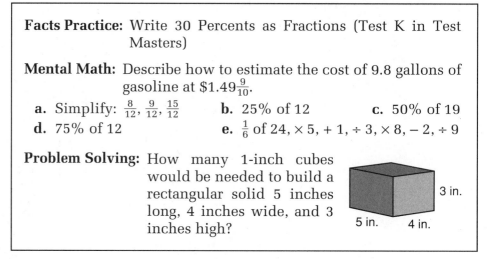

Facts Practice: Write 30 Percents as Fractions (Test K in Test Masters)

Mental Math: Describe how to estimate the cost of 9.8 gallons of gasoline at 1.49\frac{9}{10}$.

   a. Simplify: $\frac{8}{12}, \frac{9}{12}, \frac{15}{12}$ **b.** 25% of 12   **c.** 50% of 19

   d. 75% of 12   **e.** $\frac{1}{6}$ of 24, × 5, + 1, ÷ 3, × 8, − 2, ÷ 9

Problem Solving: How many 1-inch cubes would be needed to build a rectangular solid 5 inches long, 4 inches wide, and 3 inches high?

The picture below shows $1\frac{1}{2}$ shaded circles. How many half circles are shaded?

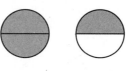

Three halves are shaded. We may name the number of shaded circles as the mixed number $1\frac{1}{2}$ or as the improper fraction $\frac{3}{2}$.

$$1\frac{1}{2} = \frac{3}{2}$$

We have converted improper fractions to mixed numbers by dividing. In this lesson we will practice writing mixed numbers as improper fractions. We will use this skill later when we learn to multiply and divide mixed numbers.

To help us understand changing mixed numbers into fractions, we will draw pictures. Here we show the number $2\frac{1}{4}$ using shaded circles.

To show $2\frac{1}{4}$ as an improper fraction, we will divide the whole circles into the same size pieces as the divided circle. In this example we divide the whole circles into fourths.

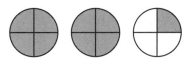

Now we count the total number of fourths that are shaded. We see that $2\frac{1}{4}$ equals the improper fraction $\frac{9}{4}$.

Example 1 Name the number of shaded circles as an improper fraction and as a mixed number.

Solution To show the improper fraction, we divide the whole circles into the same size pieces as the divided circle, in this case, halves. The improper fraction is $\frac{5}{2}$. The mixed number is $\mathbf{2\frac{1}{2}}$.

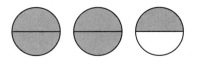

Example 2 Change $2\frac{1}{3}$ to an improper fraction.

Solution One way to find an improper fraction equal to $2\frac{1}{3}$ is to draw a picture that illustrates $2\frac{1}{3}$.

We have shaded 2 whole circles and $\frac{1}{3}$ of a circle. Now we will divide each whole circle into $\frac{3}{3}$ and count the total number of thirds.

We see that there are seven thirds shaded. So an improper fraction equal to $2\frac{1}{3}$ is $\frac{7}{3}$.

It is not necessary to draw a picture. We could remember that each whole is $\frac{3}{3}$. So the 2 of $2\frac{1}{3}$ is equal to $\frac{3}{3} + \frac{3}{3}$, which is $\frac{6}{3}$. Then we add $\frac{6}{3}$ and $\frac{1}{3}$ and get $\frac{7}{3}$.

Practice* Name the number of shaded circles as improper fractions and as mixed numbers:

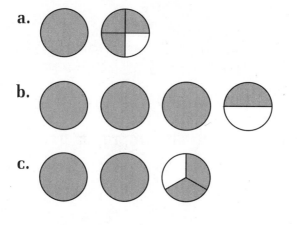

a.

b.

c.

Change each mixed number to an improper fraction:

d. $4\frac{1}{2}$ **e.** $1\frac{2}{3}$ **f.** $2\frac{3}{4}$ **g.** $3\frac{1}{8}$

Problem set 123

1. On a five-day trip, the Jansens drove 1400 miles. What
(56) was the average number of miles the Jansens drove on each of the five days?

2. Estimate the product of 634 and 186 by rounding both
(69) numbers to the nearest hundred before multiplying.

3. (a) $\dfrac{1}{10} = \dfrac{\square}{100}$
(89)

(b) What percent equals the fraction $\frac{1}{10}$?

4. The weight of an object on the moon is $\frac{1}{6}$ of the weight
(50) of the same object on earth. A person on earth who
weighs 108 pounds would weigh how many pounds
on the moon?

5. Name the number of shaded cir-
(123) cles as an improper fraction and
as a mixed number.

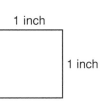

6. What is the perimeter of this 1
(60) inch square?

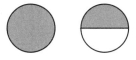

7. What fraction of a year is 3 months? What percent of a
(27) year is 3 months?

8. (a) Name this shape.
(93)
(b) How many faces does it have?

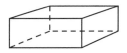

9. The denominators of $\frac{1}{6}$ and $\frac{1}{4}$ are 6 and 4. What is the
(122) least common multiple (LCM) of the denominators?

10. The arrow is pointing to what mixed number on this
(41) number line?

11. 4.239 + 25 + 6.79 + 12.5 + 986.47 + 83.925 + 43.0
(109)

12. 6.875 − (4 − 3.75)
(24)

13.
(119) $\begin{array}{r} 3.7 \\ \times\ 0.8 \\ \hline \end{array}$

14.
(121) $\begin{array}{r} 0.125 \\ \times\ \ 100 \\ \hline \end{array}$

15.
(120) $\begin{array}{r} 0.32 \\ \times\ 0.04 \\ \hline \end{array}$

16.
(104) $\dfrac{408}{17}$

17.
(104) $27\overline{)705}$

18.
(26) $5\overline{)\$17.70}$

19.
(47) $\begin{array}{r} 3\frac{7}{10} \\ +\ 4 \\ \hline \end{array}$

20.
(99) $\begin{array}{r} 5\frac{5}{8} \\ +\ \ \frac{1}{8} \\ \hline \end{array}$

21.
(70) $\begin{array}{r} 7 \\ -\ 4\frac{3}{10} \\ \hline \end{array}$

22.
(96) $\dfrac{5}{6}$ of 4

23.
(100) $\dfrac{3}{8} \times \dfrac{1}{2}$

24.
(106) $\dfrac{3}{8} \div \dfrac{1}{2}$

25. Write fractions equal to $\frac{1}{6}$ and $\frac{1}{4}$ that have denomina-
(89)   tors of 12. Then add the fractions. Remember to reduce your answer.

LESSON 124

Naming a Simple Probability

Facts Practice: Write 30 Percents as Fractions (Test K in Test Masters)

Mental Math: Describe how to estimate the product of $5\frac{3}{4}$ and $6\frac{7}{8}$. How many inches is one foot? two and a half feet?

a. $\frac{1}{8}$ of 24   **b.** $\frac{3}{8}$ of 24   **c.** $\frac{5}{8}$ of 24

d. 25% of 40, + 2, × 2, + 1, ÷ 5, × 3, + 1, ÷ 8, − 2

Problem Solving: Tamara had 24 square color tiles on her desk. She arranged them into a rectangle that was one row of 24 tiles. Then she arranged them into a rectangle that was two rows of 12 tiles.

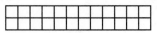

Draw two more rectangles Tamara could make using all 24 tiles.

Probability is a measure of **how likely** it is for an event to happen. We name a probability with a number from 0 to 1. If an event is **certain to happen,** then the probability of the event is 1. If an event is **certain not to happen,** then the probability of the event is 0. If it is uncertain whether or not an event will happen, then its probability is some fraction between 0 and 1.

Probability is a part of many games—card games, dice games, and spinner games. We will use a spinner to give us a better idea of probability.

The drawing below shows a circle equally divided into four parts labeled A, B, C, and D with an arrow (spinner) in the center. If this were an actual spinner, the arrow could be spun and then it would stop with its point in one of the parts of the circle (or exactly on a line, a possibility which we will ignore for now).

The probability that the spinner will stop in a certain part of the circle is equal to that part's fraction of the circle. Since part A is one fourth of the circle, the probability that the spinner will stop in part A is $\frac{1}{4}$.

Example What is the probability that the spinner will stop on each of the following?

(a) An even number?

(b) An odd number?

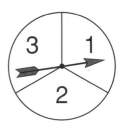

Solution (a) The circle is equally divided into 3 parts. Only 1 of the 3 parts has an even number in it. The even numbered part is $\frac{1}{3}$ of the circle. The probability that the arrow will stop on an even number is $\frac{1}{3}$.

(b) There are two parts with odd numbers in them. The odd numbered parts take up $\frac{2}{3}$ of the circle. The probability that the spinner will stop on an odd number is $\frac{2}{3}$.

Practice   What is the probability that the spinner will stop on each of the following?

   a. The number 2

   b. The number 4

   c. An odd number

   d. The number 5

   e. A number less than 5   **f.** A number less than 4

Problem set 124

1. Draw a circle and shade all but $\frac{1}{3}$ of it. What percent of
$^{(31)}$ the circle is shaded?

2. Which of these units of length would probably be used
$^{(83)}$ to measure the length of a room?

   A. Inches   B. Feet

   C. Miles   D. Light-years

3. A **line of symmetry** divides a shape into mirror
$^{(100)}$ images. Which of these does **not** show a line of
symmetry?

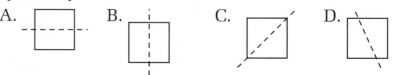

4. Michael's car can travel 28 miles on one gallon of gas.
$^{(21)}$ How far can his car travel on 16 gallons of gas?

5. Write $1\frac{3}{4}$ as an improper fraction.
$^{(123)}$

6. Write a fraction equal to $\frac{1}{2}$ that has the same
$^{(89)}$ denominator as $\frac{5}{6}$. Then subtract the fraction from $\frac{5}{6}$.
Remember to reduce your answer.

7. The denominators of $\frac{3}{8}$ and $\frac{5}{6}$ are 8 and 6, respectively.
$^{(122)}$ What is the least common multiple (LCM) of the
denominators?

8. What fraction names the probabil-
(124) ity that the spinner will stop in
the area marked A?

9. What is the probability that the
(124) spinner will stop in area B?

10. QS is 6 cm. RS is 2 cm. RT is 6 cm. Find QT.
(81)

11. 45 + 16.7 + 8.29 + 4.325
(109)

12. 4.2 − (3.2 − 1)   **13.** 0.75 × 0.05
(24)   (120)

14. 0.6 × 38   **15.** 100 × 7.5
(119)   (121)

16. $24.36 ÷ 12   **17.** 4600 ÷ 25
(103)   (104)

18. $6\dfrac{9}{10} - \dfrac{1}{10}$ **19.** $5\dfrac{4}{9} + 3\dfrac{5}{9}$
(99)   (101)

20. $4 \div \dfrac{1}{8}$ **21.** $4 \times \dfrac{1}{8}$
(106)   (100)

22. At the Little League baseball game there were 18
(107) players and 30 spectators. What was the ratio of
players to spectators at the game?

23. (a) What percent of the rectangle
(31)   is shaded?

  (b) What percent of the rectangle
       is not shaded?

24. (a) Write the reduced fraction equal to 60%.
(118)
  (b) Write the reduced fraction equal to 70%.

25. A loop of string can be arranged to
(60) form a rectangle that is 12 inches
long and 6 inches wide. If the
same loop of string is arranged to
form a square, what would be the
length of each side of the square?

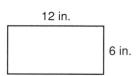

12 in.

6 in.

LESSON 125

Calculating Areas of Rectangles

Facts Practice: Write 30 Percents as Fractions (Test K in Test Masters)

Mental Math: The sides of a square are 5 inches long. What is the perimeter of the square? What is the area of the square?
How many ounces is a pound? two and a half pounds?

a. 25% of 80   **b.** 50% of 80   **c.** 75% of 80

Problem Solving: The uppercase letter B has a horizontal line of symmetry. List all the uppercase letters of the alphabet that have a horizontal line of symmetry.

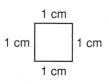

We measure the area enclosed by a polygon by counting the number of squares needed to cover the area. We agree to use squares of specific sizes to measure area.

A square that has sides 1 centimeter long is called a **square centimeter.** This is the actual size of a square centimeter.

1 cm

1 cm   1 cm

1 cm

A square that has sides 1 inch long is called a **square inch.** This is the actual size of a square inch.

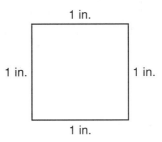

A square with sides 1 meter long is a **square meter.** A square with sides 1 foot long is a **square foot.** We use the abbreviation "sq." to stand for the word *square.* These squares are bigger than this book and are used to measure large areas such as the area of the floor of a room. Even larger areas may be measured with square kilometers or square miles.

We have noted that it is necessary to draw figures in reduced size so they will fit on a page. In the following example we have drawn the figure smaller than 2 inches by 3 inches. We do this so that the figure will fit in the space we have.

Example   How many square inches are needed to cover the area of this rectangle? (Be sure to label your answer.)

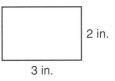

Solution   The length of the rectangle is 3 inches, so we can fit 3 square-inch stickers along the length. The width is 2 inches, so we can fit 2 square-inch stickers along the width. Two rows of three means that we could cover the area with **6 sq. in.**

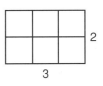

Practice What is the area of each rectangle? Draw the squares and count them.

a.
3 cm

4 cm

b.
3 ft

c.
2 in.

5 in.

d.
2 m

1 m

Problem set 125

1. Jack was 48 inches tall. The giant was 24 feet tall. How
(36) many feet taller than Jack was the giant?

2. Name the number of shaded circles as an improper
(123) fraction and as a mixed number.

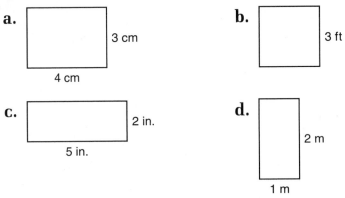

3. What fraction names the probabil-
(124) ity that the spinner will stop in
the area marked A?

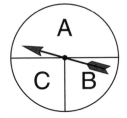

4. What is the probability that the
(124) spinner will stop in area B?

5. The arrow is pointing to what mixed number on this
(41) number line?

7   8

6. What time is $1\frac{1}{2}$ hours after 11:40 a.m.?
(29)

7. Which pair of fractions has the same denominator?
(23)

A. $\frac{1}{3}, \frac{1}{4}$ B. $\frac{4}{3}, \frac{4}{2}$ C. $\frac{1}{4}, \frac{3}{4}$

8. The denominators of $\frac{2}{5}$ and $\frac{2}{3}$ are 5 and 3, respectively.
(122) Find the least common multiple (LCM) of the denominators.

9. What is the perimeter of this
(60) rectangle?

10. How many square inches cover
(125) the area of this rectangle?

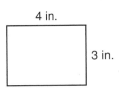

4 in.

3 in.

11. 42.98 + 50 + 23.5 + 0.025
(109)

12. How much greater than 5.18 is 6? Use words to write
(77) your answer.

13.   0.375
(121) $\times$ 10

14.   0.14
(120) $\times$ 0.06

15.   7.8
(119) $\times$ 9

16. 2340 ÷ 30
(61)

17. $18\overline{)2340}$
(104)

18. $7\overline{)8765}$
(26)

19. $\frac{5}{6} + 1\frac{5}{6}$
(101)

20. $7\frac{5}{8} - 7\frac{1}{8}$
(99)

21. $\frac{4}{5} \times \frac{2}{3}$
(86)

22. $\frac{4}{5} \div \frac{2}{3}$
(106)

23. (a) $\frac{2}{5} = \frac{\square}{15}$ (b) $\frac{2}{3} = \frac{\square}{15}$
(89)

24. In problem 23 you made fractions equal to $\frac{2}{5}$ and $\frac{2}{3}$
(101) with denominators of 15. Add the fractions you made. Remember to convert your answer to a mixed number.

25. All five sides of this pentagon are equal in length.
(60) What is the perimeter of this pentagon?

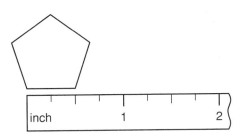

LESSON 126

Probability and Chance

Facts Practice: Write 30 Percents as Fractions (Test K in Test Masters)

Mental Math: The sides of a square are six inches long. What is its area? What is its perimeter?

    a. Simplify: $\frac{14}{12}, \frac{15}{12}, \frac{16}{12}$ **b.** $\frac{1}{7}$ of 35   **c.** $\frac{2}{7}$ of 35   **d.** $\frac{3}{7}$ of 35

Problem Solving: There are 50 pennies in a roll, 40 nickels in a roll, 50 dimes in a roll, and 40 quarters in a roll. What is the total value of two rolls of pennies, two rolls of nickels, two rolls of dimes, and two rolls of quarters?

Probability and chance are two ways to describe how likely an event is to happen. To state a probability, we use a fraction (or a fraction converted to a decimal number). To state a chance, we use a percent. The scale below shows the ranges of probability and chance.

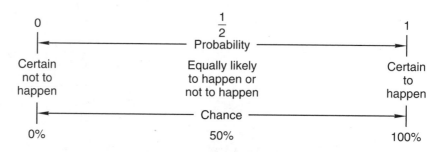

When a meteorologist states that the chance of rain is 50%, the meteorologist is saying that it is equally likely to rain or not to rain. If the chance of rain rises to 80%, it is more likely to rain. If the chance drops to 20%, then it may rain, but it probably will not rain.

Example 1   (a) What is the probability that the spinner will stop on a number greater than 1?

         (b) What is the chance of spinning a number greater than 1?

Solution   (a) There are four regions of equal size. Three of the four regions have numbers greater than 1. So the probability that the spinner will stop on a number greater than 1 is $\frac{3}{4}$.

(b) The chance of spinning a number greater than 1 is the percent equal to $\frac{3}{4}$, which is **75%**.

Example 2   (a) What is the probability of rolling an even number with one toss of one number cube?

(b) What is the chance of rolling an even number with one toss of one number cube?

Solution   (a) A number cube has six faces numbered one through six. Three of the numbers are even (2, 4, 6). So three of the six possibilities are even numbers. The probability is $\frac{3}{6}$, which reduces to $\frac{1}{2}$.

(b) The chance of the same event is the percent equal to $\frac{1}{2}$, which is **50%**.

Practice   a. What is the probability that the spinner will stop on 3?

b. What is the chance of spinning a 4?

c. What is the probability of spinning an even number?

d. What is the chance that the spinner will stop on an odd number?

e. If the chance of rain is 40%, is it more likely to rain or to not rain?

Problem set   **1.** (a) What is the probability of roll-
126   (126)   ing a six with a single toss of
one number cube?

(b) What is the chance of rolling a
six with one toss of a single
number cube?

2. The weather forecast states that the chance of rain is
(126)   60%. What is the chance that it will not rain?

3. Tapes were on sale, 4 tapes for $14. At that price, what
(55)   would be the cost of 10 tapes?

4. Two cups equal a pint. Two pints equal a quart. Four
(95)   quarts equal a gallon. How many cups equal a gallon?

5. Jubilee finished a 64-kilometer bike ride in 4 hours.
(56)   She rode at an average speed of how many kilometers
per hour?

6. How many decades is half a century?
(27)

7. Estimate the quotient of $7\frac{3}{5}$ divided by $1\frac{7}{8}$.
(111)

8. (a) A centimeter is what fraction of a meter?
(83)   (b) A centimeter is what percent of a meter?

9. Write $1\frac{5}{6}$ as an improper fraction.
(123)

10. (a) Write $1\frac{1}{10}$ as a decimal number.
(72)
(b) Write $1\frac{1}{100}$ as a decimal number.

11. 6 + 7.4 + 8.56 + 0.3 + 12.1
(109)

12. Twenty-five is how much more than twenty and five
(36)   tenths?

13.   3.6   **14.**   0.13   **15.**   4.75
(119) × 0.7   (120) × 0.7   (121) ×   10

16. 6)$\overline{\$8.76}$
(26)

17. 3751 ÷ 15
(104)

18. 30)$\overline{5970}$
(61)

19. $6\frac{11}{12} + 1\frac{5}{12}$
(101)

20. $6 - 3\frac{1}{9}$
(70)

21. $6 \times \frac{3}{8}$
(101)

22. $\frac{3}{4} \div \frac{1}{2}$
(106)

23. Write fractions equal to $\frac{3}{5}$ and $\frac{3}{4}$ that have denomina-
(89) tors of 20. Subtract the smaller fraction from the larger fraction.

Below is a magic square. In this magic square the numbers in each row and each column should add up to the same total. In this magic square there are three missing numbers.

24. What should be the sum of each
(54) Magic Square row and column?

25. What number should be written
(54) in place of the *y*?

Magic Square

2	9	4
x	y	3
6	z	8

LESSON 127

Adding and Subtracting Fractions, Part 2

Facts Practice: Write 30 Percents as Fractions (Test K in Test Masters)

Mental Math: A rectangle is 6 inches long and 4 inches wide. What is its perimeter? What is its area?
How many seconds is a minute? two and a half minutes?

a. 10% of $300   **b.** 10% of $30   **c.** 10% of $3
d. $\sqrt{16}, \times 5, - 6, \div 7, + 8, \times 9, \div 10$

Problem Solving: The local newspaper sells advertising for $20 per column inch per day. An ad that is 2 columns wide and 4 inches long is 8 (2 × 4) column inches and costs $160 (8 column inches × $20) each day. What would be the total cost of running a three-column by eight-inch ad for two days?

The fractions $\frac{1}{4}$ and $\frac{3}{4}$ have common denominators. The fractions $\frac{1}{2}$ and $\frac{1}{4}$ do not have common denominators. Fractions have common denominators when they have the same denominators.

Same denominators   Different denominators

$$\frac{1}{4} \longleftrightarrow \frac{3}{4} \qquad\qquad \frac{1}{2} \longleftrightarrow \frac{1}{4}$$

To add or subtract fractions that have different denominators, we first change the name of one or more of the fractions so that they have common denominators. The least common multiple (LCM) of the denominators is the lowest common denominator of the fractions. The denominators of $\frac{1}{2}$ and $\frac{1}{4}$ are 2 and 4. The least common multiple of 2 and 4 is 4. So the lowest common denominator for halves and fourths is 4.

Example   Add: $\frac{1}{2} + \frac{1}{4}$

Solution   Since $\frac{1}{2}$ and $\frac{1}{4}$ have different denominators, we change the name of $\frac{1}{2}$ so that both fractions will have a denominator of 4. We change $\frac{1}{2}$ to fourths by multiplying by $\frac{2}{2}$ to give us $\frac{2}{4}$.

$$\frac{1}{2} \times \mathbf{1} \frac{2}{2} = \frac{2}{4}$$

Then we add $\frac{2}{4}$ and $\frac{1}{4}$ to get $\frac{3}{4}$.

$$\frac{2}{4} + \frac{1}{4} = \frac{3}{4}$$

Practice*   As you do the practice problems, follow these steps:

1. Figure out what the new denominator should be. In these practice problems, the common denominator is the larger of the two denominators.
2. Change the name of one or both fractions.
3. Add or subtract the fractions that have the same denominators.

a. $\frac{1}{2} + \frac{1}{8}$ **b.** $\frac{1}{2} - \frac{1}{4}$ **c.** $\frac{3}{4} + \frac{1}{8}$

d. $\frac{2}{3} - \frac{1}{9}$ **e.** $\frac{1}{6} + \frac{1}{2}$ **f.** $\frac{5}{8} - \frac{1}{2}$

g. $\frac{1}{6} + \frac{2}{3}$ **h.** $\frac{5}{6} - \frac{2}{3}$

Problem set 127

1. Draw a circle. Shade all but $\frac{1}{6}$ of it. What percent of the circle is shaded?
   (31)

2. In 1875 Bret Harte wrote a story about the California Gold Rush of 1849. How many years after the Gold Rush did he write the story?
   (27)

3. (a) What is the chance of the
(126)   spinner stopping on 4?

(b) What is the probability the
spinner will stop on a number
less than 4?

4. A **line of symmetry** divides a shape into mirror
(100) images. Which of these does not show a line of
symmetry?

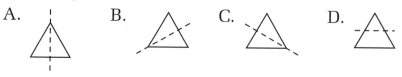

A.   B.   C.   D.

5. What time is 25 hours after 6 a.m.?
(29)

6. Name the number of shaded circles as an improper
(123) fraction and as a mixed number.

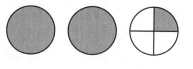

7. Alberto counted 100 cars and 60 trucks driving by the
(107) school. What was the ratio of trucks to cars that
Alberto counted driving by the school?

8. What is the perimeter of this
(60) square?

5 mm

9. How many square millimeters cover the area of this
(125) square?

10. *AC* is 70 mm. *BC* is 40 mm. *BD* is 60 mm. Find *AD*.
(81)

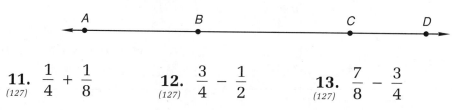

11. $\dfrac{1}{4} + \dfrac{1}{8}$ **12.** $\dfrac{3}{4} - \dfrac{1}{2}$ **13.** $\dfrac{7}{8} - \dfrac{3}{4}$
(127)   (127)   (127)

14. $\frac{3}{5} \times 3$
(101)

15. $\frac{3}{5} \div 3$
(106)

16. $3 \div \frac{3}{5}$
(106)

17. 45.275 + 16.18 + 125
(109)

18. Forty-two is how much greater than the decimal
(77) number three and sixty-four hundredths? Use words to write your answer.

19. 6.5 × 100
(121)

20. 4.6 × 8
(119)

21. 0.18 × 0.4
(120)

22. $10\overline{)\$13.20}$
(61)

23. $12\overline{)\$13.20}$
(103)

24. 1470 ÷ 42
(104)

25. Which angle in quadrilateral
(33) *ABCD* is an obtuse angle?

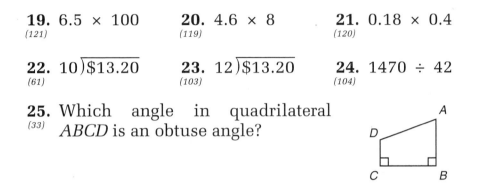

LESSON 128

Adding and Subtracting Mixed Numbers, Part 2

> **Facts Practice:** Write 30 Percents as Fractions (Test K in Test Masters)
>
> **Mental Math:** A floor tile with sides one foot long has a perimeter of how many inches? Its area is how many square feet? how many square inches?
>
> **a.** Reduce: $\frac{8}{12}, \frac{9}{12}, \frac{10}{12}$ **b.** $\frac{2}{3}$ of 12 **c.** $\frac{3}{4}$ of 12 **d.** $\frac{5}{6}$ of 12
>
> **Problem Solving:** How many 1-inch cubes can fit in a box with inside dimensions of 4 inches by 3 inches by 2 inches?

When we add and subtract mixed numbers, we first write the fractions with common denominators. We use the same method we learned in Lesson 127.

Example $3\frac{1}{2}$
$+ 1\frac{1}{6}$
___

Solution   We work with the fraction part of each mixed number first. We change $\frac{1}{2}$ to $\frac{3}{6}$ by multiplying by $\frac{3}{3}$.

$$\frac{1}{2} \times \frac{3}{3} = \frac{3}{6}$$

Then we add the whole numbers to whole numbers and fractions to fractions and reduce the answer when possible.

$$3\frac{3}{6}$$
$$+ 1\frac{1}{6}$$
$$4\frac{4}{6} = 4\frac{2}{3}$$

Practice*   **a.** $3\frac{1}{4}$ **b.** $2\frac{1}{8}$ **c.** $3\frac{1}{2}$ **d.** $2\frac{3}{4}$
$+ 2\frac{1}{2}$ $+ 5\frac{1}{2}$ $- 1\frac{1}{6}$ $- 2\frac{1}{2}$

e. $5\frac{5}{8}$ **f.** $3\frac{3}{10}$ **g.** $4\frac{7}{8}$ **h.** $4\frac{1}{2}$
$+ 1\frac{1}{4}$ $+ 1\frac{1}{5}$ $- 1\frac{1}{2}$ $- 1\frac{1}{10}$

Problem set   **1.** There were four rows of desks in the room. There were
128   (56)   eight desks in the first row, six desks in the second row, five desks in the third row, and nine desks in the fourth row. If all the desks were arranged in four equal rows, how many desks would be in each row?

2. Estimate the sum of 37.3 and 46.91 by rounding to the
(115)   nearest whole number before adding.

3. If high tide is at 9:15 a.m., at what time is low tide if it
(29)   is 6 hours and 12 minutes later?

4. A loop of string 1 yard long is formed into a square.
(83) How many inches long is each side of the square?

5. Ten of the 50 prospectors found gold.
(117)
    (a) What percent of the prospectors found gold?

    (b) What was the ratio of prospectors who found gold to prospectors who did not find gold?

6. (a) Write the reduced fraction equal to 80%.
(118)
    (b) Write the reduced fraction equal to 90%.

7. Four years in a row is how many days?
(27)

8. Write $2\frac{3}{4}$ as an improper fraction.
(123)

9. In rectangle *ABCD*, *AB* is 2 cm
(60) and *BC* is 3 cm.

    (a) How many segments one centimeter long would it take to reach around the rectangle?

    (b) How many square stickers that are one centimeter on each side would it take to cover the area of the rectangle?

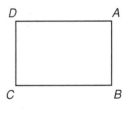

10. *AC* is 48 mm. *BC* is 20 mm. *BD* is 64 mm. Find *AD*.
(81)

$$\overset{A}{\underset{\bullet}{\vphantom{|}}} \qquad \overset{B}{\underset{\bullet}{\vphantom{|}}} \qquad \overset{C}{\underset{\bullet}{\vphantom{|}}} \qquad \overset{D}{\underset{\bullet}{\vphantom{|}}}$$

11. $\begin{array}{r} 2\frac{1}{2} \\ + 1\frac{1}{4} \\ \hline \end{array}$
(128)

12. $\begin{array}{r} 3\frac{7}{10} \\ + 1\frac{1}{5} \\ \hline \end{array}$
(128)

13. $\begin{array}{r} 4\frac{5}{8} \\ - 1\frac{1}{4} \\ \hline \end{array}$
(128)

14. $\begin{array}{r} 6\frac{1}{2} \\ - 1\frac{1}{6} \\ \hline \end{array}$
(128)

15. 29.32 + 9.3 + 16.7 + 8
(109)

16. 25.3 − (4.2 − 1)
(24)

17. 3.65
(121) × 10

18. 0.27
(120) × 0.30

19. 0.43
(119) × 0.27

20. 4250 ÷ 25
(104)

21. 12)‾912‾
(104)

22. 6 × $\frac{3}{4}$
(101)

23. 6 ÷ $\frac{3}{4}$
(106)

Read this information. Then answer questions 24 and 25.

Dan's car holds 12.6 gallons of gas. He went to the gas station and filled the tank with 10.0 gallons, costing 97¢ per gallon.

24. How many gallons of gas were still in the tank when
(54) Dan went to the gas station?

25. If Dan paid for the gas with a $10 bill, how much
(54) money did he get back?

LESSON
129

Dividing a Decimal Number by a Whole Number

Facts Practice: Write 30 Percents as Fractions (Test K in Test Masters)

Mental Math: Describe how to estimate the total cost of 32.6 liters of gasoline at 0.49\frac{9}{10}$ per liter.
How many minutes is an hour? three and a half hours?

a. 25% of $16   **b.** 50% of $16   **c.** 75% of $16
d. $\frac{1}{5}$ of 20, × 4, − 4, ÷ 4, + 4, × 4

Problem Solving: Shirts are on sale for 10% off. The regular price is $30. Ten percent of $30 is $3. So $3 is taken off the regular price, making the sale price $27. Pants are on sale for 25% off. The regular price is $40. What is the sale price?

Dividing a decimal number by a whole number is like dividing money by a whole number. The decimal point in the quotient is directly above the decimal point in the division box. The memory cue reminds us that the decimal point in the answer will be straight up from the decimal point in the number inside the division box. The symbol "÷ W" in the chart means "division by a whole number." We follow a different rule when dividing by a decimal number.

Decimals Chart

+ −	×	÷ W
Line up the decimal points.	Multiply. Then count decimal places.	up
Place decimal points on whole numbers. Fill empty places with zero.		

Example 1 $2\overline{)4.8}$

Solution   We are dividing by 2, which is a whole number. We remember "up" and place a decimal point in the answer straight up from the decimal point inside the division box. Then we divide and get **2.4**.

$$\begin{array}{r} 2.4 \\ 2\overline{)4.8} \\ \underline{4} \\ 0\,8 \\ \underline{8} \\ 0 \end{array}$$ decimal point "up"

Example 2 $0.42 \div 3$

Solution   We rewrite the problem using a division box. The decimal point in the answer is straight up. Then we divide and get **0.14**.

$$\begin{array}{r} 0.14 \\ 3\overline{)0.42} \\ \underline{3} \\ 12 \\ \underline{12} \\ 0 \end{array}$$ decimal point "up"

Practice*   **a.** $4\overline{)0.52}$ **b.** $6\overline{)3.6}$ **c.** $0.85 \div 5$

d. $5\overline{)7.5}$ **e.** $5\overline{)0.65}$ **f.** $2.1 \div 3$

g. $3\overline{)0.51}$ **h.** $4\overline{)0.64}$ **i.** $0.58 \div 2$

**Problem set
129**

1. Write the following sentence using digits and symbols:
(81)   "The sum of one sixth and one third is one half."

2. Gilbert scored half of his team's points. Juan scored 8
(54) fewer points than Gilbert. The team scored 36 points. How many points did Juan score?

3. The first day of winter is December 21. The first day of
(27) summer is 6 months later. What is the date of the first day of summer?

4. (a) What is the probability that
(126)   the spinner will stop on a
        number greater than one?

   (b) What is the chance of spin-
       ning a three?

5. Name the shaded part of this rect-
(72) angle as a fraction, as a decimal, and as a percent.

6. If each side of an octagon is 6 inches, then the
(60) perimeter of the octagon is how many feet?

7. Name the total number of
(123) shaded circles as an improper fraction and as a mixed number.

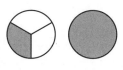

8. What is the largest four-digit odd number that has the
(2) digits 7, 8, 9, and 0 used once each?

9. In rectangle $ABCD$, which seg-
(32) ment is parallel to $\overline{AB}$?

10. In rectangle *ABCD*, *AB* is 3 cm
(60) and *BC* is 4 cm.

  (a) What is the perimeter of the rectangle?

  (b) What is the area of the rectangle?

11. *KL* is 56 mm. *LM* is half of *KL*. *MN* is half of *LM*. Find
(81) *KN*.

12. $16 + 3.17 + 49 + 1.125$
(109)

13. How much greater is 3.42 than 1.242?
(112)

14. 4.3×100 **15.** 6.4×3.7
(121) (119)

16. 0.36×0.04 **17.** $2\overline{)3.6}$
(120) (129)

18. $3\overline{)0.51}$ **19.** 13.5×9
(129) (119)

20. $\begin{array}{r} 2\frac{1}{8} \\ + 1\frac{3}{4} \\ \hline \end{array}$ **21.** $\begin{array}{r} \frac{1}{3} \\ + \frac{1}{6} \\ \hline \end{array}$ **22.** $\begin{array}{r} \frac{7}{10} \\ - \frac{1}{2} \\ \hline \end{array}$ **23.** $\begin{array}{r} 3\frac{9}{10} \\ - \frac{1}{5} \\ \hline \end{array}$
(128) (127) (127) (128)

24. $4 \times \dfrac{3}{2}$ **25.** $\dfrac{3}{4} \div \dfrac{1}{4}$
(101) (106)

LESSON 130

Dividing Decimal Numbers: Fill Empty Places with Zero

Facts Practice: Write 30 Percents as Fractions (Test K in Test Masters)

Mental Math: A square with sides one yard long has an area of how many square feet? Its perimeter is how many feet?

a. $\frac{1}{3}$ of 100   **b.** $\frac{2}{3}$ of 100   **c.** $\frac{3}{3}$ of 100

d. 50% of $\sqrt{36}$, $\times\, 7$, $-\, 1$, $\div\, 4$, $\times\, 8$, $+\, 2$, $\div\, 6$

Problem Solving: At Video World the tape costs $20. At Movie Mania the price is 10% more. Ten percent of $20 is $2. So the price at Movie Mania is $2 more than $20, which is $22. The price of a tape rewinder at Video World is $16. At Movie Mania the price of a rewinder is 25% more. What is the price of the rewinder at Movie Mania?

The memory cue for dividing a decimal number by a whole number is "up." Sometimes we need to fill empty places with zero.

If $0.12 is shared equally by 3 people, then each person will receive $0.04. The division looks like this. The decimal point is up. Then we divide and fill the empty places with zero.

$$\begin{array}{r} \$0.04 \\ 3\overline{)\$0.12} \\ \underline{12} \\ 0 \end{array}$$

Example 1   0.15 ÷ 3

Solution   The first number goes inside the division box. The decimal point in the answer is straight up. Divide and fill empty places with zero.

$$\begin{array}{r} \mathbf{0.05} \\ 3\overline{)0.15} \\ \underline{15} \\ 0 \end{array}$$

Example 2   0.024 ÷ 3

Solution   The first number is inside the box. The decimal point is straight up. Divide and fill empty places with zero.

$$\begin{array}{r} \mathbf{0.008} \\ 3\overline{)0.024} \end{array}$$

Practice*   **a.** $4\overline{)0.16}$ **b.** $0.35 \div 7$

c. $5\overline{)0.025}$ **d.** $0.08 \div 4$

e. $6\overline{)0.24}$ **f.** $0.012 \div 3$

g. $3\overline{)0.06}$ **h.** $0.009 \div 3$

Problem set 130

1.
(129) Copy the decimals chart in Lesson 129.

2.
(27) It takes 6 months to grow a watermelon from seed. Jill planted seeds in March. In what month will the watermelon be ripe?

3.
(87) The parrot weighed $\frac{3}{4}$ pound. How many ounces did it weigh?

4.
(126) If the chance of rain is 20%, what is the chance it will not rain?

5.
(118) (a) Write the fraction equal to 1%.

(b) Write the fraction equal to 2%.

6.
(83) A string 1 meter long is made into a square. How many centimeters long is each side of the square?

7.
(123) Name the number of shaded circles as an improper fraction and as a mixed number.

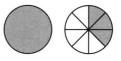

8.
(123) Write the mixed number $1\frac{1}{3}$ as an improper fraction. Then multiply the improper fraction by $\frac{3}{4}$. What is the product?

9. (a) Write $1\frac{3}{10}$ as a decimal number.
(75)

    (b) Write $1\frac{3}{100}$ as a decimal number.

10. (a) What is the perimeter of this
(60)   rectangle?

    (b) What is the area of this
     rectangle?

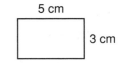

11. *QR* is $1\frac{1}{4}$ inches. *RS* is 2 inches. *ST* is $1\frac{1}{2}$ inches. Find
(81) *QT*.

Q   R   S   T

12. Jonathan was paid \$32.50 for 5 hours of work. He
(56) earned an average of how many dollars per hour?

13. $6.5 - (3.42 - 1)$
(24)

14. 0.45 **15.** 62 **16.** 0.16
(121) $\underline{\times \quad 10}$ (119) $\underline{\times 4.8}$ (120) $\underline{\times \quad 0.3}$

17. $4\overline{)0.024}$ **18.** $10\overline{)0.180}$ **19.** $18\overline{)640}$
(130)   (130)   (104)

20. $\frac{5}{6}$ **21.** $2\frac{1}{4}$ **22.** $\frac{2}{3}$ **23.** $4\frac{7}{8}$
(127) $\underline{+\ \frac{1}{2}}$ (128) $\underline{+\ \ \frac{1}{8}}$ (127) $\underline{-\ \frac{1}{6}}$ (128) $\underline{-\ 1\frac{3}{4}}$

24. $\frac{3}{5} \times \frac{1}{2}$ **25.** $\frac{3}{5} \div \frac{1}{2}$
(86)   (106)

LESSON
131

Dividing Decimal Numbers: Keep Dividing

Symmetry Trick: Materials needed: Pencil and paper, mirror or reflective surface, scissors (optional)

The word BOB has a horizontal line of symmetry because each of its letters has a horizontal line of symmetry.

-B⊖B-

If we fold under or cut away the upper half of the word along the line of symmetry, the lower half of the word looks like this: **DUD**

By placing the paper against a mirror we can make the upper half of the word "reappear."

mirror

B̶O̶B̶

Make up a word that has a horizontal line of symmetry and try the activity for yourself. How does this "trick" work?

We usually do not write remainders with decimal division problems. The procedure we will follow for now is to continue dividing until the "remainder" is zero. In order to continue the division, we may need to attach extra zeros to the decimal number that is being divided. **Remember, attaching extra zeros to the back of a decimal number does not change the value of the number.**

Example 1 $0.6 \div 5$

Solution   The first number goes inside. The decimal point is straight up. As we divide, we attach a zero and keep dividing.

$$
\begin{array}{r}
0.12 \\
5\overline{)0.60} \\
\underline{5} \\
10 \\
\underline{10} \\
0
\end{array}
$$

Example 2 $0.3 \div 4$

Solution   As we divide, we attach zeros and keep dividing. We fill empty places in the answer with zero.

$$
\begin{array}{r}
0.075 \\
4\overline{)0.300} \\
\underline{28} \\
20 \\
\underline{20} \\
0
\end{array}
$$

Practice*   **a.** 0.6 ÷ 4   **b.** 0.12 ÷ 5   **c.** 0.1 ÷ 4

d. 0.1 ÷ 2   **e.** 0.4 ÷ 5   **f.** 1.4 ÷ 8

g. 0.5 ÷ 4   **h.** 0.6 ÷ 8   **i.** 0.3 ÷ 4

Problem set   **1.** Which of these shows two parallel line segments that
131   (32)   are not horizontal?

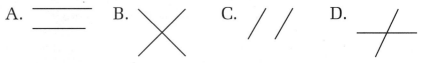

A.   B.   C.   D.

2. Estimate the product of $6\frac{1}{10}$ and $4\frac{7}{8}$ by rounding both
(111)   numbers to the nearest whole number before you
multiply.

3. How many 12¢ pencils can be bought with one dollar?
(80)

4. A line of symmetry divides a shape into mirror
(100)   images. Which of these dotted lines is not a line of
symmetry?

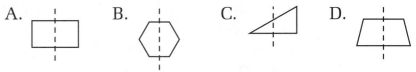

A.   B.   C.   D.

5. The first roll knocked down 3 of the 10 bowling pins.
(117)   What percent of the pins were still standing?

6. (a) Write the fraction equal to 4%.
(118)   (b) Write the fraction equal to 5%.

7. Name the total number of shaded circles as an
(123)   improper fraction and as a mixed number.

8. Write the mixed number $1\frac{3}{8}$ as an improper fraction.
(123)   Then multiply the improper fraction by $\frac{1}{2}$. What is the
product?

9. A stop sign has the shape of an 8-sided polygon. What
(39) is the name for a polygon that has 8 sides?

10. List these numbers in order of size from least to
(42) greatest:

$$\frac{5}{3}, \frac{5}{6}, \frac{5}{5}$$

11. The perimeter of this square is 8
(60) centimeters.

(a) How long is each side of this
square?

(b) What is the area of this
square?

12. 49.35 + 25 + 3.725 + 0.08
(109)

13. Subtract 1.234 from 2 and use words to write the
(116) answer.

14. 3.6 × 87   **15.** 4.2 × 100   **16.** 0.5 × 0.17
(119)   (121)   (120)

17. 0.6 ÷ 4   **18.** 0.6 ÷ 10   **19.** 24$\overline{)850}$
(131)   (130)   (104)

20. $3\frac{1}{9}$ **21.** $\frac{1}{3}$ **22.** $\frac{7}{8}$ **23.** $4\frac{1}{2}$
(128) $+ \ \frac{1}{3}$ (127) $+ \frac{5}{6}$ (127) $- \frac{1}{4}$ (128) $- 1\frac{3}{10}$

24. $6 \times \frac{2}{3}$ **25.** $6 \div \frac{2}{3}$
(101)   (106)

LESSON
132

Dividing Decimal Numbers by 10, 100, and 1000

> **Problem Solving:** A palindrome is a word like "mom" or a number like 52325 that reads the same backward or forward.
>
> **a.** Use the letters a, a, d, m, m to make a word that is a palindrome.
> **b.** What is the largest palindrome you can make with the digits 3, 4, 4, 5, 5?
> **c.** What is the smallest palindrome you can make with the digits 3, 4, 4, 5, 5?
> **d.** What is a four-letter palindrome that names a time of day?

When we divide a number by 10, we find that the answer has the same digits, but the digits have shifted one place to the right.

$$34.$$
$$10\overline{)340.}$$
$$.34$$
$$10\overline{)3.40}$$

We may use this pattern to find the answer to a decimal division problem when the divisor is 10. The shortcut is very similar to the method we use when multiplying a decimal number by 10. In both cases it is the digits which are shifting places, but we can make it appear that the digits are shifting places by shifting the decimal point instead. To divide by 10, we shift the decimal point one place to the left.

Example 1   Divide: $3.4 \div 10$

Solution   To divide a number by 10, we may shift the decimal point to the left one place. We see that the answer is **0.34.**

$$3.4 \div 10 = .34 \qquad 10\overline{)3.40}^{\;0.34}$$

Dividing by 100 is like dividing by 10 twice. When we divide by 100, we move the decimal point two places to the left. When we divide by 1000, we move the decimal point three places to the left. We move the decimal point the same number of places as there are zeros in the numbers 10 or 100 or 1000. We will remember which way to move the decimal point if we keep in mind that dividing a number into 10 or 100 or 1000 parts produces **smaller** numbers. As a decimal moves to the left, the value of the number is less and less.

Example 2   Divide: $3.5 \div 100$

Solution   When we divide by 10 or 100 or 1000, we may find the answer mentally without performing the division algorithm. To divide by 100, we shift the decimal point two places. We know that the answer will be less than 3.5, so we remember to shift the decimal point to the left. We fill the empty place with a zero.

$$3.5 \div 100 = \mathbf{0.035}$$

Practice
a. $2.5 \div 10$	**b.** $32.4 \div 10$
c. $2.5 \div 100$	**d.** $32.4 \div 100$
e. $2.5 \div 1000$	**f.** $32.4 \div 1000$
g. $64. \div 10$	**h.** $1.25 \div 100$
i. $64. \div 100$	**j.** $630. \div 10$
k. $64. \div 1000$	**l.** $5. \div 1000$

Problem set 132

1. The books were piled in four stacks. Becky counted 5
(56) books in one stack, 7 books in another stack, and 8 and 12 books, respectively, in the remaining stacks. If Becky rearranges the books so that the number of books in the four stacks are equal, how many books will be in each stack?

2. Write the following sentence using digits and
(37) symbols.

"The sum of one half and one fourth is less than one."

3. A mile is 1760 yards. How many yards is $\frac{3}{4}$ of a mile?
(83)

4. If the sun rises at 6 a.m. and sets at 5 p.m., at what
(29) time is it halfway across the sky?

5. Name the shaded part of the
(76) square as a fraction, as a decimal
number, and as a percent.

6. Tom is about to flip a dime.
(126)
(a) What is the chance that the dime will lands
"heads" up?

(b) What is the probability that the dime will lands
"tails" up?

7. Name the total number of shaded circles as an
(123) improper fraction and as a mixed number.

8. Write the mixed number $2\frac{3}{4}$ as an improper fraction.
(123) Then multiply the improper fraction by $\frac{1}{3}$.

9. (a) What is the perimeter of this
(60)   rectangle?

(b) What is the area of this
rectangle?

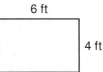

10. *AB* is 36 mm. *CD* is half of *AB*. *AD* is 68 mm. Find *BC*.
(81)

Solve problems 11 and 12 by mentally shifting the decimal
point:

11. 3.5 ÷ 10   **12.** 4.3 ÷ 100
(132)   (132)

13. 4.5 + 3.25 + 16 + 5
(109)

14. (4.6 − 3) − 1.59
(24)

15. 4.3 × 100
(121)

16. 0.37 × 0.06
(119)

17. 6.8 × 9.4
(119)

18. 4)$11.00
(26)

19. 7)8.33
(129)

20. 8)0.12
(131)

21. $1\frac{3}{5} + 2\frac{1}{10}$
(128)

22. $3\frac{1}{3} - 1\frac{1}{6}$
(128)

23. $\frac{5}{8} \times \frac{1}{2}$
(86)

24. $\frac{1}{2} \div \frac{5}{8}$
(106)

25. If $3a = 12$, then what number is equal to $10 - a$?
(20)

LESSON
133

Finding the Average of Two or More Numbers

Mental Math: The sides of a square are 12 inches long. What is the perimeter of the square? What is the area of the square?

How many millimeters is one centimeter? one hundred centimeters?

a. How much is 10% of $50?   **b.** How much is 10% **off** $50?

Problem Solving: What is the volume in cubic inches of a tissue box that is 9 inches long, 4 inches wide, and 3 inches high?

4 in.   9 in.

3 in.

We have found the average of numbers by making groups even. We have moved students from one line to another to make lines even. We have moved books from one pile to another to make piles even. We have moved water from one glass to another to make water levels even.

Sometimes it is not possible to move things around to make them even, but we can still find the average. Look at this example.

Example 1 Three boys weigh 108 pounds, 98 pounds, and 112 pounds, respectively. What is the average weight of the three boys?

Solution We cannot actually move weight from one boy to another, but we act **as though** we could. We first find the total weight. Then we evenly divide the total three ways because there are three boys.

Total weight: 108 + 98 + 112 = 318 pounds

Average weight: 318 ÷ 3 = 106 pounds

The average weight of the three boys is **106 pounds.**

Example 2 What is the average of 5, 7, 8, and 12?

Solution We can find the average of two or more numbers by following the same "add and divide" method. We add to find the total. Then we divide by the number of numbers, which, in this case, is 4.

Add: 5 + 7 + 8 + 12 = 32

Divide: 32 ÷ 4 = 8

The average of 5, 7, 8, and 12 is **8.**

Practice* Find the average of each group of numbers:

    a. 9, 7, 12, 12   **b.** 3, 3, 3, 5, 6

    c. 78, 84, 87   **d.** 300, 310

Problem set 133 **1.** Draw a quadrilateral that has two parallel horizontal
(39) sides and two parallel oblique sides.

2. Write the following sentence using digits and
(81) symbols:

"The sum of one half and one sixth is two thirds."

3. The "stars and stripes" became the official flag of the
(27) United States in 1777. The pledge of allegiance to the
flag was first used in 1892. The pledge came how
many years after the flag?

4. Name the unshaded part of the
(76) square as a fraction, as a decimal
number, and as a percent.

5. (a) What is the probability of
(126) spinning an even number?

(b) What is the chance of spinning an odd number?

6. Name the total number of shaded circles as an
(123) improper fraction and as a mixed number.

7. Write the mixed number $3\frac{1}{2}$ as an improper fraction.
(123) Multiply the improper fraction by $\frac{2}{3}$. Remember to
convert the product to a mixed number and reduce.

8. What is the average of 6, 7, 9, and 10?
(133)

9. What is the name for a polygon with five sides?
(39)

10. (a) What is the perimeter of the
(60) square?

(b) What is the area of the square?

10 mm

11. 29.325 + 7.5 + 123.7 + 4
(109)

12. 6.15 − (4 − 1.8)
(24)

13.   0.48
(121)   ×   10

14.   46.3
(119)   ×   47

15.   0.015
(120)   ×   5

16. 3.6 ÷ 100
(132)

17. 3.6 ÷ 5
(131)

18. 0.36 ÷ 9
(130)

19. $6\frac{5}{6} + 3\frac{1}{12}$
(128)

20. $5\frac{11}{12} - 2\frac{1}{2}$
(128)

21. $4 \times \frac{5}{6}$
(101)

22. $4 \div \frac{5}{6}$
(106)

23. The denominators of $\frac{3}{7}$ and $\frac{1}{2}$ are 7 and 2, respectively.
(89)   The least common multiple of 7 and 2 is 14. Rename both fractions so that the denominators are 14. Then add the fractions.

24. What temperature is shown on the thermometer?
(28)

25. Water freezes at 32°F. The temperature shown on this thermometer is how many degrees above freezing?
(28)

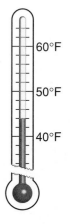

LESSON
134

Adding and Subtracting Fractions, Part 3

Mental Math: Describe how to estimate the cost for each pencil if an order for 1008 pencils costs $59.80.

a. How much is 10% of $30?   **b.** How much is 10% off $30?

c. How much is 10% more than $30?

Problem Solving: The largest and smallest five-digit palindromes that each have two different digits are 99899 and 10001. What are the largest and smallest five-digit palindromes that each have three different digits?

When we add or subtract fractions with different denominators, we sometimes need to change the name of both fractions.

The fractions $\frac{1}{2}$ and $\frac{1}{3}$ have different denominators. Before we add, we rename the fractions so that the fractions have common denominators.

$$\begin{array}{r} \frac{1}{2} \\ + \frac{1}{3} \\ \hline \end{array}$$

We choose a denominator to which both $\frac{1}{2}$ and $\frac{1}{3}$ may be changed. One way to choose a new denominator is to multiply the denominators of the two fractions. The denominators of $\frac{1}{2}$ and $\frac{1}{3}$ are 2 and 3, respectively. Multiplying 2 and 3, we get 6, which we can use for the new denominator.

Choose a new denominator.

$$\begin{array}{r} \frac{1}{2} = \frac{}{6} \\ + \frac{1}{3} = \frac{}{6} \\ \hline \end{array}$$

After we choose a new denominator, we multiply each fraction by a name for 1 which will make a fraction with the new denominator. Here we multiply $\frac{1}{2}$ by $\frac{3}{3}$ and $\frac{1}{3}$ by $\frac{2}{2}$.

$$\frac{1}{2} \times \mathbf{1}\frac{3}{3} = \frac{3}{6} \qquad \frac{1}{3} \times \mathbf{1}\frac{2}{2} = \frac{2}{6}$$

This gives us the fractions $\frac{3}{6}$ and $\frac{2}{6}$, which we add.

$$\frac{3}{6} + \frac{2}{6} = \frac{5}{6}$$

Example Subtract: $\frac{2}{3} - \frac{1}{2}$

Solution First we choose a new denominator for both fractions. One way to do this is to multiply the two denominators. We multiply 3 and 2 to get the new denominator 6. Then we multiply each fraction by a name for 1 which will make a new fraction with a denominator of 6. This gives us $\frac{4}{6}$ and $\frac{3}{6}$.

$$\frac{2}{3} \times \mathbf{1}\frac{2}{2} = \frac{4}{6} \qquad \frac{1}{2} \times \mathbf{1}\frac{3}{3} = \frac{3}{6}$$

Now we subtract $\frac{3}{6}$ from $\frac{4}{6}$.

$$\frac{4}{6} - \frac{3}{6} = \frac{1}{6}$$

Practice* Rename the fractions as necessary to add or subtract:

a. $\frac{1}{3} + \frac{1}{4}$ **b.** $\frac{1}{5} + \frac{1}{3}$ **c.** $\frac{1}{2} - \frac{1}{3}$

d. $\frac{2}{3} + \frac{1}{4}$ **e.** $\frac{2}{3} + \frac{1}{5}$ **f.** $\frac{3}{4} - \frac{2}{3}$

g. $\frac{1}{2} + \frac{2}{5}$ **h.** $\frac{3}{5} + \frac{1}{4}$ **i.** $\frac{2}{3} - \frac{1}{4}$

Problem set 134

1. (87) An elephant eats about 250 pounds of food every day. How many days would it take an elephant to eat 1 ton of food?

2. (81) Write the following sentence using digits and symbols:

"When one third is subtracted from one half, the difference is one sixth."

3. The football field is 300 feet long and 160 feet wide.
(60) What is the perimeter of the football field?

4. $\dfrac{4}{10} = \dfrac{\square}{100}$
(89)

5. Name the shaded part of this rect-
(72) angle as a fraction, as a decimal
number, and as a percent.

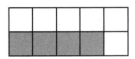

6. (a) What is the probability of
(126)   spinning an even number?

(b) What is the chance of spinning an odd number?

7. Write the mixed number $2\frac{1}{4}$ as an improper fraction.
(123) Then multiply the improper fraction by $\frac{2}{3}$. Remember
to simplify the product.

8. What is the average of 7, 4, 8, 6, and 10?
(133)

9. *AD* is 80 mm. *AB* is 50 mm. *BC* equals *CD*. Find *AC*.
(81)

$$\xleftarrow{\quad\overset{A}{\bullet}\qquad\qquad\qquad\overset{B}{\bullet}\quad\overset{C}{\bullet}\quad\overset{D}{\bullet}\quad}\rightarrow$$

10. 235 + 17.5 + 6.29 + 10.1
(109)

11. 0.2 − 0.015   **12.** 4.6 × 100
(112)   (121)

13. 0.46 × 0.04   **14.** 37 × 4.9
(120)   (119)

15. 4.6 ÷ 100   **16.** 0.46 ÷ 4   **17.** 0.46 ÷ 5
(132)   (131)   (130)

18. $\dfrac{1}{2} + \dfrac{1}{3}$ **19.** $\dfrac{2}{3} - \dfrac{1}{4}$ **20.** $\dfrac{5}{12} - \dfrac{1}{3}$
(134)   (134)   (127)

21. $4 \times \dfrac{3}{5}$ **22.** $4 \div \dfrac{3}{5}$ **23.** $\dfrac{3}{5} \div \dfrac{1}{5}$
(101)   (106)   (106)

24. If $4a = 12$, then what number is equal to $3a + 1$?
(17)

Read this information. Then answer question 25.

Nancy found a treasure map with this clue:

"Start from where the tree be dead.
Step ye right; then step ahead.
Count thy paces, four and three.
There ye find the treasure be."

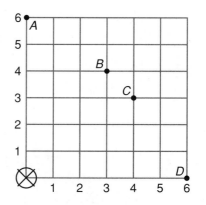

25. Nancy figured that the dead tree was marked with an
(54) X. At which point should she find the treasure?

   A. *A*   B. *B*   C. *C*   D. *D*

**LESSON
135**

Adding and Subtracting Mixed Numbers, Part 3

> **Mental Math:** Describe how to find the average height of four children in the classroom.
>
> **a.** How much is 25% of $40?
>
> **b.** How much is 25% less than $40?
>
> **c.** How much is 25% more than $40?
>
> **Problem Solving:** What was the total number of days in the years 1988, 1989, 1990, and 1991?

We may add or subtract mixed numbers just as we add or subtract fractions. Before we add or subtract mixed numbers, we make sure that the fraction parts of the mixed numbers have common denominators.

Example

$$3\frac{1}{2}$$
$$+ 1\frac{1}{3}$$

Solution We add fraction to fraction and whole number to whole number. Before we add the fractions, we change their names so that the denominators are the same. Our answer is $4\frac{5}{6}$.

$$
\begin{array}{r}
3\frac{1}{2} \times \frac{3}{3} = 3\frac{3}{6} \\
+ 1\frac{1}{3} \times \frac{2}{2} = 1\frac{2}{6} \\
\hline
4\frac{5}{6}
\end{array}
$$

Practice* Add:

a. $\quad 2\frac{1}{2}$
$\quad + 1\frac{1}{5}$

b. $\quad 3\frac{1}{4}$
$\quad + 1\frac{1}{5}$

c. $\quad 4\frac{2}{3}$
$\quad + 1\frac{1}{4}$

d. $\quad 3\frac{3}{4}$
$\quad + 1\frac{1}{2}$

Subtract:

e. $\quad 5\frac{3}{4}$
$\quad - 4\frac{1}{2}$

f. $\quad 4\frac{2}{3}$
$\quad - 1\frac{1}{2}$

g. $\quad 2\frac{2}{3}$
$\quad - 1\frac{1}{4}$

h. $\quad 6\frac{1}{3}$
$\quad - 2\frac{1}{4}$

Problem set
135

1. If popsicles cost $1.92 per dozen, what would be the cost of 60 popsicles?
(55)

2. Write the following sentence using digits and symbols: "The product of one half and one third is one sixth."
(81)

3. What is the name for a polygon that has six sides?
(39)

4. A crocodile may lay 84 eggs at a time. How many dozen eggs is that?
(21)

5. Compare: $\dfrac{\$2.50}{5} \bigcirc \dfrac{\$25.00}{50}$
(61)

6. Name the shaded part of the circle as a fraction, as a decimal number, and as a percent.
(72)

7. Sarah planned a picnic with a friend on Saturday. Then she heard that the chance of rain on Saturday is 20%. Should Sarah cancel her picnic plans? Why or why not?
(126)

8. Write the mixed number $2\frac{1}{2}$ as an improper fraction. Also, write $1\frac{1}{3}$ as an improper fraction. Multiply the two improper fractions. Then convert the product to a mixed number.
(123)

9. In rectangle *ABCD*, all sides are the same length. The perimeter is 12 inches.
(60)

(a) How many inches long is each side?

(b) How many square stickers that are 1 inch on a side would cover the area?

10. $\dfrac{5}{6} \times \dfrac{2}{3}$
(100)

11. $\dfrac{5}{6} \div \dfrac{2}{3}$
(106)

12.
(135)
$3\frac{1}{3}$
$+ 1\frac{1}{4}$
_____

13.
(134)
$\frac{3}{5}$
$+ \frac{1}{2}$
_____

14.
(135)
$8\frac{1}{2}$
$- 1\frac{1}{5}$
_____

15.
(134)
$\frac{2}{3}$
$- \frac{1}{2}$
_____

16. $30 + 4.1 + 0.43 + 0.037$
(109)

17. $0.02 - 0.019$
(112)

18. 5.7×84
(119)

19. 5.7×10
(121)

20. 0.3×0.15
(120)

21. $5.7 \div 3$
(129)

22. $5.7 \div 10$
(132)

23. $0.15 \div 3$
(130)

Read the following information. Then answer questions 24 and 25.

There are 7 children in the club. Their ages are 9, 12, 10, 10, 13, 12, and 11, respectively.

24. What is the average age of the children in the club?
(54)

25. In order of age, how old is the middle child?
(54)

LESSON 136

Dividing by a Decimal Number

Mental Math: Describe how to find the perimeter and area of a sheet of paper that is 11 inches long and $8\frac{1}{2}$ inches wide.

  a. How much is $\frac{1}{3}$ of $60?

  b. How much is $\frac{1}{3}$ less than $60?

  c. How much is $\frac{1}{3}$ more than $60?

Problem Solving: Find the four uppercase letters that have both a horizontal and a vertical line of symmetry.

We have practiced dividing decimal numbers by whole numbers. In this lesson we will practice dividing decimal numbers **by decimal numbers.**

Look at these two problems. They are different in an important way.

$$3\overline{)0.12} \qquad 0.3\overline{)0.12}$$

The problem on the left is division **by a whole number.** The problem on the right is division **by a decimal number.**

When dividing by a decimal number with pencil and paper, we take an extra step. Before dividing, we move the decimal points so that we are dividing by a whole number instead of by a decimal number.

$$0.3\overline{)0.12}$$

We move the decimal point of the divisor so that it becomes a whole number. Then we move the decimal point of the dividend the same number of places. The decimal point in the quotient is straight up from the new location of the decimal point in the division box. The memory cue for dividing by a decimal number is "over, over, and up."

$$\overset{\text{up}}{0.3\overline{)0.12}}$$
over over

To help us understand why this procedure works, we will write "0.12 divided by 0.3" with a division bar.

$$\frac{0.12}{0.3}$$

Notice we can make the divisor, 0.3, a whole number by multiplying by 10. So we multiply by $\frac{10}{10}$ to make an equivalent division problem.

$$\frac{0.12}{0.3} \times \underset{}{\frac{10}{10}} \overset{\text{}}{} = \frac{1.2}{3}$$

Multiplying by $\frac{10}{10}$ moves both decimal points "over." Now the divisor is a whole number and we can divide.

$$3\overline{)1.2} \atop {}^{\phantom{3\overline{)}}0.4}$$

We will add this memory cue to complete the decimals chart. In the last column "÷ D" means "dividing by a decimal number."

Decimals Chart

+ −	×	÷ W	÷ D
Line up the decimal points.	Multiply. Then count decimal places.	up	over, over,up
Place decimal points on whole numbers. Fill empty places with zero.			

Example $0.6\overline{)2.34}$

Solution We are dividing by the decimal number 0.6. To make 0.6 into a whole number, we move the decimal points **over** and **over**. The decimal point in the quotient is straight **up** from the new location of the decimal point in the division box.

$$
\begin{array}{r}
3.9 \\
0.6\overline{)2.3\,4} \\
1\,8 \\
\hline
5\,4 \\
5\,4 \\
\hline
0
\end{array}
$$

Practice*   **a.** $0.3\overline{)1.2}$ **b.** $0.3\overline{)0.42}$ **c.** $1.2\overline{)0.24}$

d. $0.4\overline{)0.24}$ **e.** $0.4\overline{)5.6}$ **f.** $1.2\overline{)3.6}$

g. $0.6\overline{)2.4}$ **h.** $0.5\overline{)0.125}$ **i.** $1.2\overline{)2.28}$

Problem set 136

1. Copy the decimals chart in this lesson.
(136)

2. What is the average of 5, 6, 7, 8, and 9?
(133)

3. In the forest there were lions and tigers and bears. If
(54) there were twice as many lions as tigers and twice as many tigers as bears, then how many lions were there if there were 24 bears?

4. Joey has \$18.35. John has \$22.65. They want to put
(55) their money together to buy a car that costs \$16,040.
How much more money do they need?

5. A line of symmetry divides a shape into mirror
(100) images. Which of these dotted lines is not a line of
symmetry?

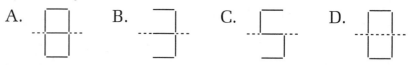

A.   B.   C.   D.

6. Write the mixed number $3\frac{1}{3}$ as an improper fraction.
(123) Then multiply the improper fraction by $\frac{3}{4}$. Remember
to simplify your answer.

7. In quadrilateral *ABCD*, which
(33) angle appears to be an obtuse
angle?

8. In quadrilateral *ABCD*, which two
(32) segments are parallel?

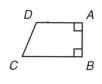

9. $3\frac{1}{2}$ **10.** $2\frac{1}{6}$ **11.** $5\frac{5}{6}$ **12.** $4\frac{2}{3}$
(135) $+ 1\frac{1}{3}$ (128) $+ 1\frac{1}{2}$ (128) $- 1\frac{1}{2}$ (135) $- 1\frac{1}{4}$

13. $3\overline{)0.24}$ **14.** $5\overline{)1.2}$ **15.** $12\overline{)0.180}$
(130)   (131)   (130)

16. $0.3\overline{)0.24}$ **17.** $0.5\overline{)1.0}$ **18.** $1.2\overline{)0.180}$
(136)   (136)   (136)

19. $\$9.75 + 78¢ + \$16 + \$0.25$
(80)

20. $(3 - 1.6) - 0.16$
(24)

21. 0.12 **22.** 0.12 **23.** 7.6
(120) $\times 0.12$ (121) $\times 10$ (119) $\times 3.9$

24. $4 \times \dfrac{3}{8}$ **25.** $4 \div \dfrac{3}{8}$
(101)   (106)

LESSON
137

Multiplying Mixed Numbers

Mental Math: Describe how to find the average length of three used pencils.

a. What number is 10% of 20?

b. What number is 10% more than 20?

c. What number is 10% less than 20?

d. $\frac{1}{4}$ of 80, × 3, + 3, ÷ 9, × 4, − 1, ÷ 3

Problem Solving: Sandra used small cubes to build larger cubes. She built a 2 by 2 by 2 cube and a 3 by 3 by 3 cube. On your paper, sketch a 4 by 4 by 4 cube. How many small cubes are needed to build it?

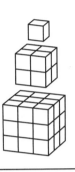

To multiply mixed numbers, we change the mixed numbers to improper fractions before we multiply.

$$2\frac{1}{2} \times 1\frac{2}{3}$$

Change mixed numbers to improper fractions first.

$$\frac{5}{2} \times \frac{5}{3} = \frac{25}{6}$$

Then multiply.

$$\frac{25}{6} = 4\frac{1}{6}$$

Then simplify.

Example 1 $\frac{1}{5} \times 4\frac{1}{2}$

Solution First we write the mixed number as an improper fraction. When both numbers are written as fractions, we multiply. We find that $\frac{1}{5}$ of $4\frac{1}{2}$ is $\frac{9}{10}$.

$$\frac{1}{5} \times 4\frac{1}{2}$$

$$\frac{1}{5} \times \frac{9}{2} = \frac{9}{10}$$

Example 2 $3 \times 2\frac{1}{3}$

Solution We write both numbers as improper fractions. Then we multiply. We simplify the answer when possible.

$$3 \times 2\frac{1}{3}$$

$$\frac{3}{1} \times \frac{7}{3} = \frac{21}{3}$$

$$\frac{21}{3} = 7$$

The product is **7**. We found our answer by multiplying. We find the same answer if we add, as we show here.

$$2\frac{1}{3} + 2\frac{1}{3} + 2\frac{1}{3} = 6\frac{3}{3} = 7$$

Practice* **a.** $1\frac{1}{2} \times 1\frac{3}{4}$ **b.** $3\frac{1}{2} \times 1\frac{2}{3}$ **c.** $3 \times 2\frac{1}{2}$

d. $4 \times 3\frac{2}{3}$ **e.** $\frac{1}{3} \times 2\frac{1}{3}$ **f.** $\frac{1}{6} \times 2\frac{5}{6}$

Problem set 137

1. Copy the decimals chart that is in Lesson 136.
(136)

2. Name this shape.
(93)

3. Write the following sentence using digits and symbols:
(4)   "The sum of two and two equals the product of two and two."

4. Which of these is not equal to $\frac{1}{2}$?
(78)   A. 0.5   B. 50%   C. 0.50   D. 0.05

5. Estimate the sum of $3\frac{1}{3}$ and $7\frac{3}{4}$ by rounding the numbers to the nearest whole number before adding.
(111)

6. If Lillian can type 2 pages in 1 hour, how long will it take her to type 100 pages?
(55)

7. In rectangle *ABCD*, segment *BC* is
(60) twice the length of segment *AB*.
Segment *AB* is 3 inches long.

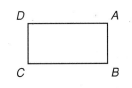

   (a) What is the perimeter of the rectangle?

   (b) What is the area of the rectangle?

8. Jason is about to roll a single number cube.
(126)

   (a) What is the probability that he will roll a prime number?

   (b) What is the chance that he will not roll a prime number?

9. An octagon has how many more sides than a
(39) pentagon?

10. What is the average of 2, 4, 6, and 8?
(133)

11. *QR* equals *RS*. *ST* is 5 cm. *RT* is 7 cm. Find *QT*.
(81)

$$Q \qquad R \qquad S \qquad\qquad\qquad T$$

12. 38.248 + 7.5 + 37.23 + 15
(109)

13. $6 − ($1.49 − 75¢)   **14.** 2.4 × 100
(24)   (121)

15. 0.24 × 0.12   **16.** 2.4 × 5.7
(120)   (119)

17. $3\overline{)0.123}$ **18.** $0.5\overline{)4.35}$ **19.** $1.2\overline{)1.44}$
(130)   (136)   (136)

20. $\quad 3\frac{1}{3}$ **21.** $\quad \frac{3}{7}$ **22.** $\quad 6\frac{14}{15}$ **23.** $\quad \frac{4}{5}$
(135) $\;+ 7\frac{3}{4}$ (134) $\;+ \frac{1}{2}$ (128) $\;- 1\frac{1}{5}$ (134) $\;- \frac{1}{3}$
$\overline{}$ $\overline{}$ $\overline{}$ $\overline{}$

24. $\frac{1}{2} \times 3\frac{1}{3}$ **25.** $4 \times 2\frac{1}{2}$
(137)   (137)

LESSON 138

Locating Points on a Coordinate Graph, Part 1

Mental Math: Describe how to estimate the area of a room that is 12 feet, 9 inches long and 9 feet, 10 inches wide.

a. What number is 25% of 80?

b. What number is 25% less than 80?

c. What number is 75% of 80?

Problem Solving: How many 1-inch cubes will fill a shoe box that is 10 inches long, 6 inches wide, and 5 inches high?

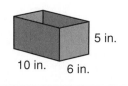

We have solved problems that asked us to locate points on a grid. For example, we located points on a map using a grid.

In mathematics we call a grid a **coordinate graph.** The coordinate graph is formed by two perpendicular number lines with marks extended to form a grid. We locate points on the coordinate graph with two numbers. These numbers are called the **coordinates.** The first number tells us how far to move horizontally from the starting point. The second number tells us how far to move vertically from there.

Look at the coordinate graph below. **The starting point is the point marked with the zero.** To find the point (4, 2), we move along the horizontal number line to the point marked 4. Then we move up **from there** to the level of the 2 on the vertical number line.

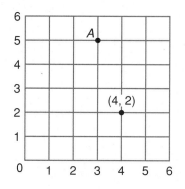

To name the location of point A, we find the number on the horizontal number line that is directly under point A. That number is 3 and is the first number of the location. Then we find the number on the vertical number line that is on level with point A. That number is 5 and is the second number of the location. We name the location of point A this way: (3, 5).

Practice   What letter names the point at each of these locations?

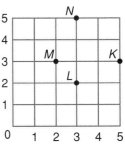

  a. (3, 2)   **b.** (5, 3)

Write the coordinates of these points:

  c. Point M **d.** Point N

Problem set 138

1. List the first six prime numbers.
(90)

2. The diameter of the tree stump was 18 inches. What was the distance from the center of the stump to the outside of the tree?
(60)

3. What is the average of 63, 84, and 102?
(133)

4. $365 + 0 = 365 \times \square$
(18)

5. Which of these does not name the part of the square that is shaded?
(76)

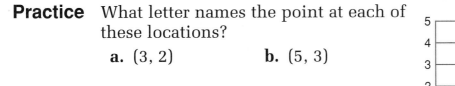

  A. 25

  B. 0.25

  C. $\frac{1}{4}$

  D. 25%

Use the coordinate graph for problems 6–8.

6. Name the shape centered at (3, 2).
(138)

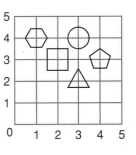

7. Name the shape centered at (4, 3).
(138)

8. Write the coordinates of the point at the center of the hexagon.
(138)

9. Fifty percent of the students were girls. If there were
(50) 30 students, how many girls were there?

10. (a) What is the perimeter of this
(60)   square?

(b) What is the area of this
    square?

12 in.

11. 6.45 + 2.1 + 12 + 0.075
(109)

12. 4.567 − (3 − 1.5)
(24)

13.   0.37
(120) × 0.12

14.   0.48
(121) ×   10

15.   0.136
(121) ×   307

16. 1.2)‾1‾.‾3‾2‾
(136)

17. 1.5)‾0‾.‾6‾0‾
(136)

18. 4)‾1‾.‾6‾2‾4‾
(130)

19. $3\frac{7}{20}$
(128)
  $+ 1\frac{1}{10}$

20. $\frac{1}{4}$
(134)
  $+ \frac{1}{5}$

21. $5\frac{4}{5}$
(128)
  $- 3\frac{1}{10}$

22. $\frac{1}{2}$
(134)
  $- \frac{2}{5}$

23. $\frac{1}{3} \times 2\frac{2}{3}$
(137)

24. $3 \times 1\frac{2}{3}$
(137)

25. $3 \div \frac{5}{6}$
(106)

LESSON 139

Recognizing Negative Numbers

Mental Math: What is the perimeter and area of a 12-inch by 18-inch sheet of construction paper?

a. What number is 10% of 40?

b. What number is 10% less than 40?

c. What number is 10% more than 40?

Problem Solving: Write a story problem that asks for the average number of students on 3 buses. Find the answer to your problem.

Numbers that are less than zero are called **negative numbers.** Numbers that are greater than zero are called **positive numbers.** On the number line below, negative numbers are to the left of zero, and positive numbers are to the right of zero.

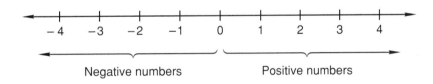

We identify negative numbers by a negative sign (like a minus sign) written in front of the digit. We may write a positive sign (a plus sign) in front of a digit to mark a positive number, although a digit without a sign in front stands for a positive number.

$$-4 \qquad \text{negative four}$$

$$+4 \text{ or } 4 \qquad \text{positive four}$$

If we subtract a larger number from a smaller number, the answer will be a negative number. Here we show the answer when we subtract 4 from 3.

$$3 - 4 = -1$$

One use of negative numbers is to identify temperatures "below zero." This thermometer shows a temperature below zero. The temperature shown is –6°F.

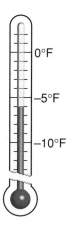

Example   3 – 5

Solution   We are subtracting a larger number from a smaller number. One way to do this is to start at 3 on the number line and count back 5 numbers. We end up at –2.

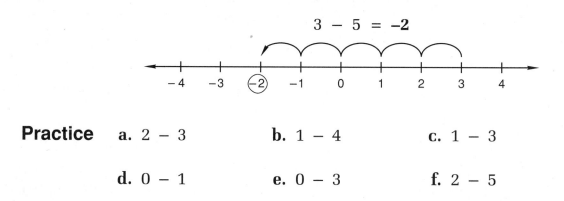

$$3 - 5 = -2$$

Practice   **a.** 2 – 3   **b.** 1 – 4   **c.** 1 – 3

d. 0 – 1   **e.** 0 – 3   **f.** 2 – 5

Problem set 139

1. There are two prime numbers between 20 and 30.
(90) What is the product of those two prime numbers?

2. Jack is 11 and Jill is 18. If Jill was 12 when Jack fell
(54) down, then how old was Jack?

3. Compare: $\dfrac{1}{2} \times \dfrac{1}{2} \bigcirc \dfrac{1}{2} \div \dfrac{1}{2}$
(97)

4. Ralph's 4 scores were 78, 81, 81, and 80, respectively.
(133) What was the average of his 4 scores?

5. Estimate the sum of 6.15, 9.96, and 7.9 by rounding
(115) each decimal number to the nearest whole number
before adding.

Look at the graph. Then answer questions 6 and 7.

6. Which letter names the point at
(138) (3, 4)?

7. Which pair of numbers gives the
(138) location of point *C*?

A. (3, 1)   B. (1, 3)   C. (3, 2)

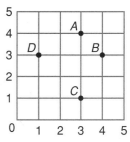

Look at the drawing. Then answer questions 8 and 9.

8. What fraction names the probabil-
(126) ity that the spinner will stop in
the area marked A?

9. What is the chance that the spin-
(126) ner will stop in area B?

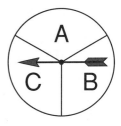

10. The rectangular ceiling of Albert's classroom is
(125) covered with ceiling tiles that are 1 foot square. Albert
counted 32 tiles along the length of the ceiling and 30
tiles along the width. What is the area of the ceiling?

11. 5.84 + 16.7 + 125 + 1.625
(109)

12. 6.2 − 4.375   **13.** 6.3 × 100
(112)   (121)

14. 0.18 × 0.12   **15.** 3.8 × 0.7
(120)   (119)

16. 4)‾1.3‾   **17.** 0.5)‾0.42‾   **18.** 1.6)‾3.248‾
(131)   (136)   (136)

19. $6\frac{5}{6}$ **20.** $\frac{3}{5}$ **21.** $4\frac{3}{4}$ **22.** $\frac{4}{5}$
(128) $+ 1\frac{1}{3}$ (134) $+ \frac{1}{4}$ (128) $- 1\frac{1}{12}$ (134) $- \frac{3}{4}$

23. $\frac{1}{5} \times 2\frac{1}{5}$ **24.** $3 \times 3\frac{1}{2}$ **25.** $\frac{5}{6} \div \frac{1}{2}$
(137)   (137)   (106)

LESSON
140

Locating Points on a Coordinate Graph, Part 2

Mental Math: What is the average number of days in the first three months of a common year?

a. What number is $\frac{1}{3}$ of 15?

b. What number is $\frac{1}{3}$ less than 15?

c. What number is $\frac{2}{3}$ of 15?

Problem Solving: A storage room of the size shown is completely filled with boxes that are two feet by two feet by two feet. How many boxes are in the storage room?

Storage room

8 ft

20 ft

10 ft

A coordinate graph often includes negative numbers as well as positive numbers. The number lines intersect at the coordinates (0, 0). This point is called the **origin.**

We start from the origin to locate points on the graph. If the first number of the coordinates of a point is positive, we start at the origin and move to the right. If the first number is negative, we start at the origin and move to the left. If the second number is positive, we then move up the graph. If the second number is negative, we move down the graph. The following coordinate graph shows the origin and four other points. Notice how the location of each point is written.

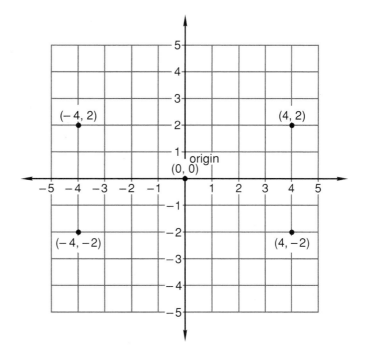

Practice   **a.** The coordinates of point A are (0, 0). What is the name for this point?

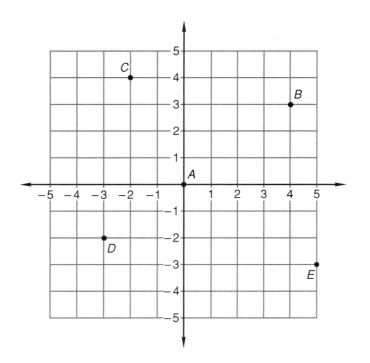

Write the coordinates of each of these points:

   b. Point B **c.** Point C **d.** Point D **e.** Point E

**Problem set
140**

1. Draw the decimals chart.
(136)

2. What is the average of 1.2, 1.3, and 1.37?
(133)

3. In three games Janet had 10 hits. Four of the hits were
(117) home runs. What percent of Janet's hits were home
runs?

Look at the graph. Then answer questions 4–6.

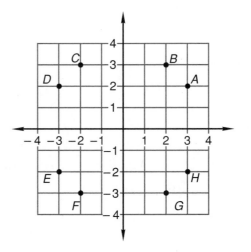

4. Which letter names point (2, –3)?
(140)

5. Which letter names point (–3, –2)?
(140)

6. What are the coordinates of point *D*?
(140)

Look at the drawing. Then answer questions 7 and 8.

7. What is the probability that the
(126) spinner will stop in the area
marked A?

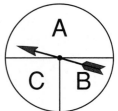

8. What is the chance that the spin-
(126) ner will stop in area B?

9. 49.37 + 0.23 + 125.4
(108)

10. 8 – (0.8 – 0.08)
(24)

11. 2.5
(119) $\times\ 2.5$

12. 0.64
(120) $\times\ 0.07$

13. 1.43
(121) $\times\quad 10$

14. $8\overline{)4.4}$
(131)

15. $0.5\overline{)0.42}$
(136)

16. $1.4\overline{)0.308}$
(136)

17. $5\frac{1}{6}$
(128) $+\ 3\frac{1}{2}$

18. $\frac{3}{5}$
(134) $+\ \frac{3}{4}$

19. $3\frac{9}{10}$
(128) $-\ 1\frac{1}{2}$

20. $\frac{1}{2}$
(134) $-\ \frac{1}{7}$

21. $\frac{1}{4} \times 2\frac{2}{3}$
(137)

22. $4 \times 5\frac{1}{2}$
(137)

23. $3 \div \frac{3}{8}$
(106)

Whole numbers greater than one that are not prime numbers can be formed by multiplying two or more prime numbers. This table shows the whole numbers 2 through 10. For each number that is not a prime number, the table shows how the number may be formed by multiplying prime numbers.

Number	Prime Factorization
2	2 is prime.
3	3 is prime.
4	2 × 2
5	5 is prime.
6	2 × 3
7	7 is prime.
8	2 × 2 × 2
9	3 × 3
10	2 × 5

24. The first four prime numbers are shown in the table.
(54) What are the next four prime numbers?

25. The number 12 is not a prime number. Write the three
(54) prime numbers that can be multiplied to equal 12.

Appendix A

Supplemental Practice Problems for Selected Lessons

This appendix contains additional practice problems for concepts presented in selected lessons. It is very important that no problems in the regular problem sets be omitted to make room for these problems. This book is designed to produce long-term retention of concepts, and long-term practice of all the concepts is necessary. The practice problems in the problem sets provide enough initial exposure to concepts for most students. If a student continues to have difficulty with certain concepts, some of these problems can be assigned as remedial exercises.

Supplemental Practice Problems
for Selected Lessons

Supplemental Practice for Lesson 5

Use words to name each number:

1. 44

2. 55

3. 110

4. 312

5. 426

6. $5.37

7. $211.25

8. $608

9. $76.27

10. $9.01

Use digits to write each number:

11. One hundred fourteen

12. Two hundred forty

13. Seven hundred thirty-two

14. Six hundred seven

15. Eight hundred sixteen

16. Three hundred eighty-four dollars

17. Four hundred eighteen dollars

18. One hundred eighty dollars and fifty cents

19. Five hundred eight dollars and fifteen cents

20. Six hundred fifty dollars

Supplemental Practice for Lesson 6

1. 3 + 6 + 7 + 8 + 4 + 1

2. 5 + 4 + 3 + 7 + 8 + 6

3. 12 + 4 + 23 + 17 + 8

4. 16 + 24 + 58 + 7 + 9

5. 56 + 9 + 31 + 18 + 7

6. 324 + 472   **7.** 589 + 723

8. 487 + 706   **9.** 312 + 58

10. 936 + 87   **11.** 43 + 246 + 97

12. 517 + 49 + 327   **13.** 625 + 506 + 84

14. 315 + 287 + 589   **15.** 643 + 420 + 708

16. 36 + 24 + 275 + 9

17. 513 + 68 + 8 + 45

18. 178 + 215 + 24 + 9

19. 47 + 6 + 428 + 14

20. 351 + 157 + 68 + 5

Supplemental Practice for Lesson 7

Use digits to write each number:

1. Seven thousand, two hundred fifty-four

2. Twelve thousand, six hundred twenty-five

3. Eleven thousand, five hundred eighty

4. Twenty-one thousand, three hundred

5. Fifty-six thousand, two hundred eight

6. Eighteen thousand, seven hundred

7. One hundred seventy-five thousand

8. Two hundred ten thousand, five hundred

9. Three hundred fifty-six thousand, two hundred

10. Nine hundred eighty thousand

Use words to name each number:

11. 6500

12. 4210

13. 1760

14. 8112

15. 21,000

16. 12,500

17. 40,800

18. 118,000

19. 210,600

20. 125,200

Supplemental Practice for Lesson 9

1.
$$\begin{array}{r} 67 \\ -\ 48 \\ \hline \end{array}$$

2.
$$\begin{array}{r} 50 \\ -\ 36 \\ \hline \end{array}$$

3.
$$\begin{array}{r} \$71 \\ -\ \$63 \\ \hline \end{array}$$

4.
$$\begin{array}{r} 413 \\ -\ 242 \\ \hline \end{array}$$

5.
$$\begin{array}{r} 531 \\ -\ 50 \\ \hline \end{array}$$

6.
$$\begin{array}{r} \$736 \\ -\ \$643 \\ \hline \end{array}$$

7.
$$\begin{array}{r} 345 \\ -\ 137 \\ \hline \end{array}$$

8.
$$\begin{array}{r} 512 \\ -\ 34 \\ \hline \end{array}$$

9.
$$\begin{array}{r} \$650 \\ -\ \$552 \\ \hline \end{array}$$

10.
$$\begin{array}{r} 300 \\ -\ 256 \\ \hline \end{array}$$

11.
$$\begin{array}{r} 580 \\ -\ 74 \\ \hline \end{array}$$

12.
$$\begin{array}{r} \$400 \\ -\ \$\ 23 \\ \hline \end{array}$$

13.
$$\begin{array}{r} 504 \\ -\ 132 \\ \hline \end{array}$$

14.
$$\begin{array}{r} 710 \\ -\ 68 \\ \hline \end{array}$$

15.
$$\begin{array}{r} \$800 \\ -\ \$743 \\ \hline \end{array}$$

Supplemental Practice for Lesson 13

1. $3.00 + $2.45

2. $6.58 + $4.00

3. $5.29 + $4.71

4. $9.15 + $10.00

5. $15.75 + $8.28

6. $27.80 + $6.00

7. $0.48 + $0.76

8. $7.00 + $12.99

9. $12.00 + $8.20

10. $0.45 + $0.55

11. $6.54 − $1.49

12. $8.29 − $1.29

13. $3.18 − $2.57

14. $5.06 − $0.27

15. $3.00 − $1.25

16. $5.00 − $4.36

17. $12.57 − $5.00

18. $10.00 − $8.54

19. $1.00 − $0.92

20. $5.00 − $4.95

Supplemental Practice for Lesson 17

1. 23 × 7
2. 6 × 43
3. 57 × 4
4. 8 × 36
5. 70 × 6
6. 4 × 78
7. 96 × 8
8. 7 × 905
9. 89 × 6
10. 8 × 709

11.
$$\begin{array}{r} \$57 \\ \times\ \ \ 4 \\ \hline \end{array}$$

12.
$$\begin{array}{r} \$34 \\ \times\ \ \ 5 \\ \hline \end{array}$$

13.
$$\begin{array}{r} \$2.78 \\ \times\ \ \ \ 6 \\ \hline \end{array}$$

14.
$$\begin{array}{r} \$8.70 \\ \times\ \ \ \ 3 \\ \hline \end{array}$$

15.
$$\begin{array}{r} \$3.45 \\ \times\ \ \ \ 9 \\ \hline \end{array}$$

16.
$$\begin{array}{r} 708 \\ \times\ \ \ 8 \\ \hline \end{array}$$

Supplemental Practice for Lesson 18

1. 5 × 9 × 4
2. 5 × 8 × 3
3. 7 × 6 × 5
4. 9 × 4 × 6
5. 7 × 5 × 8
6. 5 × 4 × 3 × 2
7. 3 × 3 × 3 × 3
8. 2 × 5 × 2 × 5
9. 6 × 4 × 2 × 0
10. 3 × 5 × 4 × 6
11. 20 × 7 × 5
12. 4 × 9 × 25
13. 6 × 30 × 5
14. 50 × 5 × 8
15. 5 × 7 × 12
16. 8 × 10 × 6
17. 54 × 9 × 0
18. 5 × 5 × 24
19. 2 × 5 × 10
20. 7 × 75 × 4

Supplemental Practice for Lesson 22

Divide and write each answer with a remainder:

1. $3\overline{)10}$
2. $4\overline{)33}$
3. $7\overline{)30}$
4. $8\overline{)51}$
5. $6\overline{)53}$
6. $5\overline{)32}$
7. $\dfrac{17}{2}$
8. $\dfrac{26}{3}$
9. $\dfrac{35}{10}$
10. $\dfrac{28}{5}$
11. $\dfrac{55}{8}$
12. $\dfrac{70}{9}$

13. $35 \div 6$

14. $32 \div 7$

15. $32 \div 9$

16. $23 \div 4$

17. $17 \div 6$

18. $35 \div 10$

Supplemental Practice for Lesson 24

1. $8 - (6 - 2)$

2. $8 - (6 + 2)$

3. $8 - (6 \div 2)$

4. $8 \div (6 - 2)$

5. $8 \div (6 + 2)$

6. $(24 \div 6) \div 2$

7. $24 \div (6 \div 2)$

8. $(24 \div 6) - 2$

9. $24 \div (6 - 2)$

10. $(24 \div 6) + 2$

11. $24 \div (6 + 2)$

12. $(24 \div 6) \times 2$

13. $24 \div (6 \times 2)$

14. $(36 \div 6) \div 3$

15. $36 \div (6 \div 3)$

16. $(36 - 6) \times 3$

17. $36 - (6 \times 3)$

18. $(36 \div 6) - 3$

19. $36 + (12 - 6) + 3$

20. $(36 + 12) - (6 + 3)$

Supplemental Practice for Lesson 26

1. $2\overline{)136}$

2. $2\overline{)356}$

3. $3\overline{)234}$

4. $3\overline{)\$4.56}$

5. $3\overline{)\$5.67}$

6. $4\overline{)\$1.24}$

7. $4\overline{)248}$

8. $4\overline{)356}$

9. $5\overline{)120}$

10. $5\overline{)\$2.30}$

11. $6\overline{)\$4.32}$

12. $6\overline{)\$8.76}$

13. $7\overline{)511}$

14. $7\overline{)847}$

15. $7\overline{)903}$

16. $8\overline{)\$4.40}$

17. $8\overline{)\$6.48}$

18. $9\overline{)\$5.67}$

19. $9\overline{)568}$

20. $8\overline{)690}$

21. $7\overline{)611}$

Supplemental Practice for Lesson 29

1. What time is shown on the clock?

2. What time was it 2 hours ago?

3. What time will it be in 2 hours?

4. What time was it half an hour ago?

5. What time will it be in a half hour?

Morning

---

6. What time is shown on the clock?

7. What time will it be in 12 hours?

8. What time was it 2 hours ago?

9. What time was it half an hour ago?

10. How many minutes is it until 1:00 p.m.?

Afternoon

---

11. What time is shown on the clock?

12. What time will it be in 24 hours?

13. What time was it half an hour ago?

14. What time will it be in $1\frac{1}{2}$ hours?

15. How many minutes is it until noon?

Morning

---

16. What time is 10 minutes before noon?

17. What time is $1\frac{1}{2}$ hours after midnight?

18. What time is 5 minutes after two in the afternoon?

19. What time is 5 minutes before six in the morning?

20. What time is a quarter after three in the afternoon?

Supplemental Practice for Lesson 30

1. 10×36
2. 47×30
3. 50×78
4. 34×70
5. 90×37
6. 45×10
7. 20×35
8. 73×40
9. 60×38
10. 74×80
11. 10×271
12. 932×30
13. 70×674
14. 465×20
15. 60×793
16. 81×100
17. 500×36
18. 64×900
19. 400×84
20. 96×800

Supplemental Practice for Lesson 34

Round these numbers to the nearest ten:

1. 46
2. 37
3. 61
4. 58
5. 43
6. 79
7. 85
8. 96

Round these numbers to the nearest hundred:

9. 375
10. 216
11. 850
12. 781
13. 460
14. 329
15. 198
16. 748

Round these numbers to the nearest ten:

17. 121
18. 127
19. 358
20. 341
21. 769
22. 532
23. 477
24. 265

Supplemental Practice for Lesson 35

1. $3\overline{)31}$
2. $4\overline{)83}$
3. $2\overline{)61}$
4. $3\overline{)122}$
5. $4\overline{)243}$
6. $5\overline{)404}$
7. $6\overline{)365}$
8. $6\overline{)305}$
9. $8\overline{)407}$
10. $3\overline{)\$3.15}$
11. $4\overline{)\$8.24}$
12. $5\overline{)\$5.40}$

13. $2\overline{)415}$ **14.** $3\overline{)920}$

15. $4\overline{)433}$ **16.** $7\overline{)\$7.42}$

17. $3\overline{)\$6.06}$ **18.** $4\overline{)\$9.60}$

Supplemental Practice for Lesson 40

1. Draw a square and shade $\frac{1}{2}$ of it.

2. Draw a square and shade $\frac{1}{2}$ of it another way.

3. Draw a square and shade $\frac{1}{2}$ of it another way.

4. Draw a square and shade $\frac{1}{4}$ of it.

5. Draw a circle and shade $\frac{1}{2}$ of it.

6. Draw a circle and shade $\frac{3}{4}$ of it.

7. Draw a circle and shade $\frac{1}{3}$ of it.

8. Draw a rectangle and shade $\frac{1}{2}$ of it.

9. Draw a rectangle and shade $\frac{1}{4}$ of it.

10. Draw a rectangle and shade $\frac{1}{3}$ of it.

11. Draw a rectangle and shade $\frac{1}{5}$ of it.

12. Draw a square and shade $\frac{3}{4}$ of it.

13. Draw a circle and shade $\frac{2}{3}$ of it.

14. Draw a rectangle and shade $\frac{2}{3}$ of it.

15. Draw a rectangle and shade $\frac{2}{5}$ of it.

16. Draw a circle and shade $\frac{1}{6}$ of it.

17. Draw a rectangle and shade $\frac{1}{6}$ of it.

18. Draw a rectangle and shade $\frac{3}{5}$ of it.

19. Draw a circle and shade $\frac{5}{6}$ of it.

20. Draw a rectangle and shade $\frac{5}{6}$ of it.

Supplemental Practice for Lesson 41

Use a fraction or mixed number to name every point marked with an arrow on these number lines:

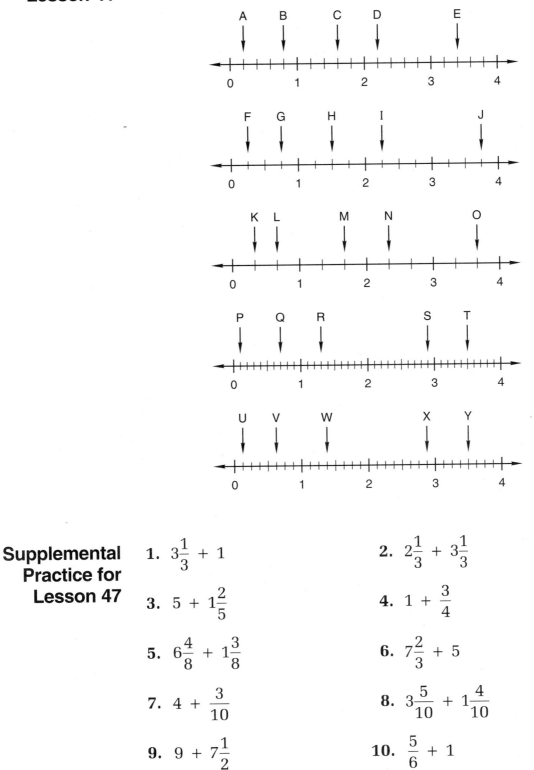

Supplemental Practice for Lesson 47

1. $3\frac{1}{3} + 1$

2. $2\frac{1}{3} + 3\frac{1}{3}$

3. $5 + 1\frac{2}{5}$

4. $1 + \frac{3}{4}$

5. $6\frac{4}{8} + 1\frac{3}{8}$

6. $7\frac{2}{3} + 5$

7. $4 + \frac{3}{10}$

8. $3\frac{5}{10} + 1\frac{4}{10}$

9. $9 + 7\frac{1}{2}$

10. $\frac{5}{6} + 1$

11. $6\frac{2}{3} - 4$

12. $3\frac{3}{4} - 1\frac{2}{4}$

13. $7\frac{1}{2} - \frac{1}{2}$

14. $1\frac{5}{8} - 1$

15. $8\frac{3}{4} - 2\frac{3}{4}$

16. $3\frac{1}{2} - 3\frac{1}{2}$

17. $10\frac{7}{10} - 1\frac{4}{10}$

18. $4\frac{3}{5} - \frac{1}{5}$

19. $9\frac{4}{5} - 4$

20. $1\frac{7}{8} - \frac{7}{8}$

Supplemental Practice for Lesson 53

Write the standard form of these numbers:

1. $(5 \times 1000) + (2 \times 100) + (8 \times 10)$

2. $(6 \times 100) + (4 \times 10) + (2 \times 1)$

3. $(4 \times 10{,}000) + (5 \times 1000) + (6 \times 10) + (7 \times 1)$

4. $(5 \times 1000) + (4 \times 100) + (9 \times 10) + (2 \times 1)$

5. $(7 \times 10{,}000) + (1 \times 1000) + (4 \times 100)$

6. $(6 \times 1000) + (4 \times 100) + (3 \times 1)$

7. $(7 \times 1000) + (8 \times 10) + (9 \times 1)$

8. $(1 \times 10{,}000) + (4 \times 100) + (7 \times 1)$

9. $(6 \times 1000) + (1 \times 10)$

10. $(1 \times 10{,}000) + (6 \times 1000) + (5 \times 1)$

Write these numbers in expanded notation:

11. 65

12. 742

13. 320

14. 506

15. 7500

16. 2001

17. 1040

18. 1760

19. 1492

20. 25,000

Supplemental Practice for Lesson 57

1. 38×49	**2.** 96×97	**3.** $\$0.78 \times 76$	**4.** $\$0.52 \times 47$
5. 63×85	**6.** 69×81	**7.** $\$0.58 \times 59$	**8.** $\$0.16 \times 74$
9. 96×36	**10.** 27×73	**11.** $\$0.85 \times 96$	**12.** $\$0.47 \times 72$
13. 74×18	**14.** 36×83	**15.** $\$0.74 \times 58$	**16.** $\$0.67 \times 64$
17. 92×47	**18.** 63×49	**19.** $\$0.18 \times 85$	**20.** $\$0.46 \times 89$

Supplemental Practice for Lesson 58

Write the value of the 1 in each number:

1. 315,275,486   **2.** 21,987,564

3. 128,675   **4.** 7,351,487

5. 125,386,794   **6.** 97,315,248

Name the value of the place held by the zero in each number:

7. 20,675,482   **8.** 123,450,683

9. 5,046,912   **10.** 17,954,068

11. 805,423,796   **12.** 8,907,485

Which digit is in the millions' place in each number?

13. 654,297,801   **14.** 37,591,846

Which digit is in the ten-millions' place in each number?

15. 752,931,468   **16.** 246,801,357

Write the value of the 5 in each number:

17. 375,286,420   **18.** 17,576,284

19. 56,234,196   **20.** 123,456,786

Use digits to write each number:

1. One million, two hundred fifty thousand

2. Five million, three hundred twelve thousand

3. Ten million, one hundred twenty-five thousand, two hundred

4. Thirteen million, two hundred ten thousand, five hundred

5. Twenty-five million, one hundred ninety-six thousand, one hundred

6. Three hundred twenty-seven million

7. Six hundred forty-five million, six hundred thousand, two hundred

8. Seven hundred sixteen million, nine hundred eleven thousand

9. One hundred twenty million, six hundred fifteen thousand

10. Nine hundred eighty-four million, two hundred thousand

Use words to name each number:

11. 1,500,000

12. 10,200,000

13. 15,352,000

14. 25,740,000

15. 42,164,000

16. 78,345,200

17. 120,000,000

18. 253,000,000

19. 412,520,000

20. 635,154,000

Supplemental Practice for Lesson 61

1. $20\overline{)420}$ 2. $30\overline{)450}$ 3. $40\overline{)\$4.80}$

4. $50\overline{)700}$ 5. $60\overline{)800}$ 6. $70\overline{)\$7.00}$

7. $80\overline{)900}$ 8. $20\overline{)560}$ 9. $30\overline{)\$5.70}$

10. $40\overline{)650}$ 11. $50\overline{)850}$ 12. $60\overline{)\$9.00}$

13. $70\overline{)800}$ 14. $20\overline{)614}$ 15. $30\overline{)\$7.80}$

16. $40\overline{)876}$ 17. $50\overline{)987}$ 18. $60\overline{)\$9.60}$

Supplemental Practice for Lesson 63

1. $\begin{array}{r} 135 \\ \times\, 246 \\ \hline \end{array}$ 2. $\begin{array}{r} 650 \\ \times\, 473 \\ \hline \end{array}$ 3. $\begin{array}{r} \$4.08 \\ \times\quad 592 \\ \hline \end{array}$ 4. $\begin{array}{r} \$3.54 \\ \times\quad 260 \\ \hline \end{array}$

5. $\begin{array}{r} 625 \\ \times\, 403 \\ \hline \end{array}$ 6. $\begin{array}{r} 754 \\ \times\, 365 \\ \hline \end{array}$ 7. $\begin{array}{r} \$3.47 \\ \times\quad 198 \\ \hline \end{array}$ 8. $\begin{array}{r} \$6.80 \\ \times\quad 743 \\ \hline \end{array}$

9. $\begin{array}{r} 503 \\ \times\, 936 \\ \hline \end{array}$ 10. $\begin{array}{r} 418 \\ \times\, 650 \\ \hline \end{array}$ 11. $\begin{array}{r} \$9.73 \\ \times\quad 409 \\ \hline \end{array}$ 12. $\begin{array}{r} \$3.49 \\ \times\quad 156 \\ \hline \end{array}$

13. $\begin{array}{r} 760 \\ \times\, 394 \\ \hline \end{array}$ 14. $\begin{array}{r} 507 \\ \times\, 938 \\ \hline \end{array}$ 15. $\begin{array}{r} \$2.43 \\ \times\quad 671 \\ \hline \end{array}$ 16. $\begin{array}{r} \$9.53 \\ \times\quad 870 \\ \hline \end{array}$

17. $\begin{array}{r} 740 \\ \times\, 698 \\ \hline \end{array}$ 18. $\begin{array}{r} 486 \\ \times\, 203 \\ \hline \end{array}$ 19. $\begin{array}{r} \$7.05 \\ \times\quad 258 \\ \hline \end{array}$ 20. $\begin{array}{r} \$5.78 \\ \times\quad 369 \\ \hline \end{array}$

Supplemental Practice for Lesson 65

Divide and write each answer with a fraction:

1. $6\overline{)19}$ 2. $5\overline{)36}$ 3. $4\overline{)27}$

4. $16 \div 7$ 5. $25 \div 8$ 6. $56 \div 9$

7. $\dfrac{10}{3}$ 8. $\dfrac{50}{7}$ 9. $\dfrac{81}{10}$

10. $2\overline{)45}$ 11. $3\overline{)46}$ 12. $4\overline{)47}$

13. $56 \div 5$ 14. $79 \div 6$ 15. $61 \div 10$

16. $\dfrac{33}{8}$ 17. $\dfrac{125}{3}$ 18. $\dfrac{95}{6}$

19. $100 \div 7$ 20. $100 \div 9$ 21. $100 \div 3$

Supplemental Practice for Lesson 69

Estimate each answer by rounding before doing the arithmetic. Round numbers less than 100 to the nearest ten. Round numbers more than 100 to the nearest hundred.

1. 36 + 43

2. 38 + 49

3. 73 − 31

4. 59 − 31

5. 51 × 39

6. 78 × 42

7. 88 ÷ 29

8. 81 ÷ 19

9. 397 + 214

10. 688 + 291

11. 687 − 304

12. 915 − 588

13. 503 × 491

14. 687 × 298

15. 395 ÷ 21

16. 589 ÷ 29

17. 87 + 93

18. 786 + 495

19. 893 − 514

20. 980 − 217

Supplemental Practice for Lesson 70

1. $1 - \dfrac{1}{3}$

2. $2 - \dfrac{2}{3}$

3. $3 - \dfrac{1}{4}$

4. $4 - \dfrac{3}{4}$

5. $2 - 1\dfrac{1}{5}$

6. $3 - 1\dfrac{1}{6}$

7. $4 - 2\dfrac{5}{6}$

8. $5 - 3\dfrac{1}{8}$

9. $6 - 1\dfrac{3}{8}$

10. $8 - 5\dfrac{5}{8}$

11. $7 - 6\dfrac{7}{8}$

12. $10 - \dfrac{1}{2}$

13. $4 - 2\dfrac{1}{10}$

14. $6 - 3\dfrac{3}{10}$

15. $3 - 2\dfrac{1}{2}$

16. $5 - 1\dfrac{1}{12}$

17. $10 - \dfrac{1}{10}$

18. $8 - 4\dfrac{2}{5}$

19. $1 - \dfrac{11}{12}$

20. $3 - 2\dfrac{3}{5}$

Supplemental Practice for Lesson 77

Use words to name each decimal number:

1. 3.4
2. 0.23
3. 12.9
4. 7.14
5. 20.5
6. 15.15
7. 10.1
8. 1.10
9. 120.8
10. 21.04

Use digits to write each decimal number:

11. Twenty-three and four tenths
12. Thirty-two hundredths
13. Ten and five tenths
14. Two and twenty-five hundredths
15. Fifty-two and one tenth
16. Five hundredths
17. One hundred thirty-five and nine tenths
18. Seventy-six and twelve hundredths
19. One and six hundredths
20. Ninety-six and five tenths

Supplemental Practice for Lesson 85

Convert each improper fraction or mixed number into a whole number or mixed number:

1. $\dfrac{8}{3}$　　2. $\dfrac{7}{2}$　　3. $\dfrac{12}{4}$

4. $\dfrac{7}{4}$　　5. $\dfrac{10}{5}$　　6. $\dfrac{100}{100}$

7. $5\dfrac{3}{2}$　　8. $6\dfrac{6}{3}$　　9. $4\dfrac{8}{5}$

10. $9\dfrac{4}{4}$　　11. $3\dfrac{11}{8}$　　12. $4\dfrac{9}{4}$

13. $5\dfrac{8}{3}$ 14. $7\dfrac{9}{5}$ 15. $8\dfrac{7}{3}$

16. $\dfrac{2}{3} + \dfrac{2}{3}$ 17. $\dfrac{3}{4} + \dfrac{3}{4} + \dfrac{3}{4}$

18. $\dfrac{2}{3} + \dfrac{2}{3} + \dfrac{2}{3}$ 19. $1\dfrac{1}{2} + 1\dfrac{1}{2}$

20. $3\dfrac{2}{3} + 1\dfrac{2}{3}$ 21. $\dfrac{5}{3} + \dfrac{4}{3}$

Supplemental Practice for Lesson 86

1. $\dfrac{1}{2} \times \dfrac{1}{2}$ 2. $\dfrac{1}{2} \times \dfrac{3}{4}$ 3. $\dfrac{2}{3} \times \dfrac{2}{3}$

4. $\dfrac{1}{3} \times \dfrac{1}{3}$ 5. $\dfrac{5}{6} \times \dfrac{1}{2}$ 6. $\dfrac{3}{4} \times \dfrac{1}{2}$

7. $\dfrac{1}{2} \times \dfrac{1}{3}$ 8. $\dfrac{1}{5} \times \dfrac{2}{3}$ 9. $\dfrac{3}{7} \times \dfrac{2}{5}$

10. $\dfrac{1}{4} \times \dfrac{1}{4}$ 11. $\dfrac{2}{3} \times \dfrac{1}{3}$ 12. $\dfrac{1}{2} \times \dfrac{1}{5}$

13. $\dfrac{1}{2} \times \dfrac{1}{4}$ 14. $\dfrac{3}{4} \times \dfrac{3}{4}$ 15. $\dfrac{5}{8} \times \dfrac{1}{2}$

16. $\dfrac{1}{3} \times \dfrac{1}{4}$ 17. $\dfrac{3}{4} \times \dfrac{1}{4}$ 18. $\dfrac{3}{4} \times \dfrac{3}{5}$

19. $\dfrac{1}{10} \times \dfrac{1}{10}$ 20. $\dfrac{5}{8} \times \dfrac{3}{4}$

Supplemental Practice for Lesson 89

Find the fraction name for 1 used to make the equivalent fraction:

1. $\dfrac{1}{2} \times \square = \dfrac{2}{4}$ 2. $\dfrac{1}{2} \times \square = \dfrac{6}{12}$

3. $\dfrac{2}{3} \times \square = \dfrac{4}{6}$ 4. $\dfrac{2}{3} \times \square = \dfrac{8}{12}$

5. $\dfrac{3}{4} \times \square = \dfrac{6}{8}$ 6. $\dfrac{3}{4} \times \square = \dfrac{9}{12}$

7. $\dfrac{1}{2} \times \square = \dfrac{5}{10}$ 8. $\dfrac{5}{6} \times \square = \dfrac{10}{12}$

Find the numerator to complete the equivalent fraction:

9. $\dfrac{2}{5} = \dfrac{?}{10}$ 10. $\dfrac{1}{4} = \dfrac{?}{12}$ 11. $\dfrac{4}{5} = \dfrac{?}{15}$

12. $\dfrac{3}{8} = \dfrac{?}{16}$ 13. $\dfrac{2}{3} = \dfrac{?}{15}$ 14. $\dfrac{1}{6} = \dfrac{?}{12}$

15. $\dfrac{1}{3} = \dfrac{?}{18}$ 16. $\dfrac{1}{2} = \dfrac{?}{20}$ 17. $\dfrac{3}{10} = \dfrac{?}{20}$

18. $\dfrac{3}{4} = \dfrac{?}{20}$ 19. $\dfrac{4}{5} = \dfrac{?}{20}$ 20. $\dfrac{1}{10} = \dfrac{?}{100}$

Supplemental Practice for Lesson 92

Find the greatest common factor of each pair of numbers:

1. 4 and 6   2. 4 and 8   3. 6 and 8

4. 6 and 9   5. 6 and 10   6. 6 and 12

7. 8 and 12   8. 9 and 12   9. 10 and 12

10. 5 and 10   11. 3 and 5   12. 8 and 16

Reduce these fractions using the GCF of the terms of each fraction:

13. $\dfrac{12}{16}$ 14. $\dfrac{12}{18}$ 15. $\dfrac{9}{15}$

16. $\dfrac{8}{16}$ 17. $\dfrac{12}{20}$ 18. $\dfrac{16}{24}$

Supplemental Practice for Lesson 96

1. What is $\frac{1}{3}$ of 9?   2. What is $\frac{2}{3}$ of 9?

3. What is $\frac{1}{4}$ of 8?   4. What is $\frac{3}{4}$ of 8?

5. What is $\frac{1}{5}$ of 10?   6. What is $\frac{3}{5}$ of 10?

7. What is $\frac{1}{6}$ of 12?   8. What is $\frac{5}{6}$ of 12?

9. What is $\frac{1}{7}$ of 21?   10. What is $\frac{4}{7}$ of 21?

11. What is $\frac{1}{8}$ of 16?   12. What is $\frac{5}{8}$ of 16?

13. $\dfrac{1}{3} \times 2$ 14. $\dfrac{1}{2} \times 3$ 15. $\dfrac{2}{3} \times 2$

16. $\dfrac{2}{3} \times 3$ 17. $\dfrac{1}{4} \times 5$ 18. $\dfrac{3}{4} \times 3$

19. $2 \times \dfrac{4}{5}$ 20. $3 \times \dfrac{3}{5}$ 21. $4 \times \dfrac{2}{3}$

Supplemental Practice for Lesson 99

Reduce each fraction and mixed number:

1. $\dfrac{2}{8}$ 2. $\dfrac{3}{9}$ 3. $\dfrac{4}{6}$

4. $\dfrac{4}{10}$ 5. $\dfrac{5}{10}$ 6. $\dfrac{3}{12}$

7. $1\dfrac{2}{4}$ 8. $3\dfrac{6}{8}$ 9. $2\dfrac{3}{6}$

10. $4\dfrac{8}{10}$ 11. $1\dfrac{2}{6}$ 12. $5\dfrac{6}{9}$

Reduce each answer:

13. $\dfrac{3}{8} + \dfrac{3}{8}$ 14. $\dfrac{9}{10} - \dfrac{3}{10}$ 15. $\dfrac{2}{3} \times \dfrac{1}{4}$

16. $\dfrac{1}{6} \times 3$ 17. $1\dfrac{1}{4} + 2\dfrac{1}{4}$ 18. $3\dfrac{5}{6} - 1\dfrac{1}{6}$

19. $5\dfrac{5}{9} + 1\dfrac{1}{9}$ 20. $\dfrac{5}{12} + \dfrac{5}{12}$

Supplemental Practice for Lesson 100

Reduce each fraction to lowest terms:

1. $\dfrac{4}{8}$ 2. $\dfrac{6}{12}$ 3. $\dfrac{8}{12}$

4. $\dfrac{10}{20}$ 5. $\dfrac{4}{20}$ 6. $\dfrac{8}{16}$

7. $\dfrac{12}{18}$ 8. $\dfrac{10}{100}$ 9. $\dfrac{18}{24}$

10. $\dfrac{50}{100}$ 11. $\dfrac{16}{20}$ 12. $\dfrac{60}{100}$

13. $\dfrac{7}{12} + \dfrac{1}{12}$ 14. $\dfrac{15}{16} - \dfrac{3}{16}$ 15. $\dfrac{3}{10} \times \dfrac{2}{3}$

16. $\dfrac{2}{3} \times \dfrac{3}{8}$ 17. $\dfrac{9}{24} + \dfrac{7}{24}$ 18. $\dfrac{17}{18} - \dfrac{11}{18}$

19. $\dfrac{6}{10} \times \dfrac{5}{10}$ 20. $\dfrac{1}{12} \times 6$ 21. $\dfrac{7}{20} + \dfrac{1}{20}$

Supplemental Practice for Lesson 101

Simplify each fraction and mixed number:

1. $\dfrac{8}{6}$

2. $\dfrac{9}{6}$

3. $\dfrac{10}{6}$

4. $\dfrac{10}{8}$

5. $\dfrac{12}{8}$

6. $\dfrac{12}{10}$

7. $\dfrac{14}{4}$

8. $\dfrac{27}{6}$

9. $\dfrac{20}{8}$

10. $\dfrac{15}{6}$

11. $\dfrac{15}{10}$

12. $\dfrac{14}{8}$

13. $3\dfrac{6}{4}$

14. $4\dfrac{16}{10}$

15. $5\dfrac{10}{4}$

16. $\dfrac{8}{9} + \dfrac{8}{9} + \dfrac{8}{9}$

17. $3\dfrac{7}{8} + 4\dfrac{7}{8}$

18. $\dfrac{3}{4} \times 10$

19. $\dfrac{6}{5} \times \dfrac{9}{2}$

Supplemental Practice for Lesson 104

1. $12\overline{)432}$

2. $24\overline{)432}$

3. $18\overline{)432}$

4. $27\overline{)432}$

5. $13\overline{)235}$

6. $29\overline{)401}$

7. $32\overline{)516}$

8. $19\overline{)399}$

9. $23\overline{)490}$

10. $14\overline{)500}$

11. $25\overline{)700}$

12. $33\overline{)1000}$

13. $41\overline{)464}$

14. $39\overline{)800}$

15. $17\overline{)422}$

16. $22\overline{)657}$

17. $15\overline{)218}$

18. $31\overline{)943}$

Supplemental Practice for Lesson 106

1. $\dfrac{2}{3} \div \dfrac{1}{2}$

2. $\dfrac{1}{2} \div \dfrac{2}{3}$

3. $\dfrac{1}{3} \div \dfrac{3}{4}$

4. $\dfrac{3}{4} \div \dfrac{1}{3}$

5. $\dfrac{3}{4} \div \dfrac{1}{4}$

6. $\dfrac{1}{4} \div \dfrac{3}{4}$

7. $2 \div \dfrac{1}{2}$

8. $\dfrac{1}{2} \div 2$

9. $2 \div \dfrac{1}{3}$

10. $\dfrac{1}{3} \div 2$ 11. $\dfrac{1}{6} \div \dfrac{1}{3}$ 12. $\dfrac{1}{3} \div \dfrac{1}{6}$

13. $\dfrac{3}{4} \div \dfrac{1}{2}$ 14. $\dfrac{1}{2} \div \dfrac{3}{4}$ 15. $3 \div \dfrac{2}{3}$

16. $\dfrac{2}{3} \div 3$ 17. $3 \div \dfrac{3}{4}$ 18. $\dfrac{3}{4} \div 3$

Supplemental Practice for Lesson 109

1. $3.47 + 6.4$ 2. $23.51 - 17$

3. $25.3 + 0.421$ 4. $6.57 - 0.8$

5. $3.842 + 1.6$ 6. $20.45 - 12$

7. $4.2 + 4 + 0.1$ 8. $5.423 - 1.4$

9. $4.28 + 0.6 + 3$ 10. $1.00 - 0.84$

11. $7.45 + 12.383$ 12. $1.000 - 0.625$

13. $3 + 4.6 + 0.27$ 14. $36.27 - 12$

15. $14.2 + 6.4 + 5$ 16. $3.427 - 1$

17. $5.2 + 3 + 0.47$ 18. $32.47 - 5.8$

19. $5.36 + 12$ 20. $16.25 - 15$

Supplemental Practice for Lesson 112

1. $0.4 - 0.15$ 2. $0.3 - 0.23$

3. $3.5 - 0.35$ 4. $4.2 - 1.25$

5. $0.2 - 0.12$ 6. $8.6 - 4.31$

7. $5.0 - 1.4$ 8. $0.75 - 0.375$

9. $0.8 - 0.75$ 10. $4.3 - 0.125$

11. $0.6 - 0.599$ 12. $1.25 - 0.625$

13. $4.0 - 1.25$ 14. $4.1 - 0.14$

15. $0.25 - 0.125$ 16. $7.0 - 1.6$

17. $0.5 - 0.425$ 18. $4.8 - 3.29$

19. $6.0 - 0.6$ 20. $0.34 - 0.291$

Supplemental Practice for Lesson 113

1. $3 - 2.1$

2. $4 - 3.21$

3. $1 - 0.2$

4. $3.45 - 1$

5. $6 - 4.7$

6. $1 - 0.01$

7. $3.4 - 2$

8. $1 - 0.23$

9. $12 - 6.4$

10. $15 - 1.5$

11. $4.3 - 1$

12. $8 - 7.9$

13. $1 - 0.9$

14. $4 - 3.99$

15. $25 - 12.5$

16. $16.7 - 8$

17. $14 - 5.6$

18. $8 - 1.35$

19. $4 - 2.77$

20. $1 - 0.211$

Supplemental Practice for Lesson 115

Round each number to the nearest whole number:

1. $7\frac{1}{8}$

2. 3.8

3. 4.18

4. $5\frac{5}{6}$

5. 5.2

6. 4.93

7. $12\frac{1}{3}$

8. 16.9

9. 14.23

10. $3\frac{2}{3}$

11. 6.7

12. 5.41

13. $16\frac{1}{5}$

14. 24.4

15. 12.75

16. $9\frac{9}{10}$

17. 9.6

18. 9.87

Supplemental Practice for Lesson 118

Write each percent as a reduced fraction:

1. 25%

2. 10%

3. 2%

4. 60%

5. 80%

6. 90%

7. 30%

8. 1%

9. 50%

10. 20%

11. 5%

12. 70%

13. 99%

14. 4%

15. 40%

16. 75%

Supplemental Practice for Lesson 119

1. $\begin{array}{r} 0.3 \\ \times\ \ \ 5 \\ \hline \end{array}$

2. $\begin{array}{r} 4 \\ \times\ 0.6 \\ \hline \end{array}$

3. $\begin{array}{r} 0.7 \\ \times\ 0.8 \\ \hline \end{array}$

4. $\begin{array}{r} 0.6 \\ \times\ \ \ 6 \\ \hline \end{array}$

5. $\begin{array}{r} 0.4 \\ \times\ 0.4 \\ \hline \end{array}$

6. $\begin{array}{r} 0.8 \\ \times\ \ \ 9 \\ \hline \end{array}$

7. $\begin{array}{r} 0.25 \\ \times\ \ \ \ 3 \\ \hline \end{array}$

8. $\begin{array}{r} 2.5 \\ \times\ \ \ 5 \\ \hline \end{array}$

9. $\begin{array}{r} 2.5 \\ \times\ 0.7 \\ \hline \end{array}$

10. $\begin{array}{r} 0.12 \\ \times\ \ \ \ 6 \\ \hline \end{array}$

11. $\begin{array}{r} 1.2 \\ \times\ 0.8 \\ \hline \end{array}$

12. $\begin{array}{r} 0.15 \\ \times\ \ \ \ 5 \\ \hline \end{array}$

13. 0.18×3

14. 4.7×0.5

15. 0.3×0.8

16. 1.23×0.7

17. 6.25×8

18. 0.15×1.5

19. 0.45×0.3

20. 0.06×8

Supplemental Practice for Lesson 120

1. $\begin{array}{r} 0.3 \\ \times\ 0.3 \\ \hline \end{array}$

2. $\begin{array}{r} 0.2 \\ \times\ 0.4 \\ \hline \end{array}$

3. $\begin{array}{r} 0.12 \\ \times\ \ 0.3 \\ \hline \end{array}$

4. $\begin{array}{r} 0.05 \\ \times\ 0.07 \\ \hline \end{array}$

5. $\begin{array}{r} 0.08 \\ \times\ \ 0.7 \\ \hline \end{array}$

6. $\begin{array}{r} 0.12 \\ \times\ 0.12 \\ \hline \end{array}$

7. $\begin{array}{r} 0.12 \\ \times\ 0.08 \\ \hline \end{array}$

8. $\begin{array}{r} 0.42 \\ \times\ \ 0.2 \\ \hline \end{array}$

9. $\begin{array}{r} 0.25 \\ \times\ \ 0.3 \\ \hline \end{array}$

10. $\begin{array}{r} 0.23 \\ \times\ \ 0.4 \\ \hline \end{array}$

11. $\begin{array}{r} 0.03 \\ \times\ 0.07 \\ \hline \end{array}$

12. $\begin{array}{r} 1.23 \\ \times\ 0.04 \\ \hline \end{array}$

13. 0.4×0.2

14. 0.25×0.1

15. 0.025×0.7

16. 6.5×0.01

17. 0.03×0.03

18. 0.01×0.1

19. 0.24×0.3

20. 0.12×0.06

Supplemental Practice for Lesson 122

Find the least common multiple of each pair of numbers:

1. 3 and 4   **2.** 4 and 5

3. 4 and 6   **4.** 3 and 6

5. 4 and 8   **6.** 6 and 8

7. 6 and 9   **8.** 6 and 10

9. 6 and 12   **10.** 8 and 10

11. 8 and 12   **12.** 8 and 16

13. 10 and 15   **14.** 5 and 15

15. 5 and 10   **16.** 5 and 6

17. 10 and 20   **18.** 10 and 25

19. 20 and 30   **20.** 20 and 40

Supplemental Practice for Lesson 123

Name the number of shaded circles as a mixed number and as an improper fraction:

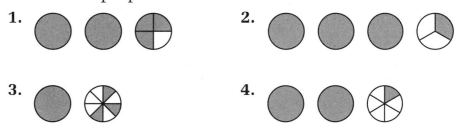

1.   **2.**

3.   **4.**

Write each mixed number as an improper fraction:

5. $3\frac{1}{2}$ **6.** $2\frac{1}{3}$ **7.** $3\frac{2}{3}$

8. $4\frac{1}{2}$ **9.** $1\frac{1}{8}$ **10.** $2\frac{1}{5}$

11. $5\frac{1}{2}$ **12.** $4\frac{1}{3}$ **13.** $3\frac{1}{4}$

14. $7\frac{1}{2}$ **15.** $3\frac{1}{3}$ **16.** $4\frac{1}{5}$

Supplemental Practice for Lesson 127

1. $\frac{1}{2} + \frac{1}{4}$ **2.** $\frac{3}{4} - \frac{1}{2}$ **3.** $\frac{1}{2} + \frac{3}{8}$

4. $\frac{5}{8} - \frac{1}{2}$ **5.** $\frac{1}{4} + \frac{1}{8}$ **6.** $\frac{7}{8} - \frac{1}{4}$

7. $\dfrac{3}{4} + \dfrac{1}{8}$ 8. $\dfrac{1}{3} - \dfrac{1}{9}$ 9. $\dfrac{1}{2} + \dfrac{1}{10}$

10. $\dfrac{8}{9} - \dfrac{2}{3}$ 11. $\dfrac{1}{5} + \dfrac{1}{10}$ 12. $\dfrac{9}{10} - \dfrac{1}{2}$

13. $\dfrac{2}{5} + \dfrac{3}{10}$ 14. $\dfrac{3}{10} - \dfrac{1}{5}$ 15. $\dfrac{1}{6} + \dfrac{7}{12}$

Supplemental Practice for Lesson 128

1. $\begin{array}{r} 3\frac{1}{2} \\ + 1\frac{1}{4} \\ \hline \end{array}$ 2. $\begin{array}{r} 3\frac{3}{4} \\ + 1\frac{1}{8} \\ \hline \end{array}$ 3. $\begin{array}{r} 5\frac{3}{8} \\ + 1\frac{1}{2} \\ \hline \end{array}$ 4. $\begin{array}{r} 5\frac{1}{6} \\ + 1\frac{1}{3} \\ \hline \end{array}$

5. $\begin{array}{r} 4\frac{1}{2} \\ + 1\frac{1}{6} \\ \hline \end{array}$ 6. $\begin{array}{r} 3\frac{2}{3} \\ + 1\frac{1}{6} \\ \hline \end{array}$ 7. $\begin{array}{r} 4\frac{3}{8} \\ + 1\frac{1}{4} \\ \hline \end{array}$ 8. $\begin{array}{r} 6\frac{3}{10} \\ + 1\frac{1}{2} \\ \hline \end{array}$

9. $\begin{array}{r} 3\frac{3}{10} \\ + 2\frac{3}{5} \\ \hline \end{array}$ 10. $\begin{array}{r} 5\frac{1}{2} \\ + 1\frac{5}{12} \\ \hline \end{array}$ 11. $\begin{array}{r} 4\frac{5}{12} \\ + 1\frac{1}{3} \\ \hline \end{array}$ 12. $\begin{array}{r} 6\frac{3}{4} \\ + 1\frac{1}{12} \\ \hline \end{array}$

13. $\begin{array}{r} 4\frac{7}{8} \\ - 1\frac{1}{2} \\ \hline \end{array}$ 14. $\begin{array}{r} 4\frac{3}{4} \\ - 2\frac{3}{8} \\ \hline \end{array}$ 15. $\begin{array}{r} 6\frac{3}{4} \\ + 1\frac{1}{12} \\ \hline \end{array}$ 16. $\begin{array}{r} 5\frac{7}{10} \\ - 1\frac{1}{2} \\ \hline \end{array}$

17. $\begin{array}{r} 8\frac{2}{3} \\ - 1\frac{1}{6} \\ \hline \end{array}$ 18. $\begin{array}{r} 4\frac{5}{6} \\ - 1\frac{1}{2} \\ \hline \end{array}$ 19. $\begin{array}{r} 6\frac{7}{8} \\ - 1\frac{3}{4} \\ \hline \end{array}$ 20. $\begin{array}{r} 7\frac{7}{12} \\ - 3\frac{1}{2} \\ \hline \end{array}$

Supplemental Practice for Lesson 129

1. $3\overline{)3.42}$ 2. $4\overline{)5.2}$ 3. $5\overline{)0.85}$

4. $6\overline{)4.2}$ 5. $7\overline{)0.84}$ 6. $8\overline{)9.6}$

7. $2\overline{)0.36}$ 8. $4\overline{)7.2}$ 9. $5\overline{)7.5}$

10. $6\overline{)1.32}$ 11. $7\overline{)12.6}$ 12. $8\overline{)3.44}$

13. $6.4 \div 4$ 14. $0.64 \div 2$

15. $6.5 \div 5$ 16. $0.63 \div 3$

17. $3.24 \div 6$ 18. $12.8 \div 8$

19. $1.44 \div 9$ 20. $23.8 \div 7$

Supplemental Practice for Lesson 130

1. 3$\overline{)0.15}$ **2.** 4$\overline{)0.28}$ **3.** 5$\overline{)1.35}$

4. 6$\overline{)0.144}$ **5.** 7$\overline{)0.63}$ **6.** 8$\overline{)0.144}$

7. 9$\overline{)0.45}$ **8.** 3$\overline{)0.012}$ **9.** 2$\overline{)0.054}$

10. 4$\overline{)0.36}$ **11.** 5$\overline{)0.30}$ **12.** 6$\overline{)0.138}$

13. 0.18 ÷ 3   **14.** 1.54 ÷ 7

15. 0.36 ÷ 9   **16.** 0.144 ÷ 6

17. 0.08 ÷ 2   **18.** 0.095 ÷ 5

19. 0.64 ÷ 8   **20.** 0.036 ÷ 4

Supplemental Practice for Lesson 131

1. 4$\overline{)3.4}$ **2.** 5$\overline{)0.12}$ **3.** 6$\overline{)2.7}$

4. 8$\overline{)0.52}$ **5.** 2$\overline{)3.1}$ **6.** 4$\overline{)0.54}$

7. 5$\overline{)0.7}$ **8.** 6$\overline{)1.5}$ **9.** 8$\overline{)3.6}$

10. 2$\overline{)0.5}$ **11.** 4$\overline{)1.5}$ **12.** 5$\overline{)0.12}$

13. 0.5 ÷ 4   **14.** 0.6 ÷ 5

15. 1.2 ÷ 8   **16.** 3.3 ÷ 6

17. 0.9 ÷ 2   **18.** 0.9 ÷ 5

19. 0.18 ÷ 4   **20.** 0.18 ÷ 8

Supplemental Practice for Lesson 133

Find the average of each group of numbers:

1. 3, 3, 6   **2.** 4, 5, 7, 8

3. 5, 6, 8, 9   **4.** 15, 17, 19

5. 21, 19, 26   **6.** 1, 2, 3, 4, 5

7. 3, 5, 7, 9   **8.** 36, 44

9. 65, 47, 32   **10.** 6, 7, 8, 9, 10

11. 112, 124   **12.** 47, 52, 54

13. 6, 6, 6, 10   **14.** 11, 12, 13, 14, 15

15. 33, 34, 35   **16.** 30, 40, 50, 60

17. 22, 24, 26, 28   **18.** 163, 197

19. 97, 101, 111   **20.** 43, 62, 56, 63

Supplemental Practice for Lesson 134

1. $\frac{1}{2} + \frac{1}{3}$ 2. $\frac{1}{2} - \frac{1}{3}$ 3. $\frac{1}{3} + \frac{1}{4}$

4. $\frac{1}{3} - \frac{1}{4}$ 5. $\frac{1}{2} + \frac{1}{5}$ 6. $\frac{1}{2} - \frac{1}{5}$

7. $\frac{1}{4} + \frac{1}{5}$ 8. $\frac{1}{4} - \frac{1}{5}$ 9. $\frac{2}{3} + \frac{1}{4}$

10. $\frac{2}{3} - \frac{1}{4}$ 11. $\frac{3}{4} + \frac{1}{3}$ 12. $\frac{3}{4} - \frac{1}{3}$

13. $\frac{1}{4} + \frac{1}{6}$ 14. $\frac{1}{4} - \frac{1}{6}$ 15. $\frac{5}{6} + \frac{3}{4}$

16. $\frac{5}{6} - \frac{3}{4}$ 17. $\frac{3}{4} + \frac{2}{3}$ 18. $\frac{3}{4} - \frac{2}{3}$

Supplemental Practice for Lesson 135

1. $3\frac{1}{3}$
$+ 1\frac{1}{4}$
     2. $5\frac{2}{5}$
$+ 2\frac{1}{2}$
     3. $4\frac{1}{6}$
$+ 3\frac{3}{4}$

4. $4\frac{3}{4}$
$- 1\frac{1}{2}$
     5. $5\frac{5}{6}$
$- 1\frac{1}{4}$
     6. $4\frac{7}{8}$
$- 1\frac{3}{4}$

7. $9\frac{1}{3}$
$+ 3\frac{2}{5}$
     8. $4\frac{3}{5}$
$+ 1\frac{1}{4}$
     9. $6\frac{1}{2}$
$+ 1\frac{1}{3}$

10. $4\frac{5}{6}$
$- 1\frac{1}{2}$
     11. $8\frac{3}{4}$
$- 1\frac{2}{3}$
     12. $7\frac{5}{8}$
$- 4\frac{1}{3}$

13. $3\frac{3}{5} + 1\frac{3}{10}$ 14. $5\frac{1}{2} - 1\frac{1}{3}$

15. $7\frac{2}{3} + 1\frac{1}{6}$ 16. $7\frac{2}{3} - 1\frac{3}{5}$

17. $4\frac{3}{5} + 3\frac{1}{4}$ 18. $6\frac{1}{4} - 6\frac{1}{6}$

19. $3\frac{1}{8} + 2\frac{3}{4}$ 20. $9\frac{3}{4} - 7\frac{3}{5}$

Supplemental Practice for Lesson 136

1. $0.3\overline{)0.15}$ 2. $0.4\overline{)2.4}$ 3. $0.5\overline{)0.15}$

4. $0.2\overline{)0.32}$ 5. $0.3\overline{)1.23}$ 6. $0.4\overline{)0.56}$

7. $0.6\overline{)0.72}$ 8. $0.7\overline{)0.98}$ 9. $0.8\overline{)1.52}$

10. $0.5\overline{)6.5}$ 11. $0.4\overline{)0.132}$ 12. $0.6\overline{)1.26}$

13. $4.6 \div 0.2$ 14. $0.64 \div 0.4$

15. $4.5 \div 0.3$ 16. $0.45 \div 0.5$

17. $3.21 \div 0.3$ 18. $1.23 \div 0.3$

19. $0.95 \div 0.5$ 20. $1.74 \div 0.6$

Supplemental Practice for Lesson 137

1. $1\frac{1}{2} \times \frac{2}{3}$ 2. $\frac{3}{4} \times 1\frac{1}{4}$ 3. $2\frac{1}{2} \times 3$

4. $4 \times 2\frac{1}{2}$ 5. $1\frac{1}{3} \times 1\frac{1}{3}$ 6. $1\frac{1}{2} \times 1\frac{1}{4}$

7. $\frac{1}{2} \times 1\frac{2}{3}$ 8. $2\frac{1}{3} \times \frac{1}{2}$ 9. $2 \times 3\frac{1}{2}$

10. $3\frac{1}{3} \times 3$ 11. $1\frac{2}{3} \times 2\frac{1}{2}$ 12. $3\frac{1}{2} \times 1\frac{3}{4}$

13. $\frac{1}{3} \times 2\frac{2}{3}$ 14. $2\frac{3}{4} \times \frac{1}{2}$ 15. $4\frac{1}{2} \times 4$

16. $3 \times 1\frac{2}{3}$ 17. $2\frac{1}{4} \times 1\frac{1}{2}$ 18. $1\frac{3}{4} \times 1\frac{2}{3}$

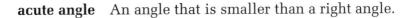

acute angle An angle that is smaller than a right angle.

acute angle   right angle

addend Any one of the numbers added in an addition problem.

$7 + 3 = 10$ *The **addends** in this problem are 7 and 3.*

algorithm A method of finding the answer to a mathematics problem.

*In the addition **algorithm**, we add the ones first, then the tens, and then the hundreds.*

a.m. Morning; the hours from midnight to noon. (Midnight is included in a.m. hours, but noon is not.)

*I get up at 7 **a.m.** I get up at 7 o'clock in the morning.*

angle The opening between two lines or segments that intersect.

*These lines make four **angles.***

area The size of the inside of a flat shape.

5 in.

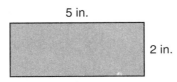

2 in.

*The **area** of this rectangle is 10 square inches.*

average   To find the average, add the numbers in a given set. Then divide the sum by how many numbers there are.

> *To find the **average** of the numbers 5, 6, and 10, add.*
> $$5 + 6 + 10 = 21$$
> *You added three numbers, so divide the sum by 3.*
> $$21 \div 3 = 7$$
> *The **average** of 5, 6, and 10 is 7.*

calendar   A chart that shows the days of the week and their dates.

SEPTEMBER 2004
S M T W T F S
1 2 3 4
5 6 7 8 9 10 11
12 13 14 15 16 17 18
19 20 21 22 23 24 25
26 27 28 29 30

*This **calendar** shows one month.*

century   One hundred years.

> *The twentieth **century** began on January 1, 1901, and ended on December 31, 2000.*

chance   How likely it is that something will happen. (We will write chance as a percent.)

> *The **chance** of snow is 10%. It is not likely to snow.*
>
> *There is an 80% **chance** of rain. It is likely to rain.*

circumference   The distance around a circle; the perimeter of a circle.

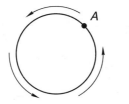

*If the distance from point A around to point A is 3 inches, then the **circumference** of the circle is 3 inches.*

common   The same; shared with another.

> *The fractions $\frac{3}{4}$ and $\frac{1}{4}$ have **common** denominators.*
>
> *The numbers 15, 20, and 25 have the **common** factor of 5.*

compare   To find out if a number is greater than, less than, or equal to another number.

> *128 > 112   This number sentence **compares** 128 and 112. It shows that 128 is greater than 112.*

congruent   Having the same size and shape.

   *These polygons are **congruent**. They have the same size and shape.*

coordinate graph   A grid formed by extending the scale marks of two perpendicular number lines.

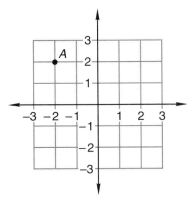

*Point A is located at (–2, 2) on this **coordinate graph.***

counting numbers   All the numbers in this sequence: 1, 2, 3, 4, 5, 6, 7, 8, 9, ...

*The numbers 12 and 37 are **counting numbers**, but 0.98 and $\frac{1}{2}$ are not.*

decade   Ten years.

*January 1, 2001, through December 31, 2010, is one **decade.***

decimal places   Places to the right of the decimal point.

*5.47 has two **decimal places.***

*6.3 has one **decimal place.***

*8 has no **decimal places.***

decimal point   The dot in a decimal number.

denominator   The bottom number in a fraction. It tells how many parts are in a whole.

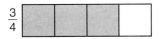

*The **denominator** of the fraction is 4. There are 4 parts in the whole rectangle.*

diameter   The distance across a circle through its center.

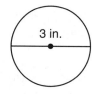

*The **diameter** of this circle is 3 inches.*

difference   The answer in a subtraction problem.

$$12 - 8 = 4$$ *The **difference** in this problem is 4.*

digit   Any of these symbols: 0, 1, 2, 3, 4, 5, 6, 7, 8, 9. Digits are used to write numbers.

*The last **digit** in the number 7862 is 2.*

dividend   The number that is divided in a division problem.

$$12 \div 3 = 4 \qquad 3\overline{)12}^{\,4} \qquad \frac{12}{3} = 4$$ *The **dividend** is 12 in each of these problems.*

divisible   Able to be divided by a whole number without a remainder.

*The number 20 is **divisible** by 4, since 20 ÷ 4 has no remainder.* $4\overline{)20}^{\,5}$

*The number 20 is not **divisible** by 3, since 20 ÷ 3 has a remainder.* $3\overline{)20}^{\,6\ r\ 2}$

division   The process of finding a missing factor.

$5 \times N = 30$	*N is the missing factor.*
$30 \div 5 = 6$	*Use **division**. Divide 30 by 5.*
$5 \times 6 = 30$	*The missing factor is 6 (N = 6).*

divisor   The number you divide by in a division problem.

$$12 \div 3 = 4 \qquad 3\overline{)12}^{\,4} \qquad \frac{12}{3} = 4$$ *The **divisor** is 3 in each of these problems.*

east   The direction to the right when facing north. East is to the right on a map.

*The sun rises in the **east**.*

*The Atlantic Ocean is **east** of the United States.*

endpoints   The points where a line segment ends.

A   B *Point A and point B are the **endpoints***
        of segment AB.

equivalent   Having the same value; equal.

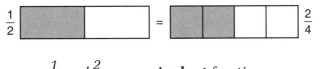

$\frac{1}{2}$ *and* $\frac{2}{4}$ *are **equivalent** fractions.*

estimate   To carefully guess how much something is.

*I **estimate** that the sum of 199 and 205 is about 400.*

even numbers   Numbers that can be divided by 2 without a remainder. Even numbers have 0, 2, 4, 6, or 8 in the ones' place.

*398 is an **even number,** but 399 is not.*

exponent   A number that shows how many times another number is a factor.

5^3 ◄— 3 is the **exponent.** 5^3 *means* $5 \times 5 \times 5$.

face   A flat surface of a solid.

*One **face** of the cube is shaded. A cube has six **faces**.*

factor   A number that is multiplied. Also, a whole number that divides another number without a remainder.

$5 \times 6 = 30$ *The **factors** in this problem are 5 and 6.*

      *The numbers 5 and 6 are **factors** of 30.*

fraction   A number that names part of a whole.

geometric solid   A shape that takes up space.

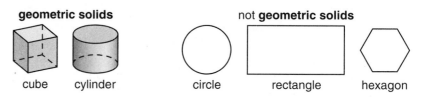

geometry   The study of shapes.

*Some of the things we study in **geometry** are lines, circles, and polygons.*

greatest common factor (GCF)   The largest whole number that is a factor of two or more numbers.

The factors of 20 are 1, 2, 4, 5, 10, and 20.
The factors of 30 are 1, 2, 3, 5, 6, 10, 15, and 30.
*The **greatest common factor** of 20 and 30 is 10.*

horizontal   From side to side.

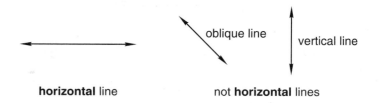

hundredths' place   Two places to the right of the decimal point.

*In 24.95, the 5 is in the **hundredths' place**.*

improper fraction   A fraction with a numerator greater than or equal to the denominator; a fraction that is greater than or equal to 1.

$$\frac{4}{3} \qquad \frac{2}{2}$$ *These fractions are **improper fractions**.*

intersecting lines   Lines that cross.

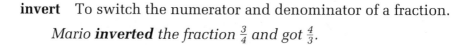

invert   To switch the numerator and denominator of a fraction.

*Mario **inverted** the fraction $\frac{3}{4}$ and got $\frac{4}{3}$.*

least common multiple (LCM)   The smallest whole number that is a multiple of two or more numbers.

> *The multiples of 4 are 4, 8, 12, 16, 20, ...*
>
> *The multiples of 6 are 6, 12, 18, 24, 30, ...*
>
> *The **least common multiple** of 4 and 6 is 12.*

length   The distance along the longer sides of a rectangle.

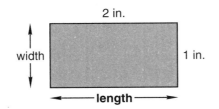

*The **length** of this rectangle is 2 inches. We can multiply the **length** by the width to find the area.*

line of symmetry   A line that divides a shape into mirror images.

lines of symmetry   not **lines of symmetry**

line segment   Part of a line.

$\overline{AB}$ *is a **line segment**.*

midnight   Twelve o'clock during the night.

> ***Midnight** is one hour after 11 p.m.*

minus sign   The symbol for subtraction. Also, a way to show negative value.

minus sign ⟶
$$\begin{array}{r} 25 \\ -\ 13 \\ \hline 12 \end{array}$$
-2

*The digit 2 with a **minus sign** in front means "negative two."*

mixed number   A number made of a whole number and a fraction.

> *The **mixed number** $2\frac{1}{3}$ means "two and one third."*

multiple   The product of one whole number and another whole number greater than zero.

$$4 \times 1 = 4$$
$$4 \times 2 = 8$$
$$4 \times 3 = 12$$
$$4 \times 4 = 16$$

*The **multiples** of 4 are 4, 8, 12, 16, ...*

$$9 \times 3 = 27$$

*The number 27 is a **multiple** of both 9 and 3.*

negative   Less than zero; the opposite of positive.

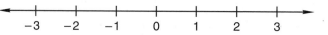

*The number –2 is **negative**. It is less than zero.*

noon   Twelve o'clock during the day.

***Noon** is one hour after 11 a.m.*

north   Toward the North Pole. North is to the top of a map.

*Canada is **north** of the United States.*

number line   A line that has marks labeled with numbers in order.

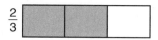   number line

numeral   A symbol for a number.

*4, 72, and $\frac{1}{2}$ are examples of **numerals.***

*"Four," "seventy-two," and "one half" are number words, not **numerals.***

numerator   The top number in a fraction. It tells how many parts of a whole are counted.

$\frac{2}{3}$    *The **numerator** of the fraction is 2. Two parts of the whole rectangle are shaded.*

oblique   Slanted or sloping; not horizontal or vertical.

oblique lines   not **oblique** lines

obtuse angle   An angle that is larger than a right angle but smaller than a straight angle.

obtuse angle   right angle

odd numbers   Numbers that have a remainder of 1 when divided by 2. Odd numbers have 1, 3, 5, 7, or 9 in the ones' place.

*467 is an **odd number,** but 468 is not.*

ordinal numbers   Numbers that tell position or order.

*"First," "second," and "third" are **ordinal numbers**. Their abbreviations are "1st," "2nd," and "3rd."*

origin   The point (0,0) on a coordinate graph.

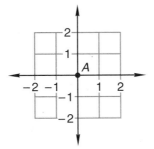

*Point A is at the **origin**. Its coordinates are (0, 0).*

parallel lines   Lines that stay the same distance apart; lines that do not cross.

parallel lines

percent   A fraction whose denominator of 100 is expressed as a percent sign (%).

$$\frac{99}{100} = 99\% = 99 \text{ percent}$$

perimeter   The distance around a closed, flat shape.

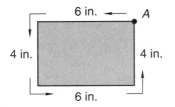

*The **perimeter** of this rectangle (from point A around to point A) is 20 inches.*

perpendicular lines   Lines that intersect and make square corners (right angles).

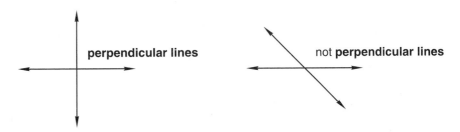

place value The value of the place a digit holds in a number.

$$
\begin{array}{r}
341 \\
23 \\
+\ \ 7 \\
\hline
371
\end{array}
$$

Place value tells us that the 4 in 341 is worth "4 tens."

Line up digits with the same place value (all the digits in the ones' place, the tens' place, and so on).

plane figure A flat shape.

plane figures   not a **plane figure**

plus sign The symbol for addition. Sometimes used to show positive value.

$$
\begin{array}{r}
12 \\
\text{plus sign} \longrightarrow +\ 20 \\
\hline
32
\end{array}
$$

$+4$

The digit 4 with a plus sign in front means "positive four."

p.m. After the middle of the day; the hours from noon to midnight. (Noon is included in p.m. hours, but midnight is not.)

I go to bed at 9 p.m. I go to bed at 9 o'clock at night.

polygon A flat, closed shape with straight sides.

polygons   not **polygons**

positive Greater than zero.

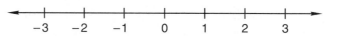

The number 2 is positive. It is greater than zero.

prime number A counting number that has only two factors, the number 1 and itself.

Seven is a prime number. Its only factors are 1 and 7.

Ten is not a prime number. Its factors are 1, 2, 5, and 10.

probability   How likely it is that something will happen. (We will write probability as a fraction.)

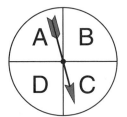

*The **probability** of spinning C is $\frac{1}{4}$. There are four letters. You will spin one of them.*

product   The answer in a multiplication problem.

$5 \times 4 = 20$ *The **product** of 5 and 4 is 20.*

proper fraction   A fraction with a denominator that is greater than the numerator.

*The fraction $\frac{3}{4}$ is a **proper fraction**; $\frac{4}{3}$ is an improper fraction.*

quadrilateral   A polygon with four sides.

quadrilaterals

quotient   The answer in a division problem.

$12 \div 3 = 4$ $3\overline{)12}\,^{4}$ $\dfrac{12}{3} = 4$ *The **quotient** is 4 in each of these problems.*

radius   The distance from the center of a circle to a point on the circle.

*The **radius** of this circle is 2 inches.*

ratio   A way of describing a relationship between two numbers. Ratios can be written as fractions.

*There are 3 triangles and 5 stars. The **ratio** of triangles to stars is "three to five," or $\frac{3}{5}$.*

reciprocal   The result of inverting a fraction.

*The **reciprocal** of $\frac{3}{4}$ is $\frac{4}{3}$.*

rectangle A quadilateral with four right angles.

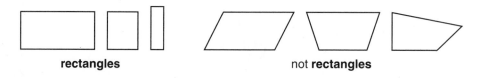

rectangles   not **rectangles**

reduce To make an equivalent fraction with a smaller numerator and denominator.

*Laura **reduced** the fraction $\frac{3}{6}$ to $\frac{1}{2}$.*

remainder Amount that is left after division.

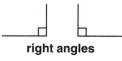

*Thirteen divided by 3 equals 4 with a **remainder** of 1.*

right angle A square angle (corner).

right angles

*A small square often marks a **right angle**.*

segment *See* **line segment.**

sequence A list of numbers that follows a rule.

*The numbers 2, 4, 6, 8, ... form a **sequence.** The rule is "count up by twos."*

side A line segment that is part of a polygon.

A rectangle has 4 **sides.**   A hexagon has 6 **sides.**   A triangle has 3 **sides.**

solid *See* **geometric solid.**

solve To find the answer to a problem. Also, to find a missing number.

4 × 3 = N   *Jorge **solved** this multiplication problem. He wrote "N = 12."*

south Toward the South Pole. South is to the bottom of a map.

*Mexico is **south** of the United States.*

sphere   A geometric solid shaped like a ball.

sphere

square   A rectangle with four sides that are the same length.

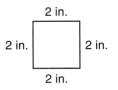

*All four sides of this **square** are 2 inches long.*

straight angle   An angle that forms a straight line.

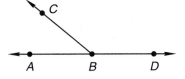

*Angle ABD is a **straight angle.** Angles ABC and CBD are not **straight angles.***

sum   The answer in an addition problem.

$7 + 6 = 13$ *The **sum** of 7 and 6 is 13.*

tally mark   A small mark used to help keep track of a count.

꒒꒒꒒ || *I used **tally marks** to count the goals scored. I counted seven goals.*

tenths' place   One place to the right of the decimal point.

45.91   *The digit 9 is in the **tenths' place.***

times sign   The symbol for multiplication.

$$5 \times 9 = 45$$

↑

times sign

triangle   A polygon with three sides and three angles.

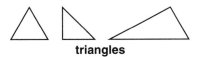

triangles

unit segment   The distance from 0 to 1 on a number line.

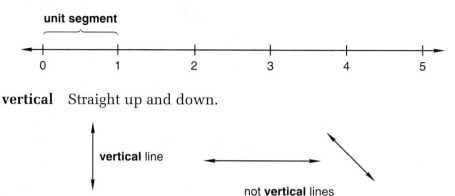

vertical   Straight up and down.

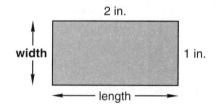

west   The direction to the left when facing north. West is to the left on a map.

*The sun sets in the **west**.*

*The Pacific Ocean is **west** of the United States.*

whole numbers   All the numbers in this sequence: 0, 1, 2, 3, 4, 5, 6, 7, 8, 9, …. Whole numbers are the counting numbers and zero.

*The number 35 is a **whole number,** but $35\frac{1}{2}$ and 4.2 are not.*

width   The distance along the shorter sides of a rectangle.

The **width** of this rectangle is 1 inch. We can multiply the length by the **width** to find the area.

Index

Symbols

◄► (arrowheads), 45
¢ (cent sign), 301
: (colon), 109
. (decimal point), 50
— (division bar), 77
⟌ (division box), 74
÷ (division sign), 77
$ (dollar sign), 8
= (equal sign), 13
> < (greater/less than), 13
– (minus sign), 29
× (multiplication sign), 50
( ) (parentheses), 92
% (percent), 117, 443
+ (plus sign), 19
√ (square root), 265

A

Abbreviations
  square units, 473
  for units of length
    metric system, 182, 313
    U.S. system, 186, 313
  for units of liquid measure
    metric system, 360
    U.S. system, 360
  for units of weight
    metric system, 329
    U.S. system, 329
Acute. *See* Angles
A.D. *See* Years
Addends. *See also* Addition
  definition of, 19
  missing, 37–38
  order of, 19

Addition
  with algorithm, 20–21
  of decimal numbers (*See* Decimals)
  of fractions (*See* Fractions)
  with missing addends, 37–38
  of mixed numbers (*See* Mixed
      numbers)
  of money
    dollars, 20–21
    dollars and cents, 50–51, 301–302
  stories
    some and some more, 40–43
  using multiplication for, 49–50
Algorithm
  addition, 20–21
  division, 97–99
  multiplication, 66–68
  subtraction, 32–35
a.m. *See* Time
Angles
  definition of, 123
  drawing of, 123–124
  naming of, 356–357
  types of
    acute, 124
    obtuse, 124
    right, 124
Areas
  calculating, 472–473
  closing in, 141–142
  units used to measure, 472–473
Averages
  calculating, 212–213, 499–500
  definition of, 212

B

Bar graphs. *See* Graphs
B.C. *See* Years

Abbreviations

U.S. CUSTOMARY		METRIC	
UNIT	ABBREVIATION	UNIT	ABBREVIATION
inch	in.	meter	m
foot	ft	centimeter	cm
yard	yd	millimeter	mm
mile	mi	kilometer	km
ounce	oz	gram	g
pound	lb	kilogram	kg
degree Fahrenheit	°F	degree Celsius	°C
pint	pt	liter	L
quart, gallon	qt, gal	milliliter	mL
OTHER ABBREVIATIONS			
square	sq.		
square mile	sq. mi		
square centimeter	sq. cm		

Equivalence Table for Units

LENGTH	
U.S. CUSTOMARY	METRIC
12 in. = 1 ft	10 mm = 1 cm
3 ft = 1 yd	1000 mm = 1 m
5280 ft = 1 mi	100 cm = 1 m
1760 yd = 1 mi	1000 m = 1 km
WEIGHT	MASS
U.S. CUSTOMARY	METRIC
16 oz = 1 lb	1000 g = 1 kg
2000 lb = 1 ton	
LIQUID MEASURE	
U.S. CUSTOMARY	METRIC
16 oz = 1 pt	1000 mL = 1 L
2 pt = 1 qt	
4 qt = 1 gal	

Place Value Chart

hundred billions	ten billions	billions	,	hundred millions	ten millions	millions	,	hundred thousands	ten thousands	thousands	,	hundreds	tens	ones	.	tenths	hundredths	thousandths	ten thousandths	hundred thousandths

Geometric Solids

SHAPE	NAME
	Cube
	Rectangular solid
	Pyramid
	Cylinder
	Sphere
	Cone

Common Polygons

SHAPE	NUMBER OF SIDES	NAME
	3	Triangle
	4	Quadrilateral
	5	Pentagon
	6	Hexagon
	8	Octagon

Measures of a Circle

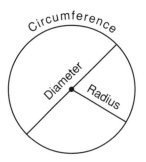

Types of Angles

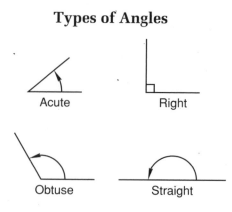

Roman Numerals

NUMERAL	VALUE
I	1
V	5
X	10
L	50
C	100
D	500
M	1000